"John Schultz, more than any other observer, covered the Conspiracy Trial in all its bizarre aspects. It was his bone-deep investigation and persistence, especially his astonishing conversations with two of the women jurors, that led to an unprecedented rehearing. This work, aside from being a profound study of fear, is investigative journalism in its highest sense."  — STUDS TERKEL

"A beautiful, compelling, tear-jerking, mind-boggling book."  — WILLIAM BURROUGHS

"The Schultz study is enormously relevant, covering as it does the jury performance under those strenuous conditions and testing realistically whether the jury today does perform the classic role (insulating the citizen from official oppression). It is therefore an important book for those who care about the jury system. . . . Mr. Schultz has written up his impressions with verve and perception. They cannot help but round out one's view of this important and perplexing case."  — HARRY KALVEN, JR.,
Professor of Law, University of Chicago

". . . he puts words together with a clarity of sense and syntax that is almost physically engaging. Yet his brilliant account of the Chicago Conspiracy Trial is strikingly nonlinear. . . . If Schultz has offered us a drama that is a metaphor for this society itself, then his intensive concern with the jurors and their own special agony is its climax."
— DAVID GRABER, *Los Angeles Times-Calendar*

"A masterful recapitulation of these anomalous events. . . . All politically literate Americans should read [*The Chicago Conspiracy Trial*.]"  — *Kirkus Reviews*

"As an historian, I am impressed with the depth with which John Schultz's book elucidates the American historical experience through a focus on this one important present-day event. . . . This book is a work to which I can turn, and to which I can direct the attention of students, for deeper understanding of the present as history and history as a way of understanding ourselves in the present."
— MARTIN J. SKLAR, Bucknell University

# THE
# CHICAGO
# CONSPIRACY
# TRIAL

By John Schultz

As Author

*Writing from Start to Finish*

*Motion Will Be Denied*

*No One Was Killed*

*The Tongues of Men*

As Editor

*f1*

*f2: Novels in Progress*

*The Story Workshop Reader*

*The Best of Hair Trigger*

*Don't You Know There's a War On?*

*It Never Stopped Raining*

# THE CHICAGO CONSPIRACY TRIAL

REVISED, UPDATED EDITION
With a New Afterword

*by John Schultz*

*New introduction by Carl Oglesby*

DA CAPO PRESS • NEW YORK

Library of Congress Cataloging in Publication Data

Schultz, John, 1932–
  The Chicago conspiracy trial / by John Schultz; new introduction by Carl
Oglesby. — Updated ed.
    p.    cm.
  Rev. ed. of: Motion will be denied, 1972.
  ISBN 0-306-80513-8
  1. Chicago Seven Trial, Chicago, Ill., 1969–1970. I. Schultz, John,
1932–   . Motion will be denied. II. Title.
KF224.C47S38   1993
345.73′0231 — dc20                             92-41323
[347.405321]                                  CIP

Portions of this book appeared originally, in different form,
in *Evergreen Review.*

First Da Capo Press edition 1993

This Da Capo Press paperback edition of *The Chicago Conspiracy Trial* is an
updated edition of a book originally published as *Motion Will Be Denied* in
New York in 1972. It is supplemented with a new introduction by Carl Oglesby
and a new afterword by the author. It is reprinted by arrangement with
John Schultz.

Published by Da Capo Press, Inc.
A Subsidiary of Plenum Publishing Corporation
233 Spring Street, New York, N.Y. 10013

*For my son, Tim,
and my daughter, Susie*

# CONTENTS

# INTRODUCTION
## The Whole World Was Watching

THE WEEK-LONG COLLISION of the Chicago police and several thousand anti-war activists that occurred during the Democratic Party's national convention in August 1968 has emerged, after all these years, as one of the crucial events of the entire Vietnam War period.

From the point of view of the U.S. Government, the irony of justifying the war as a defense of democratic values while simultaneously attacking dissent against it would thereafter be dismissed as an unavoidable casualty of a principled cause. On the other hand, after Chicago, the Government would no longer try so hard to convince the home front that the United States was fighting in behalf of Vietnamese democracy. From then on, it was just fighting to win a war whose purpose was no longer clear.

And from the point of view of the anti-war movement too, Chicago marked a sea change. The movement's original commitment to nonviolence would thereafter be pushed aside right along with its earlier shared sense of the humanity of one's adversary. From then on, the protest against the war was increasingly an all's-fair attack upon "the system." And the demand was no longer merely for the immediate return of U.S. forces in Southeast Asia, but indeed for the overthrow of the

entire American system in behalf of the imprecise but revolu-
tionary-sounding rhetoric that the movement then began to
adopt. Not quite typical but indicative of the change of mood
was the fact that by 1969 a large handful of campus newspapers
had become explicit supporters of the Viet Cong.

Given the importance of "the Chicago convention riots," as
the events of August 1968 were often labeled, we are fortunate
that a journalist of the power, insight, and ironic good humor
of John Schultz was there to describe in two remarkable books
first the week itself (*No One Was Killed,* 1969), then the trial
of those who organized the demonstrations (*Motion Will Be
Denied,* 1972), the latter being republished here in an updated
edition as *The Chicago Conspiracy Trial.*

Schultz is the ideal journalist-historian of these events, first
and last because, as the reader will see, he is a dream of a
writer with a novelist's sense of the telling detail and a critic's
ability to find the important line through the thicket of claims
and counter-claims that has built up around this case. He is
generally sympathetic toward the eight anti-war activists whom
the Government accused and in part convicted of conspiring
to riot, but by no means is he uncritical of their motives or
their conception of the strategic moment into which the trial
had thrust them. He is capable of appreciating the difficulties
of the situation of the Government's prosecutors and indeed
of the jurors who voted to convict. He is at the same time clear
that there probably was, after all, a conspiracy to create violence—but that it was the Chicago police and the Chicago
political authorities, very much including Mayor Richard
Daley, who were guilty of it.

I was outside the courtroom waiting my turn to testify when
Mayor Daley came. Two days before, I had been cozily nursing
my own movement wounds through a deep Vermont winter
when the call came from Tom Hayden, one of the eight defendants and like me a former president of Students for a
Democratic Society, a leading organization against the Viet-

nam War during the mid-1960s. Hayden had called me because the defense was having difficulty getting some of its key
witnesses lined up. The danger was that if the defense was at
any point unable to produce its next witness, Judge Julius
Hoffman would rule the defense closed. It was not that I had
anything so critical to contribute to the defense, but my testimony could be justified on grounds that I had been involved
in the demonstrations themselves as well as several of the planning meetings that led up to them. I could speak to two basic
questions: (a) Had the organizers intended the demonstrations to become violent? (b) Were the demonstrators and their
leadership the instigators of the violence that ensued? On the
first point, I testified that, as I read it from outside the organizing group, there was a sense that Mayor Daley's honor and
prestige were on the line and that, to defend them, he would
feel a need to protect the Democrats' convention by keeping
Chicago quiet. On the second point, I testified that as far as I
could see, it was a thousand times more the police than the
demonstrators who wanted and provoked violent encounters.

One example: Dave Dellinger had asked me to give a speech
at the bandshell on August 28, 1968, the third day of the convention. The scene I faced from the microphone was physically
calm to start with but emotionally tense, the crowd's jitters in
no way eased by the fact that we were surrounded by a line of
what seemed several hundred policemen with riot sticks in
hand. It was a baleful scene in which to attempt a speech, but
Dellinger and the other organizers were desperate to level out
the insane vibrations and give the crowd the reassurance of a
normal-seeming and nonviolent protest. Was it then a provo-
cateur or just an angrily thoughtless demonstrator who flung
something—it looked to me like an apple core—at the police
line from the middle of the crowd? Instantly the police formed
into a column two abreast and went wading right into the body
of the crowd in pursuit of the offender, riot sticks smashing
down to the left and right on the scores of people who had no

idea what was happening and who had nowhere to go to get out of the way. I had felt powerless before and would feel it again, but nothing compared to witnessing that scene of utter mayhem. The only thing the helpless crowd could think to do—and how little it seemed at the time—was to write the caption to the scene of its own mauling with the chant that would become the ultimate slogan of Chicago 1968: "The whole world is watching!"

That same sense of helpless dread was reawakened in me by the scene in Judge Hoffman's courtroom about a year and a half later, a cavernous neon oven with guards and plain-clothesmen everywhere, the dread deepened by the profound uncertainty in that cold Chicago winter as to how everything was going to turn out. The Vietnam War was increasingly bloody on its own terms and furthermore seemed about to escalate into a war with Red China. The Nixon administration's willingness to break the law in its effort to silence the anti-war movement rendered entirely reasonable the otherwise preposterous fear that we were on the verge either of an out-and-out police state or some new and terrible kind of civil war.

Schultz's marvelous evocation of the Chicago Eight trial has to a large degree been mellowed by the events of the 23 years that have elapsed since the verdict, if only because we are now beyond rather than immersed in that crisis and know how the story comes out. The book was conceived, researched, written, and published in an atmosphere of rising domestic tension against the backdrop of an increasingly violent war against the Vietnamese people. No one could guess then that President Nixon's re-election that year would be merely the prelude to his discovery in impeachable offenses.

A result is that *The Chicago Conspiracy Trial* reads in 1993 like a completely different book. In 1972, the end of the story of the war and the domestic protest against it was still excruciatingly in suspense; it had not even been foreshadowed. Indeed, Schultz's book first appeared in the bookstores at the same time as a White House spy by the name of E. Howard Hunt led a group of burglars with sophisticated bugging equipment, Nixon's Plumbers, into the headquarters of the Democratic National Committee at the complex of buildings in Washington, D.C. known as the Watergate. Their arrest red-handed in June of that year set in motion a tumult of events that resulted two years later in the forced resignation of President Nixon, the inauguration of President Gerald Ford without benefit of election, and thus, *finally*, to the end of the Vietnam War.

And with that, John Schultz's remarkable book had at last found its proper ending.

—Carl Oglesby
Cambridge, Mass
November 1992

\* \* \*

*Carl Oglesby was a leader of the anti-war movement as president of Students for a Democratic Society. He has written four books on political themes.*

# PART ONE
*Motion Will Be Denied*

IT IS THE NATURE of the several games of history-making—of determining the material intentions of a society—that the figures and groups of the "moribund but ruling past" will test to the utmost and in many different ways the strength of a challenger. They will not succumb or submit or negotiate until a challenger has found the will and the humor and the consciousness and earned the strength and the right to be born—to be dominant—or to change and compel the "past" to do its will. Such a figure almost wearing a sign saying "Moribund American Ruling Past" in a deadly sort of morality play might have been Judge Julius Jennings Hoffman, who presided over the trial of the Chicago Conspiracy Eight. I say "might have been" and I use the word "moribund" somewhat advisedly because, at seventy-four or seventy-five, he was a remarkably lively man, needing none of that Geritol that defendant Abbie Hoffman kept prescribing for him publicly out of the habit of media myth-making.

What Judge Hoffman lacked in physical stature—he was slight and literally wizened—he made up for in the agility and strength of his sometimes magically melodramatic voice. He pronounced karate "ka-ret" while reading the indictment of the eight alleged conspirators to the hundreds of prospective jurors. It perhaps showed how long ago Judge Hoffman ceased to look up unfamiliar words in the dictionary.

He was about seven or eight—about as old as Abbie Hoffman's son America at the time of the Conspiracy Trial—when the Wright brothers lay belly down on their contraption and flew it a hundred feet or so over the sands of Kitty Hawk. The defendants were a little older when more developed American planes put the torch to North Korea to keep firm a strategic reach of that empire with which Judge Hoffman had long ago identified his sense of honor and sense of elegance. That was about the time that Judge Hoffman, then on the state bench, through Senator Everett Dirksen, Republican, Illinois, to whose party the judge gave monetary gifts, secured from President Dwight Eisenhower an appointment to the federal court of the northern district of Illinois. Whereupon, we are told, Judge Hoffman embarrassed Senator Dirksen with the ingratitude of becoming nonpolitical in his judgments.

Judge Hoffman was described by persons both friendly and familiar with him as needing someone to pick on. Members of his staff understood submitting to that need to be part of their function. He was also an unconscionable flirt with women.

"I didn't ask for this case," he said more than once in the five months of trial. Persons familiar with the day-to-day "intense paranoia" of the federal courts of the Northern District of Illinois have said that he *did* ask for the case.

Judge William Campbell, friend of Mayor Daley, carefully guided the grand jury that brought the indictments against eight demonstration leaders and eight policemen. In April, 1969, he recused himself from any further judicial duty in these cases, ostensibly because he considered himself to be too familiar with the evidence and to have already formed an opinion. Irving Birnbaum, Chicago counsel for the defense, immediately sent one of his staff to the federal courts to make sure that the new judge would be selected according to the required lottery procedure. Birnbaum feared that the judge the government would pick if it had its choice would be Julius Hoffman. Judges are supposed to be picked for cases in Federal District Court by putting their names on strips of paper and then pasting the strips, name side down, one on top another in shuffled sequence, so that when a case needs a judge the first piece of paper on top is stripped off, turned over, and there's your judge. If the lottery was conducted as it should have been, then chance, against which nothing can prevail, picked Judge Hoffman. In times of energy and unresting social change, chance makes connections of awful potential for being arbitrarily magnified.

Most federal judges have what Chicago lawyers describe as a "cordial relationship" with the local U. S. Attorney's Office. But Hoffman favored the prosecution with a Roman sort of faith in the administrators of the empire, whether the case involved Mafia and gambling, desegregation, mail fraud, tax evasion, draft resistance, conspiracy to incite riot, antitrust, or what have you. The method of judge selection in the Northern District sent many important cases into his courtroom, including the Krebiozen cure-for-cancer fraud case and the South Holland school-district desegregation case. In the latter, called "his finest moment" by judges and lawyers whom he admired, he of course ruled for his favorite party, the United States government. Persons close to the judge say that "a perceptible change could be seen in the judge's mood throughout the year preceding the trial, and he was constantly buoyed by the school-district case." Many cases involving celebrated Mafia figures such as Anthony Accardo and Sam Battaglia had come before Judge Hoffman.

He was noted for seldom granting appeal bond, for no delay between a finding of guilty and sentencing, and for giving the maximum sentence. When the American Civil Liberties Union tried to enter an *Amicus* brief in the Conspiracy case, Judge Hoffman declared, "I'm not running a school for civil rights."

Judge Hoffman's unrelenting faith in the Justice Department showed in his pretrial attitude toward the motions of the defense to have access to the government's illegal wiretap logs of defendants' telephone conversations. The defense was given only two of several logs. An affidavit to Judge Hoffman from Attorney General John N. Mitchell, whose urging helped the labors of Judge Campbell's grand jury, affirmed that the defendants were national security risks. Judge Hoffman's law clerks asked him to dwell upon the fourth amendment implications of denial. "There's the Attorney General's affidavit," he always responded, gesturing toward his desk.

But when he said suddenly in July, 1969, "Get up an opinion denying the motion by 9 A.M. tomorrow," one of his law clerks cried out, "But, Judge, that's not fair," and the judge was seized with what was perceived with a touch of awe as a "Dickensian rage." The law clerk was told that he need not return after his vacation.

Judge Hoffman shrewdly postponed to the end of the trial the final part of the decision that denied the defense access to the logs, virtually annihilating the fourth amendment in this area for this trial.

Judge Hoffman was insistent on keeping the most current calendar in the first or second busiest federal district court in the nation. He forced cases to conclusion by arm-twisting with technicalities. But it was no surprise to find that he recused himself some time ago, on the grounds of obvious conflict of interest, from a case involving the Brunswick Corporation, in which he and his family were large stockholders. He was fond of relating that that case was settled in another judge's chambers while he got a lengthy anti-trust case in exchange. When he was asked in a pretrial motion of the Conspiracy defense to recuse himself from the Conspiracy Trial because Brunswick Corporation makes substantial money off defense contracts and that this produced a conflict of interest for him in facing defendants whose adult lives had been devoted to antiwar activity, he did not reveal the same concern for appearances. Motion was denied. In the year prior to the Conspiracy Trial, we were told, he granted only one or two pretrial motions of all defendants who came before him.

He was noted for delivering—and presumably writing— long and scholarly opinions, which somehow suited a man whose rhetoric seemed to have been conditioned irretrievably by the great Victorians. But it was really not so surprising to find that he occasionally hired a professional journalist or legal writer, and that the scholarship of an opinion usually reflected the ability of one of his law clerks. "Away with that sarcasm, sir. It will avail nothing," he said once in chastising Conspiracy Defense Counsel Leonard Weinglass. He was called "Mr. Magoo" for such remarks and for the shape of his face and the way he looked roundly through his glasses over the bench. This characterization was another one of our mildly clever ways of misconceiving our past, and of refusing to see how we thereby stay hopelessly in reflection of it. "Julius 'the Just' " was another such misconception.

In 1960, toward the beginning of our contemporary era, Judge Hoffman ruled in his chambers in favor of *Big Table* magazine, four hundred copies of which had been impounded by the Chicago post office for alleged obscenity. *Big Table,* edited by Paul Carroll, took the lead in the late fifties in publishing the first parts of William Burroughs' *Naked Lunch,* and many other new writers including this writer. Judge Hoffman said in his ruling that the Burroughs novel was intended "to shock the contemporary society in order perhaps to better point out its flaws and weaknesses." He also said that a piece by Jack Kerouac seemed to be "a wild prose picnic." Judge Hoffman concluded his ruling by quoting from the *Ulysses* decision: "Art certainly cannot advance under compulsion to traditional forms, and nothing in such a field is more stifling to progress than limitation of the right to experiment with a new technique." He could hardly have anticipated that nine years later he would face eight defendants practically spawned by the cultural and social change that began in several sources in the late fifties. They believed that you could change the first word of the sentence from the *Ulysses* decision to "Society" or "Democratic process" and have a valid principle for action. Some of those *Big Table* writers played parts in the demonstrations during the Democratic convention of 1968, furthering the spirit of the prose in whose favor Judge Hoffman had ruled. They would even appear on his witness stand in a trial in which the use of language to indicate intent was at issue.

In the week before the Conspiracy Trial I went to Judge Hoffman's courtroom to see how he handled cases that were not so immediately provocative of emotion. He was just as ready and salty of tongue and just as domineering and just as enjoying of himself when he felt himself looking good and winning, as he would be in the Conspiracy Trial. "I imagine he would be amusing to an uninvolved onlooker," defendant David Dellinger once said, wryly.

In the summer before the trial the judge was given heady anticipations from television and apparently from Justice Department "intelligence" of the defendants' plans "to disrupt" the trial. "They're going to come in naked," he said to his staff. He entertained many other expectations of startling improprieties coming from the defendants. He talked more and more in his chambers about the defendants' "plans" to disrupt the trial, with a tone and attitude as if he already thought they were guilty of contempt. He regarded himself as "the embodiment of everything federal," and the Justice Department apparently gave him every information that would enhance his suspicions.

When Judge Hoffman suppressed sudden anger, the wrinkles in his brows swirled up and down, literally swirled. "Everything we do here is for the record," he said. He showed that his central weakness, his raw nerve, was that he had to have the last word. He was meeting defendants who were also determined that they must in some way, preferably public and heard round the world, have the last word.

David T. Dellinger, Rennard C. Davis, Thomas E. Hayden, Abbott H. Hoffman, Jerry C. Rubin, Lee Weiner, John R. Froines, and Bobby G. Seale were charged with "conspiracy" and with individually crossing state lines and making speeches with intent to "incite, organize, promote and encourage" riots in Chicago during the Democratic convention in August, 1968, in violation of Title 18, United States Code, Sections 371, 231(a), and 2101. The indictment also cited the names of eighteen co-conspirators, not named as defendants, and "divers other persons, some known and others unknown to the Grand Jury." "Known" and "unknown" echoed, and the conspiracy seemed to be everywhere, as broad as the land itself, anti-war everywhere.

In his initial presentation to the jurors, Assistant U. S. Attorney Richard Schultz charged these eight men with "planning to bring people to Chicago to create a riot" during the Democratic National Convention, "to create a situation in Chicago where these people would riot." I smiled at Schultz's more than imprecise description of Convention Week and what led up to it. I smiled out of my ten-days-and-nights familiarity with that time and with almost every major confrontation in the streets and parks, as a writer for *Evergreen Review.* I had written the book *No One Was Killed*—lovely title—that writers and persons familiar with Convention Week thought was "more valuable and accurate as a factual account than the Walker Report, Theodore H. White's *Making of the President,* and the city's white paper combined." So I sat in that courtroom with certain clear memories of what happened and the way it happened during Convention Week, possessed by the immodest conviction that one man had done a better report on a historical event than the massively organized and implemented quasi-official "Walker" commission.

Then suddenly—I can still see myself sitting in that court-room pew in an indulgent sort of mood, and it was as much the earnest instrumentality of the Assistant United States Attorney's tone as the words he used—I felt the knell of a shifting of an end and a beginning in my soul, when he said that the government would *"prove"* that people *"infiltrated"* from Grant Park to Michigan Avenue for the purpose of rioting on August 28, 1968, and that Dellinger's nonviolent march in Grant Park on that day was a "diversionary action" for this "infiltration." If the government was ready to call that "infiltration." then the government was ready to send men smashing through one's door in the dark before dawn to shoot one in one's bed.

Did the jurors, at the touch of that exotic word "infiltrate," see the defendants through a mirage of TV images about spies and counterinsurgency and drug-maniacs and FBI . . . ?

I remembered that afternoon and I could see the people choking and coughing and retching with tear gas as they stumbled over the bridge south of the Art Institute onto Michigan Avenue. Their cry went up at the sight of the three mule-drawn wagons of the Poor People's March, behind which the demonstrators massed with a new enthusiasm thinking they were now at last part of a permitted march to the convention at the Amphitheatre. I should have laughed out loud at the Assistant United States Attorney's characterization of "infiltration" if it were not for his tone. By "rioting" Schultz meant the famous police attack on that crowd of determined demonstrators at Balbo and Michigan on August 28, 1968, a crowd thunderously determined to protest the merciless oversights of American political process—war, racism, and poverty.

There is often the certainty in a courtroom that "truth" is of no use to anyone, and that in the adversary system people win over each other at an insane cost of trust and perception, of blame being fixed and paid for. "Well," a lawyer said to me about both the state and the Weathermen in the hearing at the Cook County Criminal Courts building after the Weathermen's October 8–11 "Days of Rage" actions, "everybody's lying." It is no marvelous revelation that people lie or distort or posture or tell half-truths to protect themselves or help their friends in our courts. I was ready to expect general misrepresentations, omissions, and commissions for purposes high and low by most parties in this courtroom. But certainly the defense ought to have benefited if it could have shown, or wanted to show and prove, how Convention Week happened.

Defense counsel William Kunstler, for instance, sounded merely not properly informed when he referred to Convention Week violence as "a police riot." He sounded as if he accepted, and certainly as if he thought the jury might be familiar with, and accept, that most careful assertion of the best-selling Walker Report which so conveniently displaced the responsibility for continuous police attacks over a period of five days and nights. Defense counsel Leonard Weinglass improved the balance when he said that the defense would attempt to prove conspiracy on the other side, to block and attack the demonstrators.

The defense was obviously going to be cautious about exploring the courage, daring, and readiness of the people in the streets during the Democratic convention of 1968.

\* \* \*

There was a hollowness about almost every "political" action that happened in the courts and on the streets and in the media throughout the autumn and early winter of 1969 in Chicago. The "hollowness" began with the Conspiracy trial itself. Thump it and test it from every side and it gave back the same message of something else underneath—hollowness.

The hollowness was there when the Federal Grand Jury returned the indictments in March, 1969, in that the government knew that it could not give credit for the great revelatory events in the streets and parks during Convention Week to these "leaders." The plain truth—for anyone present in Lin-

coln Park—was that when Sunday, August 25, 1968, came at
the beginning of Convention Week, all seven of these white
"leaders" were in effect failures because so few people came
to Chicago to demonstrate, and because everything they
planned and hoped for and visualized had failed to happen.
For "obeying the law and playing the Pig's game and for trying
to cool it," some of them were actually discredited by many of
the young people who, in response to crowd situations of absurd and awesome power and freed from the traditional struc-
tures of demonstrations, took over the "leadership" that could
change from moment to moment in the Us and Them confrontation of police and demonstrators.

The defendants themselves referred ironically to that part
of their indictment concerning the training of parade marshals
as "conspiracy to act like a cop." Finally, more than a majority
of the people who took part in actions during Convention
Week, and certainly those who "led" the catalytic actions early
in the week, came from Chicago and nearby areas. There were
people from all over the country in the street and park actions,
but police arrest statistics and eyewitness observations do not
put them in the majority.

The Mayor's Office and the Corporation Counsel's Office
of the city of Chicago and the United States Attorney's Office
of the Northern District of Illinois did not find it useful to
understand publicly that there was an extreme division among
the demonstrators—with the "leaders" of traditional demonstration tactics, such as were used at the truly huge Pentagon
demonstration in October, 1967, on one side, and the very
young and in a few cases much older but generally inexperi-
enced catalytic persons on the other.

There was the hollowness that the government altered its
goals several times after the Grand Jury was first convened in
September, 1968. Attorney General Ramsey Clark advised
U. S. Attorney Thomas Foran, who was supposedly responsible to the Attorney General, against convening a Grand Jury.

Clark wanted to explore Convention Week happenings with an investigative staff, and with no explicitly outlined follow-up in the courts, with the possible exception of charges against policemen. Chief Judge William Campbell was Mayor Daley's friend and mainstay in the federal courts, and Tom Foran was beholden to Daley from the time Foran was Land Acquisition counsel for Urban Renewal projects in the Corporation Counsel's office of the city of Chicago. Foran was appointed U. S. Attorney at the nod of Mayor Daley.

Judge Campbell began the Grand Jury hearing in an unusual manner, out of keeping with the usage of grand juries, by directly presenting the potential indictments for the jurors to consider. The interested parties in Chicago paced the Grand Jury hearing through the long winter, past the election that Hubert Humphrey lost only because he did not have a few more days to overcome the angry divisions driven through the Democratic party by the Convention in Chicago, until the Nixon Administration took over the government, until John Mitchell took over the Justice Department. Then the government sought the Grand Jury's approval of indictments of a few media-known figures, artfully representing the spectrum of dissent in the United States in the sixties—from older pacifist, middle-class, civil rights and antiwar advocates, to student organizers and young academics, to long-haired dropout drug-culture youth, to militant self-defense blacks. The indictments were largely constructed by a narrowly gifted Justice Department lawyer, John Wall, who prosecuted Dr. Spock and his fellow defendants in Boston for conspiracy-to-aid-and-abet-draft-resisters.

The general revolt and dissent in the United States in the sixties had been growing fast, up to 1970, paralleling the inflation of the economy—which may be similar to what the economist Keynes was suggesting when he said that the great periods of artistic exploration tended to coincide with periods of monetary inflation. But the revolt's strength, once confessed, was not to be measured in the numbers of its "activists" but in the breadth and depth of sympathy and tolerance for it, the breathing time and latitude, in such areas of potential participation as communications and education. All of the professions had developed radical contingents by the end of the sixties, not to speak of the more publicly known sectors of discontent and desire to change social intentions and possibilities.

The indictments were aimed at the areas that had a broad social democratic potential. The great power of Convention Week events in drawing masses of people and involving whole neighborhoods and enlisting and unifying previously diverse groups was a prospect to be feared by many persons on all levels of government, from city to federal.

In establishing the "crime of crossing state lines with intent to incite riots," the indictments emphasized the growth of selective, arbitrary repression throughout the nation. Indict a few, kill a few, imprison more, club more yet, expel others, take candy in the form of scholarship support out of the mouths of some, beat up several, get others fired from their jobs, suspend a few from their schools, fine a few, exhaust supposed principals in endless litigation and negotiation and hearings of all kinds—the more arbitrary, the more "selective," the more the feeling that the deadly touch could fall anywhere on anyone at any time by accident of association with a person or place or activity, and sometimes the less institutionalized the repressive action, the better—*but let most participants perceive that the safe and thrilling thing to do was to move away from detectably "radical" positions,* away from the points of possible unity.

Add to this the mass infiltration—the word is here used advisedly—of "movement" groups by undercover agents and provocateurs who were there to report, to finger, to disrupt, to take over, to be potential witnesses, to betray, to actually direct and control—and the worst that can happen to a revolutionary group is to have both its daring and its common sense usurped by infiltrators and provocateurs. That was another hollowness that you could listen for, look in the eyes for, because the unceasing activities of counterintelligence and surveillance agents of all kinds in Chicago neighborhoods and Chicago organizations grew faster than those groups of people who had made any move toward national sanity.

The defendants in Judge Hoffman's courtroom were always intrigued by their indictments, and they played with the parts to make different combinations. They said that they were tried for their "identity"—for being persons who missionized a counterculture and way of life that was threatening to the parties represented by the prosecution. The prosecution countered that the defendants were tried for their "intentions." It amounted to the defendants' saying that they were tried for what was visible, and the prosecution saying that they were tried for what was invisible.

By February, 1970, the Conspiracy Trial and the many reactions to it, even in the form of riots, were positively generating the rapid polarization of American social and political life. Potential radicals hastened away from points of unity. If polarization were the *result,* it must be the *intention* of the indictments—so reasoned the defendants, who occasionally did not underestimate the farseeing intelligence of the men of the government.

In retrospect, the comprehensive purpose of the indictments emerges as a conscious and unconscious effort to extend, justify, and control a particular power struggle indefinitely by naming a people and an Unpeople.

Unpeople are *not* fully human, they are *contrary* to people, they are *not* worthy of precisely the same rights and regard given to people. Naming is powerful, and human beings both fear and celebrate it.

The people-Unpeople mechanism for obfuscating perceptions, and for dividing and controlling loyalties, is different from the Us and Them principle and different from the ancient tribal identifications, though it taps these source emotions in order to controvert and stultify their dynamism. The first step is to describe the Unpeople, point them out, name them, so that those who want to be people can identify each other and move away from them. Eventually, the slaying of Unpeople is not equivalent to the murder of people.

There can be no celebration of fact, or examination of it, where the main point of the game is to see who will be stuck with the name, title, and unprivilege of Unpeople. People and Unpeople always feel honored in their lies for their side, their omissions, their distortions, their differences of emphases, the very lapses that arouse the indignation of the other party.

Nevertheless, Unpeople are usually thought to be diabolically clever, incredibly prescient, nearly clairvoyant, and of a generally subtle, evil, and effective intelligence. That means that prosecutor Thomas Foran was represented by the party of the defense as being somewhat dull and backward and gauche, but acts of farseeing and farreaching consequence were attributed to him. To the party of the prosecution, the defendants were hardly better than a bunch of nervous pack rats, but they were diabolically capable of projecting actions from the demonstrations at the Pentagon in Washington, D.C., in October, 1967, to the corner of Michigan and Balbo in Chicago on the evening of August 28, 1968.

The government may have felt that the violence of Convention Week so stigmatized them through the media that reached into almost every home in the nation that the only way to get rid of the stigma was to name somebody else, hopefully once and for all, as the Unpeople. The power struggle controls itself, locks itself into two sides, and the group in power stays in power.

The Nixon Administration asked that Thomas Foran continue in his position as U. S. Attorney for the Northern District of Illinois for the specific purpose of prosecuting the

Conspiracy case, though he was a Democratic appointee. This also helped to keep the original stigma of Convention Week violence away from Nixon and the Republican party. A prominent legal defense lawyer in Chicago, who, despite his specialty, declared himself to be a friend of Tom Foran, said that Foran would do a "good and competent job as prosecutor but he wouldn't enjoy it." I was left to dwell on the varied relationships of lawyers. But I could see why Foran was thought by many young Chicago lawyers to be more than decent in those relationships in which he chose to be friendly or helpful.

The conspiratorial possibilities that could be fictionalized, that might have happened or be happening during this trial, were enough to boggle the consciences of journalists and jurors and any other citizens who had managed to stay selfishly innocent. If President Nixon was proud to claim that the White House played a part in getting the dismissal of charges against the eight Green Berets accused of murdering a double agent in Viet Nam, obviously regarding it as political gain in the country at large, then why should not the President also exercise influence on the Conspiracy Trial in Chicago? Tease the thought that the Nixon Administration feared for the political conventions of 1972 and was seeking, by penalizing celebrities, to forestall demonstrations, disruptions, and discreditations such as occurred in Chicago in August, 1968. Tease the thought that Judge Hoffman was just as confused by the "real" conspiracy—perhaps there were more than one—as everyone else who was not a knowledgeable participant in it.

The United States government *chose* its antagonists in the Chicago Conspiracy Trial, *chose* the game itself, aiming to split dissent off from its rapid spread into mainstream American politics, and *chose* the point of engagement. Judge Hoffman's courtroom became a theater for the telling of the people and the Unpeople.

\*     \*     \*

Defendant Rennie Davis related the story of a time in the summer before the trial when he was visiting a "hippie" friend and they both became aware that a panel Coca-Cola truck had been parked for hours outside the house and had not moved, with the driver in it. Defendant Davis said that he went out to the truck, stuck his head inside, and sure enough there was a man with earphones on his head among stacks of busy electronic equipment, listening through walls. Imagine the noises recorded of people talking, working, eating, doing nothing, making love, planning to incite riots or bomb buildings, dreaming, or whatever else people do behind the walls and windows and doors of their abodes. The fourth amendment protection against illegal search and seizure of premises, and of the persons themselves who make the noises, has been often naively thought to be clear, requiring warrants for police or other officials to intrude and severe penalties for other persons who trespass or invade. Certainly, it would seem that to record your noises as if the ears were inside your premises is a form of invasion. Yet, when government agencies and persons feel the need and are inclined to use their capabilities, this fourth amendment protection has been periodically at issue. Imagine the man-hours that intelligence agencies spend listening to and logging such recordings. Assistant United States Attorney Richard Schultz was fond of intimating that the government's illegal wiretaps of the defendants' conversations clearly revealed that the defendants were guilty.

The hollowness—the quality of being without dynamic response—was there every time a "movement" leader spoke of "the revolt of a whole generation of youth"—and the word and the phrase deserved to be qualified by quotes. The defendants savored quoting the *Time* magazine poll that said that one out of five college freshmen regarded themselves as being revolutionary, and more than half of them believed that the United States was an imperialist and racist country. I myself did not want to tell the defendants that the organizers of the October 15 (1969) Viet Nam Moratorium Day demonstrations at some of the largest universities in the Chicago area refused to announce or give any open support to the Conspiracy Eight from their stages. The students in the Moratorium audiences wanted the music and the dance, the way people in the old revival meeting wanted the release of ecstasy and tears, and probably more than one in five considered themselves revolutionaries.

Just before the trial began, Rennie Davis spoke at Mandel Hall at the University of Chicago to members of a student body that had been purified of the "radicals" who seized and occupied the Administration Building in the last winter, without a club being raised against them. "Let us alone and those students will be gone by September," the University of Chicago officials told the intensely concerned officials of the city of Chicago. The latter were anxious to send police into the building with clubs so that no one would get the idea that there might have been a wiser way for them to have approached the demonstrators during Convention Week. The "radicals" who seized the Administration Building were not equipped emotionally or politically to work with a situation in which police attack did not provide unity for a broad spectrum of dissenting students. The "radicals" were thus isolated from the far more numerous "moderates"— these terms are misnomers, with unfortunate self-congratulatory and depreciative connotations—and the process began in which the administration co-opted and used the issue by letting the students work out "changes" in the curriculum and the departments. Then the administration got rid of the "radicals" one by one, few by few, but let most participants stay in school even if they signed complicity-with-the-accused statements.

The University had not been changed in its relations to government or to corporations or to the city in which it is one of the largest landlords. But strangely in a few months the students seemed relieved at the U or C, in its Hyde Park enclave of fine homes in the midst of the largely black South Side. Moral pretensions were gone and with them went their tensions, and many of the students were secretly glad that the "radicals" with their incessant moralistic accusations and incitements were gone.

Davis spoke well of the relationship between repression in this country and the U. S. policy toward Viet Nam. He was not long back from a trip to North Viet Nam, which had required the special intervention of Thomas Foran on behalf of the State Department to get Judge Hoffman to let him go. You could see that the blasted panhandle of Viet Nam pocked with U. S. bomb craters every few feet was still stretched out before him in his mind. The audience of U of C students was quietly enthusiastic, quietly supportive, quietly in agreement with much that he said. But in the question period their caution and cool skepticism surfaced. "Well," one fellow asked defendant Davis, after Davis had described the government's "crime of intent" case, "what *did* you say during the Convention?" I was amazed that the fellow who asked the question was not hissed and booed by the rest of the audience. Instead, the students looked eagerly for an answer, and I may have been the only person in the house who appreciated the answer that came. "You've just heard me speak," Davis said. "What do you think was my intent?"

"I don't know," the young man said.

"But the government does," Davis said.

I laughed in appreciation of the answer. But the students cheered loudest when Davis said that the people who organized the Woodstock rock festival—he was working every lever on the youth culture gambit—were coming to Chicago in support of the Conspiracy. There was the wooing of the music again. Abbie Hoffman would say on the witness stand that "rock musicians are the real leaders of the revolution." Musicians would show up at the trial to testify as to why they had declined to show up in support of the Festival of Life in Lincoln Park during Convention Week—fear caused by the city of Chicago's denial of assembly permits and by the "vibrations" in the city that meant that the Chicago police intended violence.

The support of the Woodstock people for the Conspiracy did not materialize. I use the word "materialize" in the sense that magic means it. It also seemed that the support of "this generation of youth," no matter how many times it was summoned or invoked or declared, would not materialize either. "How can you be a young person," Davis said, at one point in Mandel Hall, declaring that he would continue his work even if a pistol were held at his head, "and have any other position?" There were a few fists raised repetitively, a few cries of "Right on," but by and large the audience was coolly supportive, perhaps imagining political positions other than staying where a pistol was pointed at their heads. The cool response happened in other meetings with other spokesmen, too. I had seen an audience of young people in a thundering ecstasy of aggression in the Coliseum in Chicago during the Democratic convention on the night of August 27, 1968.

The Black Panther party declared that, on the day the trial opened, they would close down high schools on the West Side and all those kids would come downtown to the Federal Building and demonstrate to FREE BOBBY SEALE and close down the trial. Teachers in the schools say it was true that on that day there were hardly any black kids in those high schools and grade schools. It was also true that on that day no such number showed up downtown to demonstrate. SDS factions variously declared that white high schools would be shut down, along with colleges. But it seemed that young black people often admired the Panther party and yet were scared by it, or turned off by it, and that the white students were often of the cool, doubtful feeling that Davis faced at the University of Chicago.

I stood in the drizzling rain outside the Federal Building and remembered the huge Peace march in April, 1969, in Chicago—more than fifty thousand people, which was maybe three or four times as many people as participated in the march in September, 1968, right after Convention Week and that march had been perhaps two or three times larger than any previous march. The growth of such mainstream sympathy in the population was one of the reasons for the indictments of the representative scapegoats of the Conspiracy Eight. I wondered why it would not have been possible for all of those people, of all ages, to be here to protest the trial at the Federal Building. But the "Movement" spokesmen insisted on a "youth revolution" that did not show up, and chance delivered a gray, drizzly day.

The police were under orders to stand very fast, and they refused to fill the hollowness with any sort of general aggressive response. But there were demonstrators in the rain— white young people literally jumping on the cops to get the cops to beat them back and arrest them, and black demonstrators taunting and threatening the white "muddleheaded Custerist" demonstrators. There had been meetings in the Chicago area in which it was impossible for the RYM-1 Weathermen spokesmen—such as Bernadine Dohrn—to be reconciled with the Panther party—Fred Hampton—on the proper approach to demonstrations about the trial. The Panthers wanted to attract as much support as possible, from as many sectors of society as possible, to FREE BOBBY SEALE. The police acknowledged that the Panthers gave valuable aid in keeping the peace that day, and the cops were so grateful that not many days later they raided and shot up the Panther headquarters on Chicago's West Side. That was the cops' continued participation in a program apparently approved by the Justice Department, of savage escalation of shooting police attacks on Panther party headquarters and apartments throughout the nation.

A young white news vendor asked me with urgency, both his hands jammed in the front pockets of his news apron, "Are they scared"?" Just then some young freaks were galloping past the tall glass of the Federal Building lobby bearing on their shoulders a huge papier-maché golden hog. "The things they do," he said. "Are they scared?" There was such force in his voice that I mumbled in response.

He asked, "Could they do it individually?"

I mumbled again.

"Could they?" he said. "It's the group, isn't it?"

"Maybe you're right," I said. How could they possibly do it individually? But I knew what he meant.

"It's the group," he said. "All those cops, guns. clubs, machine guns. Mow them down any time they wanted to. They got to be crazy, right?" He sensed the game nature of the demonstrations, and the special power and license of the society .

The Chicago police had been great teachers for the "movement." From the time that they shot black people in the insurrection that burned down wide parts of the West Side in April, 1968, to the time that their attacks upon the young people in Lincoln Park and Grant Park over a period of several days and nights in August, 1968, produced the tremendous energy of the events of Convention Week, to the time that they stood aside and were hardly to be seen during the SDS convention in June, 1969, where SDS sundered itself and the only possible focus for unified action on which the SDS factions might have agreed would have been an attack from the cops, to the Weathermen Days of Rage actions of October, 1969, where the police waited to be attacked before they fell upon the Weathermen, to the killing of Fred Hampton and Mark Clark in December 1969 and the massive media response that created a labyrinth for all contending parties, the Chicago police taught one continuous lesson—the power of *unity,* either by producing unity of peoples by attacking them or by standing aside and letting *disunity* happen to the dismay of factionalized brothers and sisters in the "movement."

The Chicago police demonstrated that the frustrated thirst of young rebels for confrontation could be easily manipulated by police attitude. They also caused enough moments of real theater with real blood that they very nearly convinced "move-

ment" people that the society was controlled primarily by
physical force, rather than by deep and pervading indoctrina-
tion principally through education and the communications
media. The Chicago police always succeeded in confusing essential issues.

There was no security of any kind at the Federal Building
in the week before the Conspiracy Trial when I went to the
trial of Policeman Arthur Bischoff. one of eight cops indicted
by the same Grand Jury that indicted the eight demonstrators.
Bischoff was being tried for depriving photographer Duane
Hall (of the Chicago *Sun-Times*) of his civil rights by beating
him on the head at the Michigan Avenue bridge on the night
of August 25, 1968. The policeman's family and relatives sat
in the right-hand section of the courtroom. The jurors could
see who the people were to whom their decision would deliver
happiness or misery.

Defense attorney James Demopolous in his summation to
the jury smashed Bischoff's police club on the table so hard
that everyone in the courtroom flinched. He did it to emphasize his point that if Bischoff had hit Duane Hall that hard
Duane Hall would not have got up from the ground so easily.
Demopolous made a blatant appeal to the jurors' sentiments
in favor of this "brave policeman" who acted to enforce law
and order on that "awful night of anarchy and insurgence" at
the beginning of Convention Week. Demopolous painted vividly for the jury the wild crowd on the bridge, their colorful
dress and long hair, their obscene epithets, their tall red flags.
black flags, and Viet Cong flags. It would not be long before
Judge Alexander Napoli in his charge would tell the jurors
that they must take into account "the total situation," the surrounding circumstances, to determine if an act of criminal nature had been committed by Arthur Bischoff. Assistant U. S.
Attorney Nicholas Etten was perhaps sincere in his prosecu-

tion but too much the awkward young man not long removed
from a college fraternity.

The jurors saw the "surrounding circumstances" clearly and
acquitted Arthur Bischoff. Bischoff darted across the courtroom and shook hands with the smiling jurors. He said that
the verdict showed that "most of the public want this kind of
justice in the streets."

Bischoff's family hurried exultantly from the courtroom,
and I talked briefly with one of his brothers, a loyal and hearty
man. There was no indication that Bischoff's family had been
given any assurance that the trial was rigged in their favor.

Seven of the cops indicted by the Grand Jury were acquitted
by their juries, and charges were dropped against one. Some
months later there was a small notice in the inner pages of the
newspapers that Arthur Bischoff, who had already been rein-
stated in good standing in the Chicago Police Department, was
granted full back pay for the time of his suspension. You
needed only to remember actions of Convention Week in
which hundreds of policemen were involved to wonder about
the justice of these indictments.

There was the very hollowness of the Federal Building itself,
curtain walls of steel and bronze-tinted glass, where all dynamic response was simply stared out of existence. "Mies Van
Der Rohe was a kraut," said Abbie Hoffman. The Federal
Building shows "that final and utterly disciplined control of
detail which is never lacking in a Mies structure" according to
the architecture critic of the Chicago *Sun-Times.* The great
lobby, three stories high, contains no offices except the information desk in the center—a sort of moat or buffer of air
between the imperial bureaucratic functions of the building
which begin on the second floor and the earth into which the
structure braces itself so firmly. Outside the building, you tend
to look up at it. Inside, you tend to look down.

Several relatively new buildings in Chicago have the moat of air between their activities and the ground: the Civic Center Building, which houses most of the city's government; the Brunswick Building, into which family and business the most colorful Judge Julius Hoffman married; the Inland Steel Building; and the new Time-Life Building. The moat of air can be traced to a concept of Corbusier's where the ground floor was meant to allow the free circulation of people. In the way in which the United States historically handles socially dynamic ideas, the concept was put to opposite purposes: to separate and protect the functions of the building from the urgencies of the people who surge in silence outside the glass. If German philosophy descended intact from heaven to earth, American business and government were evidently trying to lift themselves intact from earth to heaven.

The First National Bank, a new building, and Marshall Field's department store, an old building, did not possess the prudent trait of the moat of air between their functions and the ground. In December, 1969, a black theology student, in an impotent rage over the state killing of Fred Hampton, "held up" the First National Bank with a toy pistol as an act of protest. Another black man, late at night, took a hammer to the display windows of Marshall Field's, shattering thirteen of them one by one when the police stopped him and he announced that he had done it to call attention to the problems of the black ghetto.

Under glass, always lighted, exact copies of the Constitution the Bill of Rights, and the Declaration of Independence were displayed at the south end of the Federal Building lobby, reminding one of the way Lenin was preserved under glass in the Soviet Union. In the center lobby, two great granite circles of the two sides of the United States seal look across at each other. There was the Latin phrase *Novus Ordo Seclorum* [New Secular Order], and the American eagle clutching an olive branch for peace in one set of talons and a bunch of arrows for war or self-defense in the other. One of the women at the information desk answered a query on the day before the trial by saying, "Actually, a government check is good indefinitely."

U. S. marshals were summoned from all points of *Novus Ordo Seclorum* to guard the building. The U. S. Attorney's Office and the U. S. Marshal's Office were aware that intense ideological struggle was being waged among a few radical groups about whether now was the time of the lead-piper, the bomber, or the assassin. In Judge William Campbell's hearing in the week before the trial about banishing all radio, TV, and camera equipment from the Federal Building and its environs, a man on the witness stand, testifying why such equipment should be banished, suddenly fumbled to answer his own walkie-talkie in his pocket.

There was no hollowness in the lobby full of evening rush hour with the headlines resting on the newsstands, when I re-acted, as if slapped, to the murder of the Reverend Bruce Johnson and his wife, a few blocks away from my home in Lincoln Park on the Sunday night after the trial began. The Reverend Johnson, hoping generally to mix and temper Christianity and revolution, had helped the Young Lords, a former Puerto Rican street gang that had moved through the process of becoming a political organization. He was stabbed eighteen times in the region of the heart that night, sitting in his chair. His wife, in another room, was stabbed about eighteen times too. In the morning, the mailman found one of the little Johnson boys standing in the doorway with blood on his foot, crying that mommy and daddy would not wake up. Speculate, if you will, on the sort of fury that is indicated here, the who and why of what betrayal, construed more savagely than a lover's crime. There was no sign that the Reverend Johnson fought back against his murderer.

The full moon, with billion-dollar American footprints on it, lifted itself over the Federal Building, where the trial of the Conspiracy to assault, assassinate, and astound the Democratic party was under way during the daytime. There would be more killings and more billion-dollar footprints put on the moon before the story ended.

It was the peacemakers who were getting killed—because they advocated what the actions of the Chicago police taught: unity.

If you were one of the press who stood in line outside the U. S. Marshal's Office on the first morning of the trial, you had a U. S. Marshal's press card for Judge Hoffman's courtroom. You were "authorized." and the marshals were most concerned with that which was "authorized" and "unauthorized." But if a new marshal happened to be on duty, and you came barging by him, you might find yourself leaning against a voice that fairly vibrated with rising desire to snap your bones, and the tough hand was already touching your shoulder: "Can I help you, sir?"

Members of the press walked in and out of their entrance to the courtroom, wearing coats large enough to conceal many dangerous things, and were not searched because they could show the "card." The spectators, on the other hand, were searched, frisked, patted up and down, in and out. Knives, spoons, forks, compacts, fingernail clippers, handbags, books, attache cases, and other objects were deposited in a heap on a card table in care of the marshals by the swinging doors of the courtroom. The marshals found three or four pistols in the first several weeks of the trial.

There was "massive" security during the Democratic convention, too, and it made no sense, because a blind man could have assassinated whomever he chose if he had worn front and back a WE LOVE MAYOR DALEY sign. The trouble with American security is that it immediately becomes a matter of status to be free of it, status that is earnestly sought. During the Democratic convention, movement persons used press credentials to get inside the Conrad Hilton and the Amphitheatre.

The door for press and attorneys on the side of Judge Hoffman's courtroom opened easily. If you were late, you looked down into the face of a black marshal, a lanky former Harlem Globetrotter, "Slim," who eased the door shut. The room appeared to be designed to focus attention on the slightest movement anywhere in it.

It was two stories in height, with dark wood paneling, and ceiling-wide fluorescent lighting that shone through a sort of frosted honeycomb. "A rich man's living room," said Jerry Rubin. "A neon oven," said Abbie Hoffman. The shadows in this courtroom were bunched under tables and chairs and pews and around the feet of people. It was always high noon without glare.

Look up when you came through the door, and America erupted around you—erupted, and stood still in groups and enclaves for you to see. Past, present, and time to come, there was almost nothing of the people of the United States that was not represented bodily here, or conspicuous for its absence.

The first people who faced you from across the room were the members of the jury—ten women, two of them black women, all of them at least gently middle-aged and desperately middle-class, except for one girl in her early twenties. There were two men on the jury. The jurors had about them both the certainty and the mistrust of people who have labored earnestly most of their lives at jobs of modest reward and at raising children.

"We want the jury to become a part of the antiwar movement, we want to turn the courtroom into a schoolhouse," defendant John Froines said, speaking for the defense position just before the trial started. "If the government is going to try us for 'intent,' then we are going to show why we came to the Democratic convention in the first place, why we're against imperialism, racism, against the war."

\*   \*   \*

During jury selection the hundreds of prospective jurors in the broad ceremonial courtroom had been selected from voter registration lists. But this venire body was not truly representative of even that 64 percent majority of the American people who were registered to vote, because you really had to sift your way through the mass of faces to find a few people between the ages of twenty-one and forty.

The defense feared that the venire list of prospective jurors had been cleaned by FBI security checks, as happened in the Spock conspiracy trial in Boston. The prosecution countered that it was the defense who had performed "intelligence" on the veniremen. The defense did admit, out of the courtroom, that they tried to check some people and their neighbors to see if the FBI had checked them. The jury was obviously perceived by both sides to be the weak link in any chain of potential control over the outcome of the trial.

Defense Counsel Leonard Weinglass made an inventive motion to the effect that the defendants would be more nearly represented by those people who were not registered to vote, such as black people, young people, and dropouts and fallouts generally from the social and political system. But there was the shock of meeting the middle-aged portion of that 64 percent majority of the American people who must somehow be enabled to win themselves to the cause of national sanity. It seemed only fitting that the defendants should begin the second decade of their labors, the nineteen-seventies, facing a jury not composed of their peers, a jury not likely to understand them easily. For the mind and the soul of the jury, the prosecution and the defense and the judge and perhaps secret others would wage struggle as patriots.

The first open move to win the soul of the jury was made by Judge Hoffman, when he read the indictment to the hundreds of veniremen massed in the ceremonial courtroom. He exploited every possibility for melodramatic emphasis and rhythm and cast a spell with his voice upon the attention of hundreds of people with his reading of what was otherwise a long and boring document. With aghast fascination, I watched and heard him build the sentence that "John R. Froines and Lee Weiner, defendants herein, did teach and demonstrate to other persons the use, application and making of an *incendiary device*—" With crescendo fervor, he let the tight vowels and sibilants burst from him. William Kunstler rose and spoke with increasing anger, "I object to your honor reading the indictment in the manner of Orson Welles reading the Declaration of Independence."

Judge Hoffman looked up sharply and beamed. "I have never been so complimented," he said, "to be compared to one of America's greatest actors." Everybody laughed, prospective jurors, press, spectators, attorneys for defense and prosecution and even the defendants, albeit with some chagrin. Judge Hoffman overruled Kunstler's objection, but strangely submitted to it and did not read the rest of the indictment with such flair, as if he had been shocked into a humility about his own effect.

When Kunstler a few days later made a motion for a mistrial because of the judge's reading, he cited a former prospective juror who had declared on a TV program that after hearing Judge Hoffman read the indictment she could not have been impartial toward the defendants. Judge Hoffman refused to repent and said that he would continue to use "the vocal facilities the Lord hath given me."

The judge's marshal spun the wheel and twelve people were picked, and walked to the jury box. It is at the discretion of the judge in a federal court whether he will permit lawyers to examine jurors and Judge Hoffman did not permit it. The only questions the judge asked each prospective juror were about family and job. He did not ask any questions at all about familiarity with Convention Week and other aspects of the case. It was hard to believe that there could be any person in the Chicago area during Convention Week who had not formed some opinion about the street violence that obsessed the mind of the city while it was happening and for months afterward. Judge Hoffman also did not ask some of the questions requested by the defense such as, "Do your daughters wear bras most of the time?" The defense proposed a number of such questions on cultural issues that would have flushed out prejudices in the prospective juror.

The prosecution showed its political awareness in the way it used two of its peremptory challenges—bumped an unemployed black electrician and a young chemist. The defense used ten of its seventeen peremptories, mostly bumping persons with admitted government affiliations including a policeman's daughter whom they toyed with accepting.

I was sitting across the aisle from a small white woman who was talking animatedly with a black woman beside her. The white woman was Mrs. Frieda Robbins, who would become one of the four "acquittal" jurors, and the large black woman would become an alternate juror. The two of them had not yet been selected, and in retrospect I still remark on the accident of the two of them sitting together. Members of the Conspiracy staff saw the two talking together and assumed that Mrs. Robbins, because she was easy with black people, would be an "impartial" juror. Mrs. Jean Fritz who would become a juror, walked past the defendants carrying the James Baldwin book *Tell Me How Long The Train's Been Gone,* that she had been reading on the commuting train. She told me after the trial that she did not know that the defendants saw the book and assumed, with great excitement, that she was an "impartial" juror. The defendants, mostly men in their thirties, a maelstrom of lengthening hair and colorful clothing, stared at the jurors, trying to pick up cues. They excitedly leaned over their table to exchange many improvised sociological and psychological observations on the basis of very little information.

With seven peremptories remaining, the defense suddenly asked for a recess. They convened in a small room with one urinal in it, and proceeded to vote on accepting the jury as it stood. "That little room was the most tension-packed place I've ever been in in my life," said defendant John Froines. Chicago counsel for the defense Irving Birnbaum argued that the prosecution through the use of the investigative personnel of the government knew more about the jurors than the defense, and that there were four people on the jury that the prosecution would bump with its remaining peremptories. In a rare instance of maneuver, the defense unanimously accepted the jury and took the government by surprise. There was one young person on the jury, Miss Kristi King, and the judge's sparse questions had revealed that she had a sister in the VISTA program.

The government prosecutors appeared nonplussed by the defense's move. But Judge Hoffman was pleased with the defense for saving time, always a concern of his. Miss Kay Richards, about the same age as Kristi King, was selected as the first alternate. That marked the entrance of the young woman who would become the self-proclaimed "negotiator" of the conviction verdicts. Probably because Kay Richards was young and because there was every chance that she would in the course of a long trial take the place of a juror who had dropped out for illness or other reasons, the defense anxiously asked Judge Hoffman for his assurances that her place was secure as first alternate against future peremptory challenge.

The jurors listened day after day throughout the prosecution's case to an other-worldly parade of undercover agents who sounded so thickly ordinary. The jurors glanced at the men and women of the press section to see how they were reacting, to get some clue, some stance, some point-of-view, from someone they might trust. When the trial was most electric and the jurors could feel it—even though they were most often excused by the judge and shunted out of the courtroom away from those scenes that charged the air—they would look with great readiness at the press door when it opened, waiting for a face that might send some signals from the world of common sense and reality as they knew it. They were hearing Bobby Seale become more and more outspoken. They knew so little of the law that they had to work out their interpretations of events according to their personal awareness and, of course, prejudices.

Judge Hoffman gave the most routine instructions in a limber, emphatic, and expressive voice. But there was one particular phrase to which he gave every possible nuance of force and judgment, sometimes with a great bobbing of his head: "Motion will be denied."

# PART TWO
## *Seale*

WHEN JUDGE HOFFMAN mounted the bench in his courtroom on September 24, 1969, his marshal Ron Dobroski banged the gavel and there was the shuffle and stir of everyone rising— everyone except seven of the defendants. Judge Hoffman never seemed so slight as, with his right hand tucked in a languid Napoleonic fashion into his black robe, he looked over the courtroom. Only one defendant was standing in traditional respect to the judge, stonily, head up, at the far end of the defense table. It was Bobby G. Seale, a dark brown man, with round natural hair, National Chairman of the Black Panther party. He was leaning upon the table with one fist as if to underline that he knew why his name had been tacked onto the tail end of the indictments. The marshal called again for everyone to rise. The seven white defendants did not rise and even laughed among themselves. Judge Hoffman looked here and there with brief discomfort, and chose this time to ignore the disrespect.

From California a few days previously, Bobby Seale had been driven in chains in a car by U. S. marshals from state line to state line, from one state patrol escort to another, from jail to jail, night to night, across two-thirds of the vast continent and brought to rest in the tier for federal prisoners in Cook

County jail. Jerry Rubin was brought from California in the same manner, and the government's explanation was that it feared that if the defendants were flown by plane, the plane might be hijacked and directed to Cuba. Seale had reason to say that he had been "kidnapped" because his lawyers in California had secured a court order restraining the government from shipping him to Chicago before the car was outside the state of California. The marshals knew about the court order but kept driving anyway.

Seale had spent less than twenty-four hours in Chicago during Convention Week in August, 1968, as a last-minute substitute for Panther Party Minister of Information Eldridge Cleaver. He made one speech in Lincoln Park on Tuesday night August 27 and one speech in the middle of the day in Grant Park on August 28. He met Jerry Rubin only to say "hello" that Tuesday night but did not meet his other fellow "conspirators" until the arraignment in April, 1969.

In May, 1969, he found himself arrested for conspiracy to murder Panther party Member Alex Rackley in Connecticut. Seale was held in jail without bail in San Francisco awaiting a decision on extradition. The raids on Panther party offices all over the country, the arrests and shootings of Panthers, increased drastically with the coming to power of the Nixon Administration and Attorney General John N. Mitchell, who organized a "Panther section" in the Justice Department. Seale had few doubts about whether there was a conspiracy to put him into the electric chair if possible, or in jail for a long time.

On that first day of the trial, when the proceedings were reconvened upstairs in the large ceremonial courtroom filled with prospective jurors, the seven white defendants again did not rise when the judge appeared up on the bench. The marshals commanded several young white spectators to rise or get out. Prospective jurors looked nervously at the marshals, at the sometimes colorful clothing and long hair of the white defendants, and at the lean black man standing up alone, along with the lawyers, in the blue turtleneck sweater and black pants that he often wore. He dressed very differently, for instance, from Jerry Rubin, who was also in custody in Cook County jail, and with whom Seale was beginning to talk. Rubin's enthusiasm bristled with the new beard on his chin and the crew cut on his head. He wore an orange and red striped polo shirt that first day and laughed impulsively. Seale's stark way of dress and the way he leaned attentively backward or forward alerted people for what he had to say.

Judge Hoffman waited for the marshal to call for everyone to rise again, then warned the defendants to rise next time lest their behavior be considered contumacious. He had already exercised his willfulness in issuing bench warrants for the arrest of the four pretrial lawyers who had endeavored, as was the custom, to withdraw by telegram. On September 20, a Saturday, to be sure, the judge had been called to the courtroom to hear an emergency motion presented by Conspiracy staff member Stuart Ball Jr., for Fred Hampton, Chairman of the Illinois Black Panther Party, to be permitted to visit Bobby Seale in jail. The judge began warmly enough saying that he would hear Ball "as a human being," not as a lawyer since Ball was not yet licensed to practice. Stuart Ball's father, Stuart, Sr., was an old friend of Judge Hoffman's, and the judge would find that the father might be a distinguished establishment lawyer but he backed his son fully. Then the judge suddenly turned against Stuart Ball, Jr., and asked him who forged Kunstler's name to the motion, when Ball himself had said that Kunstler had permitted someone else to sign his name. The judge denied the motion. The incident reverberated for days. Seale was aware of the judge's arbitrariness in this matter.

With a manner of action that was dainty, abrupt, and arrogant, Judge Hoffman brought a brisk thrill of contest into the courtroom. The white defendants understood his warning and rose along with Bobby Seale the next time. They had estab-

lished that they would act differently from the way their lawyers acted.

Seale always sat somehow apart from the other defendants
and their lawyers at the defense table, absorbed in whatever
he was doing. During the melodramatic reading of the indictment, he sat with his hand shading his eyes, as if trying to
concentrate on something. He was ill, with a low fever. Judge
Hoffman—supported by a panel of judges in the Seventh U.
S. Circuit Court of Appeals—had refused to grant a continuance of the trial for six weeks so that Charles Garry could be
present as chief trial counsel for the defense in general and
counsel for Bobby Seale in particular. Garry's doctor had told
him that his life might depend upon having a gallbladder operation now, and he could not wait for the end of yet another
trial. Seale sat at the defense table among defendants and lawyers he'd never met, without the lawyer he trusted and admired. Garry had successfully defended Panthers in difficult
cases in California. Garry was known to be wise and abrasive
as a trial lawyer, and the defendants were anxious for him to
be their chief counsel. At the arraignment in April, Judge
Hoffman had found himself exercised emotionally and intellectually by a lawyer in a way in which he was not accustomed.
That lawyer was Garry. All of the defendants *wanted* and *expected* to have Garry as their chief trial counsel.

In Cook County jail Seale had to get up at about five every
morning to begin, along with Jerry Rubin, the tiresome process
of being taken to the Federal Building and to the lockup on
the twenty-fourth floor above Judge Hoffman's courtroom.
His day was half over by the time court proceedings began.

He listened to incidents during jury selection that were not
reassuring to him as a black man. When Judge Hoffman asked
veniremen to stand up if they felt they could not be impartial,
a black man asked to be excused because his wife had once
worked for Thomas Foran. "In what capacity did your wife
work for Mr. Foran?" the judge asked. "In domestic service?"

The hiss from several persons in the courtroom confused the judge. Prosecutor Foran, however, saw the stigma about to be stuck on the government and rose promptly to say that he remembered Mr. Miller's wife well. Foran spoke of her excellent work as a legal secretary and got a wave of positive sympathy from the audience.

The government exercised one of its peremptory challenges to bump from the jury an unemployed black man. He was an electrician which meant that he was "intelligent," he was black, he was male, and he was "unemployed," all of which meant that if not on the verge of rage and revolution he might nevertheless be expected to see too much sense in the speech of the defendants in general and Bobby Seale in particular. The government also challenged peremptorily a young chemist just graduated from the University of Illinois who might also have seen sense where angels feared to find substance in the defense's case. But middle-aged black women, who might well have spent their lives being frightened of aggressive "lightning rod" black men such as Bobby Seale, stayed on the jury. Judge Hoffman did not ask the questions about familiarity with the Black Panther party that were requested by the defense.

When a large black woman said that she had been a cook, Judge Hoffman said, "We don't like to see good cooks retire. Do you work for a private family or a restaurant?" His tone suggested his surroundings in his apartment in the Drake Towers. She said that her son worked for the Playboy Club, and Judge Hoffman responded brightly, "Notice any difference in him?" Bobby Seale heard the prospective jurors laugh readily at the judge's jokes.

When a man said that he had been a painter, Judge Hoffman said, "Painter? Not a painter like Picasso? You paint walls, right?" When another fellow said that he used to work for a bowling alley, the judge said with snippy vowels and lifted eyebrows, "Automatic pinsetter put you out of work?" The automatic pinsetter was the main basis for the success of

Brunswick Corporation, from which came most of the judge's personal fortune through his wife.

From courtroom to lockup, from lockup to escorted van, from van to the tank at the jail, Seale began writing the motion that he would read the next day.

The other defendants were not entirely enthusiastic when Seale showed them the motion in their conference prior to the next day's proceedings. They thought the judge was playing right into the script that they were writing, and now Seale was starting another trial within the trial. The other defendants were also worried that Seale's firing of the lawyers and the remarks about the judge's actions being "prejudicial to all of the defendants and myself" might be construed to mean that they were all "splitting," and the judge would revoke their bail. Seale was reported to have talked by phone to Garry the night before.

Seale was fastidious, even haughty, nervous, ready. Only John Froines rose with Bobby Seale this day, September 26, and Judge Hoffman both noted and warned the defendants who did not rise. Before even the summary presentations were made by the two sides to the jury, Bobby Seale, to the surprise of most persons present in the courtroom, strode to the lectern.

The courtroom, already terrorized by the judge's abrupt rulings, was also surprised that a sudden access of toleration possessed the judge huddled up there on the bench. If Garry could not be his lawyer, Seale wanted to defend himself. "If I am consistently denied this right of legal defense counsel of my choice, who is effective, by the judge of this court, then I can only see the judge as a blatant racist of the United States court."

The judge reacted violently, "Just a minute, just a minute. What's that? Read that. Watch what you say, sir." He argued with Seale, and Seale reiterated his basic statement before going back to his seat.

Kunstler tried to speak in support of Seale.

"Watch your language, Mr. Kunstler. I will remind you every time." The judge said that he had Kunstler's signed appearance for Seale.

Kunstler said that he had signed an appearance for Seale on September 24 only to be able to visit him in jail. Now Seale had fired him, and he would file a withdrawal of that appearance. Kunstler would be asked many times why he signed that appearance. On it, Judge Hoffman based his entire contention that Seale was represented by effective counsel of his choice, and after a trial begins it is "absolutely discretionary" for the trial judge to permit a lawyer to withdraw.

But the poisoned dart of that "blatant racist" remark made Judge Hoffman declare at this moment to the court that the first desegregation case in a northern state, the South Holland school case, had been tried and won in his courtroom. He mentioned the editorials in newspapers that praised the wisdom and liberality of his decision, but he did not mention the phone calls and letters that decried it. He did not mention that he occasionally said as a bit of a joke, "I only ruled that little boys and girls could go to school together, not that white women should marry black men."

Prosecutor Thomas Foran argued against Seale's motion with punch-punch emphases. Judge Hoffman denied Seale's motion. "What about my constitutional rights, Judge?"

"You have a very able lawyer to speak for you," Judge Hoffman said, and would often say, to Seale.

He would now try to hold four of the pretrial lawyers hostage in one of the most extraordinary strong-arming attempts by him or any other judge, to get the defendants to give equal consent to being represented by any other lawyers they had designated, and thereby justify his denial of a continuance for Charles Garry. Kunstler said, "Your honor, I've never been in a trial where two of the counsel have been in custody."

Defendant Thomas Hayden greeted the entering jury with a fist salute. Richard Schultz called the incident to the attention of the judge who sent the jury out and admonished Hayden for "shaking his fist" at the jury. "It is my customary greeting, your honor."

In his opening statement, Richard Schultz mentioned Abbie Hoffman, and Abbie Hoffman stood up and blew the jury a kiss. The judge said, "The jury is directed to disregard the kiss from Mr. Hoffman." Many laughed and even jurors suppressed smiles.

With Huey P. Newton, Seale hawked Red Books, the sayings of Mao Tse-Tung, to white radicals on the Berkeley campus in order to make money for a couple of shotguns for the Panther party's program for self-defense in the black community in Oakland. Now he sat without a sign of such humor, occasionally writing on paper before him.

Schultz mentioned Seale's name, and Seale lifted his hand in greeting to the jury. "Mr. Seale made this speech," Schultz said to the jurors, "telling people to pick up guns, .357 Magnums, shotguns, pistols, and go out and riot." Schultz held onto both sides of the lectern with both stiff arms and hunched earnestly toward the jury. "Mr. Seale is a very effective speaker. He's very *effective*." Rigidly and routinely Schultz nailed emphases in odd syntactical positions.

The jurors, often excused, knew little or nothing about the judge's attempts to jail the four pretrial lawyers. But they did know that only the day before Judge Hoffman had emphasized that "we are methodical here, we keep regular hours." Kunstler, when the judge indicated he should start his presentation to the jury, pointed out that it was 12:30, time for lunch break. Judge Hoffman said angrily that *he* would "watch the clock," *he* would "do the driving." Stomachs were growling audibly all over the courtroom, and I was so hungry I hardly knew whether I wanted to laugh or cry and it was difficult to concentrate on what Kunstler was saying. Then Judge Hoffman signed an order holding two of the pretrial lawyers in contempt in San Francisco. He was fulfilling a function of terror, managing a situation by exhausting its emotional energy.

Long-haired, serious of manner, Leonard Weinglass dared to tell the jurors that the defense considered them to be "the highest authority." There is a tradition in both English and American trial history that supports this view, particularly in trials concerning religious and political beliefs. The judge brusquely excused the jury and admonished Weinglass for his "contumacious conduct."

When Weinglass finished his presentation under the judge's unkind eye, Bobby Seale walked toward the lectern. "Just a minute, sir," the judge said. "Who is your attorney?"

"Charles R. Garry," Seale said, looking uncertainly from side to side.

Prosecutor Foran was already on his feet and asked that the jury be excused, and the judge complied.

Seale said, "Can't a man defend himself?"

Judge Hoffman said that he would permit Kunstler to make another statement on Seale's behalf. Kunstler said that he had been fired and he could not compromise Seale's position. Judge Hoffman got Kunstler to admit again that he had filed an appearance for Seale. Then the judge said that he could not permit Seale to make an opening statement "with his very competent lawyer seated there."

Mingling in the crowd of excited people in the hallways, the white defendants laughed at and scorned the judge for being old and irascible, while Seale understood from the beginning that the trial was really and seriously happening.

The government's first witness was Raymond Simon, Corporation Counsel for the city of Chicago. He testified largely to conversations about permits for assemblies in streets and parks during the Democratic convention. When Judge Hoffman was accused by the defense of favoring the government, he said that if all the defense's objections were bad, he had to call them that way. But law professor Jon Waltz, who had spoken and written well of this "tough, crusty little judge," now said that he "caught only one good evidenciary ruling all afternoon." He said that he had "never heard the like about the jailing of the lawyers," and that the way in which the jury was selected without any questions about familiarity with the case almost certainly constituted, given recent rulings by the Supreme Court, "reversible error." But you could see that the stricken professor feared that the contagion of irrationality might already have infected the higher courts.

"I commit them without bail. I deny the motion," Judge Hoffman said, throwing his hands in the air. Attorney Thomas Sullivan, who would years later become U.S. Attorney for the Northern District, was representing the four pretrial lawyers, two of whom, Michael Tigar and Gerald Lefcourt, were standing with him before the judge. Judge Hoffman's first contempt order had not been denied by the Court of Appeals, and he was filled with assertive ebullience. He said that he was known not to be a "bargainer" and then he said outright, "You can give them the keys to the county jail, Mr. Kunstler."

"Your honor is asking us to accept losing our sixth amendment rights," Kunstler said. The judge was also forcing Irving Birnbaum, Chicago counsel for the defense, to stay at the defense table as a trial lawyer—and lose his daily business for weeks—or be found in contempt and go to jail. Bobby Seale nodded and gestured broadly when he heard how the judge intended to clean up the record on Charles Garry and force the acceptance of Kunstler and Weinglass as sole attorneys for the defense. Tom Sullivan wailed, "Are they to stay in jail for the rest of their lives, your honor?"

"I'm not going to let these men play horse with the court!" Judge Hoffman said, adjourning the proceedings. "You've heard of nothing new under the sun; well, there it is," Sullivan said, as he ran upstairs to the higher court trying to get bail before the court closed. He succeeded in arguing his emergency motion over the phone to Judge Cummings, and the lawyers did not go to jail over the weekend.

By Monday morning the consternation about the attempt to jail the pretrial lawyers was nationwide. Judge Hoffman's contempt orders for lawyers Roberts and Kennedy were vacated by a federal court in San Francisco because they did not state an offense. It was Thomas Foran who, in conversation with Sullivan and the other attorneys for the defense, relented. This raises the whole question of the extent of the collusion between the prosecutor and the judge. The judge denied, in the face of the transcript and the memory of persons present, that he did not give Sullivan a chance on Friday to assure him that he would produce the lawyers on Monday so the lawyers would not have to go to jail over the weekend. Foran suggested in open court that the judge "might give consideration to letting these men withdraw." Judge Hoffman vacated his orders, but struck back sarcastically at requests for apology. The problem of Garry remained moot.

Seale was not certain of the course of his action now.

Now came the trauma of the trial. The jurors commuted every morning. On Monday of the second week of the trial, Kristi King and Ruth Peterson received in their family mail letters scrawled in black felt pen—"You Are Being Watched," signed, "The Black Panthers." The letters were mailed in the same place with the same kind of stamp and the same cancellation. In the judge's chambers with the lawyers and the prosecutors, and later in the courtroom itself, Seale scorned the notion that the letters were sent by members of the Panther party. He said that in the conference in the judge's chambers he felt that Foran and Schultz knew about the origin of the letters. When the defense showed Xerox copies to the press, the judge professed to be disturbed by their public action.

Seale stayed apart from the other defendants and their lawyers as they discussed what had happened. The white marshal assigned to Seale, a southerner by speech, sitting on the bench behind the prosecutors, noticed something and came up and leaned down to speak in Seale's ear. Seale laughed in response, and the marshal laughed too. Seale continued writing answers to questions passed him from press and spectators.

First, the entire jury was sequestered on the excuse of these letters, every bit of the jurors' lives to be watched over by marshals for the next five months. Then the next day Judge Hoffman interviewed these two jurors apart from the others, on a motion of the defense to determine if the letters had prejudiced them. When the letter was handed to the young, bemused Kristi King, she said that she had not seen it before. It turned out that her parents had intercepted the letter in the family mail and sent it faithfully to the FBI. There was insucked breath of suspense throughout the courtroom. But Judge Hoffman plunged onward with his questions before anyone could say him nay, and revealed to her that the letter she was holding had been sent to her. It gave her no time to think about the situation. "Having seen it," the judge said, "can you now be fair and impartial?" Almost crying, she stared at Bobby Seale, who sat silently looking at her. She said she could no longer be fair and impartial. She was excused from the jury.

Seale hardly needed any further suggestion that the letters were, as he contended, sent to prejudice the jury against him. The press gasped and hissed when Richard Schultz explained to the court how it was that Kristi King had not known about the letter. Kunstler countered that the FBI must have known that the girl did not know.

Ruth Peterson, who admitted that she had not only received but read the same letter, declared when interviewed by the judge that she could still be impartial. She was allowed on her own word to stay on the jury. She had even shown the letter to her roommate, Mildred Burns—a plain violation of the judge's daily charge not to discuss the trial in any way. Mrs. Burns too declared, when interviewed by the judge, that she could still be impartial. Now the first alternate Miss Kay Richards was welcomed by the judge onto the jury proper.

The defendants explained it all, looking darkly through their "youth fare" rhetoric, by saying that the government sent the letters to bump the one young juror because, with Kay Richards as the first alternate, there was always the chance that some juror would get sick in the course of a long trial and that would mean two young people on the jury, and two might hold out for acquittal. It was also a heaven-sent reason for sequestering the jury, said the defendants. Traditionally, sequestered juries vent their anger on the available targets, the defendants.

The jury was sequestered at the original suggestion of the prosecution on the motion of Judge Hoffman over the objection of the defense. Judge Hoffman was not without imagination, and not without the willingness to experiment with precedent, and this jury would be sequestered as no other jury before it—totally removed from any media or information that might cause them to think about "dissent," in a sort of contemporary Magic Mountain incarceration within one of Chicago's most well-appointed hotels, the Palmer House.

In early October Kunstler formally requested that Judge Hoffman permit Bobby Seale to have law books in Cook County jail so Seale could prepare his own defense. "I do not regard him as being without counsel," Judge Hoffman said. Kunstler then said that he had been fired and had withdrawn his appearance on September 26, before the first witness was called. The defense was relying upon a legal contention that the trial proper does not begin until the first witness is called. Seale also made his first motion before the first witness. Judge Hoffman did not agree with the contention. "You cannot *fire* a counsel in the middle of a trial," he said. Further, he claimed that he had no authority to permit Seale to have law books in Cook County jail.

That would be the ritualized sequence for the rest of the second phase of Seale's effort in the trial. Seale would declare that he was without counsel of his choice and wished to defend himself and cross-examine witnesses who mentioned his name, and Judge Hoffman would say that "his very able lawyer from New York" was there to speak for him. Then Kunstler, and sometimes both Seale and Kunstler, would say that Kunstler had been fired and had withdrawn and could not speak for Seale, whereupon the judge would say that he had Kunstler's appearance for Seale in his own handwriting over his signature, whereupon Bobby Seale would say that if he was denied counsel of his choice and denied his constitutional right to defend himself and denied books, he could only regard the judge as a "racist" and a "fascist," whereupon certain psychophysiological functions caused by rage, quickened in the judge. A spectator or a member of the Conspiracy staff would say, "Right on," and a marshal would threaten the person with expulsion and might enforce the threat, and the judge would furiously direct the marshals to have "that man," Seale, sit down.

Basing the legality of his contention about Seale solely upon the appearance that Kunstler had signed, Judge Hoffman virtually avoided the question of Bobby Seale's right to defend himself and the concomitant question of Bobby Seale's competency to defend himself. A judge must also weigh the defendant's right to "due process of law" and to "effective counsel." In the recent Charles Manson murder trial in California, the judge interviewed Manson at length before determining that Manson was not competent to represent himself effectively and then assigned him a lawyer whom Manson called "the worst in town" and the judge apparently came to agree with Manson. Imagine the dialogue of Judge Hoffman interviewing Bobby Seale to determine his competency to defend himself. Seale even asked the judge, toward the end of their struggle, to teach him the formalities of cross-examination.

The day after Kunstler requested law books for Seale, Judge Hoffman held Kunstler to task for "directing Mr. Seale." Kunstler denied it, and the judge ended the exchange by saying, "He'll be calling you a racist before you're through."

The most dangerous possible consequence of the indictment of Seale from the government's point of view was that it mixed radical blacks with whites and threatened to help close the political and cultural distance between the two. Practically, the government was using the white defendants to railroad Seale, but the major gain would result from identifying the growing movement among whites and blacks for peace and domestic sanity with the image of Black Panthers with guns, a vision mythologically feared in true nightmare proportions by many middle-class whites. This logic assumed that the government thought that the evidence against Seale, though sparse, might be vivid enough to secure a conviction at least on the substantive "speech" count. It would help to drive liberal Americans back into routinized electoral politics, accepting of social neglect and violence. It gave Seale reason to be suspicious of every relationship in the courtroom.

On the night of October 3, the Chicago police, encouraged by the Justice Department's "Panther program," raided the Black Panther party headquarters in Chicago. The newspapers called it a "shoot-out." That meant that the police riddled the place with bullets, and a couple of Panthers may have returned a few shots.

Members of the Panther party regularly visited the courtroom. "People should be in the courtroom and know about this shit," said John Seale, brother of Bobby, in a press conference. "Right on, right on," members of the Conspiracy staff responded with the black people's phrase that came to them through the Panthers, always anxious for the good opinion of the "vanguard party," and anxious to lessen the seeming distance between Seale and the other defendants.

Panther party newspapermen and artists appeared in the courtroom, and Illinois Party Chairman Fred Hampton came and was prevented by the marshals from talking with Seale. Many newsmen were getting first-hand knowledge of the party's programs and strategies and its seeming common sense. Seale occasionally informed partisan spectators that he wished them to be cool, and to tell others what happened in the courtroom. He also said this during the Weatherman "Days of Rage" actions, October 8–11.

Defendants, their lawyers, and other persons in the courtroom wore black armbands on the anniversary of the death of Che Guevara, who was shot at the instigation of the CIA in a schoolhouse in Bolivia, his eyes left open to stare out of photographs and posters at young people all over the world.

Robert Pierson, an agent heavy in body and speech and attitude, gave the testimony about the speech that Seale made in Lincoln Park, Tuesday night, August 27, 1968. Pierson looked over all the defendants earnestly before identifying Bobby Seale as the man wearing a black tee shirt. Seale was leaning back in his chair with his legs out thrust in Pierson's direct view all the time. "There being no other person with a black tee shirt," Judge Hoffman said, to join in avoiding the miracle of Bobby Seale being the only black man at the defense table, "I conclude the witness has identified Bobby Seale."

There was always the mild suspense of waiting for the moment of identification. In the trial of Policeman Arthur Bischoff, for instance, an important witness did not identify Bischoff, to the delight of the defense and the consternation of the courtroom.

Seale stood up when Pierson mentioned his name and said that he was without attorney. The jurors looked at Seale, perplexed, and the judge never gave them any explanation. Seale pulled out and shuffled broadly what was apparently a copy of the speech that he had made that night in Lincoln Park. He flipped pages and shook his head as Pierson testified that Seale had said to the crowd that they should break up into small groups and get .357 Magnums, .45 pistols, and other guns and surround cops and "they should barbecue some of that pork." Bobby Seale clapped the copy of the speech shut, and exchanged head shaking with Jerry Rubin, who had also given a speech that night. Pierson, over strenuous defense objection, was allowed to say that he interpreted the phrase "barbecue some of that pork" to mean "burn some pigs" or "kill some pigs."

Weinglass cross-examined Pierson on Seale's speech, not specifically on Seale's behalf, but because the testimony reflected upon all of the defendants in the general charge of conspiracy. Seale listened to the cross-examination and looked at the speech in his hands, and shook his head often.

"Barbecuing some of that pork" comes at the end of the printed version of that speech rather than in the context of the naming of the weapons. Seale insisted that he actually said that every man in the black community ought to have those weapons in his home. The printed speech says that if "some pig comes up to us and treats us unjustly, then we have a right to bring our pieces and start barbecuing some of that pork."

It was crucial to the writers of the Constitution that all citizens should have the ancient right of the nobility to bear arms. That was the constitutional basis for the Panther party's program of insisting upon self-defense. The Panthers pointed out that whites and blacks all over the country have guns in their homes.

Leonard Weinglass worked to impeach Pierson's testimony. Richard Schultz popped up, always as if slightly catapulted, objecting frequently. Then he and Judge Hoffman engaged in a charade of trying to make Weinglass look incompetent to the jury, with Schultz saying that he could show Weinglass "how to form the question" and the judge saying, "He may

not comprehend my ruling." Under such harassment, Weinglass asked Pierson if he had any definition of Black Panther
talk, and if he understood terms used by black people.
Schultz's objection was sustained. But even such a word as
"unjustly," which Pierson would not acknowledge that Seale
had used, would connote among many black people more
physical brutalization than it connotes among white people.
The judge and the prosecutors, in a trial about criminal intent
of speech, insisted that the meaning of Black Panther talk was
immaterial and irrelevant. The defense maintained that it was
a political trial but did not take the risk of asking, "Since when
were the political and the criminal mutually exclusive?"

Schultz, in arguing against Weinglass's questioning the
meaning that Pierson attributed to Seale's phrase "barbecue
some of that pork," tripped over his own speech and used the
word "interpretation." "Ah, that's a very interesting distinction
that the prosecutor makes," Weinglass said. "Interpretation,"
when Schultz said Pierson had noted and given his "interpretation" of what Seale said. But it did not stimulate the judge
to change his ruling.

With either faintly lidded or mildly sleepy eyes, FBI agent
Joseph Stanley sat at the prosecution table with his back forever to the jury. But sometimes he brought his hand to his
mouth to cover a smile at the importunate demands of Seale.
Stanley appeared to react to the reiterative and mimic-of-the-
man characteristics of black speech. Roger Cubbage, the Department of Justice attorney at the prosecution table, very
young and very skinny, also gave a smile at the same moments.
Richard Schultz leaned back in his black leather chair, with
his elbows on the armrests and his fingers tented before him,
sniffing the air and twitching his nose. His eyes actually crossed
now and then. Stocky Thomas Foran looked as if he were hiding a grin by drawing his lips and nose and face down to prevent a sneeze. The white defendants also aroused such
reactions from the prosecutors. Stanley again covered his

mouth and smiled a few days later when Seale rose during part-time FBI Agent Sweeney's testimony and said, "I can't hear the witness."

Weinglass's cross-examination of Pierson indicated that Seale's speech did not have an "immediate, perceivable effect" upon the crowd. "It scared the shit out of me," the editor of an underground newspaper told me. A woman told me that Seale urged the listeners "to battle back against the cops." "He is a very effective speaker," Richard Schultz said.

In January, when Seale returned to the trial as a witness, the defense produced a tape of his Tuesday night Lincoln Park speech. In cross-examination Schultz read to Seale what purported to be a quote from his speech the next day, Wednesday, in Grant Park. "If the police get in the way of our march, tangle with the blue-helmeted motherfuckers and kill them and send them to the morgue slab." Seale, after a conference with Charles Garry, who was present in the courtroom, took the Fifth Amendment and would not answer questions about that alleged quote.

Nevertheless, "it scared the shit out of me," was not the same as "an immediate, perceivable effect upon the crowd." It was not what Pierson tried to suggest when he said that he thought Seale's speech definitely inclined people toward violence. It was Leonard Weinglass's contention that the history of the first amendment had resulted in an interpretation where speech to be considered criminal incitement to riot must show an immediate effect. If someone had thrown a rock, or urged others to throw rocks, or picked up a gun and fired at policemen, that would have been an "immediate, perceivable effect." Pierson could not remember any such actions happening in that crowd as a result of Seale's speech. "To bring criminal prosecution for use of speech," Weinglass made a motion that would become routine due to the content of much government testimony, "is violation of first amendment right if clear and present danger in the circumstances is not present."

Richard Schultz answered, "Their First Amendment rights were not prohibited. They were permitted to speak. But if people can say anything with impunity . . ." Judge Hoffman smiled, pleased with Schultz. Motion was denied.

Seale was tired, anxious, haughty, in the way he walked with his head back, head high, in the courtroom. The judge, in his final contempt citations of Seale on November 5, did not note anything contemptuous in Seale's actions and comments from his first motion of September 26 until October 14 when Seale declared again that he was without counsel and should be permitted to defend himself. "I met with these defendants," he said, "and argued with these so-called cats about so-called defending me. I want that for the record, too."

Defendant John Froines asked me in the hallway if the press thought they saw a division, a separation between the other defendants and Seale, because it was not true, he said.

On October 20 Seale presented a more extensive motion to be permitted to defend himself. The clerk announced it. "I will hear you, Mr. Seale," Judge Hoffman said, with nearly a tone of consideration in his voice. Seale said in his book *Seize the Time* that he was now getting some help on points of law and possibilities from Charles Garry through law student Mickey Leanor, the young brown woman who was a central member of the legal staff of the Conspiracy. Defense counsel indicated to me that Seale was indeed receiving advice from Garry who was in a hospital in California.

Seale argued the motion not only on the basis of the constitutional right of any man to defend himself, but on the basis of a special Reconstruction law made specifically to guarantee the rights of black people. Title 42 US Code Section 1981, the great civil-rights act passed by Congress in 1866, concerned equal protection under the law for black people in particular. Seale argued that it guaranteed black people specifically the right to defend themselves, thus enabling them to avoid being

represented by railroading rubberstamp white defense counsels in the South.

Seale did not give up his claim to being without counsel of
his choice. He asked for relief of bail so that he could be free
to interview witnesses and pursue factual research and generally investigate his case. He answered a standing government
accusation with the words, "I am not playing no game with my
life, being stuck on the line, and I want to put that into the
record to explain my situation."

Judge Hoffman leaned forward now. "Mr. Schultz."

Richard Schultz came forward, swinging both arms together
rather than in the usual alternating rhythm, which paralleled
his emphases on words in odd syntactical positions. "This is a
ploy, your honor. It's a simple, obvious ploy." Schultz said that
the defendants were trying to create reversible error in the
record by letting Seale examine witnesses, which would in "two
minutes" cause a mistrial, because the testimony of any witness
against any one defendant reflected against all other defendants in the alleged conspiracy. Seale could not fire four of
five lawyers and then declare that he could not continue without the one lawyer. If Seale defended himself, it would deny
the other defendants their right to a fair trial. The defendants
were just trying to use this for publicity, to mock the court,
Schultz said.

Finally, in denying the motion, Judge Hoffman said, to support his contention that it would be "disruptive" to grant Seale
the right to defend himself—now watch the judge's agility—
"the complexity of the case makes self-representation inappropriate and the defendant would be *more* prejudiced were
he allowed to conduct his own defense than if his motion were
to be denied." Someone had called to the judge's attention
that he had left an aspect of Seale's contention unanswered.

But Judge Hoffman could not support such a statement that
so strongly suggested an assumption about a defendant's competency without conducting extensive interviews and investi-

gations into the defendant's abilities. Seale might have perceived at this time that Judge Hoffman was acting out of the "Superman syndrome" in which an assumption of white people is that black people are menials of body ability, but possess no mental ability comparable to that of white people.

Seale continued to argue angrily with the judge as the jury entered. He was saying that the jurors had been made prejudiced against him. "Mr. Marshal!" the judge said, warning Seale to sit down.

Rennie Davis secured a novel contempt when he tried to bring a birthday cake for Seale into the courtroom. "They arrested your birthday cake, Bobby," Davis said, sitting down by Seale at the defense table. "They arrested the cake." Kunstler made a motion again for leave to withdraw his appearance for Seale, and Seale angrily asked to answer because he had made it quite clear to Kunstler from the beginning that only Garry would be his trial counsel.

When Richard Schultz tried to bring into evidence a picture of a boy in a sweat shirt with what Schultz called "the black power symbol fist" on it, Seale objected heatedly, saying that it was the power-to-the-people sign, all people, and it was a "racist technique" to characterize it as representing "black power" and was meant to prejudice the jury against him. Seale was not mistaken about how "a black power symbol fist" would be perceived by the jury, but the fact that the fist is the traditional socialist salute, the ancient symbol of unity in defiance of the oppressor, was not suggested by anyone. Next Seale told the judge, who was disturbed by the Panthers among the spectators, that they would not take orders from "racist judges," but he could convey the orders. The judge was ruffled. "I think you should know that we support Bobby Seale in this," said David Dellinger, fifty-two years of age; "at least I do." Seale was by now clearly informed by Judge Hoffman that his conduct was often considered contemptuous.

The image of eleven marshals, mostly black men, standing
with their arms folded and legs spread between the spectator
and press sections, completely blocking the aisle, was, in that
charged atmosphere, unforgettable. By Supreme Court rulings, the "appearance of an armed camp" is frowned upon for
its prejudicial effect. Kunstler or Weinglass regularly pointed
out and counted the marshals for the record as a point of
appeal to higher courts.

Judge Hoffman said good-morning to the jury. Bobby Seale
too said good-morning and, in his exchange with the judge,
explained to the jurors his position of being without counsel
of his choice, of desiring to exercise his right to defend himself,
and that the letters signed "The Black Panthers" received by
two jurors were meant to prejudice the jury against him. Seale
spoke with righteousness both in the morning and in the afternoon to the jury about the prejudicial letters. Judge Hoffman listened silently.

During the testimony of the student undercover agent William Frapolly that day, Seale said, "What was that, Judge Hoffman? I didn't hear him." Now Seale was not permitting the
other attorneys to speak for him at all. He made a request for
Judge Hoffman to permit his wife and son to come into the
courtroom. Dellinger declared in open court that all of the
defendants supported Bobby Seale

Mickey Leanor, the young law student, sat next to Seale
accompanied occasionally by Leonard Weinglass or Conspiracy legal staff member Stuart Ball. They gave Seale assurances
and indications about the points of law on which Garry
through Mickey Leanor advised him. When the judge, on the
grounds that she was not an attorney or a defendant, required
her to sit in the first row of the press section, Seale sat at that
end of the defense table.

Frapolly started to testify about Seale's speech in Lincoln
Park, and Seale objected because "my lawyer is not here." The
judge excused the jury. "You think black people don't have

minds," Seale said to the judge. "We got big minds, good minds." The jury returned and Seale was still speaking on the same subject to Judge Hoffman: "Did you lose yours in that Superman syndrome comic-book stories?"

There were times when it seemed that there was only one relationship in the courtroom, the struggle between Bobby Seale and Judge Hoffman, and everyone else was a suspenseful spectator.

Seale began a most vigorous protest when Frapolly mentioned his name again, and demanded to be allowed to cross-examine the student undercover agent. "I admonish you, sir," Judge Hoffman said, "that you have a lot of contemptuous conduct against you."

"I admonish you," Bobby Seale said, "you are in contempt of people's constitutional rights."

It was hard to see if Seale's protests were emphasizing Frapolly's testimony, or distracting from it, in the minds of jurors and other observers.

The judge laughed uncomfortably and told the marshals to bring in the jury. Tom Hayden said, "Let the record show the judge was laughing."

Bobby Seale said, "Yes, he is laughing."

Tom Foran said, "The defendant Hayden, your honor, made the remark." Julius Hoffman admonished other people for laughing, and then he admonished anyone who caught him laughing.

He excused the weary, confused jurors for the day. Then he warned Bobby Seale that, in order to see that his right to "due process of law" was assured, the "governor" of the trial had the right and the duty to gag and bind him so he could be present at his trial. It was the Allen opinion of the Seventh U. S. Circuit Court of Appeals, done in Chicago in July, 1969, just before the Conspiracy trial, that called for the binding and gagging of recalcitrant defendants in order to provide them with their right of due process. Judge Hoffman did not men-

tion that the "recalcitrant defendants," to which the Circuit
Court referred, threw chairs in the courtroom, jumped into
the jury box, and physically shook the jurors.

"Gagged?" Seale said, always much alone when he spoke.
"I'm already being railroaded." The judge then said that the
court would be in recess, giving Seale time to think it over.
"Everyone will please rise," Marshal Dobroski said.

"I am not rising," said the dark brown man who had been
the only defendant to rise and show the traditional respect at
the beginning of the trial. "Why should I rise for him? He is
not recognizing—"

"Mr. Marshal," Judge Hoffman said.

Bobby Seale said, "I am not rising."

The other defendants stayed sitting with Bobby Seale.

The next day many young Black Panthers were jammed into
the audience. There were also more marshals. The black marshals tended to be in their early forties, with closecropped hair,
and the Black Panthers in their twenties with large round natu-
rals. Behind the custody door, before the proceedings began,
the marshals asked Seale, in the name of the judge and for
themselves, if he would caution the Panthers.

"Brothers and sisters," Seale said, and went on to tell the
young Panthers that self-defense was the principle of the party
and if a marshal attacked them they should defend themselves,
but otherwise, Seale said clearly, they should keep cool, listen,
and if a marshal should ask "us to leave, we leave." He used
the first-person plural in a strong, affectionate way.

The judge entered, the defendants did not rise, and the
judge noted them for the record. Kunstler made a motion protesting Conspiracy staff members being searched, and Weinglass counted the marshals in the courtroom for the record,
about twenty.

Richard Schultz interrupted the judge, who had called twice
for the jury, "If the court please, if the court please." Then
Schultz said that Seale had spoken to the audience about an

"attack by them." Schultz twisted the word "attack" into three utterly distorted descriptions of what Seale had said, implying that Seale had urged the audience to attack the court. Laughter came from spectators and press. "You're lying!" Seale screamed. "Dirty liar! I told them to defend themselves. You are a rotten fascist pig, fascist liar, that's what you are!"

The spectators shouted, "Right on!"

Judge Hoffman said that if the laughter occurred again, he would direct the marshals to clear the courtroom. "Let the record show," he said, "the tone of Mr. Seale's voice was one of shrieking and pounding on the table and shouting."

Schultz apologized and attempted to retract his characterization of what Seale had said. "I'm sure your honor will understand." But it was lost in the furor of the judge's indignation.

"I demand, demand, demand," Seale said, to be allowed to cross-examine undercover agent Frapolly. Judge Hoffman said, "I know this is just an entire device here . . ." Several observers have speculated that the government made Judge Hoffman aware of its wiretaps of phone conversations between Garry and conspiracy staff-member Mickey Leanor, who also consulted with Weinglass.

Judge Hoffman again threatened Seale with what would happen to him if he did not cease his "outbursts." Seale pointed to the portraits of the "slave-owning" founding fathers on the wall behind Judge Hoffman, among whom ironically were those who helped to write the Constitution that he revered and whose protection he was demanding. "What can happen to me more than what George Washington and Benjamin Franklin did to their slaves?" The marshals "struggled" with Seale. Dellinger, pacifist, placed his elbows to his sides and his hands to his face and tried to put himself between the marshals and Seale. Seale was thrown, hard, into his seat. Richard Schultz asked that the record show that Dellinger had "physically interfered" with the marshals.

"I didn't think I would ever live to sit on a bench or be in a courtroom," Judge Hoffman said, "where George Washington was assailed by a defendant in a criminal case and a judge was criticized for having his portrait on the wall."

"Mr. Seale, you do know what is going to happen to you." Seale continued to argue that he wanted and needed to represent himself. The judge excused the jury, and said to the marshals, "Take that defendant into the room in there and deal with him as he should be dealt with in this circumstance." The defendants did not rise when the court was recessed for the judge's order to be carried out.

Seale, gagged, was carried by marshals back into the courtroom, handcuffed and bound to a metal chair. The handcuffs scraped and clicked, and people squirmed. "All we want," the judge said to Seale, "is you to be respectful to the court." If Seale would promise to cease his outbursts, the judge said, he could be restored to his original physical condition at the defense table.

Kunstler described the binding and gagging of Seale detail by detail for the record. "You don't represent me," Seale mumbled through the gag. "Sit down, Kunstler." The judge asked the marshals to make "that contrivance more secure." Seale was taken behind the custody door again, where the gag was strengthened. Everybody waited until Seale was carried back into the courtroom.

When the jury was at last allowed into the courtroom, Mrs. Jean Fritz began weeping and other jurors squirmed hard in their seats at the sight. The brown woman who wore a red wig—she would vote for conviction on all counts during the jury's deliberation—refused to look at Seale. The other black woman, Mary Butler, who would vote for acquittal, was visibly upset and stole glances at Seale, wincing each time she saw him. Seale noticed the tears going down Mrs. Fritz's cheeks. He moved his gagged-and-bound head.

"The judge is not a mere moderator under the law," the judge said to the jurors, "but is the governor of the trial," to assure its proper conduct and fairness. Seale spoke through his gag, "Let me cross-examine the witness. I have a right to defend myself."

That was the image that went out through reports and artists' sketches on television and in newspapers. The black leader who demanded the right to defend himself was bound and gagged in the most notorious political trial of the century. "The most effective thing that has happened yet, politically," said one defendant. Furthering the political effect was also one way to assure that Seale would be somewhat protected from physical abuse at the hands of his captors. In these three days the white defendants would respond with actions and declarations that would come to constitute about one-third of the contempts for which they would be sentenced at the end of the trial.

"Free Bobby" demonstrators thronged the entrances to the Federal Building the next morning. The courtroom was jammed. Seale's wife Artie, composed in manner, sat in the pew behind me with three-year-old Malik, named after the murdered Malcolm X and Nkrumah, the deposed prime minister of Ghana. Bright-eyed with morning energy, Malik spilled out of her lap and crawled around the pews.

Defendant Lee Weiner used deaf-and-dumb sign language skillfully to combat the court's orders against talking between spectators and defendants while the trial was in session. He occasionally used the sign language with Artie Seale, though she did not appear to understand it as fluently as he.

The custody door opened and two black marshals bore a wooden "throne" chair into the courtroom with the gagged Seale bound into it. Artists began sketching on the big boards in their laps for the noon telecasts and noon editions. "Free Bobby," the spectators cried out, and marshals told them sharply to keep quiet or be ejected.

"Daddy, Daddy," Malik cried out joyfully, and Artie Seale, studied of face, held him back by the waist. Bobby Seale, with the large knot of the gag wrapped on top of his head, glanced once toward his son's voice and then stared up at the wall above the empty jury box. The good feeling of little Malik told me more about Bobby and Artie Seale. There was the woman who was on Seale's mind. There was the man who was on her mind. "It can be bad for a man's mind when he's locked up and taken away from good loving and good screwing," Seale said in his book. Artie Seale gave a press conference that noon in which she said that little Malik cried now and then for his daddy. She was reportedly not altogether enthusiastic about the all-involving nature of Seale's political activity.

Black marshals guarded the courtroom, and now Seale stared at a young brown woman in a brown vinyl dress, wearing a full natural, startlingly pretty, who sat down in the court reporter's position behind the steno machine below the witness box. The United States government was going to demonstrate to the assembled persons of this courtroom that black men would restrain the bound-and-gagged chairman of the Black Panther party, and a black woman with a natural would record the proceedings.

If the trial had been televised, the government might have projected its message about not one white hand being put upon Seale in the court. But it was the image of the bound-and-gagged Seale and the old, tyrannical white judge that entered the minds of most viewers and readers in the country.

Defendants Rubin, Hoffman, Dellinger, Davis, and Weiner did not stand when the unashamed judge entered, while Froines and Hayden did stand. Judge Hoffman looked down from the bench at the young brown woman in the brown vinyl dress with the full natural hair, "Let the record show that the defendants did not stand." When Froines and Hayden realized that they had been cited too, instead of correcting the judge, they sat down abruptly. They were, in fact, sentenced at the end of the trial for not rising on that morning.

When Seale moved his head as if in pain, a few women in the jury moved hard in their seats. Seale kept working his fingers because his arms, bound to the arms of the chair, were losing their feeling, going to sleep, circulation being cut off. Mickey Leanor sat near him to give him a pencil or answer his questions. When Seale made any slight movement, or even moved his fingers to try to keep feeling in his arm, everyone glanced at him.

Leonard Weinglass told the judge that the bonds should be loosened. Seale was shuffling his left arm loose. The black marshals grabbed him on either side to stop him. The chair with Seale in it started to topple into a row of reporters. Jerry Rubin and Abbie Hoffman leaped and tried to pull the marshals away from Seale. The largest marshal jammed his elbow into Seale's mouth. The toppling chair was caught by another marshal. Judge Hoffman excused the jury. "Don't hit me in the balls, motherfucker," Seale shouted. "Don't hit him in the balls," Jerry Rubin said. Reporters seated by the falling chair said that one of the black marshals did punch Seale in the groin.

There was pandemonium. The gag slipped, and Seale yelled at the judge, "Fascist dog," and a number of other things. The marshals carried him out in the chair. Artie Seale, sitting in the press section with little Malik, left the courtroom.

Tom Hayden, Rennie Davis, and David Dellinger spoke calmly to press and spectators, asking them to keep cool and report the happenings to everyone on the outside. "You're making an issue of sitting down," one spectator told the marshals. "Why aren't you making an issue of Seale?" Tom Hayden asked the fellow to keep cool. Richard Schultz asked that the record show that Miss Leanor had touched Seale's hand in "a very tender, motherly way."

Leonard Weinglass, in front of the jury, said that he could not continue his cross-examination with a man bound and gagged in the courtroom. He asked that the jury be polled to see if they felt that they could continue the trial. "The government is scraping the bottom of the barrel of its witnesses," Weinglass said Richard Schultz had told Kunstler in the elevator. Richard Schultz leaped up. "That is not true," he said.

"I object," Bobby Seale mumbled through his gag, with witty timing.

"Man does not have to sit here and be called a pig," Judge Hoffman said. Bobby Seale made a loud affirmative "rrrrrrrrrrnnnnnnnnnn" with a deep nod of yes. That would occur several times in the next few days.

"Your honor," Tom Hayden said, standing up and leaning with both arms on the defense table, "may I address the court?" Judge Hoffman, as if preoccupied, shook his head no. Hayden asked again. "No," the judge said, "I'm not allowed by the Supreme Court." Hayden persisted and the marshals moved toward him, and the judge noted Hayden for the record.

"What about the voir dire of the jury?" Dellinger said. "He hasn't ruled." He meant Weinglass's request for the jury to be polled. Dellinger was later sentenced for that statement.

If Seale moved his head, or made a noise behind his gag, he commanded the courtroom, the media, the attention of the nation. The proceedings could not be moved.

"Mr. Seale," Judge Hoffman said, "I ask you to refrain from making those comments."

The elastic-bandage gag slipped, and Seale was hauled out in the chair by the marshals through the custody door. He was yelling, "Fascist dog," at the judge, and about his right to defend himself and his right to a fair trial. "Now they are going to beat him," Hayden said. "They are going to beat him."

"You may as well kill him if you are going to gag him," Abbie Hoffman said.

Defendants Davis and Hayden walked up and down by the defense table. "Ladies and gentlemen," Davis said to the jurors, "when you are out of the room, they torture this man." Again Davis said, "They torture him when they take him into that room." The defendants' voices were flat, as if they had not yet contrived to find the distance between the emotion of the event and the audience. Tom Hayden asked the spectators not to stay sitting in protest and thus be ejected. "I ask you, Mr. Hayden," Judge Hoffman said, "not to try to fill my position."

Bobby Seale scrawled a message with handcuffed hands on a legal-sized yellow sheet that was shown to the courtroom. At the noon press conference, Jerry Rubin held it up because Bobby asked me to do it. TELL BROTHERS AND SISTERS TO COOL IT EVERYWHERE. JUST SPREAD THE WORD ABOUT HOFFMAN AND INJUSTICE OF U. S. COURTROOM. If it had not been for Seale's several urgings in previous days and on this day for the brothers and sisters to cool it, it was fairly certain there would have been murderous violence in the courtroom, outside it, and on the plaza downstairs.

"Will you continue to disrupt the trial until it's stopped?" I looked at the newsman who asked that question of the defendants and at the newspeople who awaited an answer. Bobby Seale pulled and shuffled his left arm loose in its bonds, and two or three large marshals struggled with him, and one marshal slugged him in the balls, and Jerry Rubin and Abbie Hoffman tried to pull the marshals off Seale—that was now called a "disruption." When Seale moved his little finger, it was a disruption, deliberate or not. The sudden hostility of the press's questions unbalanced the defendants. Tom Hayden had said earlier that what the press called "outbursts" were really attempts to bring order into the courtroom. Whose order, or what description of order, he did not specify.

That afternoon the marshal banged the gavel and said "this honorable court," and people giggled at the word "honorable."

The judge repeated to the court reporter the names of the defendants who would not rise. "And Mr. Seale," said David Dellinger, seizing upon the obvious, that a defendant bound to his chair could not rise in respect to the court.

Judge Hoffman pleaded again with Seale, telling him that "the burden is on the government to prove you guilty," and if he would cease his protests the gagging and binding could be removed. Bobby Seale even wrote a note, reasserting his desire and right to defend himself, when the judge asked him for his response.

Judge Hoffman attempted to move the proceeding anyway. "No, no," Seale mumbled through his gag at Witness Lieutenant Healy. Judge Hoffman said, as if speaking to the wall, "He has counsel of record in this court."

Kunstler asked Lieutenant Healy how he knew it was Lee Weiner he saw in the Grant Park underground garage. "In my function as head of the subversive section," said Healy, "I have seen Mr. Weiner's picture several times." That could have been construed as a deliberately prejudicial and highly objectionable statement. Through his gag, Seale interrupted. "I want to cross-examine the witness. I have a right to do so." The testimony at this point did not concern Seale directly, but he could argue that in a conspiracy case the testimony of any witness reflected on him, as Richard Schultz himself had argued to secure denial of Seale's motion to defend himself.

Spectators flourished the power salute when Seale was carried into the courtroom the next day. "Free Bobby," they cried. The marshals jumped toward them and told them to sit down. Artists were again sketching the image that would be a prominent visual image in the media for weeks.

"I don't need someone to come from New York to tell me the law," Judge Hoffman said to Kunstler, who was protesting again the treatment of Seale, "or wherever you come from."

"Let him defend himself."

"I have been called obscene names," the judge said, as if that answered the question of self-representation. "I do not need to put up with it."

"That's a black man reacting to a white man, your honor."

"I have had black lawyers in this courtroom who argue a case with dignity and great ability." Now what did the judge mean by that? Why the emphasis upon great ability?

"There comes a time," Judge Hoffman mused, "when a federal district judge is called a pig—" Seale, bound and gagged, nodded vigorously to affirm that Judge Hoffman was a pig "—in open court before a hundred people, publicized throughout the country, that this is a proper restraint." The judge mused away indignantly up there on the bench, "To be called a fascist racist," and Seale nodded deeply to affirm that Judge Hoffman was a fascist racist. Judge Hoffman continued musing, to himself and to everyone, then turned sharply toward the mumbling gagged Seale: "Listen to him now!"

Tom Hayden proposed to the court that a defendant go to California to see if Garry could come to the trial and take over Seale's defense. Garry would, of course, refuse, but the delay was welcome. Before court reconvened in the afternoon, Foran was pacing in the aisle, waiting for all parties. Then he spoke in support of the defense's motion. "I count sixteen interruptions of the trial by the defendant Seale," Foran said.

"I'll go along with great reluctance," Judge Hoffman said to Foran. The judge was reacting to the defendants' speeches that were more and more successful in terms of increasing audiences. "I don't want to be watching television and see one of them vilifying me or you." Tom Hayden, after conferring with the other defendants, went to the lectern to more or less assure the judge he wouldn't vilify him in any speech. "But on principle," Hayden said, "I think one gag is enough."

The jurors were downcast, angry, frightened, when they were told that the court would be recessed until Monday. Seale wrinkled his forehead and squinched his eyes before the women jurors, who stood there looking at him while they were supposed to be listening to the judge.

On Monday morning, those who arrived early were surprised to see Bobby Seale without gag and without bonds, absorbed in writing something at the defense table. If he looked up it was with the air of a man preoccupied in his papers and not seeing the curious reporters and spectators. There was the dangerous suggestion that he had won a particular struggle.

Then Weinglass read to Judge Hoffman, before the jury was called, Charles Garry's statement which Tom Hayden had brought back from California. Garry said that even if his doctors would permit him he would be guilty of malpractice if at this late date he came into a trial already plagued with "constitutional infirmities." He gave a full argument again for Seale's right to defend himself.

"If the court please," Richard Schultz argued, Seale was trying "to build in error into the record. . . . The judiciary is too delicate to be able to conduct itself with violence in the courtroom. . . . None of us like to see the defendant gagged. It is an abhorrent sight. . . ." Listening to Schultz's tone was a lesson in the "intentions" of speech.

"I implored him, I beseeched him, I urged him," Judge Hoffman wailed. He read Kunstler's signed appearance on behalf of Seale, dated September 24, 1969. "After that date," the judge said, "it is absolutely discretionary for the trial judge to let an attorney withdraw." The defense's request for Seale to be allowed to defend himself was once again denied.

Then Seale spoke to the judge of his "blood circulation" having been cut off by the elastic bandage that had been wrapped around his head. "Even if the words fascist and racist come into it, I am trying—don't you see?—to persuade you to concede my right to defend myself."

Kunstler then argued a motion for a mistrial on the basis of race, citing the Civil Rights Act of 1866 to support his argument. Foran made one statement in answer: "No man has the right to disrupt the trial." Seale spoke sharply across the aisle to Foran, "I'm hip to you, and pretty soon the people are going to be hip to you—power to the people." Spectators and others echoed, "Right on." The judge denied the motion.

The courtroom was comparatively quiet for two days. That afternoon Seale again told the jury that he was without counsel. The next morning, when the custody door opened, little Malik dashed across the courtroom towards his father, who was being escorted by the marshals. "Daddy, Daddy," and then Malik was crying, and the marshals carried him back to Artie Seale who, for a time, left the courtroom with him.

"Could you hold the witness up for a minute, Judge?" Seale then requested to be allowed to cross-examine Donald R. Townshend, a Chicago police detective. Seale had been taking notes, and rose with the papers in his hands.

"The lawyers have examined the witness," Judge Hoffman said.

"In other words," Seale said, in subdued tones, "you're going to run all the witnesses off the stand so I can't question them."

Judge Hoffman said to the marshals, "Have Mr. Seale take his seat."

"I don't know all the formalities," Bobby Seale said, standing in front of his chair by the defense table. "But I could easily learn them if you'll give me a little coaching." He said that the judge could help him ask "pertinent questions" and that he was "well aware of the charges." It was a straight-forward sounding plea. It was intriguing, in the sentiment of speculation, to wonder what would have happened if Judge Hoffman had undertaken to coach Bobby Seale in the basic rules and principles of cross-examination and direct-examination. "A mistrial in two minutes," Richard Schultz would say. But with every lawyer in that courtroom caught leaving his footprints on rules and ethics at one time or another, it was hard to believe that Bobby Seale would have done worse.

Seale said that he had not been shackled because he called Judge Hoffman a "pig" and a "fascist" but because "When a man is denied his constitutional rights—"

"Will you sit down, please?"

But Seale continued talking about the ways in which the judge was denying him his rights. "Mr. Marshal, have that man sit down." Two marshals moved toward Seale.

Seale sat down but continued talking. "You will still be considered a pig and a fascist and a racist by me. You have still denied me my constitutional rights."

The judge asked the court reporter if she got Mr. Seale's remarks, and she nodded. "For the record," Seale said about a plainclothes policewoman, "I have no desire to cross-examine the witness." There were smiles and quiet laughter.

On Wednesday morning, November 5, Deputy Sheriff Bill Ray of San Mateo County, California, testified about the time in August 1968 that he followed Seale and saw him get a ticket for a plane. That would be Seale's use of interstate commerce. Kunstler declined to cross-examine Ray, saying he would not prejudice Seale's Sixth Amendment rights. "Mr. Kunstler is playing fast and loose," Richard Schultz said. Kunstler and Judge Hoffman argued again about whether he was or was not Seale's lawyer. The judge may have wished for the jurors to hear his side of the quarrel. Then Seale made a decisive move.

He walked to the lectern to examine the witness, with notes that he spread before him. At the far end of the defense table defendant Lee Weiner flashed deaf-and-dumb signs excitedly over the heads of reporters to Sharon Avery and Artie Seale. Artie Seale shrank and scrunched down in none-too-certain anticipation of what was going to happen. Little Malik was not in the courtroom. Black marshals came and, their arms folded, stood next to Seale.

Seale asked the deputy sheriff, "Have you ever killed a black man?"

"Sit down, Mr. Seale," the judge said.

"Have you ever taken part in raids on Black Panther party headquarters?" He gave the witness just a second. "Why did you follow me, Mr. Ray?"

"Sit down, Mr. Seale," the judge said.

The jurors fixedly watched the quarrel in which Seale called the judge "a complete, overt fascist." The judge asked him again to sit down, and the marshals, with folded arms, stayed close to Seale.

Judge Hoffman instructed the witness to return at two o'clock. "We are going to recess now, young man," he said to Seale.

"Look, old man," Seale said, "if you keep denying me my constitutional rights you are going to be exposed to the world."

In the hallway during the noon recess, Tom Hayden said miserably that the judge, if he really wanted to handle the situation, should have dismissed the witness. Hayden shrugged and said he was going out for a drink, as if he had no control over what was happening and morbidity was a pleasure if it could be shared over a drink.

Seale did not want the government to perceive the situation as a hopeless bind. It may be that the government also feared for how he was affecting the jury.

Everyone whose presence was required at 2 P.M. in the courtroom was there except the judge and Thomas Foran. Foran entered just before the judge at 2:36 P.M. with an expectant air that was also in the other prosecutors. If the defense attorneys were even a minute late, the judge would read it for the record.

The judge entered, heavy with some sort of feeling. He was carrying papers against his chest, and he stooped over to let them down upon his bench. "There is a matter that I wish to take up, gentlemen, before we proceed further with this trial."

He always kept the proceedings suspenseful, avoiding the many difficulties that would have resulted if people had warning of things that he intended. He dismissed the witness "temporarily."

"I perceive it as my duty and obligation . . . that the trial to continue in an atmosphere of dignity. . . ." He ended his prologue by calling Bobby Seale's behavior a "willful attack upon the administration of justice in an attempt to sabotage the functioning of the federal judicial system."

"That is a lie," Seale said.

In what was nearly a tone of meeting of minds, Judge Hoffman said, "You are making things very difficult for me, Mr. Seale."

"You are making things very difficult for me, Judge Hoffman."

"I find it necessary," Judge Hoffman said, "that I deal with this conduct at this time, which in some instances was accompanied by physical violence."

"That is a lie," Seale said, "and you know it."

Seale interrupted Judge Hoffman's reading several times to say something was a lie.

Defendant John Froines went out of the courtroom, apparently to go to the washroom. A marshal noticed him and went out, too, by the other door. There appeared to be a number of plainclothes marshals without visible badges and also Chicago police in the audience. A plainclothes policewoman or marshal went in and out, talked to a couple of marshals, and sat in the press section with a coat wrapped up in her lap and her hands inside the coat.

Standing behind Seale's chair, Krim Ballentine, a stocky black marshal with a tough, intelligent, cynical face, took the marshal's badge that hung in its leather case from the handkerchief pocket of his suit jacket and slipped the badge into his lower jacket pocket. All over the courtroom marshals put into their pockets badges and other obvious things that might be grabbed in hand-to-hand fighting. The courtroom was jammed, with the exception of the empty jury seats along the north wall.

"I certify that I saw and heard," Judge Hoffman said, "and each constituted a separate contempt of this court." Seale sat at the defense table in his usual manner, which caused him to appear separate from the other defendants.

With mimic powers that could chill a listener, with the eerie reality of Seale's voice in his voice, Judge Hoffman read the sections of the transcript for each of the sixteen instances of contempt. The reading even seemed to be in support of Seale's contention. The only voice that the judge missed in the transcript was his own voice. He always read it so mildly, particularly when it was dialogue in which he was admonishing Seale.

There was dull, dull anger in the courtroom, with people not knowing actually what to expect. Time and again lawyers and newsmen had looked into Supreme Court rulings, and concluded that a judge could not sentence a contemner summarily without jury trial for more than six months.

In the midst of stymied conflict that afternoon, spectators, newsmen, and marshals fought the hanging drowse in the atmosphere. "That was when I was hit in the testes," Seale said aloud at one point. He occasionally noted something on paper. Foran, with his back to Seale across the aisle, was writing steadily at his table. Judge Hoffman said there were remarks in the transcripts that he would not repeat in the presence of young people in this courtroom.

Then the judge asked Kunstler as Seale's attorney to speak. Kunstler said in a tone of humility that he would be "derelict" if he presumed to speak for Seale now when it was central to the issue that he did not represent the defendant Bobby Seale. The judge then said that Seale could speak.

Seale stood up, looking this way and that confusedly, "I can speak now, but I can't speak to defend myself." Judge Hoffman simply wanted Seale to conform to the obligations of sentencing procedures and speak in mitigation of punishment. "What kind of a court is this?" Seale said. "Is this a court? It must be a fascist operation, like I see it in my mind, you know—I don't understand you"—as if he were really a little surprised to find that the actuality of the court coincided with the fascist operation he saw in his mind.

Seale said that the judge had just finished reading a whole record of him trying to speak for himself and for his right to defend himself, and that was what he would speak about.

Judge Hoffman interrupted to tell him he could speak about possible punishment.

"Punishment? You've punished black people all your life." Judge Hoffman interrupted Seale frequently, in an attempt to hold him to the empty form of speaking about punishment that was already fixed.

Judge Hoffman found Seale "guilty of each and every specification in my oral observation" and "committed him to the Attorney General of the United States for three months for each specification to run consecutively." Bobby Seale drew four years in prison for his constitutional efforts. Judge Hoffman tried to circumvent the six-month limit on summary contempt by sentencing Seale to three months for each citation. On the previous Friday, Foran said there were sixteen interruptions by the defendant Seale, but one of the sixteen contempts was that of Seale going to the lectern that morning of November 5, 1969. When was the number sixteen decided, and by whom?

But no one yet knew what the sentencing meant in the context of the trial. Seale literally shrugged at the sentencing; he was already in jail and prepared to continue with the trial. He even seemed to be no longer sitting separately from the other defendants. Judge Hoffman saved the "real shit" until the last moment.

"There will be an order for a mistrial."

Seale looked up sharply, and said with loud surprise, "What's this cat up to now?" Then Judge Hoffman said that Bobby G. Seale was severed from this case, to be tried separately at a later date. He fixed a date, tentatively, in April, 1970. If Seale was seeking a mis-trial, he was certainly surprised at this point.

Newsmen ran pell-mell, in the way of newsmen, to phone their stations, networks, and newspapers. There was no time for action from the impotent fury of spectators and others. I was seized by an urge to duck my head below the benches and yell, "Attack the court," in the hope that it might catch the spirit of the moment and impel people to do something. I was only an inch away, a jostle of the elbow, that far, from doing it. "I want a new trial now," Bobby Seale said.

"I'm sorry," Judge Hoffman said, shuffling papers together to leave the courtroom, "I can't try two cases at one time." The marshals were already guiding the confused Seale toward the custody door. "Where's my coat? I want my coat." He jerked his coat from the back of his chair.

He would return to the courtroom in January as a witness about his speech in Lincoln Park.

Lawyer observers said about the unprecedented four-year sentence for contempt, "That judge is crazy; he can't do that." Judge Hoffman was letting everyone know that precedent is so treasured in the law just because the law is so arbitrary.

Bobby Seale was gone from the trial so suddenly that the white defendants, the next morning, practically huddled at the defense table under the shock of Judge Hoffman's action. There was much pleased and relieved smiling among the prosecutors. The black people and the young Panthers were gone from the spectator and press sections. A particular feeling about the trial was gone, the feeling that it opened into many struggles in the world. A feeling of white people was here now, a closed club of limp, fearful, guilty white people.

The next day Weinglass and Kunstler made a motion for a mistrial for the remaining seven defendants on the grounds that the jury could not help but be biased against them because of their association with the severance and with the vivid acts and testimony of acts attributed to Bobby Seale. A day later a special attorney for Seale tried to argue the illegality of the four-year contempt sentence. "I have known literally thousands of what we used to call Negro people," Judge Hoffman said, "and who are now referred to as black people, and I have never heard that kind of language emanate from the lips of any of them."

Kunstler made a motion out of the presence of the jury, on the afternoon of November 7, requesting that Abbie Hoffman's remark "being treated like a bunch of rotten niggers" be struck from his speech on the government exhibit of a film of a press conference that he gave on Monday of Convention Week. The film also gave a close-up of Defendant Hoffman tapping his thigh with a small stick. Judge Hoffman was delighted to deny the motion.

Kunstler was concerned that the three black women on the jury would misconstrue the remark, and I watched their faces when the film was shown. They gave no expression at the remark, and then, after a moment, looked here or there, from one side to the other, or down into their laps. The film ended with Abbie Hoffman cut off in midsentence. The prosecutors, particularly Roger Cubbage who researched these materials, suppressed their grins. Abbie Hoffman grinned, too, and shook his head at Jerry Rubin.

Months later, in February, 1970, during the closing arguments, Richard Schultz would remind the jurors, "You may recall that expression on his face as he struck the stick against his thigh. He spoke of being pushed around like rotten niggers." The black women's faces appeared to harden. Thomas Foran also repeated it in his closing argument, talking insistently about the "hate, hate, hate" suggested by Abbie Hoffman striking that stick against his thigh.

"There wasn't any element of racism in this case," Judge Hoffman said at the end of the trial when he was preparing to sentence William Kunstler for contempt, "except that there was one defendant, if you call that racism, who was a member of the black race."

The voice of Bobby Seale rose again at the end of the trial into the voice of Judge Hoffman as he read the contempt transcript for the seven remaining defendants and their lawyers.

# PART THREE
*A Demonstration Here,*
*A Demonstration There*

FROM THE MIDDLE OF SEPTEMBER to the middle of October, 1969, in the first weeks of the Conspiracy trial, there were a great many demonstrations of different kinds and styles and intentions by different groups of people in Chicago. Many would not have happened and would have received no notice in the media if it were not for the Conspiracy trial that attracted them. Others coincided with this time, such as the demonstrations of blacks for entrance into the construction trades training programs and the counterdemonstrations of white construction workers. These last possessed such energy and potential of violent involvement from wide sectors of black and white working-class population that the city was especially fearful and touchy, causing many sympathizers with the defense to stay away from demonstrations specifically concerned with the Conspiracy trial.

The overt reasons for various demonstrations that fall were to get jobs or to keep jobs, to protest the Conspiracy trial as an injustice and a harbinger of a broad repression, to protest the imprisonment of Bobby Seale, to demand withdrawal of United States Armed Forces from Viet Nam, to call attention to issues of poverty and racism and medical care and housing and police oppression, to protest suppression of free speech, to protest the oppression of women, to protest the draft, and to start a war at home against the imperialist American war here and abroad.

Most of these demonstrations were attended by no more than a couple of thousand people, sometimes fewer. Some of them were ingenious, most were repetitive and dull, and all were at least partly planned.

The only demonstrations that possessed the power of dynamic involvement of wide population groups were those by black people, and the counterdemonstrations by white workers, over the issues of entrance and treatment of black people in the training programs of the construction-trades unions where wages were deemed to be high. The Chicago news media, full of immediate fear, put these demonstrations into the forefront of their newspapers and telecasts. But the only demonstrations that secured a dynamic response on the front pages and in the telecasts of the national media were the briefly violent Weatherman "Days of Rage" actions, which oddly enough attracted no involvement of surrounding people at all, except for high-rise apartment dwellers who threw cocktail ice down on the Weatherpeople.

The wish of every demonstration organizer and every demonstrator is twofold: they want the action of the demonstration to draw bystanders into it, and at the same time to give strong enough image and interest to the media that viewers and readers and listeners will in some way, at least in their minds and emotions, be drawn into the issue. Such public awareness also gives protection to a demonstration.

Nowadays the image for the media, the action that occurs within the frame of a picture without relationship to the wider surroundings, is often the sole aim of a "demonstration," because it offers seemingly quick results by virtue of wide dissemination.

It was the fear of the power of such images, and to preserve the order of the court and the due process of the proceedings, that Chief Judge William Campbell ruled in the week before the trial that all cameras and recording equipment in general were to be excluded from the Federal Building and its environs except for one room on the second floor. Judge Campbell named a copper property line embedded in the asphalt on the eastern side of the Federal Plaza as one of the boundaries of this exclusion.

There, in a protest press conference, media men straddled the copper line, one foot in violation of Judge Campbell's order and one foot in free territory, and took each other's pictures. There were shouts of glee as a funeral procession, led by a man with a solemn bell, laid the fair body of Free Speech to rest at the foot of the flagpole among moribund cameras and recording equipment. Media men laughed excitedly because of the witty, flattering imagery offered to their cameras by the Conspiracy staff. No one knew how strictly the government would enforce Judge Campbell's ruling. When a couple of cops shouldered their way through the crowd, the "demonstrators" hissed and jumped with mock fear and a rush of excitement. But the cops did nothing to prevent the immediate violations.

Illinois Panther Party Chairman Fred Hampton spoke here alongside Rennie Davis. Hampton was challenged by a bald-headed man with a briefcase who said that the demonstrators were getting publicity far out of proportion to what they deserved, "just like the Democratic convention." He also said that he was the father of ten kids. "All power to those ten kids, you bald-headed capon," Hampton said. When the newsmen tried to get the man's name in his heated exchange with Hampton, he called himself just a "working guy." His picture appeared in the papers. He had seized the moment to demonstrate the sentiments of many middle-class white people.

Then the cameramen and newsmen clustered about a man in a wheelchair, court researcher and gadfly Sherman Skolnick. He joked and took pictures of the cameramen as they took pictures of him. He said that, in order to make a constitutional point, he was going into the Federal Building and take pictures. He was wheeled across the plaza into the lobby, where he was indeed arrested. The picture of him and his little camera appeared in the papers and in some newscasts, and he had a case with which to challenge Judge William Campbell's ruling.

Judge Campbell's ruling, however, prevailed throughout the trial.

Jerry Rubin's hair had been cut short into a crew cut when he was in custody at the beginning of the trial, serving a forty-five days' sentence on a conviction for blocking military trains in California. He asked for long-haired kids all over the country to send him locks of their hair from which he would make a wig to wear in court. Nancy Kurshan and other Conspiracy staff dumped great loads of envelopes with "locks of hair" onto the table in a press conference before cameras, in the room set aside by Judge Campbell. Jerry Rubin began wearing a wig in the courtroom.

None of these completely manipulated demonstrations within the frame of a picture, however, could equal the effect of the image, that could not even be photographed, that could only be pictured through the drawings of courtroom artists, of the binding and gagging of Bobby Seale. None of the street demonstrations during this time could equal the actions during the Democratic National Convention for involving bystanders and giving images to the media. The city feared the potential of ever-widening involvement in the black and white contruction workers' demonstrations, and that was why Mayor Daley used his power to force conclusions in the construction trades disputes.

The most effective demonstrations appeared to be those that were prosecuted day after day over a period of time and that gained an unpredicted element, a surprise, the free play of a growing contradiction, unstymied.

The Conspiracy defendants worried over the SDS demonstrations scheduled for October supposedly in support of them. SDS had been sundered in its disastrous convention at the Coliseum in Chicago in June, 1969.

The three main factions of SDS in the ugly, shabby, nearly lightless meeting halls of the Coliseum attracted different types of people. Members of Progressive Labor, numerically the largest of the groups, allied with the Worker-Student alliance, were particularly routinized in their phrases, inflections, and the movements of their bodies. They kept sexual expression to themselves. They used the word "bullshit" frequently to characterize any contrary utterance. PL–WSA were credited with important campus actions at Harvard and Berkeley. They were strongly opposed to the use of drugs by young people, yet many of them were heavy smokers of cigarettes.

The National Collective group, whose submission but not expulsion PL was seeking, was brighter in the eye, livelier in movements, and less routinized in speech. They even laughed now and then. The NC group for more than a year had been trying to find an answer to the unity and growing strength of PL. The NC members were often sons and daughters of wealthy families, and exhibited a love of contest. They were also closer spiritually to the youth culture of American middle-class students.

In the NC caucus in the adjoining hall of the Coliseum, they went so far in their limber angry arrogance as to call themselves "the head, and the PLers the tail," because some PLers were saying in the first hall that they did not want to lose the characteristics of the NC that were attractive to many young people. Finally, the PL–WSA group in the first hall agreed to hear, without physically fighting back, the NC statement.

The NC group filed into the hall and massed with folded arms on the speaker's stand and in the area below it and in the adjacent aisles, to protect their speaker, Bernadine Dohrn. In a resonant voice, that avoided a call to battle, she read PL out of the party, so to speak. She was interrupted more and more toward the end by chants from the PL–WSA group of "Shame—shame on you, Bernadine," with thrusting arms emphasizing each "shame."

Then the NC group stalked down the long center aisle out of the Coliseum in a great ecstasy chanting, "Ho, Ho, Ho Chi Minh," while the PLers stood on their chairs yelling and stamping in opposition, "Power to the workers, power to the workers." Thus they declared their ideological differences, and there was a great beating of the air with their fists. I have never known a scene with such a divisive feeling of evil and hatred, self-righteous hubris everywhere.

The NC group attempted to hold their own convention, only to find that they too were split. They could think their way out the front door, but not out of their dilemma of trying to take action that would unearth a "revolutionary" theory of American society. Abbie Hoffman had been outside the front door of the Coliseum on the first day of the SDS convention, with a small group: "We have come to praise SDS, not to bury them." If the SDS agreed on anything, they agreed that Abbie Hoffman was silly.

The three groups, which were finally formed from the breakup of SDS, planned demonstrations associated with the Conspiracy Trial. The defendants decided not to reject the support of any group. But they were, so far as I know, absent from any Progressive Labor function. Different attitudes about the body and about self-indulgence often seemed to be the source of other differences over strategy and tactics. There was certainly no clear and dominant historical perception under which group differences could be subsumed.

On Saturday October 4, SDS–Progressive Labor held a rally in Grant Park by the Buckingham Fountain. Many demonstrations during October gave their own characteristic satirical skit. In Grant Park, the SDS–PL group conducted a football game. On the evil side were figures with signs saying Tricky

Dick Nixon, Joe Racism, Rocky, and Crazy-Legs McCarthy, and on the good side were the workers and the students and North Viet Nam. Uncle Sam was the umpire whose rulings favored the evil side. Somehow—I forget how—the good side won, to cheers and clapping, and Five, Six, Seven, Eight, Nothing to Negotiate. The young woman who spoke to this group in Grant Park about "correct ideas" and "wrong ideas" was pretty and good in feeling, in a plain way. Men near her—who later led the march to the Federal Building—made only a modest effort to disguise the fact that they were directing the women to speak because "liberated" female leaders were a "correct idea." Many plainclothes policemen with walkie-talkies stood a head taller and a hundred pounds heavier than any student on the edge of the crowd of perhaps fifteen hundred people.

Uniformed cops stood along the line of the march with their hands behind their backs. By the Walgreen's drugstore at Jackson and State, a balding man listened to the strong, uniform chants about Viet Nam—"Get out now—negotiate what?"—and said, "They think the President is going to listen to that, now?" Every time I wrote in my notebook, there was someone looking over my shoulder.

PL claimed to shun media observance. PL men wore their hair cut short. Their faces were plain, their attitudes were calm even when they made their speech in which they used the phrase "no good corporations and no good ruling class and no good cops," with an absolute lack of affect. They carried a sign saying: Bosses Profit—Workers' Pay. The apostrophe made it an odd message. In a narrow defile at the north end of the Federal Building, the marchers' voices resonated tremendously and brought smiles to their faces and energy to their step.

It was Saturday and there was no one in the Federal Building except a couple of janitors. There were only a few bystanders and a few cops and a few U. S. marshals, chatting in small groups. A great many young people were in the Loop, particularly on the State Street side of the Federal Building, laughing, skipping, talking, shopping, and their attention was not caught by the PL march.

There had been no involvement of bystanders, and no noticeable image appeared in the media.

The next Wednesday night, October 8, the anniversary of the martyrdom of Che Guevara in Bolivia, the SDS–Weatherman, having named themselves Revolutionary Youth Movement I, came pouring out of their rally in Lincoln Park across LaSalle Drive, many with crash helmets and long sticks, right in front of my car lights, to BRING THE WAR HOME in the Gold Coast streets of Chicago and in the minds of every person in the nation who watched TV or read the newspapers.

The night before, a dynamite bomb had blown the police statute in Haymarket Square a hundred feet. That meant war between the Weatherman and the police—so said representatives of police in a public statement.

It was not hard to see that the Weatherman originated from the more flamboyant National Collective group that had walked out of the Coliseum, and from a position statement made at that time. They asserted their identification with the liberation struggles and the future better life of the Third World—for rhetorical purposes that meant mainly China, Cuba, and Viet Nam. They preached that they were the vanguard that would take up armed struggle behind enemy lines here in the mother country against the imperialist and racist force of the United States. They sought to awaken and discover themselves, even sacrificially, in losing their "white-skinned privilege" and forcing the police to treat them the way police often treated black people.

Weatherman desperately wanted the support of the Black Panther party, admired by the young white Weathermen as the vanguard of revolution in the United States. Many of the

Conspiracy defendants were attracted to the daring and personal qualities but not the common sense of the Weathermen. They tried to bring about a reconciliation between Weatherman and the Panther party, between Bernadine Dohrn and Fred Hampton. But the Panther party, in the person and voice of Fred Hampton, spoke of self-defense and breakfast programs for children and free medical clinics and schools and legal defense and housing and other programs that showed that they were taking the revolutionary risk of standing against the society while involving themselves in attempts to meet the immediate needs of people. But their publicly displayed guns and their dramatic self-defense "threat," inviting trouble, caused them to repel black people as much as to attract them.

Fred Hampton, the most charismatic, visionary, common-sensical 21-year-old revolutionary in the country, was unyielding in calling the Weathermen "Custerist" and declaring that no young blacks would follow any Yellow-Hair into a Little Big Horn with the police on the Chicago streets. Defendant Tom Hayden, author of the Port Huron statement that initiated SDS in 1962, spoke to the Weatherman rally Wednesday night in the name of the sentiment but not the fact of unity of the movement. "Marion Delgado!" someone yelled the name that would become the Weatherman signature, perplexing many listeners.

The Weathermen streamed across LaSalle Drive chanting "Ho, Ho, Ho Chi Minh." Persons in the front leaped forward and hurled rocks that broke windows in the Historical Society building at the south end of Lincoln Park. They screamed with excitement and crossed Clark Street hurling rocks and bricks that broke windows of the Home Federal bank. The flashing blue lights of police cars and the wails of police sirens were sailing down nearby streets toward the scene. The police had certainly been given warning by their undercover agents and by plainclothesmen with walkie-talkies in Lincoln Park. It was my impression that they could have stopped the Weatherman attack right there if they wanted to do it. A Cook County

Grand Jury investigating police "Red Squad" intelligence found, years later, that the police had been abundantly warned and were, in effect, permitting the violence to happen.

The Weathermen felt they had to act quickly before being subdued. They lunged across North Avenue south on Clark Street. They smashed, as a matter of random choice and availability, the windows of a flower shop, the Red Star Inn restaurant, and a supermarket.

Beginning to string out now into small groups, they pounded down streets where there had been street fighting during the Democratic National Convention. That was one of the symbolic reasons that they picked Lincoln Park, but they were not able to involve bystanders sympathetically as happened so generously during the Convention Week actions.

From the little balconies of the Carl Sandburg high-rise apartments, residents threw cocktail ice cubes down at the Weathermen among stopped cars. The lead Weathermen skidded at the sight of the police blockade at Clark and Division. They dodged into the side streets of the Gold Coast, heading for Judge Julius J. Hoffman's apartment at the Drake Hotel on the corner of Oak and Michigan.

They moved swiftly. They smashed the windshields of parked cars with bricks and long sticks. They smashed windows of apartment-house lobbies and of small shops. Every windshield was smashed on a two-block line of cars parked bumper to bumper on Astor Street. Almost that completely on other streets. A woman sat in the front seat of a car, with a brick and shattered windshield glass in her lap. She cringed when anyone approached her. A doorman was dumped over a hedge. Angry people thronged street corners in the narrow Gold Coast streets.

The attack peaked quickly on Division Street near the Inner Drive, where the Weathermen tried to bring the war home to Judge Hoffman, who reportedly stayed asleep in his Drake Towers apartment a couple of blocks away. Weathermen with the long sticks flurried briefly with the police, more than half of whom were black men.

It was said that the Weathermen fired guns, and some cops were wounded. I saw one unmarked police car with siren blaring, going west on Division Street. The arm of a cop, lying in the backseat, stuck up in a helpless, unconscious way. Crowds on the street corners watched unafraid here.

All of this happened in perhaps less than a half hour. Weathermen were using cabs to get from one place to another. The police arrested more than sixty persons in the confrontations.

Many curious people were gathering back in Lincoln Park, around a bonfire made from a broken-up park bench. McIntosh apples were being passed out from plastic bags lifted out of the broken windows of grocery stores.

The enforcement of the 11 P.M. curfew had been the immediate nightly cause of confrontations in Lincoln Park during the Democratic convention. But the police did not do anything about the curfew tonight.

People ate the apples and some mused on the energy and ever-widening involvement of the night-after-night confrontations during the Democratic convention. The property of neighborhood people had not been the target; the police were the target because the police had made people the target. It was the windshields of police and National Guard vehicles that were broken then. Damage to neighborhood property would have alienated the neighborhood people, who supported the demonstrators, hid them, fed them, and gave them medical care and places to sleep.

But the media the next morning gave utterance and image to the Weatherman actions comparable to the Normandy invasion. The editors and publishers and network managers got nightmare kicks as they enthusiastically headlined RADICAL INVASION and RADICALS RAMPAGE on the Near North Side, with full reportage and photographs. It was national. The media and the police could not conceal their excitement about the windows and windshields broken. Yet a month before the Weathermen blew into town a couple of boys, as North Side residents testify, one night broke every windshield on two blocks of parked cars on Pine Grove Avenue and not only got away with it but were not commended by a single paragraph in the newspapers. The journalistic treatment given the Weatherman action was akin to the treatment given a society murder.

Throughout the week, the Weathermen continued to thrust just the right images of their mythicized intentions into the primarily pornographic and sensationalist news mind, for buyers and viewers.

For instance, less than a hundred Weatherwomen and supporters gathered the next morning in Grant Park opposite the Hilton Hotel, again a famous site of actions during Convention Week. They got front pages again, with pictures of young radical women in crash helmets and biker suits carrying clubs, trying to march to draft induction centers and meeting a line of police before they got out of the park. They were subdued by the police and dispersed. A young woman reporter, in an Army field jacket, who was present at the event, said with a curl of her lip that the Weatherwomen were a bunch "of scared little girls." But another woman who was there as a supporter said the women milled about with uncertainty until Bernadine Dohrn arrived with other Weatherwomen and made a brief stirring speech. "Marion Delgado," she cried, with the name that would sign letters for the Weathermen in the future.

RYM-I Weathermen and brothers and sisters in RYM-II planned rival demonstrations and "jailbreaks" for students in high schools, but these did not happen.

RYM-II was also composed of young people from the National Collective group and other SDS who did not agree with either side in that debacle. There was going to be much counting of heads and comparing of dominance in the media to see who would seize the chance and the insight necessary to win the loyalty of movement youth in America. RYM-II was supported by the Illinois Black Panther party.

Both RYM factions were attended throughout the week by a stupendous number of Chicago police in plainclothes and uniform, at their demonstrations and at their meeting places.

In the RYM-II demonstration in the little park opposite the huge Gothic front of Cook County Hospital, to protest medical care given to poor people, a young woman screeched over the portable speaker, "The pigs are stopping personnel from coming out of the hospital." Doctors and nurses and aides, standing on the edges of the crowd in the chilly drizzle, laughed at her. The screechy voice did not attract a rise of sympathetic feeling in the crowd that was quite mixed with young blacks, young Puerto Ricans, service personnel from the hospital, and the white students of RYM-II. There were reporters and seven TV cameras. Plainclothes and uniformed police stood down by the corner.

Police helicopters yammered overhead, making it hard to hear the voice of someone next to you. "I want to tell all you people about the guys up in the sky." The helicopters were interrupting the screechy voice as it declared that "doctors must give up their status, their high income," and everything else that doctors must sacrifice and do in order to serve the real medical needs of poor people. There was no mention of what the doctors would gain, not even spiritually. There was also no discussion of the ways of guaranteeing health care.

RYM-II gave the first witty political skit of the demonstrations that week, about a sick brown woman who came to the reception table at a hospital, holding her stomach. "I'm so sick, I don't know what to do."

The receptionist said, "We're very busy, you know."

The woman hit the table: "I'm very sick, you know."

Finally, after more clever and well-played entrances and exits in the skit, it was decided, "You've been systematized.

We've got to operate to unsystematize you. You got to be radicalized, sister." It was all delivered with the tongue-in-cheek irony of real street speech, and it got real laughs of recognition from black bystanders who were not a part of RYM-II.

Fred Hampton's voice was right for addressing the demonstration, calm and summoning of excitement. Husky, in a sheepskin jacket, he spoke out again against those "Custerists," the Weathermen, and people who had not heard the term before laughed at the wit of it. He spoke solemnly for the Panther free medical clinics and for the freeing of Chairman Bobby Seale. He was not using the microphone. He asked for "the people beat," a clapping of hands on a beat which he led with such calm, unabashed fervor that the audience hardly knew what to do with its good feeling when he finished. But that feeling made the arguments and discussion possible in clusters of people all over the little park.

"You can't point at that building," a tall doctor with a mustache said to RYM-II people at the back of the crowd, "and say the staff in it don't care."

"Maybe the food people," the RYM-II guy said, with a shrug.

"No, sir," the doctor said. "You can't point at that building and say the doctors don't care."

One of the accusations of RYM-II was that the young resident doctors experimented on black people in the hospital, performing operations that were not needed, to gain surgical experience that they would later use in the lucrative care of rich people. The RYM-II medic, who wore an armband to signal his presence in case of police use of tear gas or clubs, said he had been a resident at Bellevue Hospital in New York and that was true there. He had dropped out of the medical profession, he said. He and the mustached doctor argued and uncovered some procedural differences about residency in various public hospitals.

The RYM-II medic was not about to regard the doctor with any attitude but moral disapproval. "Would you give some time to the Black Panther Health Clinic?" The doctor with the mustache showed the first sign of uncertainty. "I work a hundred and ten hours a week over there," he said. He was asked if he would give a couple of hours a week. He said maybe if he knew more about it.

One of the three Puerto Rican guys, with no immediately perceivable organizational affiliation, spoke straight at the RYM-II accuser: "*You* give some time."

Now the RYM-II guy placed his hand upon his chest uncertainly. "I'm not a doctor," he said. "Besides, that's not the point."

"That *is* the point," the Puerto Rican guy said.

The RYM-II medic was confused.

"I'm not sure what SDS is here for," one young OB resident said, earnestly. "I'm more confident about the Panthers" for their direct concern in the health of the black community.

RYM-II focused its moralistic attack on the medical staff, with whom the students could, if they wished, share status and income. They made such accusations as black women, while groggy with anesthesia, were having their tubes tied by young residents greedy for experience in the operation. The OB resident said that, if only because there was no need to invent experiences in the world's largest public hospital in one of the largest black ghettos, the accusation was not well founded. He said it was true that a resident wants to do as many hysterectomies and appendectomies as possible. He conceded that if a resident felt a little bump on a woman's uterus, he might get her to sign a paper to perform the operation.

The doctors at the demonstration thought that the hospital was assigned enough funds but the money was diminished by graft in the Cook County Board of Commissioners. They agreed that there should be "an evolution toward a black staff." They also said that the hospital needed more of the money assigned to it in order to get more food and such things as fans and air conditioners so that a woman would not lose more water than she gained in the OB wards. They said there was not enough staff at Cook County Hospital. "Everybody is trying hard, but it is a losing battle." One of the young doctors said, "People would be dying to come," and then laughed at himself. They were hearing cliches that they wouldn't ordinarily notice, just as people giggled at the phrase "honorable court" in the Conspiracy courtroom. They said that the "nonsense garble of lies" about the Cook County medical staff turned off the young doctors who did want to do something.

RYM-II asked those in the crowd who wished to make statements to come to the microphone. The tall, large, mustached doctor, who was so articulate in defending the medical staff and stating what he thought were the substantive issues in medical care, went to the young woman who was managing the microphone and asked to speak. "A minute," she said, and she gave the microphone to others, always black people behind him or to the side of him, and then put him off again, and then when it seemed that there was nothing more she could do but give him the microphone, she called off the demonstration and turned off the portable speaker.

"They won't let me speak," he said, with a shrug of wonder.

The RYM-II demonstration at Cook County Hospital had a high degree of bystander involvement, with strong discussion of questions about medical care in the United States. But, because of sketchy research and accusations that were not always accurate, it tended to factionalize that involvement. It also suggested that such a demonstration on a specific issue would need to be developed day-by-day, week-by-week to be effective.

But the RYM-II demonstration at the hospital only made the third page of the Chicago *Sun-Times*. The mustached doctor got his picture in the paper. But the story was difficult for the newspapers and television because of the extensive discus-

sion of the aspects of the issue that developed over the afternoon. No national publicity. No sensational images.

On Saturday, October 11, there were two rival actions by
RYM-I (Weathermen) and RYM-II. The Weathermen gathered in Haymarket Square, amid the echoes from the late nineteenth century of conspiracy and protest and riot and
martyrdom. The Weatherman march had a permit from the
city of Chicago. RYM-II gathered at People's Park in Lincoln
Park. RYM-II did not have a permit.

Less than two hundred Weathermen stood shoulder to
shoulder at the pedestal, where the blasted away statue had
been. They would march toward "those buildings," the offices
of corporations and government, in the Loop. The RYM-II
march was manned by three or four thousand persons, with
the support of the Panthers and the Young Lords and other
organizations. They would march through poor white, Puerto
Rican, and black neighborhood areas, followed by squads and
busloads of cops. The Weathermen would be remembered in
the nation, perhaps for nationally self-defeating reasons, while
RYM-II needs explication to most hearers.

A dozen plainclothesmen suddenly approached the Weatherman group and pulled out and clubbed and arrested five
persons, among them Weatherman spokesman Mark Rudd,
"for probable cause of riots Wednesday night." It was strange
for me to see Assistant Corporation Counsels Steven Zucker
and Richard Elrod taking notes here, and then to see them on
films of marches during the Democratic convention in the
Conspiracy courtroom. It gave me the faintly eerie feeling of
being in a film that would be shown in a courtroom somewhere
someday.

A young Weatherman in a buckskin coat, with long fringes,
jumped on top the pedestal to emphasize that the statue had
been blasted away. The crammed-together Weathermen
hardly talked or gave any facial expression, just stared, as if

caught in the paralyzed stillness of a nightmare. A tall under-cover agent, in a black turtleneck sweater wearing a Bring-The-War-Home button, stepped away from the group and mumbled something to Zucker. Weathermen grinned behind him. Undercover agent William Frapolly, who would appear shortly as a witness in the Conspiracy trial, was also associated with the Weathermen. They took his car with them when they headed for Michigan directly after the October actions.

Then a fellow called J.J., with red football helmet, blue shirt, dark jacket, keeping his arms folded, spoke to the assembled congregation, as if standing beside the pedestal of a broken column in a surrealist painting with great, clear, traumatized spaces. "We're going to set an example for what people in this country have to do and be willing to do to change the nature and course of our lives. . . ." He was not without a conscious-ness that there should be a tone of destiny. Zucker was stooped over in the street writing on a pad on his knee. "Sounds like more coming, going Ho, Ho," he said, in a most ordinary tone. More Weathermen were marching up the sidewalk chanting "Ho, Ho, Ho Chi Minh," with fists raised, and there were shouts of greeting, "Right on." J.J. was saying, "We know to be attacked by the enemy is a good thing. . . ." The sky was so low and gray that nothing made you look up.

They moved out briskly into the street marching toward "those buildings" in the Loop. Many young men with cameras were running backward and crouching in front of them to take pictures. I saw one marcher light his cigarette with a particular nervous anticipation, and once again I was made aware that the police were letting happen what they knew was going to happen. The Weathermen turned south on LaSalle Street and marched past City Hall, respectful of the lines of policemen on the sidewalks around it.

They leaped out suddenly from LaSalle onto Madison Street, and the first window to go was that of the Canadian National Railways office. With sticks and bricks, shouts of attack, windows were broken all down the street. One black restaurant man planted himself in front of his barbecue place to protect his little window, with a long knife that he held at his side. Plainclothes and uniformed police, their sirens and voices howling with the release of incredible rage, came from everywhere. Under the long upward curve of the First National Bank building, that gave you the feeling of falling when you looked up at it, was a jam of skyblue helmets and dark blue uniforms and squadrols and three-wheeler motorcycles. There the Weathermen and the cops, in a sixty-second media message, nailed each other.

Saturday-afternoon shoppers hastened along the sidewalks toward the action, lest they miss the sights. Thousands of young people, white and black, only one or two blocks away on all sides—shopping, skipping, laughing, holding hands— knew nothing of the Weatherman action until they turned on their TVs that evening.

A few Weathermen not arrested or beaten on Madison Street convened a discussion on the Logan Statue hill in Grant Park, once again the scene of major demonstrations during the Democratic convention. A blank-faced fellow swung a soap-bubble ring and sent bright bubbles drifting through the gathering. A dark-haired young man, who could pass in any group of young people in this country, hair not too long, not too short, was speaking for the Weathermen. "We brought the movement a qualitative step forward. . . ." A bald-headed legal defense lawyer said, "Can I ask you some questions about what you believe, young man?"

*"No,"* the Weatherman said.

Even the lawyer laughed.

Then the sun came out all over Chicago, straight over the buildings onto the Logan Statue hill, so hard and dazzling you couldn't look at it. From the Outer Drive, Lake Michigan glowed green and choppy as if there were a candle in the heart of each wave. The sun poured over the quick rising green-white violence of Lake Michigan.

The Weathermen once again moved to the forefront of the national nightmare, with national headlines and prominence in national newscasts. Mayor Daley found justification in their "riot" for the way his police acted during the Democratic convention. You could hardly escape the feeling that, in the minds of some people, the Weatherman "riot" gave a special authenticity to the government's charges in the Conspiracy trial. Many liberals and leftists in the Chicago area felt bitterly betrayed by the Weathermen.

The much larger RYM-II-Panther march was noted on the third pages of the newspapers, but not outside Chicago. It received sympathetic bystander response at the moment of passing in the street, but no more.

Eleven Weathermen were finally indicted by a Federal Grand Jury under the same antiriot provisions of the 1968 Civil Rights Act as the Conspiracy Eight. Then the Weathermen disappeared "underground" in the United States. They began to play with forms of terror, notions about race and cultural destiny, and experimentation with enforced communal sex and community. The Panthers wanted publicly known guns, while Weathermen used the speech of dynamite against government and corporation property. Their ceaseless experimentation thrilled and terrified and numbed the middle-class conscience of readers and viewers of media. It is a form of pornography, where the cultural, social, and economic system by reflex selects and sells the news images that protect it. Even their "going underground" became a media image. The waves of the Weatherman bombing actions helped send masses of American youth rocking back into more cautious ways of life, even though the bombing thrilled and satisfied people's fantasies of vengeance against an oppressive government.

In Judge Hoffman's court Monday morning, there was a tight denial, a withdrawal, particularly because of the paralysis of Assistant Corporation Counsel Richard Elrod, who took a blow on the neck while apparently trying to tackle a Weatherman. Elrod and his paralysis occupied headlines in Chicago papers and prominence in newscasts. It made me want to see a headline everyday for all of the people who had been paralyzed by violence in this country.

Jerry Rubin said in the cloakroom, in front of marshals and reporters, "They brought the movement a qualitative step forward . . ." The Yippies shared with the Weathermen a concern about what happened within the confines of a media image. It was the unmistakable daring of the Weathermen that was always mentioned as the particular attribute of the "qualitative step." Within a few months, other defendants, such as Rennie Davis, would "wholeheartedly disagree."

The Weatherman daring may have shown that their identification of themselves with the Third World liberation movements was similar to the social movement in the thirties' identification of itself with another romance overseas—the Great Experiment of the Soviet Union—as a way of avoiding the process of finding our own identity in the peculiar character and magnitude of the United States in a world situation.


On Wednesday, the October 15 Moratorium Against the Viet Nam War, groups interested in peace rallied in the Civic Center Plaza. Conspiracy defendants Dellinger and Davis, against some vocal opposition, spoke to the assembly before they hurried back to the courtroom.

Demonstrators—white and black construction workers and students and others—always climbed on the Picasso statue in the Civic Center Plaza. It was a structure of oxidized brown steel, three or four stories high. During the Moratorium demonstration, the police, through a bullhorn, ordered the statue to be cleared.

"This is not a too popular place for a policeman to be," said a young cop who went past me with a detail of fellow cops toward the statue.

They talked everyone off the platform except one woman, with gray hair, in her fifties probably, in a blue coat, who would not leave. She gave the peace sign to the cheering crowd on all sides. The police again asked her to leave. She folded her arms and shook her head no, in a broad firm way. She made it plain that they would have to drag her away bodily in front of this crowd and these cameras. The two cops up there pleaded with her—you could see their embarrassment—and finally their commanding officer told them to leave her on the platform. The astonished crowd cheered. The cops formed themselves in lines between the crowd and the statue.

She placed herself comfortably against a back rail. Then she gave the peace sign again and called out for people to join her. The police commander, through his bullhorn, cautioned the crowd to stay off the statue. There she was, alone, and there was an easy and graceful feeling about her. She was cheered, and she called out again for people to join her.

The first young man who leaped through the police line and up onto the platform beside her was glowing in the face. They grabbed hands and laughed together. Then another young man ducked through the police line and leaped up there. Another. And another. "Join us, join us!" The commander on the bullhorn warned people to stay off the statue. But more and more people made the jump. Then the crowd simply surged forward, and the surrounded police did not resist, as the crowd reclaimed the statue. The commander handled the problem of the "face" of the police commitment by saying over the bullhorn, "You climb at your own risk."

If the police had dragged her away and the crowd had responded in anger, that would have been an image for TV. That was her deterrent. But though she was mentioned in the media, her story proved too long for TV and too subtle for the space available to rewrite men on the newspapers.

Authority is, at root, the authority of perception. It comes from the perception of needs and of possibilities and probabilities of solving needs, and from the indispensable ability to voice the perception so others may see, share, and, with a willingness, act for and with it in order to carry it through. That is the function of leadership, the promotion and guarantee of magic and ritual. It works in many guises and is often worked against itself because the clear, voiced perception may entail great demands of danger, loyalty, change, and implementation. Leadership of perception can and does move from moment to moment, person to person, surprise to surprise, if permitted. But that is also, paradoxically, why there are chieftains and teachers and organizations and rules: to assure the exercise and expression of perception to anyone to whom the perception occurs, to assure the order of the exchange of perception among people over time for the sake of survival and the enhancement of material and spiritual prosperity. It is not surprising that leadership and organization should be often used to conceal and suppress the very process that they were meant to aid.

It is seldom that there is an immediate commitment of large numbers of persons to the perception and the person who expresses it. The voice that expresses the perception must compel to a degree worthy of what it has to say. The first person jumps, and then another, and another, and then the surge of numbers.

The Conspiracy Trial itself was a cumulative action on the part of the defense to make it a political trial, and on the part of the government to keep it thoroughly political by denying that it was.

# PART FOUR
*The Struggle for the Laugh in the Courtroom*

"I DO NOT PERMIT hundreds of lawyers to appear before me," Judge Julius Hoffman said testily, when defense counsel William Kunstler made the deadpan announcement that lawyers from all parts of the country wished to file an amicus curiae brief, and were clamoring in the halls and on the Federal Building Plaza to come up to the twenty-third floor courtroom and offer the brief directly. The lawyers wanted to protest the judge's nearly naked attempt to strongarm the defense to relinquish its Sixth-Amendment right to counsel—his issuing an order trying to jail four of the pretrial lawyers as hostages on the excuse that they tried to withdraw improperly from the trial by telegram. In the press section, I smiled suddenly and would have laughed, as other members of the press smiled and would have laughed, except for the marshals in the aisles who stirred at the merest murmur of laughter. You need only see in your mind *hundreds* of lawyers appearing before Judge Hoffman to see why the struggle for the laugh and to suppress the laugh became principal forms of aggression and unification in this courtroom.

This story is about how every group in the courtroom found itself dividing into two sides, how each person carried two sides within himself, and how laughter exposed the allegiances—in many cases, actually enabled people to find out their allegiances—and gathered people into one or the other side and strengthened their awareness of each other. By tone, gesture, voice, by bodily expression of all kinds, by the disposition of one person to another, and the feelings about one's body and the bodies of others—that is how we shall see America becoming divided into a historical struggle.

Necessarily this story of laughter in the Chicago Conspiracy trial will be about the many kinds of expression that do not appear in the official record. Of course, the story will be about the record, too, which was "incredibly difficult and sometimes almost impossible" to transcribe, said the court reporter. The talk in the emotionally driven action often went too fast for her fingers and she had to piece together from different sources whatever had happened. Inaccuracies often happened when there was laughter. Abbie Hoffman, in his speech when he was sentenced for contempt at the end of the trial, quoted Napoleon as saying, accurately enough, "History is the sum of men's lies," not "History is the sum of men's lives," as the record reads in only one instance of inaccuracy.

The trial was experienced and perceived by human reporters, spectators, jurors, defendants, lawyers, marshals, prosecutors, and, make no mistake, a human judge. You will see how mistakes of perception also became part of the action. This story will be about what Judge Hoffman, in his preface to the contempt proceedings at the end of the trial, correctly observed—though he only dimly looked into the cause and effect, where he might have seen a familiar face, albeit shadowy, looking back at him—that no record, "no matter how skillfully transcribed," could "adequately portray" the laughter, "the constant murmurs and snickering," "the venom, sarcasm, and tone of voice," "the applause, the guffaws, and other subtle tactics employed" in the "contemptuous behavior" in the courtroom.

In many instances of direct and cross-examination through-out the trial, it became an urgent question literally of who threw the first stone or wielded the club in August, 1968, dur-ing the Democratic Convention in Chicago. Who pissed on whose shoe first, or who was the most perfect hardass in the denial of parade and assembly permits, the city of Chicago or Yippies and demonstrators? This reversed the dependable "After you, Alphonse" routine, which became "It was you who threw first, Alphonse. . . ." "Not very likely, Gaston. . . ."

But both the prosecution and the defense were largely re-lieved of the labor of putting the whole issue-by-issue, curse-to-curse, firecracker-to-pistol, park-to-park, street-to-street, day-by-day dynamic of Convention Week into evidence before the jury, relieved of analyzing that powerful rite of passage in American history by the wording and the terms of the indict-ment of the conspirators. The indictment was magnificently structured and worded, from the government's point of view, with many alternatives and possible combinations. It con-cerned itself with the "intent" of the defendants, not with their actual "acts."

The defense, of course, in Perry Mason style as prosecutor Foran accused them, wished to prove their innocence by bring-ing evidence that would convict the Mayor and other city of-ficials and police department and Democratic party officials of "promoting, organizing, encouraging, and inciting riots" during Convention Week. That was a laugh, too. Any question that reached the threshold of the decision-making processes in the Mayor's Office was caught in a cross-fire of sustained objections.

It was conceivably no accident that Miss Kay Richards, the young juror who claimed in February to have negotiated the final verdict out of what had been a hung jury for four days and nights, said she reread the indictment and then made her proposal to the rest of the jurors, who also comprehended the many possibilities for compromise. The alternatives in the indictment that were so helpful to Miss Richards and the other jurors were the parallel charges of conspiracy and individual intent.

"The substance of the crime was a state of mind," ruled Judge Hoffman in a pretrial hearing on September 9, 1969. Defense counsel Leonard Weinglass would remind that redoubtable man of that ruling several times in the course of the trial. It was an imaginative ruling, a ruling worthy of a Grand Inquisitor, a ruling that opened the trial to the imaginative thrust of both desperate parties.

The trial had to become a struggle for the literal last laugh because the prosecution had only to prove that the defendants "did travel in interstate commerce from outside the State of Illinois to Chicago, Illinois, Northern District of Illinois, Eastern Division, with intent to incite, organize, promote, and encourage a riot" and thereafter did speak to "assemblages of persons for the purpose of inciting, organizing, promoting and encouraging a riot." The prosecution was under no further burden of proof. They merely had to give appropriate meaning and connotation to words and behavior, such as arguing that when David Dellinger said "cool it" to the Wednesday afternoon rally in Grant Park, August 28, 1968, and organized a "nonviolent" march, he was really creating a "diversion" for a later gassed, confused, fragmented crowd to "infiltrate" the Loop and cause "violent" action specifically at Michigan and Balbo. If the defendants' speeches to the assemblages put almost everyone to sleep, there was still a crime for which the defendants could be tried, convicted, and sentenced if one of three persons eventually, conceivably even a year later, threw a rock that dented a car fender or scratched a person. The "three person" definition of a riot goes back a long way into English and American law. But the antiriot provisions of the 1968 Civil Rights Act, with the best ecclesiastical opportunism, appeared to separate intent from action and make intent alone the crime.

If the riot that the government alleged the defendants intended never happened, or if it happened without the presence of the defendants, or if a different riot incited by different people happened, the government was under no burden to deal with it. Of course, if the government *could* show that the defendants *did* lead or incite or abet or commit any specific "riotous" or angry action during Convention Week, it would only strengthen the government's case. If, on the other hand, the defense could show that the defendants were not present at this-or-that "riot," or that they actually tried to cool a "riot," it did not, in any equivalent sense, help the defense. The defense had to prove that the defendants did not cross state lines and speak to assemblages of people with "the state of mind" to incite a riot.

"That distinction between speech and action has got to be made very clear. There were some wild things said during that week," Dave Dellinger said in the cafeteria of the Federal Building at the beginning of the trial. He still had not comprehended the defendants' crime. The First Amendment, up to this point in our history, had come to protect advocacy, such as "wild things said," if there were no direct, immediate, perceivable effect of causing the crowd to riot.

The irony was that the defendants never caught up in their speech or action with the people in the streets and parks during Convention Week.

The event of Convention Week, the way it happened and its impact on the national consciousness, had caused such consternation to so many parties and persons in the nation that all parties were anxious to have the "facts" support their contending claims. Anyone who has ever exaggerated an event in order to entertain, or emphasized or omitted one part of an event over another, or explained in order to justify, or lied or distorted information to help one's self or one's friends or the side that one favors, is aware of the possible failings of testimony that became hugely magnified in what was called the trial of the century. An expressed "fact" can only be as whole as the acceptance and sensitivity of its perceiver. He must be aware of his needs to alter it. He must also recognize that, each time he tells it, it is paradoxically "new fact" and "old fact" at once.

When a hitherto "friendly" network newscaster finally burst out demandingly to the defendants, "Well, who did organize it?," I saw that the indictments were working their charms on the "facts" of the historical event of the Democratic convention. It could be suspected that some of the jurors lived with the newspeople's assumption, too. The defendants stammered angrily. Abbie Hoffman said, "What do you ask Mayor Daley?"

Yes, the situation was ludicrous, productive of hysteria. Assuredly, the defendants had been ambushed. Given the terms of their indictment, the rulings of the judge, and the minds of the jury, their situation was not unlike that of the geese in the folktale. When the fox surprised them and announced he would eat them all, they begged him for permission to say their prayers first, which, after a moment's thought, he granted. So far as is known they are praying yet.

Now, how do you plan laughter, or put it on tape for a courtroom? Richard Schultz, in cross-examination of Abbie Hoffman about his intentions concerning Convention Week, said, "You were secretly planning spontaneous acts of violence." Defendant Hoffman saw the easy retort, laughed, and said, "How do you plan spontaneous acts of violence?" You can, of course, set up situations where acts of violence will be very likely to happen "spontaneously." The city of Chicago showed how cleverly that could be done during Convention Week 1968, when they moved police into areas where there was no trouble and then trouble began.

You can't, of course, plan the laughter in the courtroom— you let it happen. But it takes a will and an attitude of risk to let it happen, a will to engage. The government, hard as it tried to maintain its aseptic decorum, could not stay out of the struggle—for the sight of jurors laughing at the opponents' wit strikes terror into the heart of a lawyer. It is good to laugh, and it is good to laugh with your fellows, and it is not good to be the ones laughed at or the ones left uncomprehending outside the laughter. William Faulkner once said that white supremacy in the South was so absurd that the only way it could be ended was to laugh it to death. It is dangerous to laugh at people in that way, and dangerous to cause such laughter. It was dangerous to impeach the government's case with wit that caused laughter in the courtroom.

The anthropologist Ashley Montagu, in his book *The Human Revolution,* points out that man is the only animal that speaks and the only animal that laughs. "Those, in short, who spoke their laughter were socially selected in preference to those who did not." He describes laughter as one of the main communicative capacities that helped human beings cooperate and survive.

But in a courtroom, events are generally prefigured if not preplanned, and there is little sustained spontaneity. If laughter is interpreted as laughter of impeachment, you find yourself suddenly in direct struggle with the powers that maintain the judicial format.

In a trial the prosecution and the defense share a format in which all speech can be challenged, argued, and have rulings passed upon it, a process of coming to a conclusion to which all contending parties, as assumed contractual members of the general society, must submit if the process is to work. Suppose a party or parties perceive that the process is being used against them?

"I insist on a lawyer having good manners before I find out if he is a good lawyer," Judge Hoffman said. "Our profession is first of all one of good manners." A few ironic laughs greeted this remark. Judge Hoffman would certainly argue that both

the actions of the marshals and "good manners" were necessary to keep one's concentration on the exercise of the format.

The manipulation of this format and its rules asks for a
considerable cunning, just what the folklore says about lawyers. It asks a thorough-going ability to improvise with what
counsel knows about his case, the law, the workings of groups,
and the minds of men and women. In a famous phrase, Charles
Lamb said, "Lawyers, I suppose, were children once," and the
sibilance at the end of that "once" hisses through all eternity.

Even "the heat of battle" concept, which higher courts have
held excuses lawyers for saying otherwise impermissible things,
becomes a way in which lawyers are able to get across impermissible information to the jury—information not allowed by
law as interpreted by the judge. In the adversary system, lawyers are there to win.

Spontaneous action is quickly incorporated into the format
by the response of all parties. This was illustrated when Judge
Hoffman said about a remark of Kunstler's, " 'I will imagine
so' will be stricken from the record."

"I did it involuntarily, your honor." Kunstler said.

Richard Schultz said, "I don't think Mr. Kunstler does anything involuntarily, your honor."

"You ought to talk to my wife," Kunstler said.

Judge Hoffman thought it was addressed to him. "Perhaps
I will," the judge said.

"I meant my wife would agree with Mr. Schultz, your
honor," Kunstler said. Richard Schultz laughed, others
laughed, and everyone took up his place within the format
once again.

The ancient struggle for dominance, justice by strength,
might is right, waits in every gesture, every word, every action,
every disposition of the standing and sitting person in a courtroom. The rules of the court have much of their origin in the
need to forestall anybody's impulse to make might right. Indeed, rules and balances have been pressed upon the strength

of the state by such appellants as the barons of England, who were mighty enough to make their Magna Carta stick. The Chicago Conspiracy defendants would be the first to argue that it was the United States government, in the official persons of the judge and the federal marshals, who violated the historically hard-won rule of the avoidance of physical conflict in the courtroom. If a party in the courtroom by manner and speech does not accept the rulings, the ancient struggle emerges from under the trappings, whole and shining, as if never buried. Judge Hoffman clearly heard the ancient echo, but impractically comprehended its threat.

People paying a visit to the trial for the first time generally remarked on, and felt, the nightmarish emotional involvement of everyone present, which reflected more than a little the tumultuous outrage of the "governor" of the trial. Laughter and nightmares mean guaranteed emotional involvement. So does taking sides in politics, or finding yourself, in spite of yourself, taking sides. During Convention Week itself, the day-to-day confrontations between the police and the demonstrators in the parks and streets compelled people into action with the power of nightmares. People were caught up and gloried in these events, and were caught up in the trial too, and compelled by it, beyond their ability to say yea or nay—caught up in the "scary" test and tease of strength finding itself against strength.

Early in the trial, at the time of Detective Frank Riggio's testimony of his constant tailing of Tom Hayden, in which he said among other things that Hayden let the air out of the tire of his squad car, my son, six-year-old Timmy, woke in the middle of the night from a "scary" dream and came into the kitchen where I was making a roast beef sandwich. "I like dreams," he said. "Why?" I said. "They're scary," he said. Then he told me that he and a friend were holding onto kites and flying above a beach and making the kites move in different directions by dropping boots. Then, when the kites were high up, he and his friend fell off. "But it wasn't true," he said, as we sat there eating roast beef sandwiches in the middle of the night.

The trial adjourned in consternation when Judge Hoffman tried to jail the pretrial lawyers on September 26, 1969. Abbie Hoffman spun around the defense table, saying to a friend of his who was lunging out of the spectator section, "Everybody's on LSD," and the friend answered, "Yeah, and it's a bum trip," and Abbie Hoffman said, as if taxed beyond response and yet marveling, "This is far out, man."

Nightmares can grow luminous with all that they are hiding. Nightmares can be leadenly boring, too. Out of such a situation laughter was the last resort of the will to be, both revealing and a cover-up of the action, both a distraction and one of the most substantial points of the whole proceedings.

The first witness for the prosecution was Raymond Simon, Corporation Counsel of the city of Chicago. He testified mainly about why the city was of wise and informed disposition in not giving permits to the National Mobilization to End the War in Viet Nam for a march to the Amphitheatre and to both the National Mobilization and the Yippies to use the parks for sleeping after the 11 P.M. curfew in August, 1968. If the city had granted these permits at the last minute, which, to keep the numbers of demonstrators unremarkable, was its usual tactic with planned demonstrations, it was nearly certain that the street and park confrontations would have been avoided. The demonstrations would have been more akin to the one at the Pentagon in October, 1967, with fair numbers, reasonable energy, a few "incidents," and satisfaction to all parties. That was the argument of many persons, such as Attorney General Ramsey Clark's Department of Justice personnel. That was my own observation of every day and night of action during Convention Week, though I also felt a headlong inevitability.

That was the argument of "reasonable men" that the prosecution had to refute.

The contrary argument that the prosecution would try to prove—and it took a certain blank-faced daring—was that the defendants, "these psychologists with a college education," "smart men," "*evil* men," Prosecutor Thomas Foran would say in his closing argument, made sure with their words and actions and innuendo that the city would *not* grant permits so that, with the defendants' diabolically clairvoyant "psychologists'" view of things to come, the riots that they intended were guaranteed to happen.

After a recess, the judge invited Leonard Weinglass to continue his cross-examination of Simon, who appeared to smile at Weinglass's long hair. Weinglass buttoned the button on his suit jacket, bent slightly forward at the lectern, paused, waited, and then said, a trifle concerned, "May we have the presence of the jury, your honor?" The judge stammered at his absent-mindedness. "You must expect to do well in the remainder of your cross-examination," he said, unkindly.

Weinglass's questions mapped out arbitrary adamancy on the part of the city in denying permits and all proposals and alternatives presented by the Yippies and National Mobilization.

Defense Counsel William Kunstler, tall, lean, fifty-one, starting to let his dark hair with fine gray in it grow long in conformity possibly with the style of the wigs on the Founding Fathers rather than the style of the defendants, some of whom were also just beginning to let their hair grow long, came to the lectern for his first cross-examination of the trial. He almost certainly reached down as he usually did in beginning an examination, and lifting his foot, pulled up one or both socks, while saying in a casual, resonant voice, "Mr. Simon, my name is William Kunstler. I'm one of the attorneys for the defense . . ." Often Kunstler's manner was so effective that the witness would involuntarily nod his head and start to say something in greeting. Sometimes Kunstler would have his glasses pushed back on top of his hair; sometimes he would take them off and hold them to the side of his head and slightly raise or lower his chin as he asked a question. Sometimes he would take hold of the lectern by both sides with his long arms, as if he were steering some fantastic flying machine of his fancy, no doubt designed by Leonardo da Vinci. One suspected him of having long since studied the gestures of a great actor of the English theater. But it was his voice that gave him his style and tactics in cross-examination. Warm, resonant, with a fair range, a confessor's voice, it tended to make witnesses emotionally, almost physically, trust him in spite of their better judgment. That was what he sought, the emotional involvement of the government's witness, and he often got it, where the witness would try to explain and justify himself. He got it with Raymond Simon.

Simon leaned earnestly forward with his elbows on the stand and positively batted his eyes first at Weinglass and then at Kunstler, as if hoping to dissuade them from some perverse attack. He didn't act that way with Tom Foran during direct examination. That ingratiating manner, along with the submissive tone of voice, was employed by some of the public officials and most of the long-term infiltrator agents who appeared as witnesses for the government. It was not characteristic of the ordinary uniformed or plainclothes cop, or of any witness for the defense.

"Would it be fair to say," Kunstler asked Simon, in the midst of a series of questions about Simon's relation to Mayor Daley, "that you are a protege of the Mayor's?" Raymond Simon stammered and then said, "I am proud to be that." That claimed a snicker from press and spectators, and puzzled looks at the press from jurors. Simon would show up again at the trial on the day the mayor testified, sitting with a curled-up look and feeling in the front row, which was generally used by visiting attorneys, behind the prosecution's table, while the mayor smiled solidly on the witness stand in the midst of the tumult breaking out around him.

Now Kunstler prodded Simon through the city's current rationale for not granting permits, and at the same time got Simon to say that the city could not have known, and certainly did not desire, that its denial, as Rennie Davis had warned him, should cause violence in the streets. National Guardsmen and Boy Scouts were allowed to sleep in the parks. Simon had to say that the city was appropriately horrified by the violence, and then he had to minimize the violence that happened in Chicago. That was when Kunstler closed his examination: "Tell me, Mr. Simon, in retrospect, don't you think it would have been wiser on the part of the city to let those kids sleep in Lincoln Park?" Raymond Simon stammered. "Tell it to the jury," Kunstler said firmly, nodding toward the twelve jurors and four alternates in the jury box. Simon, sounding unsure and trapped at first, as if he had let the prosecution's ball be snatched out of his hands, had to tell the jury why he thought the representatives of the city would have been "derelict" in their duty if they had permitted Yippies and Mobilization demonstrators to sleep in the parks. That got a laugh from newsmen with experience of Convention Week. Whom were the puzzled jurors to trust?

The different levels in the courtroom were so unobtrusive and yet so definite in their relationships, that they appeared to suggest certain attitudes appropriate both to promoting and mitigating the appearance of absolute authority. Only a lawyer examining a witness, or a lawyer objecting to something said or done, or a marshal guarding aisles or entrances, felt the clear right to stand erect. Most people tended to hunch or stoop a little when they got up to leave in the middle of proceedings. The defendants scurried around their table to confer with one another as if the air above their heads were filled with flying bullets. The court reporter sat in front of the witness box to the right of the judge. You did not realize until Miss

Reporter's voice broke sweetly upon a quick, strong exchange between attorneys or witnesses and attorneys—"Mr. Kunstler, I'm sorry, you're going too fast"—that the speed of her fingers on the steno machine set the limits for the possible pace of the recorded verbal action.

When the marshal assigned to the court called, "Everyone rise," Judge Hoffman often rose as if he were, by sympathetic magic, pulling the audience to its feet. The arbitrary power of this man to control people's lives was deadening.

The people in this courtroom—jurors, press, spectators, lawyers, marshals, everyone—found themselves being divided by their own laughter and terror, the kind that you feel cold or good in the gut, into two audiences. You could sit and listen to the two inside your head, as if the courtroom were a soul on display. The two audiences, perhaps two cultures, or two sides of one culture, were physically different, and they laughed at different things said by different people. Yet they came out, one against the other, one in relation to the other, one with the other, in and of the same society. The two sides had different feelings about children, about fucking, about learning, about noise, about bathrooms, about courtesy, about honor, intelligence, imagination, duty, authority, entertainment, barbecue, money, hair, skin, blood, and laughter. It has something to do with the feeling and concept of your body, and of the bodies of others, and the way you act with that feeling and concept on issues that affect the life and future of your society.

I sat and watched how the jury came out, how it began to laugh, and who laughed and smiled at whose wit and witticism, and who gave only slight indication of a turn of the lips. The map of the "hung" jury, that stayed "hung" for four days and nights until a verdict was "negotiated," was there to be seen.

Richard Schultz, a solid young prosecutor who was always being sprung up and out by his own tensions, gibed one morning at the defense, "We have no objection to another objection." There was wit enough of the moment in it that members of both audiences smiled. But the upholder of the convict-on-all-counts end of the jury smiled big at the Assistant U. S. Attorney's remark. Edward Kratzke, an elderly man who would be the jury's elected foreman during its deliberations, never laughed at wit of the defense, and sometimes that wit pained him to the point of forcing upon him a deeply red face. Mrs. Jean Fritz, on the "acquittal" end, hardly smiled, sometimes looked down, at the wit of the prosecution. But she greatly enjoyed the wit of the defense, often holding her hand to her mouth and bending with laughter. Laughter regularly affirmed allegiances that were perhaps heretofore only hinted in a person's life. With one notable exception, the jurors voted in the deliberations as their earlier smiles and laughs would indicate.

The defendants and their attorneys were proud of the comparison of the "unholy clutter" of their table with the untroubled expanse of the prosecution's table. They also considered themselves to be a clutter of life-styles around their table beside the close-clipped, but never crew cut, hair, and the suits the colors of metal and camouflage, of the prosecutors. The defendants tried to answer letters and keep up with the speeches and talks that they were giving all over the country with grinding regularity to nurture their cause and the number of their supporters and to raise funds. Tom Foran doodled horses' heads and other items when Richard Schultz was handling an examination. Kunstler claimed after the trial that the defense had some marijuana on the table under a copy of the Berkeley *Tribe,* for one day, in a silent dare to the court and the marshals to do something about it.

The second witness for the prosecution was Deputy Mayor David Stahl, a young man with a sandy look and sandy hair and a firm response. Kunstler would not accept Stahl's identification of Abbie Hoffman from the witness stand. "We will concede, your honor, that the witness pointed at the defense table and not at the bench." Play on the shared name of Hoffman would continue throughout the trial. Kunstler asked prosecution witnesses to come down from the witness stand and actually touch the named defendant. The defense hoped for a salutary shock of human recognition in the touch of shirts and flesh, and that a witness might make a mistake.

David Stahl was the principal figure with whom the defendants met to "negotiate" for permits. Leonard Weinglass asked Stahl what did he mean that he had no power to grant permits in these talks and was only "keeping lines of communication open." Communication means response and there was no response, Weinglass said. Stahl testified that the city's intelligence information found the defendants to be dangerous. Leonard Weinglass asked, "Did you take seriously Abbie and Jerry's statements about tearing down the city?"

"I did."

"Was there laughter?"

"No."

Abbie Hoffman and Jerry Rubin laughed quietly together. Tom Foran—as dapper as a firm-lipped tough-guy prosecutor could be—stooped up in a deliberate sort of way, as if he thought he should not be required to exert himself to object to such idiotically formed questions, or he wanted any observer to think he thought that way. He objected most sarcastically to the "Abbie and Jerry, men over thirty being called by their diminutive." The judge sustained the objection.

Weinglass then asked David Stahl, "Does Mr. Hoffman often speak in jest?"

"I believe," Stahl said, smiling, "that's a matter of broad public knowledge." The laugh turned against the defense, and both sides laughed.

The green-shaded lamp on the witness stand blinked now and then, causing an alert paranoid to wonder how far prosecutors and court might go to give signals to their witnesses.

Each side accused the other of giving witnesses signals. Foran was accused of tapping with a pencil in particular ways.

This was the day after the jury's sequestration, and the jurors entered the courtroom in a huff, many with their arms folded. Kunstler asked Stahl if he took seriously Abbie Hoffman saying that for one hundred thousand dollars Abbie and Yippies would leave Chicago in August, 1968. Stahl said yes. Abbie Hoffman laughed, and whispered to his fellow defendants, "It was two hundred thousand dollars." Kunstler read from Stahl's Grand Jury testimony—the Grand Jury transcript was available for each witness—where Stahl had said that he had had "mixed feelings" about the "offer." "I took it seriously when it was made," Stahl said, "but I had *mixed* feelings about it." Stahl became angry and indignant, effectively so, when pressed.

"If a man came to you," Kunstler said, "and said I want your help on routes to get to the First National Bank to blow it up, you wouldn't continue to negotiate with him, would you?" That mildly degraded the testimony of David Stahl.

"I was not a one-stop shopping center for permits," David Stahl had said. But when the defense tried to subpoena appropriate officials and records, the Departments of Streets, Sanitation and Parks were protected by the judge's rulings more than any castle defended by magic in a fairy tale. Kunstler said quite nastily, "You're not even a little *store,* are you?" The objections of the prosecutor were regularly sustained.

Stahl had testified that Rennie Davis had suggested to him that the police should be "less visible" during Convention Week to avoid violence, as if what Davis really wanted was a free hand for violence. "Did you think," Kunstler asked, "that there might be merit to Mr. Davis's suggestion that police be less visible?" Stahl grinned when the prosecutor's objections were sustained. In fact, during Convention Week whenever the police went away from the demonstrators the conflict went away, and one police commander would testify dramatically to that fact under cross-examination in the government's rebuttal case months from now.

Sometimes the marshals in the courtroom pointed at or admonished or even expelled from the courtroom a person who was laughing. But when the laughter was in appreciation of witticism from the judge, he basked in the pleasure of it as much as anyone would, and even the marshals knew that the only behavior required of them was laughter, too. The defense pointed out to the judge this unequal treatment, and he simply did not accept their view.

The marshals always voiced concern about unevenness among spectators or press. Twice, when I was leaning forward in the press section on the front edge of a pew, I was told by the most aggressively proper marshal, a clerical sort, to sit back, "Sit *back*," apparently because I was interrupting the symmetry of the pew with its other occupants all sitting back straight. Similar incidents occurred with other persons who were not sitting back evenly.

Kunstler complained to the judge of the marshals' strictness with the spectators on the matter of laughter and making "sounds." Judge Hoffman, after defending the marshals vigorously, finally conceded, "If a marshal told any spectator not to utter a sound, I will use my authority to vacate that order."

The same marshal who told me to sit back counseled the spectators before the trial began on the day Mayor Daley testified, "If you have any laughter, *control* it," almost as if he were saying if you are rich enough to possess any laughter, *save* it. Two of the jurors whom I interviewed after the trial said that this marshal was "good" at all times to them. He also talked warmly with David Dellinger about places to send his daughter to college, asking Dellinger's opinion. "That's a good school," Dellinger once told the marshal, "a friend of my daughter once went . . ." The marshals generally said that they had great respect for "that man, Dave Dellinger."

Sometimes with every burble of laughter, the marshals stirred furiously and sought to squelch it. Reporters would often duck their heads between their legs or behind a bench to let loose a laugh that could not be denied.

FBI Agent Stanley held his hand to his mouth to cover a smile at long-haired Leonard Weinglass when the judge sustained prosecution objections preventing Weinglass from getting answers about permit "negotiations" that would reveal information about the city's intentions that were as well known to Agent Stanley as they were to Weinglass and the grinning David Stahl.

Plainclothes Policeman Murray and Policewoman Dahl could have been close kin or neighbors of some of the white jurors. Murray testified that he saw Jerry Rubin in a football helmet with 88 on the back flip a lighted cigarette at cops, and inciting other people by the field house in Lincoln Park Sunday night August 25, 1968, to flip lighted cigarettes. The defense tried to prove that Jerry Rubin, because he was sick, was not even in Lincoln Park that night. With permission of the judge, they threw open the courtroom doors to reveal, in a helmet, one of two other men periodically regarded as Jerry Rubin by the police during Convention Week. Murray folded his arms indignantly and said no. The audience was laughing and stirring with the thrill of what two of the jurors later called "a cheap trick."

Murray, at Kunstler's request, uncomfortably showed how he pressed a marijuana joint between two fingers and "pretended" to suck at it in a circle of young people in Lincoln Park. He gave an inoffensive description of Lincoln Park in the daytime during Convention Week, with young people sleeping and talking and smoking dope and "making love," the latter being far rarer in my observation of activity in the park than he seemed to suggest. You hardly noticed the introduction of the themes the government would amplify. Of course, the young people were sleeping so they would be awake for fighting cops that night, and they were talking to make plans for that fighting, and smoking dope to enflame themselves, and "making love" to enflame the cops and the city and cause riots that would wreck a great political party.

Kunstler asked Murray how he knew an antipolice person when he saw him at night in Lincoln Park. "When they open their mouth and yell, 'Kill the pigs,' I assume they are antipolice." Murray got the laugh, and there were neighbors on the jury who were pleased at the way he handled the New York lawyer. Murray admitted that he had not thought about any of these incidents until he talked with "Mr. Cubbage" long after Convention Week.

Mary Ellen Dahl was a doll, a pretty, blond plainclothes policewoman. She testified that, early Tuesday night, August 27, 1968, wearing a World War I helmet, she sat toward the front of a group clustered around Abbie Hoffman who was telling them to get missiles to throw. "Tomorrow we're going to storm the Hilton." There was "still light in the sky," she said. Abbie Hoffman said in the hallway that he was at the Coliseum at that time. He was, I remember, at the Coliseum not long after that time. By Tuesday night of Convention Week, a great many people in the streets and parks were making more daring threats and readying for streetfighting *that* night, not "tomorrow."

Every day the trial was about the many aspects of expression—language—speech—the magic of language, nuance of language, language of law, the power of language to invoke and evoke, to project and betray the intentions of the human voice and spirit.

Policewoman Dahl was trying to chew gum discreetly in the witness box when Richard Schultz asked her what Abbie Hoffman had said in Lincoln Park.

"Did he say blank?" "Blank" was the word Schultz used.

"No."

"Did he use a four-letter word?"

"Yes."

"Did it begin with *f*?"

"Yes."

Other undercover informants testified that the defendants throughout Convention Week were "f-ing this and f-ing that." Another plainclothes police lady, Barbara Callender, said that in one of Jerry Rubin's speeches "every other word was the *f* word." A plainclothes U. S. Navy agent said that a defendant's speech was "laced with *f* stuff." When Barbara Callender testified that she was attracted to following Jerry Rubin in Lincoln Park because he was "a very obnoxious man," Kunstler could hardly believe his good luck and asked her, "Do you often follow obnoxious men?" The laughter from the audience that supported the defense was obvious and costly, while there was haughty discomfort among jurors who sided with the prosecution. Expression that affirmed one side often negatively affirmed the other.

Mrs. Callender referred to the "beady eyes" of Tom Hayden, whom she had also seen in Lincoln Park. "You don't like these defendants very much, do you?" Kunstler said. But the prosecution's jurors simply did not see or feel the bias of the lady plainclothes cop in the way suggested by Kunstler. They were discomforted and angered by Kunstler's making fun of her.

Kunstler asked her why she had said nothing about Rubin's use of "obscenities" in her testimony to the Grand Jury. He had the transcript of it before him. Richard Schultz objected to Kunstler's question, and Judge Hoffman became very angry with Kunstler for making the point in spite of the objection being sustained. That was true of other agents' testimony about the defendants' abundant use of obscenities. Their Grand Jury testimony showed no mention of it.

Toward the end of its case the prosecution apparently realized that some members of the jury were not so prissy, so the prosecutors permitted their witnesses to say that the defendants said "fucking this" and "fucking that." Abbie Hoffman said on the witness stand that he liked that word "fuck," he liked what it meant to him. The prosecutors decided to give that word to the defendants with a special emphasis when they charged the defendants with such intentions as inciting youngsters to "*fuck* on the grass" in a public park. In fact, alleged obscenity and obnoxiousness of language, with or without socially redeeming value, were very much at issue throughout the Conspiracy Trial.

Weinglass asked U. S. Navy Agent Schaller, who testified to defendants' speeches being replete with obscenities, if the order of a mayor of a major metropolitan area to-shoot-to-kill-all-arsonists-and-to-maim-all-looters, and the use by United States armed forces of napalm on civilians in North Viet Nam, were obscenities? "Mr. Weinglass," Mr. Schultz said, "can't be serious in contending that these questions are proper on this recross-examination." The judge sustained the prosecution's objection.

"That," Weinglass answered, "was perhaps my most serious question of this trial." There was no laughter at all in the courtroom.

During the defense's case Richard Schultz told Witness Norman Mailer that he should give only the facts, and Mailer responded, "Facts without their nuance are nothing, sir." Assistant U. S. Attorney Schultz proved it with the tone and inflection that he gave to the word "infiltrate."

The large undercover agent Robert Pierson strove so heavily to speak grammatically at all times that he once said "whom I do not know his name." Barbara Callender, in trying to answer questions about the frequency of the *f* word in one of Jerry Rubin's speeches, said that every time you have a verb the *f* word was the adjective, and then corrected herself abruptly, as if she feared she were being grammatically twisted beyond being able to understand herself—"I mean every noun," she said, and then grimaced as if there were something sour in her teeth.

Defense Counsel Leonard Weinglass observed in his closing argument that "men of strong convictions use strong language." The prosecution needed to change the relationship of the objects of repression to the public at large so that the "strong convictions" of Abbie Hoffman and Tom Hayden became the "evil intentions" of Mr. Abbott H. Hoffman and Mr. Thomas E. Hayden.

The prosecutors and the judge created a contextual vacancy around a remark to summon the contextual nuance that would stimulate the jury's deep suspicions. For instance, an FBI informer, who described himself as a New York advertising executive—moonlighting as an informer for kicks, cash, and country—stated on the witness stand that Tom Hayden said in a July, 1968, speech to the Fifth Avenue Peace Parade Committee in New York City that "because the Vietnamese are shedding their blood, peace demonstrators in this country must be ready to shed their blood, too"—presumably in Chicago in August, 1968. The informer was eager to call the speech "the most inflammatory" he had ever heard, but he offered the words entirely truncated and extracted from their verbal and situational and political context. Judge Hoffman would not allow any answers to defense questions over prosecution objections to elucidate Hayden's "intent." Hayden apparently meant that people should not avoid demonstrations just because the Chicago police were threatening to crack heads. If he meant more than that, if he meant that people should defend themselves or attack police, that too was not elucidated. There was no way for the observers in the courtroom not to feel that Judge Hoffman's interpretation of the Rules of Evidence, however arbitrary, had absolutely prevented an understanding of the meaning of the words and of the intent of the defendant.

Truncation and extraction of language from context were applied to film, tapes, witness testimony, every form of evidenciary material. The prosecutors played a tape of a radio interview with Abbie Hoffman during Convention Week. "They care more about a City Ordinance than they do about the destruction of Chicago," Abbie Hoffman said, and *bloop* the tape ended. The prosecutors were grinning, particularly Roger Cubbage, who had researched these materials. Abbie Hoffman was grinning and shaking his head.

Reactions to testimony caused expressive slips of the tongue that caused more contradiction. For instance, Schultz objected heatedly to Weinglass's questioning Sergeant Murray on whether he ever saw Jerry Rubin with a weapon in his hand among Yippies in Lincoln Park. Schultz delivered the phrase "the crowd throwing objects at the crowd," instead of at the police, which was what he would say he meant. Weinglass delightedly called the slip to Schultz's attention, because Schultz's slip was a description of what often happened during Convention Week. But Schultz, to avoid the impeachment of being laughed at, ferociously accused Kunstler of having used the phrase first.

Slips of the tongue sometimes appeared to indicate a larger or at least more ambiguous perception on the part of the person whose tongue betrayed him.

Slips of ruling on the part of the judge usually favored the defense. For instance, in Kunstler's cross-examination of Murray, Schultz objected to a question. Judge Hoffman appeared a little bemused as he leaned forward. "I overrule the objection," he said.

With that ruling, if it became a pattern, the game of the trial would change. Kunstler, hunched at the lectern, paused, becoming aware of what he had heard, and said, "You mean the witness can answer the question?"

Judge Hoffman stammered, correcting himself. "I sustain the objection." If he dreamed occasionally, it was only reasonable that the courtroom should be the scene.

Undercover Agent Robert Pierson had been "bodyguard" for Abbie Hoffman and then for Jerry Rubin in Lincoln Park. Nods and laughter greeted his description of letting his hair and beard grow and of "purchasing the attire of a motorcycle gang member."

He was a heavy witness in more ways than one. He gave testimony about most of the defendants, but principally about the behavior and speech of Jerry Rubin and Bobby Seale. He too was ingratiating and submissive toward the cross-examiners, until they asked questions that implied a long psychiatric history, suicide attempt, and strange reasons for leaving the employ of the Palmer House. Then he stared with stolid hurt at the defense.

Pierson testified that he saw Rennie Davis on a bullhorn Monday afternoon August 26, 1968, at the head of the Free Hayden march. But Pierson gave no testimony of angry marchers calling Davis a "pig" for keeping them on the sidewalk in conformity with requests of the police. "Conspiracy to act like cops," the defendants said, with great irony. Pierson testified that Rubin said on this march, "Let's go to the Hilton," and then other marchers started saying it. "Better than Iwo Jima," he quoted Rubin as saying when marchers swarmed with flags up the hill in Grant Park onto the equestrian statue. Rubin denied everything of Pierson's testimony, "Total fantasy trip," but he thought the Iwo Jima remark was too good not to claim it.

Pierson said that Jerry Rubin showed people in Lincoln Park pictures of newsmen being beaten by police. "Now we've got the newsmen on our side." Pierson said that Rubin spoke of burning the city of Chicago. Pierson said that Rubin said that putting the Yippie pig on the Grant Park bandshell stage would cause the police to come into the bandshell area and bring about a confrontation.

Pierson said *f* to denote Rubin's use of the word fuck. When Pierson stood by the map of Grant Park in front of the jury, he kept his hands clipped together in front of him and looked down as only a big, awkward man can act demurely. Anyone possessing a personal familiarity with Convention Week smiled when Pierson said that cops hit demonstrators with their clubs only when they were hit with "objects" thrown by the demonstrators. He himself threw a bottle of paint at a squad car. The bottle was given to him by Nancy Kurshan, and he said Jerry Rubin threw a bottle at the same time. It was revealed that Pierson told the Grand Jury that Rubin wanted to avoid all possible contact with the police. He claimed to have stolen a diary of Rubin's that proved intentions to create riot.

Pierson usually repeated Kunstler's and Weinglass's questions. He seemed to try to pre-guess and predetermine his gestures and facial expressions, stereotyping his voice and his tone, loud and clear on direct, almost inaudible on cross-examination, so that the pre-guessing often did not fit the situation that came up, which caused him a sort of slow pain. But it was partly because he seemed victimized by the defense that he conveyed sincerity to the prosecution jurors, and partly because he sounded so ineptly manipulative that he gave an insincere impression to a few other jurors.

On the morning of October 15, David Dellinger began reading from the list of the war dead on both sides, for the Moratorium Against the Viet Nam War. The marshals, in a brief tug-of-war with Abbie Hoffman, removed the Viet Cong flag draped over the defense table. But, with wonderful absentmindedness, as Abbie Hoffman pointed out, they left the American flag untouched. Then they removed it.

The judge excused the jurors, who literally stumbled to get out of the courtroom. Foran was on his feet yelling at Kunstler for wearing a black armband, for being a "mouthpiece." That means a lawyer who does whatever his clients ask him to do. Judge Hoffman said, in one of his pious astonishments, "to place an enemy flag on the defense table!" Tom Hayden said, "Are they your enemy?" Several of the defendants then made it plain to the judge that the United States had not officially declared war against the people represented by that flag, which was one of the issues that caused all of them to be assembled in this courtroom. Kunstler asked the judge to admonish Foran for calling him "a mouthpiece." Judge Hoffman said, "I do *not* admonish the U. S. Attorney for properly representing his client, the United States of America."

Tom Hayden, who had stayed scrunched up morbidly chewing at his nails and hangnails for the first couple of weeks of the trial, was now brighter, easier, quicker. He smiled as Leonard Weinglass asked Detective Frank Riggio if, in the three incidents of the crowd surging around him in Lincoln Park in protest of Hayden's arrest, he saw *so much as a pebble thrown at policemen? a policeman shoved? a policeman hit?* Foran was on his feet objecting, the judge was sustaining the objections, but there was a quickening in the courtroom with the marksmanship of Weinglass's questions. Detective Riggio defined an agitator as "anyone who causes me problems, anyone who fights or stirs up problems."

The prosecution did not feel so easy when the "agitators" heckled them in whispers across the aisle between the two tables. Rennie Davis and Jerry Rubin were particularly willing to accept the onus of reminding the prosecutors of their mortality. They heckled them the way a catcher tries to get a batter to lose his cool, out of the hearing of the umpire.

Foran said on a TV show after the trial that Davis made continuous remarks across the aisle about Foran's "sexual prowess" while he was at the lectern cross-examining a witness. You could wonder how much this, along with all the rest of the marshaling of the rhetoric of two sides of sexuality and sexual morality, influenced Foran in making his amazing, hot statement after the trial, "We have lost our kids to the freaking fag revolution."

In the first days of the trial the prosecutors were deprived of the appearance of personal ability or power by the lack of contest, caused by the judge's rulings being so consistently in their favor. The defense attorneys at the same time, under the constant goading and denial and harassment, grew stronger.

"Free press and fair trial might include fair free press," Foran said to the judge, both of whom were personally chagrined by the images of a bizarre struggle between good and evil that the defense was able to project into the media. Early in the trial, the prosecutors sought and got a ruling in law that forbade the attorneys to speak publicly about events in the courtroom. But every attempt of the government to maintain its version of order pushed the press toward the defendants, not that the reporters were uniformly thrilled by the proximity. The prosecutors were anguished by the way wit and laughter in the courtroom affected the newsmen, and by the constant exchange between the defendants and the press. The prosecutors isolated themselves behind the protection of the ruling that forbade them to talk.

The lack of humor on the part of the government was illustrated by almost every incident. Rennie Davis distributed jelly beans from a large box to spectators and reporters one morning. Davis said, to the marshal who stopped him, "No, no, I won't throw them on the floor." Davis was smiling.

In the proceedings, Foran objected furiously to "that claque over there giggling and groaning"—and he pointed with his whole stiff hand at the defendants' table and at the press section alongside it—"and that claque over there, giggling and groaning"—and he pointed at the press, staff, and family section in the back of the defense table with his whole stiff hand. That sort of behavior on the part of a defense attorney would have merited a contempt citation.

Richard Schultz frequently complained to the judge about how difficult it was to concentrate on one's cross-examination, with the defendants making continual comments and laughter in the courtroom. Right in front of the jury, he likened it to the way demonstrators provoked police during Convention Week.

Toward the end of proceedings one day, Judge Hoffman characteristically admonished Kunstler and Rennie Davis for laughing, when in fact they were only smiling and whispering together. Then the judge looked down from his bench and saw a most extraordinary sight—Tom Hayden lying veritably with his back on the bottom of his chair and his legs sprawled with his knees up far out in front of him, and with his hands crossed on his stomach. "Look at that man there," the judge said, "lying down there as if he's on the ground."

"That's the way I feel, your honor."

"Sit up, sit up."

"It may reflect his attitude, your honor," Kunstler said, "to what is going on in this courtroom."

"Oh," the judge said, "I think it does reflect his attitude, I think it does."

"Then it is free speech," Kunstler said.

"And that attitude will be appropriately dealt with," Judge Hoffman said, bobbing with fury. When provoked about the Constitution, he acted the way cops acted toward demonstrators, with guilty rage. Then he said, as if a little confused, "Can't three marshals back there deal with this matter?" Newsmen were scribbling wildly in their notebooks. The three marshals standing in the aisle between the press and spectator sections moved hesitantly. The judge looked at them a moment, they were not sure if they had received an order, and then he adjourned the court.

In the elevator, with observers who were still trying to figure out what had happened, Abbie Hoffman said, "Well, what do you expect the judge to do? With Tom lying there like that, with his pants open, playing with himself?" The judge had indeed acted as if that were the magnitude of Hayden's offense against the court. Sit right, sit nice, sit polite, sit back, sit up.

Some of the government's witnesses could be impeached with laugh after laugh for the parties sympathetic to the defense. Many women in the jury were discomforted when the slender, copper-haired policewoman Barbara Callender took the stand and young women of the Conspiracy staff were talking in tones that could be overheard of "male supremacy," calling her "the nearest thing to a whore I ever saw."

There was a sort of hissing from all sides when she described how she dressed for her "work" in Lincoln Park during Convention Week, wearing "hippie clothes," white bell-bottoms, and carried a .38 Colt in her bag. What gave her, or any policeman, the right, when a defendant would have been damned to prison for carrying a weapon for self-defense? Hesitantly, then resolutely, she poked her finger in Abbie Hoffman's and Jerry Rubin's backs to identify them, which caused smiles and laughs, and she touched Hayden and Davis, too.

Then Mrs. Callender answered Kunstler's questions about a speech of Jerry Rubin's concerning Pigasus, the hog that was the Yippies' candidate for President of the United States. Kunstler said, "Do you understand what a satire is?"

Mrs. Callender said this was somehow different, this candidate for President.

"Did you support Pigasus?"

"No," she said. Then, after a second, "Certainly not." There was laughter at her straight answer and then her double take. Kunstler held onto both sides of the lectern with his long arms.

"Did you oppose him?"

"No," she said. She was doing her best to answer according to the yes or no instructions, uncomfortably, as if hoping the prosecutor would object. It must have been especially satisfying to Jerry Rubin to see the myth of Pigasus still doing its work, now a satire on the rules of evidence.

"You were neutral, right?"

"Yes," she said. The completion of the game was so perfect that the laughter was wide and silent, a part of the game, never letting her know the import of what she had said. The game was even more delightfully consummated because Kunstler was whiling away minutes until adjournment and dominating her and toying with her. It was possible that a number of women in the jury really hated the "New York lawyer" for using her so blatantly.

But the laughter was godsent to make dubious her so careful testimony about Jerry Rubin urging kids in Lincoln Park to "arm themselves" and wait for the "big day, Wednesday," to "disrupt the Convention." In cross-examination, she admitted that she did not tell her police superior about any of these remarks at the time.

There were times when the defense won the laugh and made the prosecution look foolish but lost the credibility of the impeachment. Richard L. Thompson, a plainclothes black Chicago policeman with a compelling, self-conscious style of dress and manner, gave testimony about a speech of Rennie Davis's in Judd Hall at the University of Chicago in November, 1967. Officer Thompson had shown his style when he stepped down from the witness stand to identify Davis and Hoffman. He made his hand into a pistol and put it right into their backs neatly. It got a laugh. Thompson's testimony about Davis's speech, and the resulting controversy between the prosecution and the defense over whether Davis said "disrupt the Convention" or "disrupt the sham of the Convention," reverberated throughout the trial. "Did you understand," Kunstler asked, "what he meant by civil disobedience?"

Richard Schultz jumped up. "Objection."

Judge Hoffman leaned forward to rule. "Your honor," Kunstler said, "I think the grounds for that objection should be stated."

Richard Schultz stammered, "I withdraw the objection," and sat down. There was a lot of laughter in the courtroom because most observers had registered that Judge Hoffman would have sustained the objection. But Officer Thompson proceeded to give an honest description of civil disobedience and the motives of those who might engage in it. It gave credence to what he had said about what Davis had said. It hurt. The defense was never completely able to impeach his testimony, partly because the other audience felt a picayune condescension in any attempt to make distinctions about the use and meaning of the words "disrupt" and "sham."

The phrasing and tone of an item of testimony could lend as much to the credibility, and to the finding out of your allegiance in reaction to it, as the supposed substance of the testimony itself. Dwayne Oklepek, the slight student undercover newspaper reporter with an unusual summer job of infiltrating movement organizations for Columnist Jack Mabley of *Chicago Today,* testified that "Mr. Hayden was considered violent by all his intimates." Laughter came particularly from newsmen, spectators, and persons familiar with the defendants. The word "intimates" gave a sexual suggestion that was pricelessly funny, and the close-lipped feeling of the witness in speaking the close vowels gave connotations to the testimony that were unwelcome to the prosecution. If Oklepek had said instead, "Tom Hayden was considered violent by all his friends," there might have been laughter but it would have been for a different image and reason.

Nevertheless, Oklepek was one of the most verbally agile of the government's witnesses, and that differentiated him from the undercover police agents. He testified that Tom Hayden said, "The Mobilization should train an army," and he attributed similar paramilitary declarations to Davis. He said that Davis said about the use of expressway viaducts along the route of the big march to the Amphitheatre, a march that never materialized, "We'll put marshals on those things, and they'll shoot the shit out of any of them," presumably meaning the police.

Kunstler asked Oklepek if he ever saw a Mobilization person wearing a gun and Oklepek said not that he could see.

"Not that you could see," Kunstler said. "Are you saying you saw outlines under their coats?"

"I saw bulges under their coats," Oklepek said.

"Oh, you saw bulges. Did you say to yourself at that time, 'Those are guns'?"

"I said to myself at that time, 'Those are bulges.' "

That was the rare wit in this trial that got genuine response from everyone. But, oddly, because of his close-lipped feeling, Oklepek did not invite laughter and even though his remarks might be very funny he did not receive the fullness of audience response that, for instance, Judge Hoffman and William Kunstler welcomed.

"Did you tell the Grand Jury anything," Kunstler asked, "about guns emanating from Mr. Hayden's mouth?"

"That question will look awfully bad on paper, Mr. Kunstler," the judge said. "Nobody objected to it, but I just want you to have a good record."

Kunstler presented Oklepek with a series of Oklepek's FBI interviews. "Do you remember" such and such? Kunstler would say.

"No, I do not."

Then Kunstler would hand him an FBI interview. "Does that refresh your memory?"

"Yes, it does."

The defense tried to get across to jurors and observers that Oklepek first told the FBI that he did not consider the Mobilization to be "violent," and told his *Chicago Today* employer Jack Mabley on August 21, 1968, the same. The defense tried to suggest that it was after a great many interviews with the FBI that Oklepek apparently changed his characterization of the defendants and their intentions.

When Oklepek stepped down from the witness stand at the end of his long testimony, the prosecutors, all four of them, looked as if their faces would explode with jubilance. Oklepek looked back over his shoulder as he unclipped the rope to go down the aisle. He looked back not at the prosecutors, who were not looking at him, but at the defendants. They too were not looking at him, and there was a feeling of the damned in the room. It was that he had been "used" by the prosecution that gave, or took away, the credence of his testimony, depending on which side you felt it.

William Frapolly, the young student undercover police agent, caused intense emotional reaction among some jurors with sons and daughters who were students. The convict-on-all-counts jurors believed every word he said, and the ones who held out for acquittal of the defendants were horrified and repelled by a young police agent growing long hair and becoming a student in order to spy on the activities of other young people, even his roommates. Foran asked, "Now, during this period of time has your appearance altered any?"

Frapolly said, "I have grown sideburns approximately to here. My hair is exceedingly long, I have grown a goatee, I have grown a mustache." Foran always enjoyed the agents' descriptions of their long hair. When Frapolly stepped down to the defense table to touch Rennie Davis, the defendants said, "Oink, oink."

Frapolly testified that Rennie Davis said that the young supporters of Senator Eugene McCarthy's campaign for the presidential nomination would be "lured" to Lincoln Park by rock music and sex, and the music would keep them after the 11 P.M. curfew and the cops would arrest and injure people in clearing the park and that would get sympathy for the National Mobilization. In cross-examination, Kunstler and Weinglass brought out that Frapolly did not tell the Grand Jury about "luring the McCarthy kids with music and sex." There were many other lurid items that he neglected to tell the Grand Jury but remembered in time for the Conspiracy trial.

Frapolly testified that David Dellinger said at the Wednesday morning, August 28, meeting that his march would be a "diversion" to get people "out of Lincoln Park. I'm sorry, Grant Park," he corrected himself.

Frapolly testified that he saw John Froines throwing rocks on Tuesday night of Convention Week.

Kunstler disclosed that Frapolly was suspended for one year at Northeastern Illinois University because he was in a group that pushed the president of Northeastern off a stage. Weinglass showed Frapolly how his suggestion in parade marshals' training in Lincoln Park for using a grappling hook on barbwire on vehicles could be incitement to violence, and if it had in fact been tried, might have caused worse violence from Guardsmen and police than occurred during Convention Week. Frapolly said that he did not think the suggestion would work, and he gave it just in order to be a seeming participant. He said that Davis said, "That's a good idea." If so, Rennie Davis must have been trying inordinately hard to encourage responses in that meeting.

The undercover agents were a little confused every time it was shown to them that a particular action of theirs would be considered criminal if it had been done by one of the defendants.

Kunstler said, "Fifty to a hundred thousand people would snake dance through the streets of Chicago, is that what Mr. Hayden said?" Foran objected to the question. The laughter from the defendants was caused by actually seeing in their minds a hundred thousand people snake dancing through the streets of Chicago. Judge Hoffman admonished the laughter. The defendants' memories of events compared with the agents' testimony and interpretation of the same remarks and events caused much of the reaction that the defendants, of course, wanted the jurors to see.

When Judge Hoffman, in acidly discussing the "open-the-door" rule of evidence with Weinglass, said, "Very often it kicks back in your face," he could not see that his remark incited Weinglass to say, "The door in this courtroom seems

to swing in one direction." Weinglass was later sentenced for
that bit of contumacious behavior. Both the judge and Frapolly
said that it was their intentions, and their positions of responsibility within the society, that made the difference between
the nature of their actions and the actions of the defendants.
It amounted to a confession that it was one's position toward
society, not whether one's behavior incited other people, that
determined whether one's intentions were evil or not.

Lieutenant Healy, head of the subversive section of the Chicago Police Department during Convention Week, defined a
subversive organization as "any organization that might create
a problem for the city or the country." The notion that the
government, with its policies and its lack of policies concerning
money and work and the right to live, racism, and war, might
be creating problems with which people and "organizations"
were trying to cope, passed the understanding of the side represented by Lieutenant Healy. His testimony echoed Detective
Riggio, who defined an agitator as "anyone who causes me
problems, or stirs up problems and fights." Lieutenant Healy
said that he personally had the power to define any organization as subversive, and the director of intelligence of the Chicago Police Department had the same power. When Healy
said, to identify Lee Weiner, that he had seen "Mr. Weiner's
picture many times," in the files of the subversive section, you
could wonder how that statement affected some jurors. But a
few jurors, with Bobby Seale bound and gagged across the
room, looked warily from under their brows at Lieutenant
Healy, as if they were becoming suspicious of positions and
intentions in and toward society.

Thomas Foran yawned mightily through a motion by Weinglass for a mistrial because of "government invasion of the
legal camp of the defense." Weinglass said that Conspiracy
mail, addressed to their office at 28 East Jackson, had been
opened, wastepaper and garbage examined by police agents,
phone conversations tapped, and that the court possessed a

government-affirmed affidavit that the government acknowledged having opened the envelope containing the Conspiracy telephone bill. Weinglass said that the government admitted wiretapping six or seven defendants, three wiretaps the prosecutors even conceded to be illegal and three they contended were legal for national security reasons. Foran, throughout Weinglass's motion, held his chin in one hand and tapped his lips rhythmically and stiffly with the first finger. Richard Schultz was fond of intimating that the information in the wiretaps would convict the defendants.

Schultz, to answer Weinglass's motion, began by saying with a pious sort of threat that he would not repeat himself the way Weinglass repeated himself. Judge Hoffman leaned forward and beamed at Schultz. But when Weinglass spoke the judge folded his arms and leaned back and grimaced continually.

Schultz said that if the elevator operator at 28 East Jackson actually saw police go through the wastepaper, as the defense contended, then the defense should have brought the elevator operator to testify. Cubbage and Foran were grinning as they looked straight at Weinglass, who was saying, "For some reason the government never feels the need in this case to answer any legal argument."

The defense isolated Irwin Bock as a probable agent by narrowing down the persons who had been present at certain conversations indicated in the indictment. Leonard Weinglass and Irving Birnbaum extracted from Bock in June, 1969, a statement to the effect that to the best of his knowledge the defendants were not guilty of intentions to incite riots during Convention Week.

Bock's hair stayed short and his dress and manner suitably middle class as he infiltrated the movement to the point of becoming a member of the Executive Committee of Veterans for Peace and of the Executive Committee of the Chicago Peace Council and the Steering Committee of the New Mobilization to End the War In Viet Nam. He came through the door of the courtroom in his hunched forward, rolling, on-the-balls-of-his-feet walk. The defendants had long suspected and awaited him, and murmured excitedly and laughed among themselves. In a recess, Bock walked fast in that rolling way down the corridor to a private elevator, craning a glance over his shoulder as if to see if anyone might be coming after him.

Bock's testimony was long, covering parade marshals' training and many meetings. He had trouble recalling the names of defendants present at each meeting, and sometimes appeared to recall them at the suggestion of Richard Schultz. He was often slow and repetitive in his attempts to be precise in answering a question, "an automaton," the defendants suggested, "trying to remember his script." Bock sometimes took so long to begin answering a question that the cross-examiner would prompt him with a glance or a word. Further, he developed a sore throat that made it hard for him to speak audibly during cross-examination. He too was submissive and ingratiating in tone and manner. Not the least of an undercover agent's job is the guilt that he must bear.

In cross-examination, Kunstler first explored the affidavit that Bock had signed in which he stated that the defendants were peaceful in their intentions. Bock said that his "control officer" told him to make a statement that would not reveal he was a police officer. Kunstler elicited the fact that in other instances Bock was not "above lying if it suited his purposes."

Kunstler and Weinglass used Bock's testimony to impeach or cast doubt on the testimony of Oklepek and Frapolly. Bock was present at meetings with Oklepek and Frapolly. He could not remember Davis's saying that National Mobilization would use music and sex to lure the McCarthy kids to Lincoln Park or that marshals would build barricades in Lincoln Park or that marshals on the overpasses of the Dan Ryan Expressway would "shoot the shit" out of soldiers or police. It would be interesting to see the agents' reports on the behavior and "intentions" of each other. It must have delighted their control officers.

Weinglass, in his cross-examination, established that Bock could always move freely and talk freely with the defendants and so could anyone. There was no secrecy. Weinglass asked, "Did you see any of them hit a policeman?"

"No, sir."

"Did you see any of them throw a rock or any other sort of missile?"

"No, sir."

Weinglass positively insisted that Bock remember that the Mobilization parade marshals were trained in keeping groups of demonstrators "peaceful and orderly." "Did you ever receive instruction as a marshal to take action against the police?"

"Not personally," Bock said. Yes or no was the answer that the judge would require of the defense's witnesses. But Bock was permitted to say "not personally."

During Kunstler's cross-examination of Bock, Richard Schultz objected to audience laughter at the witness, and the judge admonished the audience and told the marshals to take care of it. Kunstler protested Schultz's objection, and Schultz retaliated by asking that the audience be put on the record for laughing. He also said that the defendants laughed at Bock's testimony to influence the jury to think that the testimony was absurd.

Bock recounted vividly, matter-of-factly, and carefully a speech that Tom Hayden gave to a party in Evanston about the effects of the United States's bombing of North Viet Nam. There was solemnity in him, and in the clear and intense listening in the courtroom.

When Kunstler dwelled on Bock's testimony about Rennie Davis saying that Nixon and Humphrey represented no choice for young people, Kay Richards leaned far forward in the jury with her hands laced together on her knees, and seemed especially moved and attentive.

Rennie Davis had befriended and defended Bock among movement people—because of the movement's need to cultivate middle-class support—long after many persons in the Mobilization became suspicious of him. Now Davis declared in open court, "Why don't you arrest this lying police spy? He has filed an affidavit."

Foran rose and said in a level tone of anger, "I would like to have those remarks on the record, Miss Reporter." Foran and Schultz appeared to keep track of the contempt possibilities.

"I suggest to you, Miss Reporter," Kunstler said, getting to his feet across the aisle from Foran, "that no one has the authority to ask you to put those comments in the record."

Foran's tone stayed level as if he did not care who found out that he was running this court. "The remark was, 'Why don't you arrest that lying police spy,' Miss Reporter."

"And that district attorney who is teaching him to lie," David Dellinger said.

"Take that also, Miss Reporter," Foran said.

"That is a fine way to get to be senator," Dellinger said.

Two or three times in the course of the trial the judge had admonished Tom Hayden for "trying to fulfill" his, Judge Hoffman's, function—in each case Hayden was trying to cool some heated activity—but the judge might as well have been asleep on the bench when Foran gave the orders to the Court Reporter.

Toward the end of the cross-examination of Bock, the judge cautioned the defendants not to raise their voices. Without looking up, Dellinger and Hayden continued to read magazines and manuscripts. Davis and Weiner continued writing on pads of paper. Abbie Hoffman looked up from his newspaper with a preoccupied, uncomprehending air at the judge.

Agent Stanley, with FBI files flashing in his mind, smiled at Weinglass's questioning of Bock on what Dellinger said about combining "militant nonviolent action with mobile tactics" on the morning of the fateful Wednesday, August 28, 1968. The judge often instructed the prosecution in its possibilities. He craned his head this way and that around Weinglass at the lectern in order to catch Richard Schultz's eye. The judge grinned as Schultz registered the signal and objected to Weinglass's question.

In the men's room on the twenty-third floor, Rennie Davis, while combing his hair carefully as he did each day before facing the women of the jury, said that the trial was now boring to him, "at its lowest ebb" for the defense, "not political now." Tom Hayden, slumped in his chair in the court, was chewing on his nails and hangnails again. The defendants did not flourish, spiritually or physically, unless they were involved in political confrontation.

The movement seemed so riddled with agents, and fear of agents, that when Kunstler in cross-examination of Frapolly said Chicago Police Council instead of Chicago Peace Council, there were snorts of recognition in the audience. Frapolly asked politely and earnestly if Kunstler had said "Chicago Police Council," and Kunstler denied it and hostilely suggested that Frapolly had said it. It was an inspired slip of the tongue.

Bock attempted to make the parade marshals' training in Lincoln Park seem somewhat surreptitious. Frapolly made it sound as if it were hand-to-hand combat training. All of the agents testified to the violent, conspiratorial nature of the training. In fact, the training was defensive and done in the open on a ball field in a well-frequented park, with an ever-present audience of dozens of plainclothesmen, uniformed police, newsmen, TV camera crews, Lincoln Park citizens, and other spectators. But by the wording of the law and the indictment the government needed only to prove that the defendants conspired that "instructions would be given in techniques of resisting and obstructing police action." The jury, in its compromise verdict, acquitted the defendants of this charge, though eight of the jurors actually believed they were guilty of it.

This writer witnessed the training in the time period mentioned in the indictment, during the week before Convention Week. The agents never admitted in either direct or cross-examination that the trainers of the parade marshals used the words "defensive" or "we want to avoid violence but if it comes here's how to protect yourself," and the agents could not remember any training in keeping demonstrations "peaceful and orderly," words that I heard used to preface and explain every part of the actual training. "Conspiracy to act like a cop," the defendants said, wryly, ironically, and not very pleased with themselves.

The purpose of the marshal training was manyfold. First, the city of Chicago had been effective in its campaign to scare demonstrators away from Chicago. The Chicago police, with mounting intensity through 1968, showed that they would administer arbitrary punishment in the form of clubbing, tear gas, mace, and other brutal actions right there on the streets. In other words, clubbing was not used merely, as the police training bulletin prescribes, to subdue a person for arrest. The demonstrators needed to feel that something was being done to enable them to take care of themselves in the face of the armed might and provocative attitude of the police. In legal terms, the parade marshall training was meant to enable demonstrators to avoid being punished without due process of law.

There was training for keeping crowds "orderly" and "peaceful," and in how to handle provocateurs. The training was also a charade to get images into the media that would cause a high degree of audience involvement. You get two lean, hard-muscled black guys, for example, to stand before the white demonstrators and show off some rather startling karate tactics. The black guys are well trained, they yell and leap dramatically, they look good, and they give a vivid image for the screen in everybody's living room. Such an image—two skilled *black* guys training *war protestors* in exotic deadly *karate* (Judge Hoffman's *ka-ret*)—excited strong feelings of fear and anticipation for most viewers in most living rooms. The image of the pale, flabby, generally unathletic marshals wobbling as they tried to balance on one foot, falling over, sweating, panting, would not be so satisfying because it allowed for the safe feeling of ridicule and boredom and was not guaranteed to fascinate an audience. The parade marshals were supposed to be trained in a few sessions in a few days to use these tactics for self-defense *and then* turn around and magically train all marchers in parades to use them, too. Absurd. For the most part, the marshals' training was a charade for TV, and a charade to lift the mental outlook of the marchers, to put-on the city and maybe give confidence to the marchers.

The agents testified time and again, and the prosecutors recalled time and again, that David Baker, an unindicted co-conspirator, showed parade marshals how to use a rolled-up magazine to deflect a blow from a police club, and then how to give a special kick in the groin that required a high degree of balance and physical sureness and coordination to deliver if the cop would stand still long enough to receive it. The agents did not hear Baker saying in preface to each training demonstration, "We are not looking for violence, but if it happens, here's one way to protect yourself."

In any case, the current of Convention Week took such a sharp turn on Sunday, August 25, 1968, that all of that training, except for the first-aid training, some of which was given by Irwin Bock, became irrelevant. Except for the Wednesday afternoon rally in Grant Park, the National Mobilization parade marshals were largely derided and ignored by the angry people sometimes in their late thirties, who seized the high spirit of the event in shifting confrontations brought about by police pressure and attack. "Mobile tactics," for the prosecution during the trial, meant the breaking of windows, setting off of fire alarms, and such harassments. "Mobile tactics," to most young people in Lincoln Park, meant small groups harassing police. No windows of homes and only two of businesses were broken throughout Convention Week.

If the agents saw and heard such a distorted version of the marshal training, with such significant omissions and apparent commissions on their part, it was likely that their testimony about what was said in other meetings would be faulty in the same way. I interviewed a young woman on the Conspiracy staff, Donna Gripe, an unindicted co-conspirator, who knew Frapolly, Oklepek, and Bock. She knew Frapolly when he first joined student peace groups at Northeastern Illinois where she also went to school, and said that he was not only with the group that pushed the president of Northeastern off the stage, but it was Frapolly's initiative and he was the one who did the pushing. I can only say that I had an interviewer's sense for the authenticity of what she was saying. What did he feel about what he was doing, a criminal act in his own mind for an angel's purpose? She also suspected Oklepek when he showed up in the Mobilization meetings, but she felt differently about "Dwayne" because he initially reported that the Mobilization was peaceful. She was convinced that it was the FBI with its "series of interviews" that changed his mind.

Donna Gripe said that at the Counter-Inaugural demonstration in Washington, D. C., in January, 1969, where Bock was responsible for putting up the tent and sound equipment, he was openly writing in a notebook at the oddest times and butting into people's conversations at inappropriate moments. She warned Rennie Davis again that she was sure Bock was an agent. Agents, because they were in effect being paid to do the work, were able to take positions of trust and responsibility because most people could only work part-time and felt guilty and pressed about it.

How do you know agents? "You just know," she said. "They're just not right, something's wrong about them." She said to Rennie Davis, "Now, *who* knows agents?" But she suspected that she had missed on the "really big ones," the long-term undercover agents of the FBI and CIA. Most people in the movement have been suspected at one time or another.

There was talk throughout the trial of one or more of the defendants being agile-coin agents, for the double purpose of spying and of actually controlling the actions and directions of "dissent." There came the moment in the government's case when the government had called its next witness, and the defendant most frequently suggested as a possible agent got up suddenly and went out the side door, apparently to the bathroom. The other defendants, Conspiracy staff members, and some newsmen literally held their breath for fear that he would come through the front door and take the stand for the government.

Undercover agents are some of the bravest men in police work, said the prosecutors. Their work is dangerous, demanding, valuable, and they need to have their wits about them. They are some of the filthiest and nerviest paranoids ever to insinuate themselves into the friendship, trust, and loyalty of persons whom they are going to betray with lies, distortions, and fabrications, said the defense.

If you have ever been lied about by someone taking a phrase out of context and giving it a different meaning, and you suspected that he had only an insecure notion of the difference between what happened and what he says happened, you have an idea of the sort of psychopathic persons that the defendants said these agents were.

The domestic undercover agent is used in a special relationship to facts and the power of facts. Nothing is more unsettling to political, social, cultural, ideological, and psychological systems, stances, and positions than a "fact." A "fact" that is perceived and accepted and communicated clearly, which is a further and continuing process of perception, causes necessary changes in the behavior and the consciousness of as many people as share in the process. A "fact" here has the same potential as a "myth" to Abbie Hoffman. He would even say that he used the term "myth" because there was no such thing as "truth." It was not clear whether by "truth" he also meant "fact."

There was a "fact" and there were "facts" of the Democratic convention, incompletely but strongly perceived by a large number of people, many of them influential in the information processes of this country. These "facts" were acting as catalysts on many systems of mind from the left to the right of the political and cultural life of this country. The catalytic reactions to these "facts" were particularly dangerous to those people who insisted, in their own view of their threatened lives and of the lives of others, on "control" being present in all events. The "fact" of the Democratic convention, that it was a powerful "uncontrolled" event, was not accepted. Because that "fact" was not accepted and most groups reacted against it, it burned its way through the consciousness of most groups in American society. It was "uncontrolled," but that does not mean that planning, hopes, intentions, organizations, and "leadership" were not part of it. It means that response was free and strong and took the direction of real possibility, shaped by all contending forces present. The "fact" of the Democratic convention became everyone's skeleton in the closet, first to be hidden and then to be used as a "myth," to be interpreted and described in whatever way in order to protect and expand each system and stance.

The undercover agent played an utterly crucial role in this process. He brought back what he was sent to see, what he was sent to hear: the evidence, the guarantee, that the government's purported perception of the fact was true and actual. Therefore appropriate political, judicial, and police actions were not merely indicated but justified. The agent brought back the evidence that "control" was present and necessary in all human affairs.

The undercover agent characterized the government's relation to "fact." The movement's perception of the government characterized its relation to "fact." That constituted the contradiction with which both had to struggle.

The "fact" exists to challenge the limitations of the winner.

With the testimony of Irwin Bock, Judge Hoffman apparently realized that the government's case was factually weak and not likely to improve. Now laughter often exacted sharp reactions from him.

The judge usually ended proceedings at 4:30 P.M., sometimes virtually in midsentence. The two or three exceptions were always significant. In November, when Bock was on the witness stand with a bad sore throat, Kunstler requested an earlier recess so the defendants "who had spent much of their adult lives in antiwar activity" could catch their planes to go to Washington, D. C., for the Moratorium Against the Viet Nam War. The jury was in the courtroom.

Judge Hoffman vehemently denied the request for such a recess. Foran smiled in that wide and steady way of his. He was probably furious with Kunstler for telling the sequestered jury about the Moratorium, and particularly about his defendants' noble motives for wishing to be there. To keep bail privileges the defendants had to file their travel plans with Foran's office. Perhaps, in some way, the judge had also found out what time their planes departed O'Hare airport.

Kunstler protested to an irate Judge Hoffman that the defendants wished to exercise their constitutional rights to protest the war in Viet Nam in Washington. Foran rose, stooping as he often did, and asked that the jury be directed to disregard the comments. Judge Hoffman sarcastically directed the jury to "disregard all that talk about Washington and constitutional rights." Spectators and press laughed hugely. The marshals stirred furiously in the aisles and by the doors. It was one of Judge Hoffman's most magnificently masochistic comments. Then he was sharp with the reaction. He thought the defendants were principal participants. He promptly named Jerry Rubin, Lee Weiner, and Abbie Hoffman. I could see those three defendants clearly and they were not, and had not been, laughing. I was shaking my head vigorously no, no, no. The defendants attempted to say that they had not been laughing. But their attempt was not accepted, and the request for recess was again denied.

Everybody in the courtroom watched the clock as Kunstler continued asking questions of Bock. The defendants were restless as 4:30 came and went. Kunstler even asked Bock, who had just "blown his cover" a few days before, if he was going to be present the next day in Washington as a member of the Steering Committee of the New Mobilization. That got a few ironic laughs.

The trial was recessed at 4:54. The defendants did arrive at the huge Moratorium demonstration in Washington, D. C.— five hundred thousand strong—only somewhat delayed.

Stereo speakers were set up in the courtroom to play the cassette tapes of U. S. Navy Intelligence Agent Schaller. The sounds of helicopters yammering constantly overhead, and the voices of the crowd in the Grant Park bandshell, brought Convention Week played live, its sense of dread and destiny, into the courtroom. I had been there, and I remembered the fear and hopelessness of the crowd after the police attack. I concluded the government offered these speeches of Wednesday afternoon, August 28, 1968, into evidence in order to prevent the defense from presenting them first to prove the opposite of the government's case. "We have decided to move into their space in any way we can, to defend ourselves in any way we can." That was perhaps that afternoon's most inciteful statement, made by Tom Neumann, who wasn't even indicted. The government declared he was the mouthpiece of that master-plotter David Dellinger, pacifist. Tom Hayden followed, declaring "if blood is going to flow, let it flow all over the city."

Witnesses on the stand for the government could take advantage of wit, too, not necessarily because their relation to their testimony was so pure. Deputy Superintendent of Police James M. Rochford was a large man, with a large sloping forehead and thinning reddish hair that he combed straight back, and his ears appeared to point backwards. Kunstler asked Rochford, who was in general command of police around the Conrad Hilton and in Grant Park during Convention Week, to explain why a request for a permit to march to the Amphitheatre was denied on Wednesday afternoon, August 28. Rochford had said that he himself could let a march happen if he judged it to be safe. That took the mayor off the hook for having denied crucial permits. Rochford said that one of the reasons the march was denied was that its route would go through areas of "lower socio-economic groups." Laughter came at such insight into the mind of the government. "We had information . . ." and Kunstler cut him short, "I know you had lots of information." Rochford, taking just a moment to be incensed, said snappily, "A great deal," and turned the put-down back at Kunstler. The jury's future foreman, Edward Kratzke, smiled at Rochford's comeback.

Kunstler continued cross-examining Rochford about the time when police stopped Dellinger's "nonviolent" march inside Grant Park along Columbus Drive. The jurors looked apathetic and weary, except for Mrs. Fritz and Kay Richards. Kunstler said to the Deputy Superintendent, "You saw the crowd?"

"Yes. They were dribbling about."

"Were you aware of gas from the National Guard?"

"Yes."

Kunstler now began to stake out his ambush. "Did you order any arrests made?"

"No."

"Did you see any arrests made?"

"No."

"You didn't see any reason for arrests, is that right?"

Rochford grinned. "I sure did." He explained about the "massive movements of people," implying that the police did not make legitimate arrests in order to avoid provoking the demonstrators. Rochford grinned at the jury. Once again the future foreman of the jury smiled at Rochford's comeback. Kunstler did not look good. He often overreached in his questioning and offered the chance to undercut his point.

Rochford continued to testify in a low voice that he had not used so gently in front of the Conrad Hilton in August, 1968. Defendant Lee Weiner, who was usually reading a work in social science, looked up and spoke quietly to Kunstler: "Bill, the executioner is mumbling. Could you have the judge tell him to speak up?" Kunstler delivered the request. Judge Hoffman, apparently unaware of Weiner's quiet remark, asked Rochford to raise his voice. Then Foran, scorekeeper of contempt possibilities, rose, stooping, and asked that Weiner's remark be put into the record. This would be Specification 5, for which Lee Weiner would be sentenced one month in his contempt citations.

With his great head of springy black hair and black beard, he stood up and willingly repeated his remark in a raised voice for the judge. "I said, 'Bill, the executioner is mumbling. Could you have the judge tell him to speak up?' " In the jury box, Mrs. Jean Fritz, who had not heard the remark the first time, ducked her head and laughed behind her hand. Beside her, Kay Richards also laughed. Kay Richards talked and whispered only with Mrs. Fritz in the jury box, in an especially friendly way.

Now Foran protested what he called the defendants' constant flippant interruptions and heckling and harassment. Kunstler, on the other hand, protested what he called Foran's "constant schoolhouse episodes" and called Foran a "schoolmarm"—echoing frontier-western movies—for the offense he took at "mirth" in the courtroom, especially if the "mirth" was at the government's expense. At the "schoolmarm" remark of Kunstler's, Jean Fritz and Kay Richards ducked their heads and laughed. Two other jurors, who would be among the "holdouts" for acquittal, also smiled. The other jurors and the jury's future foreman looked glumly upon the scene.

Rochford said that, in the famous "massacre" of demonstrators by police or the famous "riot" of demonstrators against police on the evening of August 28, 1968 at Michigan and Balbo, which he pronounced "Balboa" as a native Chicagoan—setting himself off from "New York lawyer" Kunstler's pronunciation—only a few officers used their batons in skirmish line I, and only a few in skirmish line II. Rochford called it "a natural thing to raise the baton," and he lifted his arm to demonstrate as he said it. There were wry laughs and smiles in the audience, even among the jurors sympathetic to the defense. Judge Hoffman looked askance at the laughter but made no admonishment.

Rochford testified that Sidney Peck, a Mobilization organizer who tried along with David Dellinger to negotiate with Rochford for a permit for the march back in Grant Park, screamed, "I told you this would happen!" Peck was beating Rochford on the chest "hysterically" in front of the Conrad Hilton Hotel. Peck was arrested for assault and battery.

Rochford was seen at Michigan and Balbo pulling his cops off demonstrators and yelling, "For Christ's sake, stop it! Stop it, damn it, stop it!" Kunstler asked Rochford now, "Were you yourself shocked at what you saw Chicago police officers doing to civilians in the streets of Chicago?"

Rochford said, "Did I say that?," as if he really wondered.

Kunstler repeated the question.

After a pause, Rochford said, "I was hurt." He was sensitive to the very different connotations of "hurt" and "shocked." Kunstler would have done better if he could somehow have quoted the line, "For Christ's sake, stop it!" assuming he knew about it.

"The blinking lights in rooms" of the Hilton during Convention Week were "signals," Rochford said, portending action somewhere; he implied the signals were from the young people in the Hilton to the demonstrators in Grant Park across the street. In fact, spokesmen for the demonstrators—I remember especially Julian Bond—asked through the portable speaker for Convention delegates and campaign workers in the hotel to blink their lights to show their sympathy. Laughter of wry amazement came from people in the courtroom, with hopelessness in it, because Rochford, on the street with the police, could hear Julian Bond's voice as clearly as anyone. I remember that on Tuesday night a few room lights blinked in answer, and on Wednesday night when the call for blinking in sympathy was sounded the lights of the fifteenth floor—campaign headquarters of the avowedly antiwar candidate Eugene McCarthy—blinked jubilantly.

If Rochford really believed his melodramatic interpretation of the "blinking lights," his testimony may have been revealing of the way the whole audience for the prosecution throughout the nation saw Convention Week, as a strange code for evilly planned and projected actions.

Rochford was also asked if he heard or knew of "orders" given by demonstration "leaders" for demonstrators to go to Michigan Avenue and riot. "I'm sure they were there," he said. "But I did not hear them." Again, the judge would have required defense witnesses to answer yes or no.

Rochford would also not admit in his testimony that the use of tear gas changed the character of the crowd in Grant Park. Weinglass then read from the report that Rochford wrote on the day of the event. "Frontal attack and release of gas caused complete collapse of order." Rochford now testified that he did not see either the police attack or the gas, and he did not appear to be embarrassed by the apparent contradiction.

Reluctantly, after prodding from Weinglass and becoming aware that the government would not object to the question, Rochford said, "Yes," that the demonstration parade marshals were keeping very good order in the march in Grant Park up to the point when the march was stopped by police. Then it began to disintegrate.

Kunstler, in questioning Rochford about the "intelligence" information that caused him to consider the defendants dangerous and to deny marches, said, "Did you also hear about ten thousand naked people walking on the waters of Lake Michigan?" Great laughter came from the audience for the defense, even from some jurors who ordinarily laughed on the side of the prosecution. Kay Richards and Mrs. Fritz enjoyed themselves. But the deep end of the convict-on-all-counts jurors looked pained, and the word and image of "naked" possibly pained them as much as the laughter itself. Miriam Hill, a large blond woman, called "Mrs. Wallace," referring to "America First" presidential candidate George Wallace, always folded her arms and looked about the courtroom huffily at such images and such laughter.

Rochford smiled and seemed to wink at the judge at the end of one day's testimony.

Later in the trial, in cross-examining another police commander during the government's rebuttal case, Kunstler would call attention to the fact that Rochford received a promotion directly after he testified. The promotion was, at the very least, inappropriate timing on the part of the city.

The form, the process, the rules of the court give rise to esthetic demands. When Judge Hoffman quashed defense subpoenas for undercover materials gathered by government in-

vestigative agencies during the period covered by the indictment, his ruling was called "beautiful" and "clever" by observ-
ing lawyers. That was because the judge reasoned elaborately
that the defense had a right to such information but there was
also the matter of "public interest," and by the end of his ruling
laymen and defendants were still wondering, "Did he rule for
or against?"

Judge Hoffman often used the word "elegant" to describe,
in part, what he thought was needed at a particular moment,
the way a scholar uses "elegant" to describe an argument or
a proposition. Toward the end of the prosecution's case, in
the first week of December, 1969, Department of Justice attorney Roger Cubbage—observers speculated that he might
be the direct liaison to Attorney General John N. Mitchell—
came up with more film for the prosecution. He admitted in
court that he had first looked at the film only a few days before.
That lent support to the contention of those who said the
prosecution was extending its case, filling it out. If that was
true, if the judge had signaled to the prosecutors that he
thought their case was not factually good enough and if he
really had not otherwise communicated personally with Foran,
then he gave the signal by saying to the defense that perhaps
he "would allow their motion for a directed judgment of acquittal" at the end of the government's case. The prosecution
became sloppy as it slapped together more materials, and
Judge Hoffman became sharp in his demand for "elegance."

"I don't know what the word 'buildup film' means," he said,
as if the close vowel in "means" were a thin piece of steel
vibrating between his front teeth. "I prefer the word 'foundation,'" he said to Richard Schultz, who was answering a defense objection to admission of a film into evidence. "It is more
elegant and more accurate." It was one of the few times that
Judge Hoffman's tone was one of chastisement toward the
Assistant U. S. Attorney, in whom the judge was generally well
pleased.

It all began the day before when Roger Cubbage tried to introduce that film into evidence—to support Rochford's testimony, one supposes. Cubbage was young, extremely skinny, bouncy and quick. He had very little trial experience, as you will soon see. Judge Hoffman cringed with a personal chagrin whenever Cubbage attempted to introduce exhibits for the prosecution.

This particular film was, in the usual way, shown to the court out of the presence of the jury. Then Kunstler conducted a voir dire examination of Cameraman Roy, at the end of which he objected to the admission of the film into evidence to be shown to the jury because the film was cut and spliced, containing only ten minutes of more than two hours of actual film. In addition, the parts of the film that had been used on TV newscasts, presumably the most vivid parts, were not even in this spliced presentation and could not be located. Cubbage, in trying to answer the grounds of Kunstler's objection, suddenly found himself alone and far from the sight of help.

Cubbage was arrogant and helpless enough that he simply asserted the materiality and admissibility of the film. Earlier in the trial he had tried to get a tape introduced by simply declaring, with a shrug, "There was mob actions Monday night." Judge Hoffman tried to get Cubbage to answer Kunstler's objection, but Cubbage was unable to muster any significant argument of law or fact. If he expected Judge Hoffman to rule in favor of the prosecution without a prima facie fulfillment of form, he was wrong. Judge Hoffman began to show that nothing aroused his indignation so much as what he called "inelegance." The situation became awkward. Kunstler could not help smiling though his voice stayed mild as he gave each objection. Cubbage displayed a sort of petulant astonishment that he was being done this way. The sight of it was most satisfying to the defendants, their lawyers, and members of the press and spectators. They were all laughing at Cubbage, who did not know how to play the game, and perhaps showing that the common interest that they all shared *was* the game—its risks, rewards, and supposed guarantees.

Back at the prosecution's table Richard Schultz was also laughing with Foran, who was both smiling in that way of his and somewhat chagrined at Cubbage's debacle. Schultz, still laughing, moved toward the bench. "I see some reserves have moved up from the rear," Judge Hoffman said. Most parties to the scene continued to laugh now and then for a few moments as Schultz began to answer Kunstler's objection to the admissibility of the film.

To a certain extent, Schultz met the esthetic demand of argument for the admissibility of the film. He sounded good. That's important. But Judge Hoffman found that he had to do it himself—had to find for the government the basis in law for admission into evidence of this partial film. The judge used the example of the portion of a film that showed Jack Ruby shooting Oswald, but Kunstler said that he himself had argued the Ruby appeal and there was no need of the film in that case because Ruby admitted killing Oswald. Oh, the echoes of assassination and conspiracy in this courtroom. There were smiles all over the courtroom because it seemed that Kunstler was forcing the government and the judge to incredible lengths to gain admissibility of a film that did not, to the eye, appear to be any kind of good evidence.

Judge Hoffman finally said—it was near the end of the day's session and the jury was there to be dismissed—that he would reflect on the defense's objection overnight. Kay Richards and Mrs. Fritz, in the jury, were laughing at the end of that exchange, at Cubbage's debacle and the judge's wry remarks, with recognition of the exposure of raw assertion beneath the elegant face of argument. In any case, they had heard more of a voir dire argument than they were supposed to hear. Thomas Foran and Richard Schultz smiled together. Kunstler smiled at Leonard Weinglass. Everybody knew that the judge would keep his law clerks at work that night to find some basis in law to deny the defense's objection.

The next day began with laughter. Every morning when the jury came Indian file into the jury box and stood in front of their seats and faced the judge, he would say, "Good morning, ladies and gentlemen of the jury," and the jury would answer in tones that you could not help but liken to a children's choir, "Good morning, your honor." The defendants had long ago extended the act and they echoed, in their sweetest voices, after the judge and jury, "Good morning," reminding the jurors that their responsibility did not stop at the judge. The surprise this morning was that Kay Richards and Mrs. Fritz looked directly at the defendants, particularly at Rennie Davis, and, while the other jurors said good-morning to the judge, addressed their good-mornings to the defendants. Davis was so struck by it, so ready to laugh his head off with embarrassment, that he went swiftly to the other side of the table, grinning wildly with Lee Weiner.

The film would be shown over defense objection. The judge said, "I do not think that it would be appropriate for the court to cite authorities at this time. Hence, I will merely make a decision on the offer of this exhibit." Without further ado, he admitted it into evidence for the government. The film was originally in color but this spliced version was black and white—shot from the north side of the center tower of the Conrad Hilton Hotel fronting on Michigan Avenue and Grant Park across the street. The film went dark and fuzzy so you could barely see the cops' helmeted heads bobbing about in the street and the park every time the cops were on the move in that scene of Wednesday evening, August 28, 1968. If its purpose was to suggest general confusion in the event from which a viewer such as a juror might draw a conclusion according to his or her allegiance, then possibly it succeeded. Possibly the government intended for the image of confusion to work against the clearer and more definitive films that the defense would show.

Cameraman Roy was dressed in a red shirt open at the neck without a tie. In cross-examination, he was more relaxed and informal than most government witnesses. He gave to Kunstler figures and estimates of time periods covered by film on several reels, and of time elapsed while reloading reels. Judge Hoffman waxed irritable as both he and Kunstler tried to do the arithmetic to arrive at an estimate of time of action represented by the film. "If your honor will multiply it," Kunstler said, "I will swear by it." This was one of the rare moments when members of both sides, though mostly defense persons, laughed. But Cameraman Roy also joined them.

It was Cubbage's document that was being introduced, so he would handle the objections to Kunstler's cross-examination. Department of Justice Attorney Cubbage usually sat at the end of the prosecution table farthest from the judge. But when one of his films or tapes was being brought into evidence, he sat in the chair in front of Richard Schultz on the aisle side of the table. Schultz, slumped rather precisely in his chair with his fingers tented before him, casually bumped the back of Cubbage's chair with his knee to tell Cubbage when to object. Cubbage dutifully jumped up each time, and sometimes he seemed hardly to know what he was saying, "I object, your honor," and occasionally glanced back in bewilderment at Richard Schultz.

Judge Hoffman was not pleased with Cubbage's awkwardness, lack of trial expertise, and general inelegance of presentation. Judge Hoffman denied several of Cubbage's objections, and sustained several moves of the defense. Weeks prior to the showing of this film, when Cubbage was introducing a tape and the man who recorded the tape was being cross-examined, Cubbage jumped up to object, and Schultz pushed the chair with his foot so it bumped the back of Cubbage's legs. "Sit down," Schultz said. When Cameraman Roy came down from the witness stand, he nodded his head at Richard Schultz who nodded in return, clipped glad-to-have-helped-you-nods.

Kay Richards, in the jury, sat leaning forward with her elbow on her knee and her head tilted in her hand. She often sat or disposed herself in ways that differed from the other jurors, who generally sat up straight with their heads up and back. No marshal told her to sit back, sit nice.

The trial was riddled with conflicting notions of appropriate behavior and its epitome of elegance.

If there was anything the defense could do that would expose or suggest debility of mind in the seventy-four-year-old judge, it had much to gain in the minds of many observers, and possibly of jurors, and on the record too.

Later that day there was another exchange in which Judge Hoffman asked Kunstler, "Do you adopt the objection of your colleague, Mr. . . . uh . . . uh . . . uh . . . ?"

"Kunstler, your honor," William Kunstler said, in his most compassionate tone, removing his glasses and holding them off to the side of his head in a stylized way

Those jurors sympathetic to the defense laughed, but those who generally laughed at the judge's jokes seemed offended and soured by Kunstler's tone and gesture. There was no gain made among people present in the courtroom, but it might look good on the record. It might contribute to the weight of possible reversible error for appeal purposes, in particular to the charge that the judge was emotionally involved and biased against the defense. Kunstler's name slipped the judge's mind several times. Every time the judge forgot it, Kunstler used a similar routine, and got exactly the same laughs. Sometimes he spelled his name for the judge: K-U-N-S-T-L-E-R.

In this instance, the judge saw how he had been used. "Do you adopt the objection?"

"Wholeheartedly," Kunstler said.

"I'll accept your adoption without the adverb," said Judge Hoffman, getting what was most essential to him, the last word.

Once he got the last word with Leonard Weinglass only by saying in an aggressively bitter tone, "I accept your correction."

Kunstler's name the judge forgot, but he wronged Leonard Weinglass's name many times throughout the trial. Even when he sentenced Weinglass for contempt he got it wrong again, saying "Fineglass" and "Weintraub" and "Weinrus" and "Weinrob," and Weinglass said to him, "I would think after five months of trial the court would at least get my name right." The judge seemed positively hostile about Weinglass's name, but only conventionally bereft when Kunstler's name slipped his mind. Weinglass's long hair, even though it was rather well styled, was as much abrasive to the sight of the judge as Weinglass's name was to his ear and his tongue. He was overheard once in the elevator, in the early days of the trial, talking about "that wild man, Weinglass."

In the beginning of the trial, the tone of Weinglass's approach was not guaranteed to make the judge feel that he was regarded highly. But no one tried harder than Leonard Weinglass in the course of the trial, poring over the transcript of daily proceedings, to find a pattern to the judge's rulings which, if approached correctly, would prove to be unbiased. He was not successful.

Judge Hoffman himself was not unaffected by attempts upon his name. Abbie Hoffman declared early that he no longer had a last name, that his name died with truth in this courtroom. Judge Hoffman said in an aside at the end of the trial that he didn't think he deserved such treatment so early in the case and it had hurt him deeply.

The judge several times called Dellinger "Derringer" and "Dillinger" right up to the end of the trial. Such slips would seem to indicate a particular attitude toward Dellinger.

But the judge's "slips of ruling" always favored the defense. I do not remember his ever departing from this pattern in his slips of ruling.

He was not merely an advocate of "manners" and of "elegance" in the courtroom. In one of his asides to the assembled courtroom about the kind of mail he was getting, and that there was too much of it for him to answer and that he answered some letters and not others, he said about one letter, "I didn't know the man, but he had engraved stationery, so I thought I would give the courtesy of a reply." Members of the audience for the defense smiled and nodded knowingly. They overlooked that they too depended upon stereotypes for identifying their people.

Judge Hoffman was not senile, and he could have said as fully and as complacently as Whitman or Nietzsche, "I contradict myself?—very well then, I contradict myself."

The most interesting aspect of Judge Hoffman's sense of form and elegance was his demand for a spirited, hopeful, persuasive defense. It thrilled one's sense of contest, passed the time, and relieved one's dreary sense of guilt by giving a feeling of authenticity to the charade. He often admonished defense counsel not to be "so pessimistic," which triggered smiles of differing irony among the prosecutors and the defendants and the two audiences. Leonard Weinglass made a motion to have a surveillance witness's testimony precluded on the basis that twenty-four-hour-a-day surveillance was as unconstitutional as unlawful search and seizure. Judge Hoffman retorted initially by referring to the case cited by Weinglass and ruled upon by the Supreme Court, sharing their mutual knowledge as men of the legal profession, "Was your client playing golf?"—because FBI agents had followed the man in the case cited through games of golf. Then Judge Hoffman addressed himself to Weinglass's claim of the unconstitutionality of such surveillance testimony.

"If that is true," the judge said, "a great many men are languishing needlessly in penitentiaries."

"Right on," the defendants said.

Weinglass said, "I hope we won't add to that list, your honor."

Judge Hoffman returned forcefully, "Don't be so pessimistic, sir."

Foran was smiling widely, as if feeling physical hate for the long-haired defense counsel. Several times Judge Hoffman said such things as "Your clients have pleaded not guilty, sir. Don't be so pessimistic." Or, he said more than once, "Don't be so pessimistic. Perhaps at the end of the government's case I will allow your motion for a directed judgment of acquittal."

Suppose the defendants in such a trial believed and acted as if they believed that there was not a chance for their advocacy to win for them; the credibility of the process would be given a bad appearance. Any posture or display that indicated apathy, or lack of faith or hope in advocacy, would, on the face of it, be profoundly inelegant, a mockery of the necessary appearance. The fact was that the defendants vacillated from hope to disbelief and despair several times about their advocacy having a chance.

Behavior on the part of the defendants and their supporters that invited punishment was most inelegant, first because it called for inelegant action on the part of the court and second because inelegance in a court is equivalent to lack of substance and credibility.

The suspected hollowness of the indictments may have been an affront to the judge, and even more of an affront because of his trust in the Attorney General's affidavit that the defendants were national security risks. He maddened himself with his own inelegance in his readiness to give the appearance of substance and authority to the evidence in the case presented by the party with which he had identified his historical fate.

The prosecution, toward the end of its case, put another city official, Albert Baugher, onto the stand to testify about permit negotiations. Baugher was there to corroborate the earlier testimony of David Stahl, and to firm up the foundation for all the rest of the prosecution's case. Baugher was a man with a large mustache and an evident sense of humor. Kunstler was questioning Baugher once again about the fabled ploy of Abbie Hoffman: "Give us a hundred thousand dollars and we'll leave town." The prosecutors must have felt that many of the jurors, no matter what they believed about the question, would at least be hostile to its flippancy. Kunstler said, "Did Abbie Hoffman say give us the money and we'll go away? Did you take that seriously?"

"I took it seriously," Baugher said.

"Did he tell you that Spiro Agnew offered him two hundred thousand dollars to come to Chicago?"

Oh, there was laughter in the courtroom, and Kay Richards and Jean Fritz were laughing, and Shirley Seaholm and Frieda Robbins were smiling. Miriam Hill folded her arms and looked huffily about. But, oh, the prosecution's witness, Albert Baugher, with the large mustache, he too was laughing. Prosecutor Foran must have felt a cold fear upon his heart and he had to do something about it. He had to give his witness an obvious signal.

Foran rose and objected, and said that Baugher was laughing at Kunstler and not at the remark. Kunstler immediately asked Baugher, and Baugher said, nodding, laughing, that he was laughing at the remark. Foran went smooth and chagrined before the acknowledgment of his own witness, and sat down without a word. Baugher once told some defendants during Convention Week, "Shove it"; no reason why he wouldn't say the same thing to the United States Attorney, even though they were both comrades in Mayor Daley's Cook County Democratic party machine. But Foran should not have been so unhappy. The witness for the government looked good. Foran's objection showed his fear that the persuasive power of laughter might be greater than the substance and appearance of testimony.

Laughter enabled people to discover to which audience they most belonged, and then sharpened the aggressive division and regularly affirmed each audience's consciousness of itself and of its representatives and its opposition.

In most "movement" trials and hearings that I witnessed, a ritualistic set of characters and situations emerged every time. The spectators vociferously supported the "movement" defendants, while the prosecutors and the court, perhaps willingly even if unconsciously, were scapegoated by the spectators. The most vocal satisfaction went to the losing side. The supporters of the prosecution's side simply rested or squirmed silently on the presumption of their power. When vocal supporters for the government started to show up, it indicated an increase in the perceived power of the "movement." They never showed up in the Conspiracy trial.

There were a few jurors and other spectators who now and then laughed on both sides of the line, at wit that was opposed to the party with which their expressions generally identified them. One juror on the defense's side was unexpressive, and another on the prosecution's side was so cool you wondered if he was in the same courtroom with everyone else.

The joker, in response to jokes, of course, was Kay Richards, the young woman in her early twenties who laughed—with a will, one is tempted to say—on the side of the defense. It made her apparent betrayal of her laughter in the jury's deliberations worthy of meditation and possibly investigation.

The ones who laughed most heartily and most openly were the jurors at the two extremes. Taking sides in itself may be such a physically rooted and emotionally gripped thing that it means the person becomes more easily susceptible to laughter that convulses the body, lifts the spirits, and brings about a sense of unity.

The defense won its "hung" jury and earned its laughter from its cross-examination of the government's case—the hard way. It performed better, as the movement of rebellion in

American life generally performed better in responding to the initiative of the enemy than it did when it must take the strategic initiative itself. So the "movement's" most aggressive actions paradoxically brought it again into defensive positions where it could react in ways that seemed immediately productive. Like most participants in this consumerist society, the "movement" was not well trained in working toward a broad-based, more distant goal.

The defense was always in danger of regarding laughter as its substitute for policemen, as its counter to police suppression.

The defendants and defense counsel debated whether they should give the case to the jury when the government rested. From a lawyer's point of view, said Leonard Weinglass, "that might be the best thing to do." The defense and many observers were convinced that the jury was a hung jury. But the defendants felt that the political effect of the trial was just beginning to be locomotive in the consciousness of the nation.

Even if it would have been wiser not to take the risk of sacrificing their side of the hung jury, and to admit that it was most unlikely that they could win the whole jury, they decided to go for broke.

# PART FIVE
*The Struggle for the Spirit of the Courtroom: The Defense's Case*

EVERYTHING WAS NOT WELL at the Conspiracy office at 28 East Jackson, where the staff members and the defendants, not wholly happy with their tasks or each other, tried to put together and keep together a tenuous and hectic combination of development of the legal case, of publicity and political action, and of fund raising for everything. The defense enjoyed none of the financial support from public funds or staff support from federal agencies, and the millions of dollars, that went into the government's case.

The defense relied upon volunteers, friends and family, and a few staff members who were paid a few dollars a week for "subsistence." They often slept on the floor of the more or less communal apartment rented by Leonard Weinglass in Hyde Park. Kunstler and Weinglass were paid a minimal salary of one hundred dollars per week by the Conspiracy Defense Fund.

The Conspiracy had to raise funds to meet a variety of expenses, not only ordinary and extraordinary office expenses such as huge phone bills, but expenses for transcript and for the transportation and housing of witnesses. Lawyers and legal staff members and advisers needed copies of the transcript of daily trial proceedings for constant reference and study. By the end of this five-month-long-trial, one full transcript at fifty cents a page cost nearly twelve thousand dollars. After the trial, the cost of the copies of the transcript needed for the appellate case exceeded one hundred and twenty-five thousand dollars. In order to further their supporting political case and to raise funds, the defendants accepted schedules of speeches and other conspiratorial activities such as parties that turned many of the staff members into attendants and secretaries. That was not the sort of work that the young staff members had anticipated when their sense of adventure brought them to the Conspiracy cause. Most of the work that supported the defense's case could be considered drudgery, from the interviewing of possible witnesses to getting out mailings and typing letters.

They rejected the need of leadership, then succumbed to despair, obsessive bitterness, competitiveness, and confusion about aims, necessities, tasks, and priorities. "If only there had been a word of gratitude from the defendants now and then," said Donna Gripe, in explaining what happened in the Conspiracy office. She asked Hayden and Davis to take more of a sympathetic interest in the young people on the staff. The answer she got was that the staff members ought to be able to "hack it" in the work of a revolution, without needing such support.

The defendants perhaps put an unfortunate value upon the preoccupying strangeness of their consuming roles as national scapegoats. The after-the-trial analysis of staff members along with outside spokesmen of the movement was that it was too much "leadership" and "male chauvinism" that was the problem that drained the energy and goodwill of the staff. "Why should I type Rennie Davis's letters?" Susan Hathaway said. Staff members were not inclined to consider that their troubles may have stemmed from a lack of liberating and unifying authority of concept and perception, collective or otherwise.

In white movement groups everywhere, a sort of moralistic cannibalism—a seeking of instant satisfaction in accusing and baiting one's fellows, an abysmal acceptance of the national impotence, a craven submission to a perverted puritanical conscience and to a debased egalitarian rhetoric that turned out to be a veil for endlessly bitter personal competition—was once again consuming the energy and purpose of American radicals as surely as the god Moloch consumed the children of Babylon.

The defense went into its case without a clear theory of what happened during Convention Week. Jerry Rubin wanted a strategy that would bring "five big witnesses" to the stand, and that would be it. He became depressed for weeks, it was said, when his plan was voted down. Tom Hayden, acting in many ways as a third attorney, carried a pad of yellow paper on a clipboard with areas of strategy blocked out and the names of witnesses and the kinds of testimony that would be useful in each part of the case. The defendants were looking for witnesses for the first part of their case only a couple of weeks before the case began.

Like medical patients taking an active part in their own treatment, which is supposed to be a very good thing, the defendants were actively involved in the decision-making and development of their case. Twenty years later Nancy Kurshan said, "A lot of the decisions got made by the defendants themselves concerning trial strategy and conduct during the trial. Tom was the most legalistic. He wanted to get the trial over with and get on with the revolution. Abbie and Jerry said 'The revolution is NOW, is what we're doing *now*.' There was not a lot of love between Tom and Jerry. However, the defendants pretty much agreed that they needed The Whole World Is Watching strategy, the political publicity."

My book *No One Was Killed* appeared in the fall of 1969. One day I saw copies of it on the defense table. The defendants passed it around, glanced into it, and Rennie Davis read passages during the trial session. I was fascinated at his concentration and the way his eyes moved in jumps, an eye span that took in almost half an entire line. Most of the defendants wanted me to be a witness, because I had been on the streets and in the parks every day and night of Convention Week and had an empirical thesis for what had happened and how it happened.

I sat down to lunch in the Berghoff near the Federal Building with Leonard Weinglass and Tom Hayden. Weinglass said to me, rather uncomfortably, as if he'd been dragged there by Hayden much against his will, "You're the one who saw all those rocks thrown." He felt my testimony would be vulnerable on the most serious points of demonstrator provocation. However, Hayden felt that the fact that I saw largely unplanned, "leaderless," spontaneously reactive actions by demonstrators in response to police attacks, was a plus. Also, I could testify that in each instance that I had witnessed, the defendants were actively trying to avoid violent confrontation, even to dissuade the more reckless young demonstrators from it. Weinglass raised the possibility that I would not be allowed to testify because I had been present in the courtroom. Traditionally, it was thought that a witness, if he had been present in the courtroom, could shape his testimony according to the needs of his party, a reasonable assumption. But the defense wanted to challenge such disallowing because there were several Convention Week eyewitnesses among the press who were also writing news that was creating "The Whole World is Watching" context, and traditionally, people should be allowed to continue making their livelihood and defendants should not be denied important testimony. At one point, Weinglass said to Hayden, about my potential testimony, "I don't see anything evidential here." But Hayden prevailed. It was apparent that he could make the decision.

At his sparely furnished apartment in Hyde Park, Weinglass began interviewing me only a few days before I would go on the stand. His Berghoff attitude had changed, and he was a warm, interested, challenging interviewer who took extensive notes on one yellow legal pad after another. Then, after a couple of nights of such work, he came up to me at the trial and said that Hank de Zutter, reporter for the *Chicago Daily News*, had been disallowed from testimony because he had been present in the courtroom. There was no point in continuing our interviews. I got the impression that Weinglass was mildly relieved that my testimony, which would necessarily include accounts of rocks and firecrackers being thrown by some demonstrators (usually after the police had made the first violent moves), would not be subjected to cross-examination and heard by the jury.

The defense attorneys were conservative in that they were wary of presenting to the jury and the public witnesses who saw daring actions by young people in the streets. They chose, finally, in their confusion and uncertainty, to use the semi-official *Rights in Conflict* concept of "a police riot"—which in the same breath excuses the police by describing the allegedly intolerable provocations that young people visited upon the cops—as if concerted police attacks upon demonstrators over a period of five days and nights could properly be called a "riot" with the word's implication of acting irrationally upon incitement but without orders. Many reporters and writers familiar with Convention Week, including this writer, have pointed out that exaggeration, distortion, reporting of events that did not happen and of other events out of context or out of sequence, and seeming careful manipulation of the content in general, riddle the Report. But *Rights In Conflict* was well publicized, and presumably its phrase "police riot" might have already affected the opinions of many jurors. During the defense's case, witnesses who testified about riotous actions in the streets described police attack and police brutality. Unlike *Rights in Conflict,* they reported few, if any, provocations by young rebels.

Another part of the overall strategy was reserved for the "state of mind" witnesses, since the defendants were explicitly accused of crossing state lines, in whatever form of transportation, with the "intent," the "state of mind," to incite riots. In addition, these witnesses would give testimony to neutralize the charge of conspiracy.

The "state of mind" witnesses were roughly divided into four categories. First, there were the witnesses for the Festival of Life in Lincoln Park—the "state of mind" of the Yippies, in other words. Allen Ginsberg, Timothy Leary, Country Joe, Judy Collins, Pete Seeger, and other "entertainers"—as Richard Schultz referred to them—were witnesses to the dark or light "intents" of the Yippie mind. Such witnesses as Stewart Meacham, of the American Friends Service Committee, and Donald Duncan, the ex-Green Beret, were witnesses for the "state of mind" of David Dellinger. Carl Oglesby was a witness for the "state of mind" before Convention Week of Tom Hayden and Rennie Davis. All of the defendants wanted "youth culture" and "expert" witnesses who would testify to the defendants' general "state of mind" concerning the Viet Nam war, racism, poverty, and the suppression of physical and spiritual joy in the United States. Two defendants were in the final category of "state of mind" witnesses, Abbie Hoffman for the Yippies' side of life and Rennie Davis for the organizers of the National Mobilization to End the War in Viet Nam.

Many of the "state of mind" witnesses, such as Franklin Bardache for "youth culture," and Staughton Lynd on the American Revolution and its parallels with present-day events, were examined on voir dire and then not permitted to give testimony to the jury because the judge determined, on the motion of the prosecution, that what those witnesses had to offer was "immaterial" or "irrelevant." Even so, Judge Hoffman said that he regarded these voir dire examinations as "intellectually stimulating."

The defense also sought, with perhaps not enough fervor, testimony to rebut the government witnesses on the defendants' speeches both before and during Convention Week. They could call up celebrities or friends or the friends of friends for the "state of mind" case, but the legwork and research necessary to explore the relationships between their "intentions" and their speech and the street and park actions of Convention Week was something "a volunteer staff can hardly do," said Irving Birnbaum, Chicago counsel for the defense. The defense, in order to build its case that what the defendants said was protected by the First Amendment no matter what their "intentions," needed to show clearly that there was no "immediate, perceivable" effect of incitement to riot upon the crowd. But the defendants were more curious and more desperately involved in the immediate political and media reverberations of the trial than in the development of a legal case. There was protection in developing the publicity effects, and they were trying to retrieve and develop a constituency. Like an avalanche, the work of factual and legal research fell upon Leonard Weinglass and a few staff members and family such as Mickey Leanor, Stuart Ball, Ann Froines, Nancy Kurshan, Linda Miner, Susan Schultz, Donna Gripe, and a few others.

It was therefore surprising that the defense's case—though erratic, hastily researched, and conservative in concept—was often powerful, largely because of the intelligence and the insight of many of the participants, witnesses and lawyers.

The defense's case was an attempt at magic, an attempt by organizers to summon, invoke, exorcise, instill, and instruct.

Dead, dark Chicago winter surrounded the defense's case. With their foreheads aching from the cold, people hurried to open their packages and briefcases for the marshals' inspection inside the revolving doors of the Federal Building.

In the numb atmosphere in the days after the state murder of Fred Hampton, chairman of the Illinois Black Panther party, the defense called its first witness to the stand. Edward Sparling, president emeritus, Roosevelt University, headed the citizens' commission that investigated the police attack on the April 27, 1968, peace march—harbinger of Convention Week. The commission published the report *Dissent and Disorder,* which appeared in early August, 1968. The report concluded that the police attack occurred with the knowledge and approval of the highest ranking officials of the Chicago Police Department and the city administration. Police superintendents had been seen watching the attack with folded arms.

The defense wanted to use *Dissent and Disorder* to show the state of mind of the city administration about Convention Week, and that it influenced the defendants' attitudes toward demonstrations and parade marshals' training. Foran objected repeatedly, and the judge sustained him repeatedly, saying that there was no foundation to show that the defendants had the report *Dissent and Disorder* in mind when they made their plans for Convention Week.

"If you won't let me question this man on this matter," Kunstler said, with angry frustration, "well, then, I have no further questions." It was an excellent example of a Kunstler provocation, controlled within the confines of what he perceived to be the truth of the situation, but clearly provocative from the point of view of the judge.

The judge told the defense to hurry up and put its next witness on the stand. "You should anticipate the court may rule against you." That got downright guffaws from the defendants.

Cook County State's Attorney police, on December 4, 1969, had either stood on a ladder outside the window of Hampton's bedroom or in the doorway in the dark before dawn and, in the midst of that night's dreams, gunned him, sent bullets ripping through his head. He had hardly a flicker of knowing what was happening to him. The evidence that the police could have stood on a ladder and fired through the rear window was that the glass of that window and of the rear kitchen window was broken in from the outside, and there were two long ladders in the backyard. Machine-gun bullets, from the other direction, also came through the wall alongside his bed. The young woman beside him was pregnant. She says that she threw herself on top of him, and he looked up, that was all, he just looked up, and it was over. His blood and his dreams and his compelling sense of humor poured into the mattress. Other police slammed into the apartment from front and back doors, "good decent kids thinking they were shooting each other," U. S. Attorney Thomas Foran would say, months after the Conspiracy Trial, at the end of the Federal Grand Jury hearing that returned no indictments on the killings. The "good decent kids" were close to or over forty years of age. Foran had objected to the conspiracy defendants being called "kids."

Mark Clark, Panther defense captain from Peoria, was killed toward the front of the apartment. Panthers said that Hampton was drugged with Seconal in his food by an undercover agent before he went to bed that night. They said that an autopsy suppressed by the Coroner's Office revealed it. The evidence of bullet holes indicated that no more than one shot could be attributed to the Panthers. Some of the Conspiracy defendants had been talking with the young chairman only a day or so before he was killed.

"There's a Them and there's a We," Hampton had said on the first day of the trial to a rally of mostly young blacks for Bobby Seale and the Conspiracy Eight at the bandshell in Grant Park. "And I don't have to go into any detail explaining how we know there's a Them. Them are on our backs."

For a long time after December 4, 1969, I did not go to bed at night without experiencing the memory and anticipation of what happened to Fred Hampton. Not a day passed that I did not confront the vulnerability of the human being, of Fred

Hampton, to the formidable power of the government and its forces to do whatever it wished.

The Hampton murder deepened the defendants' morbid belief that the government's repression would carry them away into jail, where they too might be found dead in their cots one day. Such a vision may also have given them some gloomy relief from the feeling that the bullets in Hampton's body were meant for them or caused by a government reaction to them.

The defense wanted to construct in the beginning of its case a descriptively and thematically strong image of the August 28, 1968, Wednesday afternoon rally in Grant Park, then move to the earlier scene in Lincoln Park. The Grant Park rally was the one event of Convention Week for which there had been a Park District permit. An employee of a candy company gave vivid testimony of cadence-counting ranks of cops "chopping" their way through the crowd in the Grant Park rally. He was reportedly fired in reprisal for his testimony. Anne Kerr, a member of British Parliament, was not permitted to sing on the witness stand "We Shall Overcome." She said she sang that song when police heaved her into a paddy wagon outside the Conrad Hilton Hotel that Wednesday. There were other witnesses who testified to the generally peaceful determination of the marchers and the violence of the police.

Mrs. Kerr also revealed her point of entrance into the spectrum of political action by her choice of a song that was despised by the young people in Lincoln Park, where the energy of Convention Week was birthed. Three kinds of music declared commitment to one of three degrees of action in the streets. Among older people, with memories of the civil rights movement in the early sixties, "We Shall Overcome" echoed still. Among the students were such songs as "Blowin' In The Wind," most often heard in front of the Conrad Hilton. In Lincoln Park loomed the stern and demanding beat of African drums.

The government and the judge took the evidenciary position that speech was words, not voice, tone, inflection, or music. Yet the government tried to prove at times that there were intentions in the defendants' words that were expressed by heated emotion, gesture, or "noise level" in surrounding circumstances. You need only recite to yourself the refrain of "Blowin' In The Wind," and then sing it, to see and hear how specious was the argument of the government and the judge. The recited words of the song are interesting but very few people knew all of the words. They knew only the refrain, "The answer, my friend, is blowin' in the wind." It was the refrain and the music that gave a poignant concentration to many of the preparatory lulls of Convention Week actions. The intentions of the demonstrators during Convention Week were to be heard in the music, from the towering drumbeat of Lincoln Park to the melancholy singing in front of the Hilton after midnight.

But there was another reason, a tactical need in the courtroom, for having the songs sung rather than recited, and the judge and the government committed their evidenciary wrong because of it. The defense often forced the government into contradictions and dilemmas where the government annihilated its own base of legitimacy in order to protect itself. If laughter activated and confirmed one side or the other, it seldom moved both sides of the jury in the same way. People can take sides about music too, but there was the chance that really compelling song from the voices of Country Joe, Phil Ochs, Judy Collins, or Pete Seeger might send a sympathetic current through both sides of the polarization of the jury. That alone could not persuade the jurors to appreciate the possibility of the defendants' innocence. But it would open up the chance of connecting artistic relationships with verbal, psychological, and political intentions and relationships. These connections were important to bringing forth an understanding of Convention Week that would be very different from the description so far constructed in this courtroom.

Now defense testimony moved into what could be called the struggle to name the nature of human beings. An authoritative description of human nature is regarded by most people as prescriptive of behavior. For this reason, a party in power may seek to suppress a naming of the nature of human beings. Every political movement fields a prescriptive description of "human nature" in order to clarify its opposition and its points of unification and growth. A political movement can become moribund simply because its prescriptive theory cannot cope with its social and historical situation.

Naming is powerful, gut-known and gut-feared. Children play a game of "What's your name?," in which the child being victimized answers with his name again and again and is broken down into sobs by the other children shrieking each time, "*That's* not your name!" You make war with naming. You attack and deprive the enemy with naming. You take away someone else's power by naming. You strengthen yourself by naming. But the danger is that naming your enemy, or *an* enemy, may strengthen him as much or more than it strengthens you.

In cross-examination of Linda Morse, a young girl with long blond hair who came from Quaker background and now admitted practicing with an M-1 to be able to defend herself, Richard Schultz asked, "With regard to the revolution that we are talking about, you are prepared to die and to kill for it, isn't that right'?"

"Yes," she said.

"And the more you realize that our system is sick, the more you want to tear it limb from limb, isn't that right?"

Linda Morse agreed with Richard Schultz in a lengthy, passionate, articulate answer. It was stricken by the judge as "unresponsive."

Everything done in this court was naming.

It was little noticed by observers in the courtroom that the defendants had come to feel that Weinglass was their most dependably effective counsel, while Kunstler generated "Whole World is Watching" publicity on TV. Weinglass examined the witnesses who gave the most lengthy testimony for the defense, including Allen Ginsberg.

When Ginsberg took the stand, the defense made a bold move into the field of naming. Ginsberg named the people in Lincoln Park as "a gathering together of younger people aware of the planetary fate . . . a gathering of the tribes of all of the different affinity groups—political groups, spiritual groups, Yoga groups, music groups, and poetry groups." That was his description of what was "intended" by himself and the defendants for the Festival of Life in Lincoln Park. It "would turn everybody on . . . uplift everybody's spirit and show . . . what we were actually feeling . . . delight instead of the horror that was surrounding us."

Then the bearded compelling poet named the enemy. He said that he had been worried about violence in Lincoln Park in August, 1968, "worried whether . . . the government would let us do something that was funnier or prettier or more charming than what was going to be going on in the convention hall."

Prosecutor Foran sought to impeach Ginsberg as a mover of religious inspiration at the Festival of Life. He did not spend one question on the substantive testimony that Ginsberg gave of his attempts to secure permits for assembly from the representatives of the city of Chicago, of events in Lincoln Park, and of his use of the Hindu *om* to quiet crowds. When he tried it to calm down a colloquy between the judge and Kunstler, Ginsberg's *om* reverberated in the courtroom. He was condemned by the judge for it.

Foran called Ginsberg's attention to his testimony about himself sitting next to Abbie Hoffman at the Coliseum and kissing him on Tuesday night of Convention Week, at the Unbirthday Party for Lyndon Johnson. Then he asked Ginsberg to read aloud his poem "The Night Apple." Then Foran asked what the religious significance of that poem was. Ginsberg seriously and therefore wittily said that the poem was an account of a wet dream. He delivered a small, useful lecture on how exploring connections in dreams and waking life could expand and support consciousness, and was therefore "religious."

The poet Allen Ginsberg took the prosecutor's questions literally, answered them seriously, and created a tour de force of a record, fascinating to read.

Foran asked Ginsberg to read altogether three poems to the jury that appeared to be homosexual, bisexual and transsexual in content. The magnificent "Love Poem on Theme by Whitman" was among them. Foran was heard to mutter what he really wanted to call the poet, after Ginsberg left the stand: "Goddamned fag."

Ginsberg recited his poems "The Night Apple" and "In Society," and then gave the following answers to the prosecutor's questions:

> It is a record, a literal record of a dream as the other was a literal record of a dream.
>
> Q: Can you explain the religious significance of that poetry?
>
> A: Actually, yes.
>
> Q: Would you explain it to the jury?
>
> A: Yes, one of the major yogas or yoking—yoga means yoke—is bringing together the conscious mind with the unconscious mind and is an examination of dream states no matter how difficult they are, even if they include hysteria, sandwiches of human flesh, which include dirty ass holes, because those are universal images that come in everybody's dreams.
>
> The attempt in yoga is to enlarge consciousness, to be conscious that one's own consciousness will include everything which occurs within the body and the mind.

As part of the practice of poetry, I have always kept records of dreams whenever I have remembered them and have tried not to censor them so that I would have all the evidence to examine in the light of day so that I would find out who I was unconsciously.

Part of Zen meditation and part of yoga meditation consists in the objective impersonal examination of the rise and the fall and disappearance of thoughts, whether they be thoughts of sleeping with one's mother, which is universal, or sleeping with one's father, which is also universal thought, or becoming an angel, or flying, or attending a cocktail party and being afraid of being put down, and then getting hysterical. In other words, the attempt is to reclaim the unconscious, to write down in the light of day what is going on in the deepest meditation of night and dream state—so it is part of a yoga which involves bridging the difference between public, as in this courtroom. and private, subjective: Public, which is conscious, which we can say to others in family situations, and private, which is what we know and tell only our deepest friends.

Q: Thank you. . . .

Q: You also wrote a book of poems called *Reality Sandwiches,* didn't you?

A: Yes.

Q: In there, there is a poem called, "Love Poem on Theme by Whitman"?

A: Yes. . . .

Q: After having refreshed your recollection, would you recite that to the jury?

Ginsberg then recited the poem.

Q: Would you explain the religious significance of that poem?

A: As part of our nature—as part of our human nature—we have many loves, many of which are suppressed, many of which are denied, many of which we deny to ourselves.

He said that the reclaiming of those loves and the becoming aware of those loves was the only way that this nation could save itself and become a democratic and spiritual republic.

He said that unless there were an infusion of feeling, of tenderness, of fearlessness, of spirituality, of natural sexuality, of natural delight in each other's bodies, into the hardened materialistic, cynical, life denying, clearly competitive, afraid, scared, armored bodies, there would be no chance for spiritual democracy to take root in America—and he defined that tenderness between the citizens as, in his words, an "Adhesiveness," a natural tenderness, flowing between all citizens, not only men and women but also a tenderness between men and men as part of our democratic heritage, part of the Adhesiveness which would make the democracy function: that men could work together not as competitive beasts but as tender lovers and fellows.

So he projected from his own desire and from his own unconscious a sexual urge which he felt was normal to the unconscious of most people, though forbidden for the most part to take part.

"I'll go into the bedroom silently and lie down between the bridegroom and the bride."

He projected as he did in another poem, orgy, City of Orgies, as he called New York, he projected physical affection even to the sexual—or his phrase is "physical affection and all that is latently implied" between citizen and citizen as part of the Adhesiveness which would make us function together as a community rather than as a nation "among the fabled damned of nations," which was his phrase in the essay "Democratic Vistas."

Walt Whitman is one of my spiritual teachers and I am following him in this poem, taking off from a line of his own and projecting my own actual unconscious feelings of which I don't have shame, sir, which I feel are basically charming actually.

THE COURT: I didn't hear that last word.

THE WITNESS: Charming. . . .

Foran used naming with several witnesses, while with yet other witnesses he would attack the details of their testimony inch by inch, step by step, which was in fact another form of naming. He attacked literally inch by inch photographer Duane Hall's picture of a woman who had been thrown over the railing of the Grant Park underground garage by police. But when Professor Donald Kalish gave important testimony about the intentions of the Mobilization defendants, and about the alleged plot to kidnap Superintendent Rochford at the Logan Statue on Thursday of Convention Week, Foran totally ignored it in his cross-examination. Instead, he asked Kalish such questions as "Did you pay the rent for the Resistance in Los Angeles?" and several other questions that appeared to name Kalish as a Professor Moneybags supporting "radical" causes and organizations. Yet, I had witnessed that "kidnapping" event, and Kalish told it pretty much the way it happened.

Foran tried to cope with truly substantial and dangerous testimony in one of two ways. If possible, he ignored it and, instead, named such people as Ginsberg and Kalish as "fags" or as "moneybag professors" or any other common caricature that would serve, sometimes using information supplied by wiretaps and FBI investigation. The other way was to work over a witness's testimony in the manner of a boxer with his opponent trapped against the ropes. The manner of working over was more important than the substance of it. If Tom Foran worked on a witness step by step, it meant something was wrong and corrupt in that witness. If Tom Foran ignored a witness's testimony, it meant something was wrong and corrupt in that witness, and he proved it by naming them according to their activities. This was the prosecutor who periodically chastised William Kunstler and Leonard Weinglass for not being "lawyers" and for not knowing how to use the "rules of evidence which have taken five hundred years to achieve."

On December 17, 1969, the jury was excused for a voir dire examination of a film in which National Guardsmen appeared to be threatening a woman who was simply trying to drive her car full of little children out of Grant Park. "Now he's putting a grenade launcher through the windows . . ." says a voice on the sound track. Foran asked the large, confident cameraman Perez if that was a voice of persons present on the scene. Foran laughed in finding that the defense was trying to sneak a strong naming remark of Walter Cronkite's to the jury. "Since Walter baby is not here for cross-examination," he said, "we object." He laughed again, in an aside, and said, "Mr. Schultz told me it was Walter Cronkite." The jury was shown the film with Cronkite's voice deleted.

Another film was soon shown to the jury of Dellinger at the head of that careful march moving down the sidewalk along Columbus Drive in Grant Park. The green of the park, the green of that August afternoon that I remember, came into the windowless courtroom. David Dellinger, with his thinning hair and his everlasting tweed jacket, sat at the defense table watching a thinner Dellinger with a firm voice saying through the speaker at the head of the march where it met the line of police: "We are maintaining our cool . . . We have been told there is no march today by Deputy Chief Riordan . . . We may be nonviolent, but we are stubborn . . ." A great many young people were angry with him because they felt nonviolence to be a humiliating posture.

*That's not your name,* the government said of Dellinger, with the amoral conviction of total power. *We're naming you something else. Let's see. Let's name you something really bad.* That's *your name.* The prosecution said of Dellinger that he knew and intended what was going to happen when this march was denied by the police, that the marchers would eventually riot at Michigan and Balbo by the Conrad Hilton Hotel. *That's your name,* the government said. That was the reason for the righteous rage that triggered the quavering in Dellinger's voice in the courtroom. Naming is a personal and social source and weapon of power and powerlessness.

"Did you hear them call police pigs, fascists, s.o.bs., and other profane terms?" Richard Schultz asked Photographer Paul Sequiera about young people in confrontations late Wednesday night on Michigan Avenue. Kunstler objected, saying that fascist and pig were not profane words. He was counternaming the party of the government for not being knowledgeable of language, not being sophisticated, and perhaps being entirely opportunistic in what it attributed to the use of language. He was once again in danger, in front of the jury, of naming himself as an urbane "New York lawyer," not to be trusted. There is a fundamental political difference, not just a nuance, Kunstler was saying, between calling a man a sonofabitch and calling him a fascist. Further, newspapers use the word fascist all the time, Kunstler argued, so the word fascist could hardly be considered a profane word.

Judge Hoffman, who feared that he was the person that the newspapers called fascist, said he hadn't noticed. "I direct your attention," Kunstler said, "to the morning *New York Times.*" Judge Hoffman said, though there was no reason for him to assume it, "Oh, they call me a fascist there?" With whatever degree of justification, he felt rage at being named a "fascist," and perhaps his hypocrisy, if any, only intensified it.

Judge Hoffman extricated himself this time. "No, I've been called worse things than that," he said.

Tom Foran was a leader in the deathly art of naming, matched only occasionally by the Yippies, Rubin and Hoffman. The spectacle of the photographer Duane Hall being closely examined by the United States Attorney was a further mirror-house effect of the Grand Jury's indictments, because Duane Hall was the man on whose behalf the U. S. Attorney's Office prosecuted Policeman Arthur Bischoff for having deprived Hall of his civil rights by clubbing him.

I witnessed those actions on Wednesday night, to which Duane Hall testified. He either left out or did not see many important moments, but otherwise his descriptions were good and vivid. I wondered why they did not seem to add to the defense's case. It was more and more apparent that the defense accepted no powerful notion of what had happened during Convention Week.

With their cosmopolitan sentimentality, their acceptance of the honor of the indictments in order to gain a constituency, the defense persisted in virtually agreeing with the prosecution's contention that the actions of Convention Week were done by strangers to the city, by agitators from the iniquitous coastal Babylons on the edge of our country's threatened integrity. They played right into the native Chicagoan's defensive tribal disdain of such outsiders. It would have been strategically more effective to let native Chicagoans impeach the administrators of their city for denying permits for parade and assembly, and there were plenty of Chicagoans involved in organizing activities before the convention and in the streets and parks during the week itself. Well over half the people arrested during Convention Week came from the metropolitan Chicago area.

Every time Judge Hoffman referred to Kunstler as a "New York lawyer, or wherever you come from," you could see Kunstler being cut out of Chicago sympathies. It was particularly deliberate on the judge's part, it seemed, when he once assured Kunstler that "we know about the Constitution out here in the Midwest, too." Kunstler protested, but the derogation was done.

Foran and Schultz often made direct or indirect reference to the questionable geographic origin of counsel for the defense. Of course, the reference reflected upon the defendants who "had no right to come into our living room," the lakefront parks, as if public parks were the same as private houses. It went little noticed that the prosecutors were also appealing to group loyalties, and were creating, unearthing, a tribe or "nation" or "state of mind" as they went along.

For instance, when Ed Phillips, a medic with the Medical Committee for Human Rights, testified about actions in Lincoln Park, Kunstler asked him, "What contact between police and people did you see?" Phillips answered, "I saw contact between clubs and heads." It got a good laugh from the defense's audience, smiles from the defense's jurors, silence from the prosecution's audience, but look at the distinction Kunstler made between "police" and "people" and look who he called "people."

Foran asked Phillips in cross-examination about his "auditing" of classes at the University of Chicago, and thereby placed him in the category of the ungrateful student who lives on the fringes of the university community, does not pay his tuition, and causes trouble to society. It went to the heart of some of the hardworking jurors.

Judge Hoffman, because of some Latin words that Kunstler had used, told him that he should put on "striped trousers" and be a professor. The judge appealed to a sense of vaudeville wherever he found it. Mrs. Peterson and other "conviction" jurors laughed loudly at the judge's humor. But Kay Richards laughed, and Mrs. Fritz smiled, when Kunstler at about the same time retorted that some mumbling of Foran's was "an anticipatory objection."

## Full-Time Defendant Hoffman Takes the Stand

When Abbie Hoffman lifted his arm to be sworn, he flexed his fist briefly, suspensefully, in the power salute. Then, at the end of taking the oath, he flexed his fist again, and there were smiles among those who knew what he was doing. He found the cultural contradiction in the correspondence of the two gestures of the lifted arm. That contradictory correspondence wherever he could find it became the basis for contest.

For instance, first-naming was seldom a public issue in a court trial before this trial. The formal address has been generally accepted by all parties in the courtroom, and those persons unfamiliar with it have been coached by their lawyers. Yet the formality of this respect runs counter to another trend in American society where if you do not first-name a person at the right time, usually soon in a relationship, you have placed yourself in a lower status position and no useful exchange will occur. To set up a contest where no contest previously existed, you bring one trend of society into contradiction with another, both trends being culturally justified and culturally backed. In Lincoln Park, before Convention Week, the 11 P.M. closing time, the curfew, had never been an issue with either police or residents. People had always walked dogs, necked in cars, or just strolled in the park anytime after 11 P.M.

But the city administration chose to make the curfew the basis for confrontation. It created a contest that had not previously existed, along with other powerful contradictions, in Lincoln Park residents and demonstrators. If the established power, such as the city administration, does not perceive the cultural contradiction as a contest, there is no chance for the new opponent to gain strength.

"My name is Abbie," he said. "I'm an orphan of Amerika."

"Abbie, will you tell the court . . ."

"He isn't Abbie," Richard Schultz objected, "he's a thirty-three-year-old man who should be called Mr. Hoffman." These were not kids, these youth revolution advocates, these were men who could be held responsible to the fullest degree for their actions. In his cross-examination of theatre director Paul Sills about Monday night August 26, 1968 in Lincoln Park, Foran said to Sills, because Sills had testified that most of the people confronting the police at the barricades were young, "You're no kid, and you were there."

Abbie Hoffman described his residence as "Woodstock Nation," a tribal grouping of young people who constituted "a nation, a state of mind," such as the Sioux were a nation, a state of mind, that went with them wherever they went. There were a couple of "prosecution" jurors who steadfastly refused to look at Abbie Hoffman while he was on the witness stand, as if they were frightened by the offense and pain they felt, and frightened by how close they came to getting involved in his humor.

On the morning of December 30, Richard Schultz objected violently to Weinglass's "not laying proper foundation" for Abbie Hoffman's testimony about Blackstone Rangers in Lincoln Park. Schultz, in his tirade, left the jury with the impression of Blackstone Rangers with guns in Lincoln Park on the side of Yippies and demonstrators. David Dellinger rose at the defense table to protest Schultz's "untruths" about Blackstone Rangers defending the park with guns on Tuesday night. I myself saw no such weapons in Lincoln Park that night, except in the hands of policemen. Most black kids thought the white kids were taking foolhardy risks that would get black kids shot. "The truth about anything could not be allowed in this courtroom," Dellinger said.

Judge Hoffman ordered "that man" to sit down and shut up, and ordered his marshal Ron Dobroski to make "that lawyer," Kunstler, sit down too. Dobroski moved toward Kunstler and said under his breath, pleading, "Mr. Kunstler." Kunstler gestured to reassure the marshal that he would in a second sit down.

Then Weinglass continued his questioning about Rangers and guns with Schultz objecting regularly and successfully. The jury was left with the impression of Blackstone Rangers and drug-crazed kids possibly defending Lincoln Park with guns that night. "Terror is boring," I wrote in my notebook.

Abbie Hoffman vividly recounted the speech that he gave in Grant Park in front of the Conrad Hilton Hotel on Wednes-

day night where he spoke of the Babylonian king Nebuchad-
nezzar who resurrected the god Moloch and instructed the
Babylonians to throw their children to it. Most of the jurors
were truly horrified by the image of children being thrown to
a cannibal god. Even Miriam Hill, named "Mrs. Wallace" by
the defendants, who usually folded her arms and would not
look at the witnesses for the defense, was staring at Abbie
Hoffman and listening to the analogy of the god Moloch and
the United States.

"Did you come to Chicago," Weinglass asked Abbie Hoffman, "in agreement with Dave Dellinger, Jerry Rubin, Lee
Weiner, John Froines, Tom Hayden, and Rennie Davis to
commit violence in this city?"

"An agreement? We couldn't agree on lunch!" He got the
laugh, but the declaration was unfortunately true.

*Cross-Examination for the Hell of It*

Now comes a contest of the trial that would seem to have
had influence on the political thought of some of the defendants. Richard Schultz had apparently read everything in print
by Abbie Hoffman, and made many notes on the rich imposition of meaning that he gave to Hoffman's writings.

The defendants thought that Richard Schultz had come to
be visited by doubts about the guilt of a couple of them, particularly of Abbie Hoffman. Not long after Schultz's cross-examination, there happened an accidental meeting on a Sunday
at the Museum of Science and Industry, where Schultz said,
probably flippantly, to Hoffman and Rubin, "When I was in
college, I might have been with you." But Schultz reacted with
his own concomitant feeling of guilt in the courtroom the way
a cop, feeling guilt, often acts in the street. With meanness
and rage.

The contest between Abbie Hoffman and Richard Schultz
was deadly sport, "for the hell of it," the way the Native Ameri-

cans would sometimes gamble their bodies or parts of their bodies. Abbie Hoffman needed such contest to be in touch with the best of his abilities. The laugh was his momentary trophy.

Schultz addressed him as "Mr. Hoffman" at all times. "One of the purposes of the Grand Central demonstration," Schultz said flatly without rising inflection so that it could hardly be called a question, "was to create a 'liberated area.' " He looked up over the lectern at the witness in the stand. The Grand Central demonstration occurred in March of 1968 in New York, when Yippies and young demonstrators "took over" Grand Central Station. There then came a considerable police attack, clubbings and arrests.

"Yes," Abbie Hoffman said.

"And in a liberated area," Schultz said, with the same flat tone that could not be contradicted, "anyone does what they want to do." There was the crime. There was his theme. Schultz, unashamed, knew there was nothing more feared by most of the jurors.

Abbie Hoffman saw instantly the trap, and the damage that was being done to the jury's possible estimation of the "intentions" of him and the other defendants. He tried to explain what he meant by people doing what they want to do, and what the title of his book *Revolution for the Hell of It* meant. He persisted in trying to explain these things over Schultz's objection that he was going beyond the question. Judge Hoffman asked the court reporter to make sure that Abbie Hoffman's remarks were on the record.

About the implicit contempt threat, "Let's have it out now, your honor," Kunstler said, unsuccessfully, but entering into the record for appeals' sake the signal that Judge Hoffman was postponing the contempts and not dealing with them summarily.

Schultz glanced firmly at his personally and carefully annotated copy of *Revolution for the Hell of It*. He then stated, in the flat tone, that a "liberated area is only the beginning of expansion to other areas." He sounded the threat to the jury's sense of its cultural space, to the jury's sense of its name, to the jury's sense of America being invaded from within and without by licentious Communist untruth.

When he said "Grand Central Massacre," his tone implied the annihilation of peoples and cities. He did not mention, of course, that it was the police who attacked the young demonstrators in Grand Central Station. Then he began to question Abbie Hoffman on the Central Park Yip-Out that occurred a few weeks after the "Grand Central Massacre." He put the tone of annihilation on all the activities that he listed for the Central Park Yip-Out, such as "smoking dope, sexual intercourse on the grass."

Schultz was once again emphasizing New York and Chicago differences. Look what happened, he said, when the New York police because of the "Grand Central Massacre"—meaning because of the public response to the police attack—stayed away from the Central Park Yip-Out and let the Yippies "do what they wanted to do." Kids were smoking dope and fucking on the grass.

Kunstler said he knew of no New York law forbidding sexual intercourse on the grass. That got a laugh from his audience. It got no laughs from the majority of Chicagoans on the jury. But Judge Hoffman won a few smiles from those jurors when he said sharply to Kunstler, "When we want you to help us interpret New York law we'll call you."

Schultz, to corroborate his statement, read the phrase "fucking on the grass" from *Revolution for the Hell of It.* By the time the trial was over, Richard Schultz would use the word "fucking" in public as if it were natural to him. Right now he made the word sound awkward, edgy, as if he were uncomfortable with it, as if it were that four-letter word that Abbie Hoffman said he liked. "If the police do not allow you to have liberated zones," Richard Schultz said, "you will fight for that right. Right?"

"We will fight for our right to assemble."

The prosecution wanted to show that the defendants used "sex and music to lure" young people, particularly the young campaign workers for Senator Eugene McCarthy, to Lincoln Park where they might be injured by police and incited to riot. "You use entertainers to attract young people from all over," Schultz said. Abbie Hoffman spoke around the question before he finally said, "Rock musicians are the real leaders of the revolution."

Schultz was out to develop the theme and image of the crime of "doing what you want to do in a liberated area." He stated that Abbie Hoffman had said that peeing on the walls of the Pentagon gave "a sense of integration."

"I said that combining political necessity with biological necessity gives a sense of integration."

Schultz asked about Abbie Hoffman's "symbolic" act of urinating on the walls of the Pentagon.

"Did I symbolically urinate on the walls of the Pentagon?" There was general laughter.

"Are you done, Mr. Hoffman?"

"I'll be done when you are."

"You had a good time at the Pentagon, didn't you, Mr. Hoffman?"

"Yes, I did. I'm having a good time now." Abbie Hoffman turned to Judge Hoffman. "I feel that biological necessity right now. Could we take a recess?" The defense's audience was laughing, and Kay Richards and Jean Fritz were hiding their laughter behind their hands.

"You knew you could get many young people to come by having a rock festival." Richard Schultz was speaking of the Yippie plans for the Festival of Life. He recited the Yippie publicity promises of five hundred thousand young people coming to Chicago, public fornication, and many other marvelous, horrible events.

Kunstler remarked that "a young man could be a dirty old man." In front of the jury, the judge retorted to Kunstler that he had seen some documents in evidence that were "not exactly exemplary." Abbie Hoffman had testified that he had received eight hundred to one thousand dollars from the city of New York for his pamphlet *Fuck the System.* "I like that four-letter word," he said.

Schultz said that the city of Chicago could not permit these Yippie events to occur in Chicago parks and that was why permits were denied. Kunstler said, "They permitted them to do it in a tree, your honor. Policeman right under the tree looking." Kunstler pointed up, as if into a tree. "He testified to it right here on this witness stand."

"The last observation of Mr. Kunstler may be stricken from the record," Judge Hoffman said.

Richard Schultz continued to prime the "liberated area" with images of young people doing what they wanted to do. He was showing the jury what would happen when "liberated areas" started to expand. "There was LSD to your knowledge in both the honey and some brownies? Isn't that right?"

"I would have to be a chemist to know that for a fact. It is colorless, odorless, and tasteless."

"Didn't you state on a prior occasion that Ed Sanders passed out from too much honey? . . . And that a man named Spade passed out on honey?" Abbie Hoffman said yes and grinned. He said that he made up that name, Frank Spade. It was weak winnings, though, because there was now as much hell as for-the-hell-of-it in Schultz's cross-examination.

"Didn't you state as a part of your myth of coming to Chicago that we will fuck on the beaches?" To develop his case about Yippie myth and Yippie intentions, Schultz was working from an article in the *Realist* that the judge had not permitted to be admitted into evidence for the defense on direct examination. Schultz's case charged that the Yippies used their myths and promises in order both to *attract young people to Chicago and to make sure that the city would not grant any permits which, when the young people gathered, would create a tense crowd situation.*

Schultz said that Abbie Hoffman himself withdrew his suit for a permit from Judge Lynch. Abbie Hoffman responded that he withdrew the suit because he found out that Judge Lynch was a former law partner of Mayor Daley and that Lynch had already denied the permit request of McCarthy campaign workers and so a long-haired Yippie was wasting his time.

Leonard Weinglass, in his redirect examination after Schultz's cross, lost no time in establishing that the city of Chicago, in the months prior to Convention Week, never made any attempt to get in touch with Mr. Hoffman about permits to assemble and sleep in the parks, while Hoffman and the Chicago-based Yippies made weekly attempts. Richard Schultz, with his saturation objections, and Judge Hoffman, with his sustaining rulings, together guarded the threshold of the citadel of the city of Chicago's guilt or innocence. Kunstler pointed out, for the record on behalf of his colleague, that when the government was answering a defense objection the judge never ruled until Schultz or Foran had said their say, but he hardly permitted Leonard Weinglass even to begin to answer a government objection.

Weinglass asked a rapid-fire series of questions over objection about when permits were granted for the Pentagon demonstration, the Yip-Out in Central Park, the April 27 peace march in Chicago, and others. "The day before," Abbie fired back the answer for each one.

In contesting with Richard Schultz for the appropriate meaning and description of the term "disruption," Abbie Hoffman recounted an incident in which newsmen during Convention Week were asking him a similar question. He said that he pointed to all the TV cables and other equipment blocking the sidewalk and the street. "Look at all this equipment all over the sidewalk. This is disruption."

Richard Schultz accused Abbie Hoffman of trying to create a situation where troops would be posted all over the city. "You can do that with a Yo-Yo in this country," Abbie said. "Look at this courtroom. There are troops." With a slight gesture of his hand, he indicated the many marshals.

"To your knowledge, a majority of the young people coming to Chicago smoked marijuana?"

"A majority of the people in this room smoke marijuana." The general laughter from spectators and newspeople may not have helped the defense with the jury, some of whom, after the trial, expressed their disapproval and fear of drugs.

Kunstler objected to the constant "prurient interest" of the government. Schultz countered that these statements about smoking dope and fucking in the park were made deliberately by Abbie Hoffman so the city would not grant permits for sleeping in the parks. Further, Schultz indicated that the self-defense parade marshals' training in Lincoln Park was displayed purposefully as being of a violent nature so the city would not grant permits.

Abbie Hoffman, however, could not admit to Richard Schultz that the flyer which was circulated on Saturday, August 24, and Sunday, August 25, in Lincoln Park and in the nearby Free Theater was a cool-it statement. It dishonored him to admit now that he and Jerry Rubin, with their flattering statements about the daring of the demonstrators, had been trying to cool the increasingly feverish situation in the park, partly because they were afraid the demonstrators would be wasted by the police, people would be scared away, and there could be no large protests or actions on Wednesday night, nomination night, of Convention Week. They did not understand what was happening in Chicago.

Abbie played into Richard Schultz's game of projecting the "real" intentions behind his seeming efforts to cool the violent atmosphere of Convention Week.

"You are an intelligent man, sir," Judge Hoffman often admonished defendant Hoffman. "Listen to the question. Or I will have to deal with it in some other way."

Schultz showed the extent to which he had visited his imagination upon the detail of this case when he said, "You told your tails that you had had a fight with Rubin, in order to destroy any charge of conspiracy." It took Defendant Hoffman back for a second; he blinked, and then he beamed. "I like that." he said, smiling. He and Rubin had quarreled in the middle of Convention Week and did not speak to each other for weeks.

Schultz was learning, from the book that he spent so much time reading, how to create a myth and the use of myth and the way myth brought things together and grew with the contradictory responses in the minds and actions of its perceivers. All that morning of December 31, 1969, he was pressing his examination of Yippie myth, telling a story, and he was winning. He was packing into his own Yippie myth all the Unpeople characteristics, for *his* people, that he could find.

"Did you ever say to the city that it was just a Yippie myth?"

"It never came up," Defendant Hoffman said.

Schultz repeated the question. "Did you ever say to the city that it was just a Yippie myth?" Schultz was getting his story told and winning all morning. Then about noon, as if he could not stand the continuing movement of winning, he became tiresome, repetitive, moralistic, as if it were easier to lose. Now Defendant Hoffman was involving the listeners in *his* view, *his* story.

"Do you remember Davis referring to the Amphitheatre as the War Zone?" Defendant Hoffman grinned and, at the defense table, Rennie Davis grinned and shook his head, barely glancing up from his papers.

When Abbie Hoffman attempted to explain his intentions, Judge Hoffman said angrily, "The question, sir, is did you use those words, not what did you mean?" Yet the judge had ruled that the crime concerned what the words meant, what they were expressive of, what the defendants intended. "The substance of the crime was a state of mind," he had ruled.

"Did you not say that if you didn't get electricity you would tear the park apart?" It was delivered without rising inflection, as a statement.

Defendant Hoffman answered no, but added, "I'm glad you consider it a fight. That's what I meant by fight, fight for electricity, et cetera."

"And you considered it pretty exciting, didn't you?"

FBI Agent Stanley was taking notes on points for which he would call upon all the resources of the FBI to find rebuttal material and witnesses.

"The first person you saw bleeding in Chicago on Sunday was Stew Albert? . . . You and Mr. Albert were united in your determination to smash the system. Weren't you? Was this your thought?" Abbie Hoffman took a pause before he said, "Is a dream the same as a thought? Yes, I had such a dream." That was a moment of solemn listening in the courtroom.

Assistant U. S. Attorney Schultz was making "thoughts" and "dreams" and "intentions" synonymous in his cross-examination. But earlier in the trial when Leonard Weinglass argued that the government was indeed, under the cover of the word "intention," prosecuting men for their thoughts, Schultz argued that the defendants were being tried for their intentions, not their thoughts.

"Isn't it a fact that you said that a society of love must be brought about with violence?" Defendant Hoffman laughed, so complex was the possible answer that, in the situation of this courtroom, it was only that most specifically human response, the laugh, that could give any comprehension of the implications of that question.

Then Schultz did something that the defendants were waiting for in their despair. He read from a speech given by defendant Hoffman just before the trial, nearly a year after the Democratic convention, in which defendant Hoffman gave instructions in how to make Molotov cocktails to people coming to Chicago to demonstrate against the trial. "Did you not say that if they wanted a society of love it would have to be accomplished by violence?"

With a feeling of hopelessness, Weinglass objected to the use of a speech given more than a year after Convention Week to prove intentions before and during Convention Week. But Judge Hoffman ruled, "I will let him answer.

Abbie first tried to deny it by saying that the University of Maryland sponsored and paid him for the speech. Then he explained his speech: "I said that in order to love we had to learn how to survive, and in order to survive we had to learn how to fight."

Then Prosecutor Schultz questioned what Abbie Hoffman meant when he wrote that on the plane from Chicago to New York at the end of Convention Week he wondered "what the fuck we would have done if the city had let us sleep in the park. As usual, the cops took care of the difficult decisions." Weinglass objected because the book from which Schultz was reading was *Revolution for the Hell of It* and the defense had tried to have it admitted into evidence so the jury would be able to see defendant Hoffman's statements in context.

"Mr. Marshal," the judge said, "will you ask that lawyer to sit down? There will be no argument after the court has ruled."

"Yes, I made that statement," defendant Hoffman said. "So what?"

The judge said, "The words 'so what' may go out, and I direct the jury to disregard it."

Then Schultz said, "Mr. Hoffman, you wanted to wreck this society." Abbie Hoffman said, "I feel that in time the society will wreck itself, and our role is to survive."

"Did you say, 'We are going to wreck this society or it will wreck itself so we might as well have some fun doing it.'?"

Weinglass and Kunstler objected together because Schultz was lifting a quote from Abbie Hoffman's statement to the Walker Report Task Force, and the interviewees had been guaranteed immunity for their statements. The judge denied their objections.

Defendant Hoffman said, "I cannot answer that question unless I can explain what it means."

The judge allowed him not to answer the question.

Daniel Walker, soon-to-be Governor of Illinois, made no statement publicly about the use of the materials for which he and the staff members of his Task Force had assured immunity.

"Mr. Hoffman, you felt you won a great victory in Chicago. With a small number of people you did damage to a huge and powerful party, and that you stopped Hubert Humphrey from being elected." In that statement was an admission by Assistant U. S. Attorney Schultz that the defendants had been unsuccessful in bringing large numbers of people to Chicago to demonstrate.

"Some people think," defendant Hoffman said, after long moments of comprehending the question, "that the mess that we created was chiefly responsible for the defeat of Hubert Humphrey."

Abbie Hoffman would have to explain who he meant by "we" and what he meant by "created" before his statement could be anything but arrogant, self-serving and self-defeating. Did the "we" mean the few thousand demonstrators in Chicago, and the two or three hundred "leaders"? Did the "we" include the police and city and government officials? If the "we" meant the defendants, which was exactly what the jury would think, then it was a loser's statement by a man who had been otherwise alert in his answers.

"By Thursday the twenty-ninth you knew you had smashed the Democratic candidate."

Defendant Hoffman said, "No, we would win, as in jujitsu, where you let the opponent destroy himself. Let his body destroy itself. Like in this trial."

Richard Schultz spoke of a victory celebration with champagne at Mobilization headquarters on the night of August 29, 1968. This would balance the statement by Renault Robinson, a black Chicago policeman who headed the Afro-American Policemen's Association, that there were police celebrations after Convention Week in which the men yelled "Sieg Heil" to their commander.

When Richard Schultz questioned Abbie Hoffman on the move to "kidnap" Deputy Superintendent Rochford at the Logan Statue on August 29, defendant Hoffman said abruptly, "If you got it, let's play it."

Weinglass had tried to question Abbie Hoffman on Yippie myth, but Schultz's objections were consistently sustained, largely on the grounds that documents of which the witness is the author are "self-serving" and can be used only for purposes of impeachment in cross-examination. The most prominent of evidence authorities, McCormick and Wigmore, do not agree with the judge and the prosecutor, who often enough cited these authorities too. In a legal system where the defendant is presumed to be innocent, no presumption of guilt should be visited upon the defendant's writings or other forms of expression.

The defense let many questions be asked by Schultz, in the hope that the very consequential subject of Yippie myth could be opened up for redirect examination, the scope of which is roughly determined by the scope of the cross-examination.

In trying to introduce into evidence the Yippie film about Convention Week, Weinglass said that Abbie Hoffman was the producer and that the film would reveal its producer's "intent." The film was shown out of the presence of the jury so the opposing side could determine if it objected to the admissibility of the document. A few reporters sat in the empty jury seats for a clearer view of the showing. I myself sat in Kay Richards' seat, with the feeling that I was in a director's chair.

Both audiences in the darkened courtroom laughed when the voice on the sound track of the film said, "Official Yippie campaign promises ranged from eternal life to free pay toilets." The men of the government, Thomas Foran, Richard Schultz, Roger Cubbage, and FBI Agent Stanley, laughed and snickered many times with pleasure in the visual wit of the film, showing the courtroom how sophisticated they were. The moment the showing was over, Richard Schultz, with laughter still in his face, objected to admission of the film. Hardly even self-serving. Immaterial. Irrelevant.

"Nothing shows Yippie intent better than this film does," Weinglass answered the objection. "Nothing better explains Yippie myth, Mr. Schultz's own word. Nothing has greater weight, or is more probative in this trial of intent, than this film. To exclude it will cut the heart out of the Yippie defense." Judge Hoffman, the only person in the courtroom who did not openly enjoy the film, sustained the government's objection briskly. "If you will get that apparatus out of here, sir," he said nastily, meaning the projector and screen and sound equipment. It was a loss to the art of jurywatching that observers were precluded from seeing the jurors' reactions to the film.

Weinglass tried, nevertheless, to get many questions answered about Yippie myth. Defendant Hoffman described what he called a "famous experiment in psychology": a fast, brief film in which a white man in a business suit stabs a young black man. Most white viewers change it around in their minds so that when queried on what happened, they answer that the black boy stabbed the white man in the business suit. The victim becomes the criminal, the guilt-projection, controversion, of those in power. The Conspiracy, he said, is the guilt-projection of the city of Chicago and the United States government. Yippie myth makes use of the probability that the viewer will controvert whatever he perceives in order to make it acceptable to himself.

For two weeks Abbie Hoffman was on the witness stand, though he was in the hospital with bronchial pneumonia part of that time and Christmas also intervened. His testimony was terminated abruptly, so Abbie Hoffman said, by the defendants, who did not believe that he should continue. He had been on the stand for nearly two weeks. He acted clownishly chagrined in the halls for several days.

Nevertheless, the defendants drew political notions from the magnification and distortion that Richard Schultz gave Yippie myth, particularly the ideas about liberated space and doing what you want to do, and the combining of political necessity with biological and personal necessity.

Thomas Foran cross-examined Theater Director Paul Sills about the pink piece of mimeographed paper that was authored by Abbie Hoffman and Jerry Rubin and handed out at the Free Theater on Wells Street opposite Lincoln Park on Saturday, August 24, 1968. Foran dwelled on such phrases in the document as "we are a revolutionary new community" and "we will decide when the battle begins." Those phrases, meant to forestall immediate battle in Lincoln Park, as Sills pointed out, were now used to show overall intent to incite to riot.

## Daley Day

Below-zero frost whitened the plaza of the Federal Building and the streets around it on the day that Mayor Daley testified. Lyndon Johnson, former president of the United States, had been called, too, since he was deemed to be knowledgeable of the government's attitude and planning for Convention Week. The defense's subpoena for LBJ was quashed, and that alone was enough to make one wonder why the subpoena for Mayor Daley was not.

The defense was trying to bridge the widening historical distance between the reality of the case and the reality of the "crime." Imagine, trying to take testimony from the man for whom the Conspiracy was, according to Abbott H. Hoffman, a "guilt-projection." In short, why did the mayor accept the invitation to be possibly bearded in Judge Hoffman's courtroom?

Many spectators passed the frigid night in sleeping bags at the northeast door of the Federal Building in order to keep their places in line. Newspeople entered by the northwest door. The marshals frisked the spectators one by one, but not the men and women of the press.

In the courtroom, the marshals moved the Conspiracy staff members and family over their protest into the seats in the very last row. That put several benches full of reporters, plainclothes police and marshals, between the mayor and any "planned spontaneous actions." You could feel the excitement in the courtroom the way you sense and see bubbles before water boils.

Prosecutor Foran argued that defense flyers and propaganda characterized Mayor Daley as a "hostile witness," that the defense's purpose in calling Daley was to generate antagonism in the court and prejudice the government's case, and that if defense counsel made a motion for the mayor to be declared a "hostile witness" so he could then be examined according to the rules of cross-examination, the motion must be made out of the presence of the jury. The judge warned counsel for the defense to act accordingly. Several of Mayor Daley's entourage were already present in the courtroom.

The mayor entered briskly, in bullish good health with, so help me, a sort of blue aura about him, suggested perhaps by the color of his suit and a slight powdering of his eyebrows. He put together in the nineteen-fifties, to "save" Chicago's business and industrial "life," the most powerful big city political machine in the country. He kept it together. In his first election as mayor, his majority came, ironically, from Chicago's black community. Among the wonders and horrors of his credits, he was the kingmaker, both in nomination and election, of at least one president, John F. Kennedy. During Convention Week he committed an awesome slip of the tongue: "The police are here to *preserve disorder,* not to . . ."

Kunstler stood at the end of the defense table farthest from the mayor. The defendants gathered near him, urgently whispering and sometimes even pulling at his sleeve. Kunstler again and again asked the mayor to raise his voice, as his questioning went nowhere.

For instance, William McFetteridge, deceased by the time of the trial, had been Superintendent of the Park District, which had given no response to the defendants' requests for permits for assembly. Kunstler asked Mayor Daley, "Is this the same William McFetteridge that nominated you in 1954?" Prosecutor Foran's objection was sustained. "Is this the same William McFettridge who said parks are not for dissenters?" Foran got a lot of knee-bend exercise standing up to object to each question.

"Do you know a federal judge, Judge Lynch?" The mayor paused as if he expected the usual objection, but it did not come and so he had to answer. "Yes," he said.

"Did you ever practice law with him?"

Foran's objection was sustained. The defense could only hope that the jury felt there was a significant connection between Mayor Daley and the Judge Lynch who, as they should know from previous testimony, denied the suits of the defendants in federal court.

Kunstler suddenly asked, "Mayor Daley, what is your relationship to Mr. Foran?" Foran did not object, so the mayor had to answer. "I think he's one of the greatest attorneys in the United States . . ." The mayor said it heavily. When he was asked about his relationship with David Stahl, who had been the government's second witness, Mayor Daley said, "I think he's one of the finest young men . . ."

A hissing came from the back rows of the press and staff section. Kunstler called attention to the very back row where a marshal was asking a young woman to leave. Kunstler kept looking in that direction and making comments, and so everyone in the courtroom kept watching what Kunstler was watching. The marshal pushed sideways through the rows packed with people, to pull out the young woman, a young man, and another young woman. The Conspiracy staff members and family on that bench complained loudly.

When Kunstler asked that Daley's remark about being "very proud" of his position in the Cook County Democratic party be stricken, Judge Hoffman, to the surprise of many, struck it. Mayor Daley, with one of his rare hints of his own feeling, turned and looked across the bench at the judge as if ready to say that only a seventy-four-year-old Republican who was a federal judge could enjoy that license in the city of Chicago.

The courtroom was stuffed with a suppressed hysteria. Kunstler was unable to question Daley about his shoot-to-kill-all-arsonists-and-shoot-to-maim-all-looters order given after the black insurrection that followed the assassination of Martin Luther King, Jr., in April, 1968. The defense was ready to argue that Daley's order was meant to prepare the attitude of the police and the city toward antiwar demonstrators during the Democratic convention in August.

Kunstler moved to have the mayor declared a "hostile witness," first in front of the jury in violation of the judge's direction. Then, after indignant comments from Foran and Judge Hoffman, and after trying to ask a leading question in order to have the point for argument, he asked that the jury be excused so he could argue the question. He wanted to be able to ask those leading, suggestive, and offensive questions that were permitted by the rules of cross-examination. Out of the presence of the jury, the motion was denied. "He has answered in the manner of a gentleman," the judge said, in declaring that nothing in the mayor's behavior justified calling him a "hostile witness." The defense tried to show that Mayor Daley "must be considered hostile by reason of his clear alignment of interest with the other party." Kunstler was citing the rules of civil procedure, while Judge Hoffman was relying upon the rules of criminal procedure. The New Proposed Federal Rules for both criminal and civil proceedings, produced by an eminent commission of establishment lawyers at the behest of the Supreme Court, agreed completely with the defense's argument.

Kunstler set himself to attack Daley by whatever means might convey appropriate information to the jury. In the contempt proceedings at the end of the trial, he would be cited for asking "no less than eighty-three leading and suggestive questions." There was nothing Kunstler could do toward laying a foundation for these questions. But later in the trial, when the defense objected to a leading question by the government, Judge Hoffman said, "Oh, evidence authorities are not much against leading questions these days."

"Did you say to Senator Abraham Ribicoff, 'Fuck you, you Jew sonofabitch'?" Foran objected furiously, and everyone gave a reaction from a hiss, to a stir, to other noises. "But, your honor," Kunstler said mildly, "there was a lipreader there." He was referring to the remark that Daley shouted at Senator Abraham Ribicoff of Connecticut when the latter gentleman chastised Daley on the convention floor at the Amphitheatre for using "gestapo tactics" in the streets and parks of Chicago. In the witness stand, Daley flushed, an indication that he needed to be protected from speaking at length on any question.

"I have no sensitivity," Judge Hoffman said about a defense protest.

"You can say that again," Rennie Davis muttered.

Kunstler tried to question Daley about a letter, signed Abe. Daley received it from Federal Judge Abraham Marovitz on September 18, 1968, about the Grand Jury, impaneled on Sep-

tember 8, that finally brought the indictments against the Conspiracy Eight, now Seven.

You could see and sense right there in the courtroom the
vast complex of Daley's friends, cronies, and proteges in political, judicial, and business office, protecting him, using him,
protecting themselves.

At the lunch recess, the mayor went quickly out the back
door with marshals following him. That door was ordinarily
used only by the judge and jury and the marshals and the
judge's employees.

The defendants were glum and quarreling during lunch in
Berghoff's near the Federal Building. They could not find a
way of confronting the mayor at the point of his guilt.

Daley, even though he had said very little, did not look or
act or sound particularly good or bad on the witness stand.
But in the press he would look good enough that a Yippie
heart would quail to think of it. That was the tone of the Chicago press by the end of the day, too. MAYOR EMERGES UN-
SCATHED. That was surely the reason that he accepted the
subpoena.

Toward the end of the noon recess, the mayor settled himself early in the witness stand, with his hands folded in front
of him, before the judge or prosecutors entered. Then Abbie
Hoffman slouched into the gathering courtroom and moved
here, there, around the defense table, hesitating at the end
farthest from the mayor. He caught the mayor's eye, then
slapped his hips as if for six-shooters and said, "Why don't we
just settle it right here? To hell with this law stuff." The mayor
laughed, and the press and spectators and marshals laughed.
The mayor really enjoyed it. Who should know better that
might is right at the heart of the courtroom process?

Out of the presence of the jury, Kunstler made an extensive,
detailed offer of proof, modeled somewhat on the indictments
against the defendants. Obviously it had been prepared before
the mayor appeared on the stand. It charged the mayor with

crimes of conspiring with other notables to cause violence during Convention Week. The judge sustained the government's objection.

Foran asked only one question of the mayor. "In your conversation with anyone, did you ever tell anyone to deny them their permits?"

"No," the mayor said.

He went out the back door rapidly with marshals around him. The defense was left with the bleak problem of disproving an unreal case.

In the hallway during the immediate recess, "Why didn't you cross-examine Daley?" defendant Hoffman asked Assistant U. S. Attorney Schultz.

"I was so intimidated by him," Schultz threw his arms up stiffly as if holding a globe over his head, "I couldn't ask a question."

Defendants and prosecutors laughed.


*Enforced Companionship and Friends as Witnesses*

The morning after the mayor's appearance the atmosphere of the courtroom was so downcast that it was peaceful, almost pleasant, purged, orderly, quiet.

It was intolerable for all parties to be in such close proximity over a period of months in the courtroom with people who were their enemies and to sustain continually a hostile disposition and deployment toward them. It brought about a dreary, weary, brutalizing contemptuousness of feeling during the last weeks of the trial, along with sudden, odd flashes of compassion, humor, and comradeship. No better demonstration could be given of the powerful grip of any political and economic system upon its individuals than the fact that the simple sharing of space in the courtroom forces people to discover moments of comradeship in enemies, in persons of alien parties and opposing roles. Powerful forces and powerful restraints in the courtroom cause this to happen. The resulting guilt suffuses every word and action.

Marshals tended to feel friendly toward the defendants, not so friendly toward the defendants' wives and the Conspiracy staff members. Nancy Kurshan, sitting in the front bench behind the defense table on Daley Day, cried out in disgust at one point, and "Slim," the tall black deputy marshal who had once been a Harlem Globetrotter, said, "All right, Nancy, let's go," gesturing with his thumb toward the door. She folded her arms, and would not look at him, and shook her head no. He repeated, "Let's go." She shook her head without looking at him again, showing that he would have to pull and carry her out. Probably because of the disposition indicated by the familiarity in his tone, he accepted her threat and relented. Marshals often said to defendants and their lawyers and friends, "We're just doing our job," or, "It's our duty." But marshals often did their job with energy and determination.

The brutalization of feeling was intensified by the unbaptized freshness of friends of the defendants who appeared as witnesses. The contempt of the prosecutors for these witnesses was analogous to the regard that the defendants gave to the agents during the government's case. The prosecutors were quick to intimate that the information of wiretaps and FBI reports gave them reason for their contempt, just as the defendants' memories of conversations gave them reason to despise the testimony of the agents. But the individually responsive, "unrehearsed," and in some cases positively unprepared manner of the defense witnesses sharpened the prosecutors' rage. Most of these witnesses mistrusted the government, and feared it. They were confronted by a scene that they could hardly understand, where defendants, defense counsel, prosecutors, jurors, and judge were bound by this time into nearly irreversible, contradictory dramatic relationships in which the arrogance and self-righteousness of all parties were only heightened by fresh feeling on the witness stand.

Figures from the civil rights, student, and peace movements of the sixties came to explain themselves and their associates at the defense table. Carl Oglesby, with monkishly thinning long hair and the manner of an aggressive scholar, managed to make the full case for the "intentions" of Tom Hayden and Rennie Davis in coming to Chicago to demonstrate against the Viet Nam war, racism, poverty, and the deterioration of the enjoyment of life in the United States. Oglesby used the requirement of Judge Hoffman's interpretation of the rules of evidence better than most witnesses, by saying repeatedly, "Hayden said . . ." or "Hayden further argued . . ." or "Davis said . . ." in recounting extensive conversations over many months prior to the Democratic convention. At the defense table, Tom Hayden shook his head often during Oglesby's testimony as if he did not want anyone to believe that he had ever been so naive about possible police violence in Chicago as Oglesby made him sound.

Judge Hoffman again and again admonished Oglesby to answer questions yes or no, and finally Oglesby said with sharp irritation, "Why is it impossible for this court to tolerate an explanation of reality that goes beyond yea or nay?" He might have addressed that admonition to the movement itself.

Tom Foran, as if he were standing in a reptile house looking through glass at a cobra, stood at the lectern and asked Oglesby if he had ever heard any defendant, Rennie Davis in particular, say that getting people clubbed by police, especially getting McCarthy workers clubbed, would have a positive political effect.

Foran used Oglesby's presence in Grant Park as an occasion to read to the jury excerpts from several speeches made on Wednesday afternoon of Convention Week. Among them was the speech by Tom Neuman, which came toward the end of the afternoon when the nonviolent march was being formed. "We have been told to sit down. [Dellinger had asked the angry crowd to sit down after the police attack, and Neuman was angry at Dellinger.] When the pig runs, we will run. When the pig crawls, we have won. When they push us out of our space as they have now done in this park, we will move into their space. We are no longer waiting for them to make moves. We have decided, some of us, to move out of this park in any way that we can, to move into their space in any way that we can, and to defend ourselves in any way that we can." Foran asked Oglesby, after each excerpt, "You didn't hear that?" The judge restrained Oglesby from answering other than yes or no when Oglesby tried to comment on the context and assumptions of each speech. Oglesby saw how Foran was using him, and how the judge supported the prosecutor's "naming" activity. Oglesby said that he had left the bandshell after giving his own speech. He said with distilled distaste that the only reason he could see for Foran reading these excerpts off to him was to get his comment on them because he didn't hear the speeches in Grant Park, and he had said that he didn't hear them. That meant that by the Rules of Evidence he couldn't be questioned about them and Foran was reading them in an attempt to prejudice the jury against him and his powerful testimony.

Weinglass objected to a part of Foran's cross-examination because apparently the prosecutor was using information from a wiretap that had not been disclosed to the defense. That meant the defense had no way of knowing if the prosecutor's use of the information was accurate, or if it conformed with a pattern of distortion.

"People work very hard in jobs that are boring, that they don't believe in, in order to buy goods that are only one step away from becoming garbage," Franklin Bardache said. He was not permitted to testify to the jury on the salient rhetoric of what was called the youth revolution. Weinglass argued, on behalf of the offer of proof, that perhaps the Supreme Court's ruling that the violation of law must be weighed against the enormity of the crimes or social conditions being protested could be considered for application in the Conspiracy case because the defendants were accused of marching and assembling without permits. It was so early in the morning that the level of self-righteousness in the courtroom did not rise significantly with Bardache's speech.

Peter Martinsen and Donald Duncan had participated with David Dellinger in a war crimes tribunal in Denmark. They came to witness for his intentions and the defendants' intentions in general in demonstrating against the war in Viet Nam. "I know what Mr. Kunstler is trying to do," Assistant U. S. Attorney Schultz said, during Duncan's testimony. "He's trying to bring the Viet Nam war into this courtroom."

"Where it properly belongs," Kunstler said.

But when Martinsen described the use of electrical field telephone wire on genitals of Viet Cong prisoners by American interrogators, Judge Hoffman asked, departing from his manner of judicial disinterest, "Were you present when that was done?" "Yes," Martinsen said. The judge listened intently, with tightly wrinkled forehead, rubbing his finger on his upper lip. He seemed to believe Martinsen, and to wish to avoid the implications of believing him. Foran listened to the description of torture with a pursed expression, similar to the expression that stole into his face when he suspected "faggotry." It was a solemn moment. Listening was intense in the courtroom.

When Kunstler attempted to get the news of the My Lai massacre to the sequestered jury earlier in the trial, referring to the "slaughter of Vietnamese civilians by American soldiers," the jury's foreman was seized by a choking fit. His face flushed so deadly red that the judge excused the jury and recessed the trial for several minutes. The same sort of choking fit seized the future foreman, though not serious enough to cause a recess, when Martinsen gave his testimony about tying wires of a portable field telephone around genitals of prisoners.

But the defendants' feelings and ideas about that arduous and bloody imposition of American imperial power upon that little country on the far edge of the Pacific, and the resulting consequences within the United States, were not allowed to become evidenciary for their intentions about the Democratic National Convention of 1968.

James Simon Kunen, author of Strawberry Statement, reported that Jerry Rubin said in a speech in New York, which was cited in the indictment, " 'Hubert Humphrey is an asshole.' Very specifically, he said, 'Not the buttocks or anything but the hole. A nothing. Sold his soul to the great corporation of the U.S.A.' " The laughter from the defense's audience was rich and mean. FBI Agent Caspar had testified, in the government's case, that Jerry Rubin recommended bullets instead of ballots, but Kunen said that a similar phrase was used by another speaker. "Did you see anybody there who looked like a conception of an FBI agent? Like Mr. Stanley here," Kunstler said, pointing at Agent Stanley at the prosecution table. There were heated objections from the prosecutors and admonishments from the judge.

Stewart Meacham and Donald Kalish gave testimony for the plans and intentions of defendants associated with the National Mobilization to End the War in Viet Nam. Meacham, with the air and looks of a classically distinguished white-haired AFSC executive, turned to the judge once when he was asked to answer a question yes or no, "Judge, I haven't answered the question, sir. I can't really answer the question that way, sir. I feel quite awkward, sir. What do I do?" Judge Hoffman said that he could not help him, as if offended by being so close to the veritable image of the White Anglo-Saxon Protestant conscience.

Clark Kissinger, an organizer of the April 27, 1968, peace march, testified that Thomas Foran had been special assistant corporation counsel in charge of land acquisition for urban renewal. Kissinger was asked to describe "nefarious buildings" near the Civic Center. "Well," he said, with Foran present, "Chicago Title and Trust, which is where the politicians hold their slum land holdings in secret trust." No one seemed to remember or connect with significance, if any, that Tom Foran, former land acquisition counsel, met undercover agent William Frapolly in the library of Chicago Title and Trust to discuss the agent's testimony.

Other friends, artists, scholars, writers, and politicians who appeared for the defense included Julian Bond, Arlo Guthrie, Paul Krassner, John Sack, Arthur Waskow, Richard Goodwin, Donald Peterson, John Conyers, Judy Collins, Mark Lane, Dick Gregory, Stewart Potter. They were blocked by many government objections and rulings by the judge, but nevertheless they testified vividly, haplessly, wittily, and perhaps futilely because the government, by the law of the antiriot provisions to the 1968 Civil Rights Act, did not even have to prove that the defendants intended the actions that occurred, but merely that they crossed state lines with intent to cause a "riot" and that some actions did occur at some time. The government, however, did worry about the resolution of the jury, and protected the jurors as much as possible from prejudicial information.

Even the judge needed to relieve himself occasionally of the responsibility of maintaining angry pressure against the defense attorneys. During Leonard Weinglass's direct examination of Carl Oglesby, Judge Hoffman said, in a tone astonishing for its quiet friendliness, "The form of that question is not good, Mr. Weinglass. Try it a different way." It gave a peep into a possible world of positive interaction among the people of this court. But it was only minutes before that strange moment of friendliness was wiped out.

"For instance," Weinglass said to Judge Hoffman, in speaking against an objection by Foran, "I would like to know what you understand by the word 'movement'?"

"I've told you again and again," the judge said, "that I am not here to be questioned. I sustain the objection."

   Jerry Rubin said something to Richard Schultz and Schultz
laughed and pointed at the custody door beside the defense
table. Jerry Rubin simmered for a minute or so. Judge Hoffman had ruled that morning that the defendants should use
the bathroom behind the custody door. In order to expedite
proceedings, the defendants had waived their constitutional
right to be present at all times in the courtroom so they could
use at will the regular Men's Room in the hall. The judge was
probably trying to stop the defendants from conferring and
dreaming up actions with each other and with staff members.
Jerry Rubin stood up and asked the judge to admonish Schultz
for telling him to go to the bathroom behind the custody door
"in the jail." This caused a flurry of angry remarks.

   Schultz finally apologized to the judge by saying that he had
succumbed to the sort of tactics the defendants had used
against authorities all their lives. In the jury, Jean Fritz was
laughing silently behind her hand at Richard Schultz's embarrassment, and Kay Richards buried her head in her hands on
her knees. Ruth Peterson hid her mouth with her hand, and
Shirley Seaholm and others were smiling. The word "bathroom" kept recurring in the altercation before the bench. Weinglass and Schultz were laughing, and then the defendants
got into the quarrel and were arguing and laughing, too. Eve-
rytime someone mentioned the word "bathroom" they all dou-
bled up laughing. Judge Hoffman also said something about
having "nothing against bathroom jokes."

   Judge Hoffman regarded the two defense lawyers differently. Kunstler angered him often, but Weinglass infuriated
the judge. The only way he could assert control was to rule
arbitrarily and adamantly, cutting off Weinglass's argument.
That was odd, because Leonard Weinglass tried to avoid conflict, whereas Kunstler, the more the trial progressed, seldom
avoided it. Several lawyers have observed that Judge Hoffman
did not show a firm grasp of the law in this case. The judge's

fury with Weinglass may have come because the younger defense counsel always argued the law.

The judge's attitude toward Kunstler showed itself in one
of those musing moments when the judge found himself saying, during the examination of Pete Seeger, "I know more
about music than you do, Mr. Kunstler. I know that may come
as a surprise to you." Earlier in the trial Kunstler and the judge
had exchanged comments about the Chicago Symphony Or-
chestra. The judge implied then that Kunstler was an eastern
chauvinist and Kunstler protested that he found the Chicago
Symphony to be very good. Now Kunstler heard the need for
regard and warmth in Judge Hoffman's voice. "Not at all, your
honor," he said, inviting the judge to say more. Judge Hoffman
recovered himself quickly.

In a recess Abbie Hoffman and Rennie Davis performed
some "karate" horseplay, a brief satirical comment about one
portion of their indictment. Schultz and Cubbage laughed as
if marveling at the defendants' attitude in the face of the im-
pending end of the trial.

Foran and Kunstler occasionally shared a comment at which
both smiled. Foran initiated one such exchange, and Kunstler
pushed his chair on its casters across the aisle to be close to
Foran. They were easy together, sharing this moment.

The law was Leonard Weinglass's rod and his staff, and the
judge and the prosecutors were not comforted in exchanges
with him during legal argument. He was intellectually and be-
haviorally consistent and not blessed with many moments,
oiled and fired with guilt, of comradeship with enemies in the
shared rules and format of the courtroom game.

"I wish I had the capacity to grow long hair," the judge
suddenly said when Irwin Bock was testifying about long hair
in the government's rebuttal case. The judge leaned over and
grinned down at the defendants eagerly, with great wrinkles
in his bald head. The defendants virtually did not notice his
belated invitation to be appreciated. I wondered at the time

what would have happened in the trial if they had consciously ingratiated themselves with him.

These momentary releases from adamant points-of-view became more frequent toward the end of the trial, but only because the brutal exchanges and pressures became more frequent, too.

The courtroom became a sort of diving bell, trapping all occupants in a plunge into the American psyche and the undercurrents of American history.

Artists on the witness stand consistently made use of attitudes, speech, manners, conventions, and bodily dispositions that were different from other witnesses. For instance, most witnesses simply raised their right arms and took the oath administered by the clerk. "Do you swear to tell the truth, the whole truth, and nothing but the truth, so help you God?" Pete Seeger answered with clear, almost liturgical enunciation, "I swear, before this court, to tell the truth, the whole truth, and nothing but the truth."

In the witness stand, he leaned forward on his elbows with his chin raised, his hands clasped before him, and beamed with an expression of utmost piety and attention upon the courtroom and his examining lawyer, Bill Kunstler. Seeger was there to give testimony to the lively, but peaceful intentions of Jerry Rubin and Abbie Hoffman for the Festival of Life in Lincoln Park. He managed to do something at all moments that quietly excited anticipation in the courtroom.

The defense attempted ritually to get each singer who took the witness stand to sing for the jury those songs that were particularly significant for the movement and for the intentions of the demonstrators during Convention Week. In Seeger's case, Judge Hoffman said, "I instruct the jury to disregard—I don't know how to characterize it—the *sounds* made by the witness."

Country Joe came into the courtroom moving his mouth as if chewing long and slow and deep on gum. By the time he reached the witness stand and raised his right hand, everyone in the courtroom was watching the movement of his mouth. The clerk, about to give Joe the oath, said across Judge Hoffman's head, "Will you please take the gum out of your mouth, sir?" There was then a stillness of watching and listening as in a classroom when a teacher has warned a student. Then, most laconically, Country Joe said, "I ain't got any gum in my mouth." The implication was that he could have swallowed it or there had not been any gum in the first place, and the court would never know.

He gave his name as "Country Joe." Schultz, writing on a clipboard, said, "May we have the witness's full name?"

Judge Hoffman said, "I'm assuming Country is his Christian name," and got laughs from both sides.

Country Joe McDonald spoke slowly with heavily laconic pauses and tones. He was asked to give his Viet Nam song, and he looked down, and then began to sing strongly, "And it's one, two, three, what are we fighting for?" Judge Hoffman cried out, "Whoa, stop." A marshal held Joe by the chin. Country Joe then recited the words of the song.

He said that he could not get music groups to come to the Festival of Life, and would not sing there himself, because of the very uptight vibrations from police around the city.

"You don't mind if I call you Mr. McDonald, do you?" cross-examiner Schultz said, and soon asked a question in which the word "fornication" was mentioned. Country Joe took a long, long moment before he turned to Judge Hoffman and said, "Your honor, in my part of the world, the hippie underground, words may have different connotations." Fornication was such a word, he indicated, unsuccessfully.

Schultz asked a question about people fighting police in order to dispel the suggestion in Country Joe's testimony that it was the police, on orders from the city of Chicago, who brought the attitude of violence into the streets and parks. Country Joe would not acknowledge that that question was "rational."

With continuous gesture of voice and body, the artists took and kept attention in the courtroom.

### Rennie Davis

Roger Wilkins, director of Community Relations Service of the Department of Justice under Attorney General Ramsey Clark, and Wesley Pomeroy, a police-work expert with the Department of Justice, met with Rennie Davis in Chicago prior to Convention Week to discuss the prospects and organization of demonstrations. The eight-page memorandum that Wilkins wrote to Ramsey Clark at that time revealed their good feeling about Rennie Davis and expressed concern about the intransigence of Mayor Daley. The memorandum was not allowed into evidence to be seen by the jury. Wilkins and Pomeroy were also only partially successful, in the face of objections and rulings, in giving testimony. Wilkins and Pomeroy said to reporters in a press conference that they might as well have been speaking "Urdu" to Mayor Daley.

Rennie Davis on the witness stand managed to recite most of his all-American boy-next-door qualifications, including being a member of a 4-H club and a chicken judger. Making a show of weariness with the on-the-face-of-it sentimentality, Foran objected to the "chicken judger" statement as obviously irrelevant. "If that is part of the background," Judge Hoffman answered calmly, "I will let him say he was a chicken judger, and anything else of importance he may have done during his career."

The defense tried for the last time—they had also tried with Stewart Meacham and Donald Kalish—to place the "Lake Villa" document, authored by Davis and Hayden, into evidence for the intentions of the demonstrators in coming to

Chicago. It was written in March of 1968 at a conference at Lake Villa, Illinois, a 125-page position statement for the workers of the National Mobilization to End the War in Viet Nam. Its very first sentence was: "The campaign should not plan violence and disruption against the Democratic National Convention."

Weinglass argued strongly against Foran's objection, saying that where defendants were presumed to be innocent until proven guilty, documents authored by defendants were admissible. Judge Hoffman grew heated and initiated a side exchange with Weinglass that really obscured his attention to Weinglass's argument. The judge claimed that Professor Wigmore, the great authority on evidence cited by Weinglass, was a former employer of his.

The judge undertook to "read" the by-now legendary "Lake Villa" document. Rennie Davis, with his chin on his forearms on the side of the bench, watched him. The judge appeared to concentrate for a minute or so, then turned pages of the 125-page document rapidly. He sustained Foran's objection quietly and abruptly.

Weinglass asked, "Has your honor read the document?"

"I have looked it over."

"You didn't read it," Davis said. "I was watching you, and you didn't read it."

The judge stood up and leaned over the bench. "Did you get that, Miss Reporter?"

"With all due respect to the court," Weinglass said, "that was my impression, too."

Davis then repeated what he had said to the curious audience. Every juror, with the exception of Mildred Burns and Miriam Hill who refused to look at Davis, listened intently to his explanation about the judge not reading the document.

That was the last attempt to put the document before the jury. Weinglass pressed his forehead between his thumb and fingers. In the last weeks of the trial, the defense was blocked from placing in evidence one important document or testimony after another. The "Lake Villa" document would be presented out of the presence of the jury as an offer of proof that afternoon.

Weinglass tried to introduce into evidence a round object, a little bigger than a baseball, that was a bomb-within-a-bomb. It contained myriad razor-sharp slivers of steel. When the main canister exploded, these round objects were rained upon an area about as big as a city block. They in turn exploded and cut to shreds any living thing within their reach. Their slivers even sliced through walls. Rennie Davis had brought it back from North Viet Nam as evidence that the United States bombed that country with the intention of wiping out populations, not just "military targets" as the Pentagon usually claimed. This supported the defendants' intentions for coming to the Democratic convention to demonstrate against the near genocidal intentions of the United States in Viet Nam. The object was not allowed into evidence. The defendants laughed as they tossed it from one to another, from Froines to Dellinger to Abbie Hoffman to Jerry Rubin.

In cross-examining Davis, Foran, always hunched at the lectern, said angrily, "The Viet Nam War has nothing to do with traveling in interstate commerce to incite a riot!" There was a gasp of horror in the courtroom at Foran's desperation in front of the jury.

"Didn't you say on November 20, 1967, at Judd Hall," Foran said, "that demonstrators should disrupt the Democratic convention in any way possible? Didn't you say that?"

Davis tried to develop his differing phrase of "disrupt the sham" in answer.

"You are a highly intelligent man," Foran said. "You know how to answer a question yes or no."

Davis was earnest and courteous and insistent in his testimony, always aware of the nuance of phrasing.

"Isn't it a fact," Foran said, "that you told Dave Stahl on August 12 when you asked for a permit that you told him there would be civil disobedience?" Davis corrected Foran politely by saying that he had said that there would be "civil disobedience at movement centers," in churches and other community buildings around the city, not on marches. If Davis had answered "No" to that question, it would have been a partial misrepresentation; if he had answered "Yes" it would also have been a misrepresentation, and one that would convict him. If he tried to say what he actually said to Dave Stahl, he appeared to be flaunting the court. Kunstler also tried to use the Yes-or-No trap with witnesses, but the judge didn't let him get away with it.

"Don't call us if you're going to have a nice peaceful thing. Didn't you hear that?" Foran repeated it, suggesting that the defendants had been belittling anyone at a Mobilization meeting who wanted peaceful demonstrations. "Did you ever hear that said, 'Don't bother to call the medical committee if you are going to have a peaceful thing'?"

"No," Davis said.

"What I have underlined there is," Foran said, finally giving Davis the Mobilization document to read, " 'If you are going to have a peaceful thing where you do not predict any medical emergencies, please don't call us.' "

"Yes," Davis said, reading from the document, "and then: 'If it turns out that you need us, we'll come.' " The struggle for the soul of the future was being waged over nuance and phrasing. Foran's suggestions about the quote and its context were never quite dispelled.

"Did you say that at the Pentagon you planned both active confrontations with the warmakers and civil disobedience?" Davis said that the gist of what he meant on the radio program just before Convention Week was that the Pentagon demonstrations were essentially peaceful and that was what the Mobilization intended for Chicago.

"Now isn't it a fact," Foran said, "that the Pentagon was the blueprint for Chicago? That is a fact, isn't it?"

"That is absolutely not a fact," Davis said. "That fact is turned on its head, Mr. Foran, and that is what I'm trying to—that is what I've been trying to tell you all morning."

Foran threw both arms stiffly upward. "Did you hear yourself make that Freudian slimp—*slip*," he jerked his head down to correct himself, "when you made that slip on the film saying Pentagon instead of Amphitheatre?" Foran said on a TV show after the trial that Davis, when Foran was cross-examining other witnesses, heckled Foran from behind in whispers about Foran's "sexual prowess." That, along with Foran's amazing, hot statement after the trial, "We have lost our kids to the freaking fag revolution," made the "slimp" worth wondering about.

"No," Davis said, "I didn't hear that. What does that mean?"

"Your honor," Weinglass said, "there has only been one Freudian slip in this trial and that is when Mr. Foran said the court should disregard the jury instead of the jury disregard the statement." That got laughs for Weinglass.

"The Pentagon was a model for Chicago, and you know it," Foran said, obviously incensed at his own "slimp" of the tongue. Laughter and hisses came at him from the defense's audience.

"It's very simple," Davis said; "the Pentagon and Chicago are two different things."

"Yes," Foran said, "you would like to explain away Chicago, wouldn't you?" This writer thought that evidently everybody wanted to explain away Convention Week. Foran hunched even more at the lectern as Weinglass objected to the prosecutor confusing "apples and pears" with the two very different events of the Pentagon and Chicago.

"Isn't it a fact," Foran said, "that your plans at both the Pentagon and Chicago was to broaden the movement—in the words of Dellinger: 'Combine the peacefulness of Dellinger with the violence of active resistance'?" He would soon be setting forth Dellinger's ideas about "the synthesis of Gandhi and guerrilla." Smiles and shakings of the head flickered throughout the audience.

Foran, in his attempt at perfect paranoia, was implying that the defendants were perfectly clairvoyant, coordinating plans from the massive Pentagon demonstrations in October, 1967, to the Convention Week actions in August, 1968. That the defendants spoke of the Pentagon as an example of successful demonstrations at that time of history was beyond the logic of this courtroom situation. The ready marshals stirred and acted upon every burble of laughter. Judge Hoffman ritually instructed Davis to pay attention and not go beyond the question.

"I'm sorry I keep wanting to put everything back into context, Mr. Foran. I know you don't like that." Davis made a gesture with both hands as if putting something back on a shelf.

Foran's wife, with tall blond hair, and his young daughter, and other family members of the prosecutors, had an armored, heroic disregard for anything but the performance of their favored ones in the arena. Only Foran's daughter, very pretty, dark hair, in her early teens, allowed herself the flicker of a secret smile when she felt her father was doing well. Anita Hoffman, with a good sense for family and tribal relationships, found a son of Mayor Daley sitting with the Forans one day. Rennie Davis's family, father and mother and sister, observed the proceedings. "That's my sister they're taking out," Davis said, pointing at the marshals removing a girl for speaking too loudly. Many of the women jurors watched the women of the defense with curiosity.

Foran hit back at Weinglass with a phrase that the defense often directed at the prosecution: "I think Mr. Weinglass should get a license as a professional witness."

"I think I know where I could apply," Weinglass said, and there was lots of laughter.

"I think I know too," Foran said, pleased with a jerky surprise at his own wit, "but I can't comment on it because I would prejudice his case before the jury."

Davis attempted to say that Boy Scout groups and National Guard were permitted to camp and sleep all night in the parks. "The Yippies talked about a Festival of Life and love and—"

"They also talked," Foran interrupted Davis, "about public fornication and about drug use and about nude-ins on the beach. They also talked about that, didn't they?"

"They talked about love, yes, sir." Davis was insufferably witty at times, with his ability to give a phrase the turn that would relate it to three or four audiences.

"You and I have a little different feeling about love, I guess, Mr. Davis."

"Oh, I don't know," Davis said.

Foran said, "Mr. Simon offered you the Grant Park bandshell anytime you wanted it, didn't he?" Yet the prosecution had contended throughout its case that the city of Chicago could not give permits for a Chicago park, that it had to be done by the Park District.

Davis was unbelievably unabashed when he said to Judge Hoffman in a dulcet tone, "Originally you were to hear our case for permits and we might not have had this trial if we had been before you. You might have granted the permits."

*"Well,"* Judge Hoffman said, surprised and pleased, brimming with the ingratiating respect given him by Davis, "isn't that—that is one of the first nice things that anyone has said. I can't assure you that you are right or would have been right." The judge added that he had not known that he was scheduled to hear the permit case because he went on vacation and Judge Lynch heard it on August 22, 1968.

Not long afterward Kunstler requested that the judge admonish Foran for muttering over the lectern to the jury about Davis's testimony. Judge Hoffman, perhaps because of the feeling that welled up from Davis's "nice" remark, astonished everyone by admonishing Foran for muttering to the jury. Foran stayed hunched during the judge's admonition.

Davis had testified about most of the meetings and conversations that figured in the testimony of Bock, Frapolly, Oklepek and other agents. Foran accused Davis of having made his testimony similar to the agents' testimony but differing in small important essentials. "That's not true and you know it," Davis said.

"Isn't it a fact," Foran said, "that you wanted violence in order to impose an international humiliation on the people who ruled this country? Isn't that a fact?"

"It is my belief," Davis said, "that it was you wanted the violence, Mr. Foran, not me."

Davis took Foran by surprise when he said, "I hope after this trial you can properly respond, Mr. Foran. I really do. I hope we have that chance."

Foran said, as if aside to the judge, "I don't know what he is—what are you—?"

"That you and I can sit down and talk about what happened in Chicago and why it happened."

"Mr. Witness," the judge cautioned.

"I would like to do that very much." Davis said.

Foran read from a speech that Davis gave exactly a year after Convention Week, on August 28, 1969, in which Davis called for the whole country to mutiny the way Company A had mutinied in Viet Nam. Specifically he called for young people "to become a part of a growing force for insurrection in the United States."

For a majority of the jurors this speech, as revealed in posttrial interviews, was the most important item in convicting Rennie Davis and, by association, other defendants.

"I was standing right beside Fred Hampton when I said that," Davis said. Davis and Kunstler, in the colloquy that followed, got information of the Hampton murder to the jury.

The defense lawyers were depressed and incensed that the government would use, and the judge permit, as evidence of "intent," speeches given a year after the alleged crime.

But the defendants felt so good about Davis's testimony in general that they discussed briefly the possibility of each defendant taking the stand.

## Moments of Truth in the Presence of Evil

Norman Mailer absolutely magnetized the courtroom, drawing laughs and responses from both audiences. He came briskly down the aisle poised high on the balls of his feet. He was wearing a very white shirt over a noble belly, and suit and tie. Everyone's excitement rose with the risks that he took in answering every question.

When he recited his works from *The Naked and the Dead* to the new book on the astronauts and the shot that put footprints on the moon, it was as if someone had declared that the last twenty-five years had been real and were now gone. Strangely, he neglected to mention his book, *Why Are We in Viet Nam?*

"I met Abbie Hoffman at Provincetown Airport when I refused to see him at my home," Mailer said. Abbie Hoffman laughed. So did Richard Schultz. So did everybody. Mailer glanced about, warily pleased. There were a couple of times when Richard Schultz was hardly able to overcome his laughter sufficiently to state his objection. "We don't need a story for every answer," he said. He would soon use the cover of his apparent admiration for Mailer to make some important connections in the government's case. "You're too high-priced a writer to waste a story on every answer," Judge Hoffman said.

"I don't want to take up the court's time," Mailer said.

"Please don't, please don't," Judge Hoffman said.

Schultz objected that Mailer was giving a personal impression of Jerry Rubin instead of reporting a conversation. The question was repeated. Then Mailer, to satisfy and satirize the rules of evidence, testified, "I said, 'Mr. Rubin, it is a pleasure to talk to a man who is so objective and has such a command . . .' " The courtroom went up in laughter. Schultz laughed again, and objected again. "Is he beginning at the end of the conversation?" Schultz said. More laughter. "This witness cannot testify," Schultz said, "about what Mr. Rubin said about Mr. Dellinger's intents at the Pentagon."

*"Wow,"* Mailer reported himself as saying when Jerry Rubin projected plans for Chicago and the Democratic convention, in which a Youth Festival and the presence of one hundred thousand young people "would cause the establishment to do all the violence in Chicago." "Secret guilt" would cause the establishment to crack up in the face of the Youth Festival and smash the city.

Chagrin hit the courtroom, as if the audience were watching a racing car that after a couple of breathtaking turns of the track was suddenly plunging over an embankment. The prosecutors stayed cool at their table. It was hard to see how Kunstler was reacting to his witness. "That was a foolish remark of Mailer's," Jean Fritz said, after the trial, "but not really so important." But the prosecution would lean upon Mailer's testimony in their summations. The listening in the courtroom to this most ambiguous and revealing moment was solemn and intense.

Informed by the judge about the requirements of the "rules of evidence," of testifying to what he perceived with his senses, he responded with a poignant authority that he had spent most of his life on the problems of perception and the nuances of expressing perception. "Facts without their nuance are nothing, sir," he said to Richard Schultz.

Mailer seemed to report himself saying in his speech in Grant Park on Wednesday, "Chicago was run by a man who began as a giant and ended as a beast." FBI Agent Stanley, nonplussed, whispered to Schultz. Schultz rose quickly and ob-

jected, saying that Mailer's remark was made on Thursday
night of Convention Week, not on Wednesday. "Yes," Mailer
said calmly, "that's what I was trying to tell you." Agent Stanley's research was occasionally impressive in its detail.

Both Kunstler and Schultz went laughingly and admiringly
to the witness stand to reassure Mailer during a recess.
Mailer's strong presence was catalytic of good feeling, of ami-
able regard and exchange, among the many parties of the case
in the courtroom and in the hallways.

Then Mailer testified to what he saw of the Balbo-Michigan
"massacre" from his nineteenth floor Hilton Hotel window.
Intensely involved in "seeing" in his mind, in his voice and
with the use of his hands and body, he described the police
attacking the mass of demonstrators at Michigan and Balbo,
cutting groups "mathematically" into two parts, then four
parts, then eight parts and beating them "systematically."
Agent Stanley, the coolest man at the prosecution table,
looked with dropped-jaw astonishment at Foran and Schultz,
as if to say that that did not agree with his research at all.

In cross-examination, Schultz lost no time in going for the
nerve of Mailer's testimony about Rubin. "Did he say that the
presence of one hundred thousand young people would pro-
voke the Establishment to violence? To smash the city?"

"Yes, he said that," Mailer said solemnly, as if he realized
the import of it, "because the Establishment was so full of guilt
that they would act like guilty people." Again there was a per-
fection of listening, a sense of danger, in the audience. It was
always that way when a truth was spoken in this courtroom.
The truth always cut an opening for the thrust of both parties.
Schultz proceeded to use the catalytic potential of Norman
Mailer's presence and testimony to put the prosecution's fabu-
lous case together.

Schultz, showing an occasional lightness of hand, asked
Mailer about a speech that Mailer made during Convention
Week to demonstrators in Grant Park. "Did you tell them,

'You're much, much better than you were at the Pentagon'?"
Agent Stanley's research was fascinating in its detail, and dis-
combobulating in its interpretation. This came right after
Foran's cross-examination of Rennie Davis about the Pentagon, and there was nothing, in honesty, that Mailer could do.
"Yes—they were better looking," he said. Both audiences,
both sides, laughed, and Mailer smiled big. But the prosecutors
were laughing because Schultz had used Mailer to make an
important connection between Chicago and the Pentagon for
the government's case, while the defendants were laughing,
out of an odd pain, because they were flattered by Mailer's
wit and because they realized what Schultz had gained.

Schultz queried Mailer again on his testimony that Rubin
had said that one hundred thousand young people in Chicago
would so "intimidate" the establishment that they would, because of their secret guilt, smash the city.

Mailer started out winning with the spirit of the courtroom
when he undertook to explain that he, Norman Mailer, would
use such a word as "intimidate" because he was a bully, but
he didn't think Jerry Rubin would think that way or use such
a word. Mailer began plucking phrases out of the air. He entertained the many ways in which Jerry Rubin might say something, each wittier than the last, and Mailer obviously began
to enjoy himself. Then he said of Rubin, "He thinks of people
becoming aroused. Their very innocent presence would,"
Mailer paused for the funniest phrase, *drive them out of their
bird.*" The courtroom burst out in laughter. But when Mailer
said the word "aroused," somebody in the back row of the
press section said, "There goes the ball game."

Richard Schultz folded up his papers and walked, at ease
and cool, back to the prosecution table. He capped his pen
and exchanged a glance with Foran. Mailer took an electric
intensity of listening out of the courtroom.

In the hallway, Jerry Rubin, with his arm about Mailer's
waist, thanked him. In a press conference in Room 204A on

the second floor of the Federal Building, Mailer spoke of this generation of kids "surrounding the fortress and making faces at the people inside and letting them have nervous breakdowns." Conspiracy staff women were flattered. Mailer was slumping a little, perhaps losing spirit.

I was dwelling on an idea that moments of truth were most useful to evil. I was also seeing that the danger of artistic truth and artistic "lies" that cut both ways was why art and artists were high on the annihilation lists of totalitarian governments.

## Seale Returns

On January 29, 1970, Bobby Seale returned to the trial as a witness called by the defense. Just prior to the examination, the judge looked down to see Charles Garry, Seale's attorney, standing at the lectern. Garry was thus affirming his position as a lawyer of record in the case for Bobby Seale. Only after a certain amount of discussion, in which Garry showed that it was at least momentarily possible to be quite firm with Judge Hoffman without being deliberately provocative, did he move away from the lectern and sit at the defense table. The judge hardly needed more than an intimation or a tone of provocation, so Garry's attitude was all the more remarkable. There was laughter when the judge asked for the witness's name.

The defense played a tape of Bobby Seale's speech in Lincoln Park on Tuesday evening, August 27, 1968, for the jury, and passed out copies of a transcript of the tape. The tape had been given to the defense by the prosecution and was apparently the same as the tape that the defense had secured from a radio station in California but which the government would not accept because no qualifying witness could be produced for it.

In the speech Seale was addressing black people in general rather than the mostly young white people who were congregated in Lincoln Park during most of Convention Week. There were black people who came to Lincoln Park especially to hear him, though they were not present for the confrontations later that night. There were passages that could be construed as being inflaming of emotion in the situation in Lincoln Park. The passages concerning guns and self-defense were directed toward black people, and no wording of the speech was directed toward immediate incitement of the people in the park.

Seale, according to the tape that was played and the transcript of it, said in Lincoln Park, "But if a pig comes up to us and starts swinging a billy club, and you check around and you got your piece—you gotta down that pig in defense of yourself. . . . Wait a minute . . . You gonna take that club, whip him over his head, lay him out on the ground and then this pig is acting in a desired manner."

In cross-examination, Assistant Prosecutor Schultz asked Seale what he meant by the phrase "acting in a desired manner." Seale tried to explain it in a behavioral sense, in the sense of acting in a just and respectful manner.

But Schultz asked, "Now you said in your speech that was just played before the jury that Huey P. Newton was busted and charged with making a couple of pigs act in a desired manner, did you not, sir?"

Seale said, with an attempt at a broad air, "I am a comedian. . . . Actually, the man was charged with shooting a policeman."

"And he was charged then in your language the way you said it here," Schultz said, " 'with making a couple of pigs act in a desired manner.' Right?"

"Yes," Seale said.

"So when you said that 'individuals should make pigs act in a desired manner' you were referring to shooting policemen in defense, if necessary, isn't that right?"

The defense objected, and Schultz chose to rephrase the question several times, and the implications for the jury mounted with each rephrasing. Seale could only answer Yes or No and so he was at the mercy of the implications.

Schultz let Seale explain at length to the jury Black Panther revolutionary tactics. Seale spoke against "spontaneous mass riots" and for political actions, petitioning, and working in small groups. It was true that Tuesday night in Lincoln Park the young people did act in small groups in the streets, effectively reinforcing and extending the experience of previous nights.

Then Schultz asked, "Now when you told the people in Lincoln Park that they should spread out everywhere and stop running in large groups, you were referring to that revolutionary tactic you have just described to the jury, is that right?"

"Yes," Seale said.

But in the transcript of the speech he appears to be addressing black people in general, not the young people in Lincoln Park at that time.

"When you told the people to get the .357 Magnums, the .45s, the M-1 rifles, you were referring to the revolutionary tactic that you have just described to the jury?"

"I was referring to another because I said—"

Schultz welded one powerful, out-of-context connection to another, one after another, until he had made a bridge on which he could walk from the wording of the indictment to the evidence as presented, to infer intent.

Schultz moved to the speech that Seale made at noon of Wednesday, August 28, 1968, in Grant Park. He purportedly quoted Seale: " 'If the police get in the way of our march, tangle with the blue-helmeted motherfuckers and kill them and send them to the morgue slab.' . . . And you were pointing to policemen at that time, isn't that a fact?"

There was colloquy, consternation, and discussion between Seale and Garry. Then Seale, on the advice of Garry, took the Fifth Amendment and its protections rather than answer the question and possibly incriminate himself. The examination ended.

It was not cross-examination. It was disembowelment.

Many months before, in his opening statement to the jury on September 26, 1969, Schultz tied together phrases from different contexts to make what he passed off as a direct quote from Seale's speech in Lincoln Park. " 'If a pig comes up to us unjustly,' he [Seale] said, 'if he comes up to us unjustly, we should bring out our pieces and start barbecuing that pork, and if they get in our way, we should kill some of those pigs and put them on a morgue slab.' "

In October, Schultz explained to the judge Seale's statements to the Panthers in the spectator section, with three controversions of the way Seale used the word "attack," and so contributed tremendously to the dynamic process that led to the binding and gagging of Seale.

Any answer to why the defense called Seale to testify only reinforced the question. As Leonard Weinglass said to me in the Men's Room in the twenty-third floor of the Federal Building the next day, "Oh, I would say we got nicked yesterday."

## Slipping Toward the End of the Trial

Judge Hoffman's slips of the tongue, his slips of ruling, and his slips of mind showed what a terrifying judge he might have been to all practitioners of untruth.

The defense simply could not equal the prosecution and the judge for slips of the tongue.

Judge Hoffman permitted a voir dire examination of Ramsey Clark, out of the presence of the jury, after heated argument between the two sides about whether the former attorney general could testify for the defense. "Mr. Marshal," he said, "will you bring in the jury?"

"Your honor," Richard Schultz was seized with an agony that the man who had been attorney general of the United States during the time of the Democratic convention would be heard by the jury.

"What did you say?" Judge Hoffman said. "Oh, that's right."
"You meant the witness," Schultz said.

"I am so used to saying, 'Bring in the jury,' " the judge tried
to chuckle the slip away, "and I don't have to. Will you call
your witness?"

If the content of Judge Hoffman's slip had prevailed, the
jury might have heard Ramsey Clark's opinion of Mayor
Daley's "shoot-to-kill" order, of government planning for the
Democratic National Convention, of positive reports on National Mobilization from Department of Justice personnel in
Chicago in August, 1968, of FBI wiretap requests concerning
the defendants, and of Clark's opposition to the Grand Jury
investigation that resulted in the indictments brought against
these defendants. The jurors would also have come to understand that Clark, who personally requested the indictments
against Dr. Spock and his co-defendants in their conspiracy-
to-aid-draft-resisters case in Boston, considered that the antiriot statutes, under which these seven defendants were
indicted, could not be constitutionally applied because of the
protections of the First Amendment.

Judge Hoffman's slip concerning Ramsey Clark echoed in
his slip on the morning of his exclusion of Ralph Abernathy
too—a restful morning. Attorneys from the office of Cook
County State's Attorney Edward Hanrahan—his police conducted the raid in which Fred Hampton and Mark Clark were
murdered on December 4, 1969—sought a motion to quash
defense subpoenas for certain documents in their offices.

The judge also heard an urgent request from Kunstler for
the resting of the defense's case to be delayed because SCLC
leader Ralph Abernathy was on his way from O'Hare airport.
Few noticed that the judge denied Kunstler's request until, "I
am trembling because of this outrage," Kunstler said, at the
lectern. "When an Attorney General of the United States
walked out of here with his lips so tight that he could hardly
breathe . . . His wife said that . . . You can put me in jail," he

declared to Judge Hoffman, "I don't care . . . No American court has ever done what you have done. I know this is not a fair trial . . . I know it in my heart . . . You are doing a disservice to the law to say that Ralph Abernathy cannot testify . . . That everything I have learned in my life has come to naught . . . If because of the technicality of my representation to your honor on Friday [that the defense would rest its case], and my not knowing until Saturday that Ralph Abernathy would be in the country . . ." Spectators shouted, "Right on! Right on!" and marshals plucked them out of their seats and moved them out of the courtroom, one, two, three. Reporters pounded out into the hallways to phone the incident to their media. Kunstler refused to rest the defense's case.

In the peculiar atmosphere, with a particularly calm enunciation, Judge Hoffman said, "Motion to quash subpoena will be denied." The courtroom stirred with the usual hope that the game was changing. A lawyer for the State's Attorney's Office, perhaps with a floating sensation in his stomach, came forward hesitantly to ask for a "clarification" of ruling. Judge Hoffman stammered and corrected himself. His slip was caused by his reaction to Kunstler's direct accusatory response to the exclusion of Abernathy.

Kunstler, as if unburdened, told the judge that if he wanted the case rested, he would have to do it. "If Dr. Abernathy is here," Richard Schultz said, "let him go on the stand." Judge Hoffman was not one to shy away from a collision course for sweet reason's sake. "Let the record show," the judge said, "that the defendants will not proceed, have, in effect, rested." The judge, at the request of the prosecution, ordered Kunstler not to mention Dr. Abernathy in front of the jury. Kunstler assured the judge that he would not abide by the order.

A noise and a shuffle started up in the hallway outside during the rebuttal testimony of Deputy Chief Lynskey. Through the courtroom doors edged a black man with an enormously wrinkled face, looking down at a piece of white paper in his hands. He had shared the motel room with Martin Luther King, Jr., in Memphis, Tennessee, when King, out on the balcony, was hit by a bullet. He had held King's head in his lap trying to stanch the blood with towels. Abernathy, succeeding King in the Southern Christian Leadership Conference, drove the lead wagon in the Poor People's mule train behind which the demonstrators marched to Michigan and Balbo. The defense wanted him to testify against the government's contention that the blacks on the wagons were afraid of the demonstrators—that in fact the blacks were afraid of police violence.

Kunstler came happily to greet him in the middle of the aisle, and told him that he could not testify. Most of the jurors were watching Kunstler and Abernathy rather than witness Lynskey. I registered the distressing suggestion that Kunstler should have asked Abernathy to stay instead of leave. Lynskey was still testifying. Kunstler gave Abernathy a big hug, and was admonished almost hysterically by the judge. There were two black women on the jury.

Just after Abernathy left the courtroom, Richard Schultz said, in front of the jury, that Abernathy might have been able to testify after Lynskey. Kunstler responded that he would go get him. Judge Hoffman denied it.

In the afternoon, possibly at the suggestion of Foran, Judge Hoffman said that because Kunstler's embrace of Dr. Abernathy "may have so prejudiced one or two members of the jury," Abernathy would be permitted to testify the next day. But Ralph Abernathy was already flying to the South, and he could not return.

Chicago *Tribune* Reporter O'Brien declared that he saw a rain of bottles thrown by young demonstrators at the corner of LaSalle and Eugenie on Monday night, August 26, 1968. He said he had to duck into a car, and bottles were hitting the roof. This rebutted the defense testimony of Albert Stuart

Braverman, a U. S. army doctor, who said he saw nothing thrown by demonstrators at that corner. I was at that corner that night, too, where one red-faced cop pointed his pistol at me and another gave me a rap on the back of the head with his club. A stifling amount of tear gas drifted from the heavy gassing in the park, burning the eyes, nose, throat, and twisting the bronchials. There was no mistaking the raging energy of the cops or the daring of the demonstrators. Bottles, firecrackers, and other objects were thrown by the demonstrators.

But Dr. Braverman's testimony was otherwise so accurate, and Reporter O'Brien's testimony of the one truncated moment was also accurate, if exaggerated, that to compare the two gave an insight into the way that fact and bias mix, even unconsciously, to provide testimony for each side. The worst implication was that the Conspiracy trial had reduced itself to the absurdity, the supposed letter of one part of classic riot law, of who threw, and who apparently intended to be thrown, objects at any moment during five days in August, 1968.

Slipping of the tongue flickered all around O'Brien's testimony. "Go ahead with the cross-examination," Judge Hoffman said to Kunstler. Kunstler said, uncertainly, as if a Star Chamber proceeding would not surprise him, "Can we bring in the jury?"

The judge was only slightly startled. "You want to bring in the jury? Yes. Bring in the jury."

O'Brien smiled slightly when the defendants oinked at him on his way out between the prosecution and defense tables. But Schultz jumped up indignantly. "Your honor, would you instruct the witnesses please not to—I mean the defendants not to oink at our witnesses as they enter or exit the courtroom? . . . I don't think that it is fair to Mr. O'Brien," continued Schultz intensely, "for example, to have to walk by the witnesses and be oinked at," Schultz jerked to correct himself again, "by the defendants as he leaves the courtroom. I think that it is just—it is just not treating him as a human being should be treated."

Judge Hoffman joined in the contagious slipping. "I would request of the witnesses not to do that." He did not notice his slip. The judge and the prosecutors apparently considered the defendants to be moral observers.

Weinglass, after standing at the lectern hesitantly, said that the testimony of a long-haired Baltimore, Maryland, police cadet about a speech by Abbie Hoffman given more than a year after the alleged crime was "so wholly improper" to show the state of mind and intentions of a defendant crossing state lines before Convention Week that he refused to dignify it with a cross-examination.

According to government testimony, Jerry Rubin flipped lighted cigarettes at cops who were surrounded by young people near the field house in Lincoln Park on Sunday night, August 25, 1968. Kunstler and Weinglass questioned Commander Clarence Braasch of the 18th District about his testimony to the Walker Report commission. He astonished the audience by agreeing that he had said that he came up to the sergeant in charge of the encircled cops and said, "What's the problem?"

The sergeant gestured at the cops surrounded by an excited crowd in the dark. "Well, this is it."

"Then there is no problem," Braasch said. "You can march your men out of here." Another group of police came up to Commander Braasch. "Did you not say to the new group," Weinglass said, " 'There is no problem. Break off contact, get out of here'? And that was it?"

"Yes," Commander Braasch said.

Weinglass then asked, "Was Abbie Hoffman courteous with you?"

"Yes, he was," Braasch said.

Braasch was remembered in the Lincoln Park area as a cool, game-playing professional during Convention Week. He did not look to either side at prosecution or defense as he marched out with his commander's hat under his arm. Braasch was hit by a corruption investigation not long after the conspiracy trial.

A truth had been spoken again, and once again the problem for both sides was what to do with it, how to convert it or controvert it.

Dave Murray, a white-haired Chicago *Tribune* reporter, appeared on the stand to rebut defense testimony that no objects were thrown in front of the Hilton Tuesday night, August 27, 1968. The prosecution witnesses always saw showers of objects in the magnitude of flights of arrows darkening the moon. The defense's witnesses usually saw no objects thrown at all. I remembered that night, and remarked on the extended naivete of the defense.

Murray said that a whiffle ball, nails driven through it, bounced on Michigan Avenue and hit him in the leg. Reporters, spectators, jurors, marshals were being tugged down toward drowsy depths during his testimony. "By the way, Foran said to Murray, "throughout all this time was traffic moving?"

"No," Murray said, with righteousness, "traffic was not moving." Interstate commerce was being interrupted. "Looking toward that scene," Foran said, "what did you see, if anything?"

"Looking toward that scene," Murray said, closing his eyes, "I saw a police officer fall."

"Did you go over to that scene?"

"I sure did, sir."

Murray described the policeman, hit by a reinforced piece of concrete. A muffled cheer came from some part of the courtroom, and the judge looked up at it.

"The two bags that landed close to me . . . had . . . uh . . . had . . . human *body* disposal."

"You mean," Foran said, "defecation? Human excrement?"

"Yes."

The audience for the defense laughed.

Murray had used binoculars to help the police locate the hotel windows from which objects were being thrown. From the fifteenth floor, he testified, from the headquarters of the anti-war McCarthy campaign, from the rooms and the hearts of liberal young people, came those bags full of . . . uh . . . uh . . .

But seated in the front row of the courtroom was a black artist, with drawing board in his lap, sketching courtroom scenes for TV. He had been a reporter during Convention Week, and it was reporters he'd seen throwing things out of the fifteenth floor windows at the police below, perhaps in vengeance for all the reporters beaten in Lincoln Park, perhaps to create news, perhaps for the hell of it. He could not testify because he had been present in the courtroom.

In cross-examination by Kunstler, Murray described a Viet Cong flag as a "black flag," to hoots of derision and delighted laughter. "Not all black," Murray said, cautiously. More laughter.

Foran, on redirect examination, asked Murray to describe the Viet Cong flag. "Red, not all red, with a symbol in it," he said. Foran went so far as to try to describe the VC flag for Murray, and the defendants hooted at him and at his description. "Ladies and gentlemen of the jury," the judge said, "perhaps a recess will cure this trouble."

"He'll find out in the recess what a Viet Cong flag is," Jerry Rubin said across the aisle, within the hearing of the jurors.

Yes, after the recess, Murray was able to describe the flag. He explained that a policeman pointed it out for him on Monday night of Convention Week. "That's hearsay," Kunstler objected. Judge Hoffman irritatedly overruled his objection.

Murray closed his eyes often before answering a question, as if struggling to see the original event. He had testified that five thousand people were throwing objects at police that Tuesday night. Weinglass produced the FBI report in which Murray said five hundred were throwing objects, and five thousand were present. Now, in cross-examination, Murray again reversed himself, back to five hundred throwing objects.

Weinglass said, "Have you seen ten people throwing things?"

"Yes, sir."

"And this was fifty times as much?"

"Yes, sir."

Murray sounded silly to many observers. Weinglass showed Murray other inconsistencies between his FBI report and his current testimony.

"I think the question was not responsive," Foran objected with an odd slip of the tongue. The judge corrected him.

"Mr. Murray," Kunstler said. "I would like to see your scar; may I?" Judge Hoffman was furiously trying to admonish and stop Kunstler, but Murray was pulling up his pants leg to show his scar. In the jury, Kay Richards was laughing and Jean Fritz was laughing behind a handkerchief. Shirley Seaholm was ducking her head and smiling. Frieda Robbins was smiling. Judge Hoffman concluded dryly that the harm was done and he directed Murray to show his scar to the jury. Many jurors were amused.

"There is perjury here," Kunstler said, in Perry Mason style, about Murray's testimony. "I'll stand on the transcript."

"I direct the jury," Judge Hoffman shrieked, "to disregard that statement as very, *very* improper."

Jerry Rubin stood up, as Murray passed, to shake his hand. There was no stopping the laughter. Abbie Hoffman pulled out a five- or ten-dollar bill and thrust it toward Murray. Richard Schultz screamed, throwing his arms up in the air in his habitual gesture, "These men who protest they have such love and compassion for mankind . . .

The courtroom was left in a quiet stammer.

Judge Hoffman soon tried to address Kunstler.

"Mr. . . . uh . . . uh . . ."

"Kunstler, your honor."

\* \* \*

The defense had wished to use the October, 1967, Pentagon affair as an example of a reasonably peaceful mass demonstration by the National Mobilization that was revealing of their "intentions" in Chicago. Kunstler was cross-examining young, thin, sharp-featured, cool FBI agent Joe Mahoney on his testimony about violent actions and intentions at the Pentagon demonstrations, when Judge Hoffman suddenly said, "Sustain the objection," for no apparent reason.

Kunstler looked up, bemused. "I didn't hear an objection, your honor."

"Uh . . . uh . . . uh . . ." The judge rocked back and forth.

Foran rose and nodded. "It's an objectionable question."

Deputy Chief James D. Riordan testified that Dellinger led a group with flags away from the disintegrating march in Grant Park toward the Illinois Central bridge, headed for Michigan Avenue. "Oh, bullshit," Dellinger said, in a quiet voice.

"Did you get that, Miss Reporter?" the judge said.

"Oh, that's an absolute lie," Dellinger said.

"Get that," the judge said to the court reporter.

"Let's argue about what I stand for and what you stand for," Dellinger said to Riordan, "but let's not make up things like that."

"Right on," a spectator yelled and was arrested on Judge Hoffman's order.

"We had to sit here," Richard Schultz said intensely, "with our lips tight while Hayden and Hoffman perjured themselves on that stand." When defendants and reporters laughed at his slip, "*Davis* and Hoffman," he corrected himself. The defense lawyers demanded that Schultz apologize. If he was referring to out-of-court evidence he should say so. Schultz apologized and said that he was not referring to out-of-court evidence.

In the confusion, Rennie Davis stood deliberately and aggravatingly close to Richard Schultz. Schultz asked the judge to order Davis to move away.

That afternoon Judge Hoffman, in his wisdom, sent the jury away until ten the next morning. Then he revoked Dellinger's bail, supposedly to maintain order in the courtroom. The defense lawyers contended that the judge actually revoked Dellinger's bail for a recent speech highly critical of the judge given by Dellinger at Marquette University in Milwaukee. Judge Hoffman had previously referred to that speech with a warning implication. "Your honor," Kunstler said, "is there not going to be any argument on this?"

"No argument," the judge said.

The action that was meant to maintain order caused incredible protest in the courtroom. Marshals were expelling people, and people were resisting. "Hitler," "Fascist," and "Prick" were shouted from all sides.

"This court is bullshit," Davis said.

"There," Judge Hoffman said, "he is saying the same words again."

"No," Davis said, "I say it."

"That was the defendant Davis," Richard Schultz said.

"Everything in this court is bullshit," Rubin said. "Why don't you put us all in jail?"

"Your honor," Schultz said, "I ask that you not do them that favor."

"You can't stand there and insult the United States District Court," Judge Hoffman said.

"I am not insulting you," Kunstler said.

"Yes, you are."

"Everything in this case is an insult," Kunstler said.

"This case is recessed," the judge said. "Bring in that young man," meaning the one taken into custody earlier.

Throughout the disorder David Dellinger sat with an appearance of release, of peace. It was marvelous to believe that all of this resulted from the use of the word "bullshit" once and once only and quietly. But by nightfall, just to prove that the trial was about speech and First Amendment protections, the news media of the nation convened editorial conferences from coast-to-coast to determine whether to treat explicitly, or euphemistically, what both the *New York Times* and Judge Hoffman called "a barnyard epithet."

That night Jerry Rubin and Abbie Hoffman argued that all the defendants should disrupt the trial so that Judge Hoffman would revoke their bail and put all of them in jail, giving thereby a correct and powerful image and "myth" to cause people to organize and free Dellinger. The other defendants felt that such actions might discredit the court's authority but could in no way affect its actual power and the defendants might lose important support in some sectors of American society.

Rubin and Hoffman decided to dash themselves against the appearance of the court anyway. The next day Kunstler argued that the only legal basis on which Judge Hoffman could possibly revoke Dellinger's bail was to prevent "flight from the court's jurisdiction." He let himself be forced by the marshals on the judge's orders to sit down.

"Julius Hoffman is equal to Adolf Hitler today," Jerry Rubin shouted.

"You're trying to put us away on contempt," Abbie Hoffman said, "because you can't do it in a jury trial. You know it's a hung jury."

"You're the laughing stock of the world," Jerry Rubin said. "Every kid in the country hates you."

Rubin and Hoffman repeated the remark about the "hung jury" several times.

Barbara Lawyer, a cocktail waitress, one of two or three "ordinary" citizens who appeared as witnesses for the government, listened with a smile. She was testifying to the manner and kind of hippies who plunged through the broken Haymarket Lounge window in the Hilton Hotel on Wednesday night,

August 28, 1968. The window was broken by the pressure of the crowd reacting to the police attacks.

The jury was marched out. The other defendants and the defense lawyers, who did not agree with the two Yippies, listened as spectators too. There were only two voices in the courtroom.

"The judges in Nazi Germany," Jerry Rubin declared, "ordered sterilization of defendants. Why don't you do that, Judge Hoffman?"

Abbie Hoffman was slumped in his chair, as if situated there positively forever, with his hands in his lap. "You'll have to cut out our tongues," he cried, without moving a finger. "We should have done it, then, with Bobby Seale. It's the shame of this country that this building wasn't ripped down when that happened."

The judge remonstrated several times with Abbie Hoffman and Jerry Rubin. Then, possibly advised by Foran and Schultz, he just sat behind his bench and made no response for the first time since the beginning of the trial. No other emotion was expressed or aroused in the courtroom, as if there were no way for anyone even to feel anything if the judge did not react. The strange silence began to fill up every crease and corner. A marshal, on his own, without orders, said brutally, "Shut up," to Abbie Hoffman.

"I will not shut up," Abbie Hoffman said. "I'm not an automaton such as you are." The judge still said nothing. The sound of tears, the feeling of impotence, welled up in Abbie Hoffman's voice.

"Shanda fur de goyim," Abbie Hoffman shot at Judge Hoffman. Shame before the goyim, front man for the Protestant elite. He was hoping to hit Judge Hoffman's sensitivity about his Jewish background. "How many blacks own stock in the Brunswick Corporation? How many blacks in the Standard Club?" These "contumacious" questions haunted mainstream politics in coming years.

Judge Hoffman called a recess.

Jerry Rubin shouted, "Tyrant!"

Judge Hoffman noted Rubin's name for the record, coolly.

The Yippies started wearing black robes the next day. "These are judge's robes," Jerry Rubin said.

The Court of Appeals refused to vacate Judge Hoffman's order revoking Dellinger's bail. Leonard Weinglass explained dismally, without being protective of the two Yippies, that the Court of Appeals felt that their rebuke, if they vacated Judge Hoffman's order, would only add to "the public furor created by Abbie and Jerry." The Court of Appeals thereby protected its man in the field. Judge Hoffman, on his assurance that the revocation was necessary to preserve order in the courtroom.

"Jesus, Abbie, these robes are hot," Jerry Rubin said, pulling at the neck of his robe, outside the Court of Appeals.

Much of the government's rebuttal appeared to be aimed at the defense's wondrously prevailing innocence about objects having been thrown during Convention Week, about fenders dented, about cops wounded or knocked to the ground. The letter of the law was such that even a single rock thrown from a group of three persons or more could be considered a riot, if the rock dented a fender or bloodied a head. The most daring approach that the defense could have undertaken would have been to try to put Convention Week into evidence detail by detail, day by day, as a way of proving that the defendants were without intention of inciting these actions. That would not have solved all of their problems with the antiriot statutes, but it would have left their testimony less vulnerable, and would probably have strengthened their argument that the defendants' speeches were protected, in any case, by the first amendment.

For instance, a Chicago policeman, Officer Layden, testified that demonstrators threw bricks at his squad car on LaSalle Street south of Lincoln Park. "Did you take a lie detector test?" Kunstler asked, in what certainly seemed to be either flippant or desperate cross-examination.

Schultz jumped up for redirect examination. "Were you asked to take a lie detector test?"

"No, sir."

"Would you have taken it if asked?"

"Yes, sir."

Both sides became intensely concerned literally with who threw the first stone in Layden's testimony. There was direct, cross, re-direct, re-cross, re-re-direct, re-re-cross, re-re-re-direct, and re-re-re-cross, as defense and prosecution vied for the last positive effect on the jury.

Kay Richards, in a bright yellow blouse, slumped with her head on the back of her chair. She did not give undercover agent Irwin Bock a single fair glance when he returned to the witness stand. Jean Fritz looked down at her feet. Most of the jurors would not look at Bock. But Miriam Hill, "Mrs. Wallace," who seldom looked at a defense witness and even folded her arms and looked haughtily away from them, did look at Bock, her man on the stand. A couple of other jurors who would be convict-on-all-counts jurors looked at Bock, too.

Sydney White, a young man in training as a Navy equipment operator and going to Viet Nam, was the prosecution's display of loyal young America for its last witness. He testified that on August 28, 1968, while he was walking south on Michigan Avenue with some friends, he saw a young man come running and fall down as if hurt onto the sidewalk. Photographers took pictures and then the young man jumped up and ran away. "I could not see any apparent injuries," White said.

When White drew his map of Michigan and Balbo, Foran spoke directly to Jean Fritz (he was supposed to regard her as the "rock" of the holdouts for acquittal): "Can you see that?" he said. She shook a little to have Foran speaking to her. "Yes, sir," she said.

Kunstler asked White about the chants of the demonstrators at Michigan and Balbo, "How come you remember only the derogatory chants?" such as Fuck LBJ.

The defendants' women were lined up in the front row behind the table for the defense. There was Susan Schultz for Rennie Davis, the blond young woman at whom Tom Hayden stared lengthily, Sharon Avery for Lee Weiner, Nancy Kurshan for Jerry Rubin, Anita Hoffman for Abbie Hoffman, Ann Froines for John Froines, and Betty Dellinger and daughters.

While young Sydney White testified, Susan Schultz sat in the front row behind the defense table with her little son crawling eagerly in her lap. Some of the women in the jury looked at Susan with sympathetic interest, almost with tears in their eyes, and a few looked away as if to say that they would not be duped. Susan pointed, for the boy to see, at the Stop-the-Trial button with Judge Hoffman's face on it, on her sweater. Then she pointed at Judge Hoffman up on the bench. The judge himself moved his head quickly to the side to look around Kunstler at the little boy, with an expression of affectionate interest, which he squelched as soon as he saw it was Susan Schultz. "I wanta go back in," the little boy protested as she took him out, because he was crawling under the benches. Several jurors were watching.

"Did you ever," Weinglass questioned Sydney White, "attend a demonstration against the war in Viet Nam?"

"No."

"Did you ever attend a demonstration against racism at home?"

"No."

Judge Hoffman tried to bargain the defense into resting and forgetting about Dr. Ralph Abernathy. The first appearance of the bargaining tone in Judge Hoffman's voice caused groans and laughter in the courtroom. The judge, really red with fury, denied the defense motion and took back his offer.

On Monday morning William Kunstler attempted to rest the defense's case subject to a sort of unsuccessful protest at the exclusion of Abernathy's testimony.

# PART SIX
*The Struggle for the Soul of the Nation*

*Like the Last People on the Face of the Earth*

"WHEN I WAS ON JURY DUTY," said Shirley Seaholm, "it was the first time I was afraid of our government." She was sitting in the living room of the home of sister juror Jean Fritz, on a green and pleasant street in the Chicago suburb of Des Plaines. It was now two and a half months after the trial. Now they themselves were going to give testimony that would expose important questions about the trial.

This was the first interview—the first of three given to this writer—that these two jurors had granted to anyone who might publish what they said. For this writer, who had been present in Judge Hoffman's courtroom from the beginning to the end of the trial, the interview was bringing at long last a sense of reality to the public knowledge of what happened in the Conspiracy jury. I had felt no clarity about the jury since February 18, 1970, when the jurors found Dave Dellinger, Rennie Davis, Tom Hayden, Jerry Rubin, and Abbie Hoffman guilty of crossing state lines with the intent to incite people to riot during the 1968 Democratic convention, but innocent of the conspiracy count to do the same. John Froines and Lee Weiner were found innocent on all counts.

I had been certain that the jury was a hung jury, by the way they laughed, smiled, and expressed themselves throughout the trial. Now I was told that four of the women on the jury believed, and still believed, that the seven defendants were innocent on all counts, and five of the jurors believed, and still believed, that all of the defendants including Froines and Weiner were guilty on all counts. Three jurors were satisfied with the verdicts.

Shirley Seaholm, a payroll and budget control clerk, was a widow with a grown son and daughter. Jean Fritz shared the work of an auto supply store with her husband in Des Plaines. They had four children, the youngest being a lively boy named Dan, ten years of age, who often listened attentively to the interviews. For weeks, the two jurors had refused all interviews with journalists, who soon gave up entirely. Mrs. Seaholm's son went to Columbia College, where I chaired the Writing/English department. Students told me of his stories about impermissible things marshals said to his mother when they brought her home on weekends. I sensed, from Mrs. Seaholm's voice on the phone, that she wanted to speak but needed time. The jurors' motivation to give the interviews was stimulated by their children's eagerness for the story to be told.

On that early spring evening in the living room in the house in Des Plaines, Mrs. Fritz, in her husky compelling voice, agreed with Mrs. Seaholm. "I came to fear our government for the first time."

The four "dissenting" women—three white women and one black woman—realized the defendants were, as they saw it in the "evidence" given to them, innocent. It would seem that the plain shock of this realization actually, paradoxically, fearfully, motivated them to reach the compromise verdict. It would seem that way, yes, but when we get into their experience we find that in fact their courage was not so lacking. What they lacked was a certain amount and quality of information. Throughout the trial they were within arm's reach, they stood

face to face with persons who could have given them the information they needed, and we see what happens when people
make decisions within an actual context of larger information
that could be, but isn't, made available.

The parade of undercover and plainclothes agents and their
testimony meant, to those four jurors, that the government's
operations were probably more underhanded and skulking
and distorted than anything the defendants could do or con-
jure. It meant the government did not trust its people. It meant
someone next-door to you, or nearby you, in trust or proximity,
perhaps someone on this jury itself, could be posing as your
friend or helpmate in order to do you grave harm.

Shirley Seaholm asked me at one point in the first interview,
"Does the government have us on its lists now?" She said the
day Mayor Daley testified was "like being in prison. It frightened me that the mayor of my city felt that he needed such
security."

The two jurors were frightened by the implications of the
electronic surveillance that the government could visit upon
anyone it chose. Phones could be tapped, walls were not im-
pervious to electronic ears, mail was opened and copied, and
people were assassinated or removed in other ways. "How long
after we were home," Jean Fritz said to Shirley Seaholm, "were
we careful about what we said on the phone?" They listened
to what was said in court, and they concluded that there was
no restraint upon the government. The government could do
as it wished, play as it wished, make up its own rules, and then
break them and make them again as it saw fit.

"What was frightening to me," said Mrs. Fritz, who had
children in college, "was that there are young people who will
go to college and let their hair grow long and then report back.
What is happening to our country when your roommate in
college may be reporting back to the government? When the
government can tap anybody's phone? Or do anything it wants
to do?" She was thinking of the student undercover agent,

William Frapolly, and the young undercover newspaper reporter, Dwayne Oklepek, and the other young agents who
showed up at the end of the trial in the government's rebuttal
case. Mrs. Fritz noted that Frapolly said on the witness stand
that it was a joke when he told the story that his father told
him of the girls at Mundelein College who jammed toilets by
pushing balsa wood balls down into them. "When Frapolly
says it, it's a joke. But if John Froines says it, it's a crime. I
don't like that."

The two jurors wanted to ask questions about many things
throughout the trial. They did not know that there was precedent in common law for jurors asking questions about anything
that they feel needs explanation. The use of this right has at-
rophied in this country, but in days when the courts deal with
"political" cases, American citizens may consider that, if they
become jurors, they have an ancient right to ask questions
when they feel they need information or explanation. It is a
right that has always been associated in English common law
with political and religious dissent.

"We wanted to ask questions, lots of questions," Shirley
Seaholm said. Though the defense made motions asking that
the judge permit jurors to ask questions and to take notes, the
defense never got across to the jury that they as jurors had the
right to ask questions and have those questions answered.
What would have been the effect on the Conspiracy trial if, in
the midst of the tumult when Bobby Seale was being forced
back into his chair by federal marshals because he was insisting
on his right to defend himself, Mrs. Seaholm had said, as she
had wished to say, "Why can't Bobby Seale defend himself?"

The account of these two jurors differed considerably from
the accounts, published serially in the Chicago *Sun-Times* and
other newspapers, by Kay Richards, who claimed to have "negotiated" the verdicts. Kay Richards said that the jury took
several ballots on Saturday, February 14, but no more. The
dissenting jurors do not disagree that ballots were taken on

Saturday, but they add that *two hung-jury messages were actually sent to Judge Hoffman* on Sunday and Monday. Kay Richards did not find it appropriate to mention, for national serialization, the two hung-jury messages refused by Judge Hoffman.

Mrs. Seaholm asked me during the interview, "Did the defendants have drugs in the courtroom?" It turned out that the incident in which Abbie Hoffman opened a package sent to him at the Federal Building and found that it contained what he called "an unknown green substance," which he promptly turned over to the judge, had been related to one of the jurors by one of the marshals. All of the jurors soon heard the story and believed that the defendants had drugs in the courtroom. They were not left with any impression of the conventional responsibility that Abbie Hoffman showed in reporting the package.

Drugs in the courtroom were the finest sort of corroboration of some of the prosecution's points, and must have anesthetized any last quiver of skepticism in the minds of the more conservative jurors. Nevertheless, these two jurors were anxious to say that the marshals who watched over them so diligently were good and true men doing an ambiguous job. The jurors would hardly tolerate any inference that the marshals had anything but tolerable motives.

Kunstler would say after the trial that the defendants did have marijuana on their table under a copy of the Berkeley *Tribe,* as a dare to the court, for one day apparently.

From the beginning the jurors found themselves divided, almost unconsciously, into two factions, by attitudes about the body, about laughter, and about the raising of children. "The five of us always ate together almost from the beginning," said Mrs. Fritz. Kay Richards always ate with "the four."

The way people feel, and conduct themselves as parents, about the raising of children appears to be more indicative of their politics than any other factor. It is as if their politics proceed directly from their deep feelings about the raising of children rather than the other way around.

The most simplistic division on the raising of children is that one side believes children must be beaten and controlled and commanded to be or become "good," and the other side believes that not only do children not have to be beaten to be "good" but that beating itself is "bad" and produces "badness," that clarity and authority are not produced by physical force. Within this simplistic division are contained different attitudes toward authority in general, about the future, whether you hold tight or open up, save or spend, look for definite payment for each response or simply respond with payment as an issue with no immediate priority. You could not be present in the homes of these two jurors without realizing that they were warm and generous people, who had raised warm and generous children.

Kay Richards reported in her serialized account that there was a clash at the jurors' dinner table one night over the issue of raising children. She gives the impression that the clash occurred between the two factions. Fritz and Seaholm say that that particular clash stayed wholly within the "other" group, where voices were raised about being tough with children to make them "good." One juror told the others about the time the juror's daughter was taken to a psychiatrist and the doctor said that what the girl needed was "love and patience" and the juror threw the money down on the doctor's desk and walked out saying that what the girl needed was to have it "shoved down her throat." The convict-on-all-counts jurors believed, in their varying degrees, that being tough and punishing children was the way to raise them right. Mrs. Fritz says she yelled once over this issue at the juror who thought that what his daughter needed was to have it "shoved down her throat."

The issue of the raising of children was, of course, basic in the trial because of the emphasis by the defense on "youth revolution," "youth culture," and the supposed "gap" between the generations' understanding of themselves and their world.

I asked them about their impressions of the "governor" of the trial. "The one side of Judge Hoffman we saw we didn't like," said Mrs. Fritz. "He gave me the impression from the beginning that he thought they were guilty. The way he read the indictment. He read it as if they were already guilty."

How were the two jurors chosen, after being picked supposedly at random from voter registration lists'?

Shirley Seaholm received her questionnaire in February of 1969 and Jean Fritz hers in the summer of the same year. They remember the following questions: How old are you? Do you work? How long have you been in residence at present address? What is your education? This is said to be the standard juror questionnaire in this district. But there was nothing standard—if a fair trial by a jury of peers of the defendants was at issue—in the jury selection that began with the responses to this questionnaire. The hundreds of prospective jurors were remarkably middle-class and middle-aged .

"I know," Mrs. Fritz said, "some of them sat down in the jury room on the first day of the trial thinking they're guilty." She said that she had seen Dellinger, Rubin, and Abbie Hoffman on TV in the spring before the trial, and she didn't particularly like the impression they gave. At the selection of the jurors, she said that she looked at those three men and asked herself if she could be fair and then concluded, "Yes, I can be fair." For this writer, it was hard to believe that there could be anyone in the Chicago area who had not formed some opinions about the causes of the street violence during the Democratic Convention of 1968.

Mrs. Fritz remembered saying to Ruth Peterson about the so-called Black Panther letters, "Did you actually get a letter?" Mrs. Fritz also said, "Ruth was very frightened at first. I remember asking Milly [Mrs. Burns] if she got one too." The jurors Fritz and Seaholm said that they personally thought the letters were crank mail.

"It wasn't possible for this jury to give the defendants a fair trial," Mrs. Fritz said. "Every one of us except one was over forty—except Kay—and there was no one with a college education. Oh, Kay had a couple of years at that school in Michigan. That was all. There was no chance for the defendants to be understood by such a jury." In addition to being over forty, almost all of the jurors came from suburban or outlying districts of Chicago.

Mrs. Fritz and Mrs. Seaholm point out an interesting sociological factor: the convict-on-all-counts jurors tended to be people who had moved recently from the city of Chicago itself to the suburbs. They were the hard-line we-worked-hard-and-won-our-way-according-to-the-standard-rules-of-social-mobility people. These were the jurors who believed that parents should be tough and strict with children. In the deliberating room, they were the jurors who were most likely to say about the defendants, "Walk through a Polish neighborhood, and they'd shoot them." The "acquittal" jurors tended to be those who had been longer situated in the suburbs or outlying parts of the city, and were easier in their attitudes about the raising of children.

These twelve people, picked from a venire body constituted from social groups most likely to be prejudiced against the defendants, became nevertheless severely split over the issues of the trial. The government definitely needed a catalytic person—whether it got that person by accident, by persuasion, or by intention—to declare and make use of all the negotiable alternatives in the indictments.

"We [the four] felt funny about Kay from the very beginning. We didn't trust her, and we didn't know why," Mrs. Fritz and Mrs. Seaholm said. The other two "acquittal" jurors, Frieda Robbins and Mary Butler, agreed with them. They said that they tried to act and speak with discretion in Kay Richards' presence.

The sequestration was implemented in an emotionally disruptive way. The jurors have conflicting feelings about whether the government was planning and ready for it. Beginning on the south side of Chicago they traveled in a wide arc in a bus until late in the night, to pick up essential belongings of each juror, accompanied by marshals every minute until they reached the Palmer House, where, along with the time in the Federal Building, they would spend the next five months.

Shirley Seaholm asked me, "Who wanted us sequestered?"

Even though Judge Hoffman had said that they were being sequestered on his own motion over objection of the defense, the jurors still wondered if the defense wanted them sequestered. This confusion resulted partly from their consternation—I still remember their reactions—at the announcement of the sequestration.

In fact, the defense mightily objected to sequestration, because sequestered juries are more likely to find defendants guilty. Judge Hoffman relieved the prosecutors of being a focus of the jurors' discontent by telling the jurors that he was doing it on his own motion.

Lawyers, steeped for years in the language of their profession, do not realize the extent to which ordinary people—even intelligent ordinary people, such as these jurors and most of the journalists in the courtroom—both fear and do not clearly comprehend everyday legal language and court proceedings. For instance, the defense lawyers thought it was an unusual hint of fairness on Judge Hoffman's part that he consented to say "over the objection of the defense." In fact, the remark did not convey to the jurors why they were sequestered or who wanted them sequestered. They ached to ask questions.

Journalists could always ask questions about the meaning of legal terms. But the jurors were not permitted to ask for

clarification. For instance, the jurors did not understand the
term "voir dire," which means an examination out of the presence of the jury to see if evidence can be admitted. Journalists
asked questions to find out what voir dire meant, while the
jurors continued to be mystified when they were excused to
let a voir dire examination take place.

The conditions and restraints of their sequestered lives—
the very word conjures glooms and glens and suggestions of
forbidden delights in sun-shot glades—would not encourage
the feeling among the jurors that they were safely free to deliver a verdict as they perceived it. They knew that their mail
was being opened. Their phone calls were monitored by marshals who listened to every word. Their conversations with
family visitors were conducted in the immediate presence of
marshals. When they were permitted to go home on Sundays,
marshals accompanied them every step and minute of the way:
married jurors were not permitted what were called "conjugal
rights." "You could not," Mrs. Fritz said, "help but get the
feeling deep inside you that the government wanted awfully
bad to win this case, when you're surrounded by government
marshals, government people, taking such good care of you."
They had their choice of the finest food the Palmer House
offered. "Crab Rangoon," Mrs. Fritz said, with a laugh and
mock sigh of delight. So the jurors were not entirely displeased
by their sequestration. "Having it thrust upon us helped us to
accept and enjoy it," they said. But they also were oppressed
by it, as if subjected to an indefinite convalescence.

Nothing so reveals the government's lack of humor—and
lack of sensitivity to "intentions"—as an account by Shirley
Seaholm about the "hacksaw" she requested for lunch. Kay
Richards, taking initiative as usual, was writing down orders
for lunch at the Federal Building one noontime. She asked,
"Do you want anything special for lunch?" Mrs. Seaholm said,
"A hacksaw." Kay Richards dutifully went along with the joke
and wrote it down and presented the list to the cafeteria man-

ager, who promptly notified the U. S. Marshal's Office about a juror's request for "a hacksaw." Marshals came quickly to find out which juror wanted a "hacksaw" and why. They simply could not see the request with Shirley Seaholm's sense of humor.

Nevertheless, the jurors' experience would appear to be, in some respects, supportive of a positive attitude toward sequestration and its supposed benefits for the judicial process. The problem of bias may be greatly stimulated by "the good care" given by government people, unsupervised by persons of the defense. Many comments by marshals to jurors would have been prevented if defense supervisors had also been present. Marshals, who were often singularly rough with spectators and Conspiracy staff, were uniformly "nice" to the jurors.

"If we had gone home every night," Mrs. Seaholm said, "we wouldn't have been able to give the trial the attention we gave it." Mrs. Fritz agreed: "Being sequestered helped me concentrate." She said she would have felt guilty leaving her husband alone each day as she went to the trial, and that the jurors would have felt guiltier about time they would be spending away from home. The two jurors agreed that, if they had not been sequestered, there would have been a lot of phone calls and talk with friends and families. "There would have been a lot of illness if we hadn't been sequestered."

The jurors' experiences also suggests that sequestration causes a jury to form itself as a group and to act as a group. "We had a lot of good laughs together," Jean Fritz said. The group would have loyalties and guilts of its own.

If they had gone home each night, there would, of course, have been much more chance for them to find out about all the happenings in the courtroom that were kept from them, and those they had only hints of from hearing raised voices through the courtroom door, among them those things they were eager to question. They would have known, as they wished to know, much more about Bobby Seale and his struggle to defend himself. They would also have learned in the newspapers or on TV or by word of mouth, even though the judge would ritually remind them not to read anything concerning the trial, about the Weatherman actions of October, about the October and November Moratorium Against the Viet Nam War demonstrations, about another Apollo flight to the moon, about the state killing of Fred Hampton and Mark Clark, and about the exposure of the My Lai massacre of Vietnamese civilians by American soldiers in Viet Nam. It was the opinion of Jean Fritz and Shirley Seaholm that news of the My Lai massacre would have seriously affected this jury. Kunstler's indirect reference to Son My was not successful.

But they felt angry about their sequestration, too, and in the predictable ways. "We felt like the criminals, while the defendants were wandering the streets." Apparently no rational interpretation will prevail with sequestered jurors anywhere, and they will, perhaps in some inversion of guilt about their roles in relation to the defendants, always blame the defendants rather than the judge or the prosecution for their confinement. Nevertheless, around Christmastime, when the defendants out on the street held up a sign LET THE JURY GO, the jurors in the big yellow bus laughed and waved.

The jurors, when traveling between the Federal Building and the Palmer House, strained to see headlines at street corner newsstands. One juror might catch a couple of words of a headline and then ask another juror, "Did you see the rest of it?" They also tried to see newscasts on TVs in display windows at the Palmer House. But they never learned much in these ways.

They were not allowed to read any literature that dealt specifically with "dissent" or the issues and persons of the trial. But they were permitted to watch endless James Bond movies, where they could compare the government's undercover agents with spying viewed in a favorable way. They were also permitted to see *Oklahoma,* a movie that must be one of the great sentimental celebrations for a generation of white people whose youth was spent during the "heroic" days of World War II and directly afterward. Mrs. Seaholm read a book about John Adams, which was apparently the most demanding reading undertaken by any juror.

When they were not sunk in the proceedings in the courtroom, the convict-on-all-counts jurors played a lot of cards, mostly pinochle. Shirley Seaholm occasionally joined in a game of cribbage. Frieda Robbins, who was one of the four, sewed and embroidered. Jean Fritz kept a notebook in her room in which she wrote her impressions of witnesses, especially "the ones that bothered" her. Kay Richards could be heard typing alone in her room at night. Sitting in the jury seats was not good for Jean Fritz, and she contracted phlebitis in the legs. She had to lie in bed with her legs propped up by pillows as she wrote in the notebook. The notebook was invaluable for refreshing her memory because the trial was so long and there were so many witnesses.

"Every time we found a rubber band or a paper clip," said Mrs. Seaholm, "we'd save it. Like we were the last people on the face of the earth." The last people on the face of the earth were afraid their rooms were bugged. They lived with fears of surveillance for five months, day and night.

They made a game of ordering from a Sears, Roebuck catalog. They actually received some items from that world out there from which they received nothing else for five months.

In an effusion of eager feeling, Kay Richards asked Mary Butler what she wanted to be called—a Negro? a black woman? a what? Jean Fritz was pleased to report that Mary Butler answered ironically, "Call me an American."

The two factions found each other almost as soon as the trial began. Most of the jurors thought that Kay Richards was on the side of the defendants because of the way she acted and the way she always associated with "the four." So it was a surprise in the deliberating room when Kay Richards came out suddenly as a convict-on-all-counts juror. "You could tell just by the way people looked after a certain witness and by a lot of other things how they felt," said Mrs. Fritz.

What events or information caused, helped, or revealed the split in the jury? What witnesses were most effective for the prosecution and for the defense? Undercover agents Frapolly, Pierson, Oklepek, and Bock convinced the convict-on-all-counts jurors, whereas the "acquittal" jurors were largely turned off, frightened, and not at all convinced by the agents' testimony. Often, the "acquittal" jurors had violently negative feelings, and they speak of the agents with distaste and distrust. For instance, Louis Salzburg, a photographer who was supposed to have been so friendly with the defendants in past times, said on the stand that he couldn't live without FBI money that was paid him. "That really disgusted me," said Mrs. Fritz. To the "acquittal" jurors, the agents often seemed "mechanical" in telling their stories.

"Timothy Leary, Paul Krassner, such witnesses hurt the defense badly. Any man who advocates drugs to young people is wrong." About the colorful, powerful testimony of Allen Ginsberg, Mrs. Fritz said, "I know that quite a few of the jurors were horrified. l liked him." After Ginsberg's testimony, when the jurors were at the Palmer House, "We sat on the floor and tried to imitate the om-m-m and meditate."

They were not so critical of the testimony of Deputy Superintendent James M. Rochford, and of other police commanders, as they were of the undercover agents. They did not believe that the commanders intended for their men to beat people in the streets of Chicago. The two jurors were "very impressed" with the surprise testimony on cross-examination of Commander Clarence Braasch, in which Braasch testified forthrightly that, in Lincoln Park during Convention Week, when the police went away the problem went away. The jurors wanted to give the impression that they listened to both sides, and that "both sides must listen to each other." They were not inclined to impugn the integrity of conventional authorities in conventional dress. But they were more impressed with long-haired defense counsel Leonard Weinglass, with his "sincerity," than with any other lawyer in the courtroom. Kunstler was sometimes more commanding of attention, but he did not establish a sense of trust with the "acquittal" jurors.

The two jurors mistrusted flamboyance in general. For instance, Jerry Rubin may or may not have been in Lincoln Park Sunday night, August 25. But the defense's dramatic presentation of the "other Jerry Rubin" in the helmet with 88 on the back was regarded as a "cheap trick" by the two jurors. They were more impressed, more trusting, of Leonard Weinglass's seemingly close attention to facts and the law.

The convict-on-all-counts jurors believed Foran and Schultz, equally.

The testimony of two women from Lincoln Park in Chicago impressed the two "acquittal" jurors: Mona Cunningham's testimony of herself and friends being chased by police who said that Lincoln Park was no longer "your home, motherfuckers," and Ruth Migdahl's testimony about her experience as a medic for the demonstrators and what she saw of police brutality to demonstrators. It made me think that my perception in the middle of the defense's case, that the witness stand should have been inundated with Chicago witnesses, was accurate.

Tom Foran asked David Lee Edmondsen if, after the police first asked him to come down off the Logan Statute, he climbed back up on the horse and thrust up both arms with the fingers of each hand in a V sign to the cheering crowd. Films had shown that incident to the jury. "I have no recollection of that," Edmondsen said. "I've been told that I did that and I've been shown photographs," but he said that he had "blacked out" on the event. There was the sudden feeling that he had blown the trust in the listening in the courtroom, even though he may have been sincere. The two jurors did not believe him.

Most observers thought Rennie Davis did a superb job on the witness stand—really addressed himself to the needs of the case—when he testified for himself and the defense. But these two jurors said that Davis hurt the defense's chances with the jury more than any other witness, partly because he seemed "too clever" with some of his answers, "too pat" with other stories, and because he said and affirmed—and Richard Schultz repeated it—the words about supporting "insurrection" on the campuses. The problem once again was one of feeling or not feeling the sincerity of the witness. However, both Mrs. Seaholm and Mrs. Fritz say that they themselves were impressed with Rennie Davis, handsome-young-man-next-door. Mrs. Fritz sank back a little in her chair and smiled as she said it.

It would seem that Davis confirmed—froze—the polarization of the jury. He was the most disliked of the defendants by the majority of the jurors, and yet the most liked by the four "acquittal" jurors.

Nothing was said among the jurors about Abbie Hoffman's testimony as definite as the things they said about Davis. A couple of the jurors were turned off by Abbie Hoffman's saying, " 'Work is a dirty word instead of fuck is a dirty word,' " and these were people who had worked hard all their lives. They didn't miss one thing Foran or Schultz said, but they would not listen to the defendants. Nevertheless, the jurors didn't think Abbie Hoffman was "evil" the way Prosecutor Foran had said.

"Conduct, deportment, language, style of life were important," said Jean Fritz, "in determining the attitudes of the other jurors, even though they said it didn't make any difference. When Dellinger said, 'Oh, bullshit,' and when the defendants used colorful language and actions, it certainly affected the majority of the jurors adversely in their attitudes toward the defendants." The "adversely affected" jurors were the suburbanites who had moved to the suburbs from Chicago after having lived most of their lives in the city itself. The testimony about the young people in the streets during the Democratic convention flying black, red, and Viet Cong flags, and the account of the taking down of the American flag in Grant Park, strongly affected these jurors against the defendants.

Most of the jurors simply would not hear anything good about the defendants. When the Yippie flyer "Impossible Dream" was admitted into evidence and the jurors read it, the convict-on-all-counts jurors saw only the word "fucking" and the "impossible" things on the Impossible Dream side of the flyer, and would not turn the page over to see what the Yippies recommended as a national program in lieu of being able to satisfy the Impossible Dream. "The other side was marvelous," declared Jean Fritz, "but they wouldn't even take the time to look at it." Twenty years later many items in the Yippies "other side" national program became central concerns of mainstream American politics.

Judge Hoffman constantly, each and every day, reminded the jury not to discuss the trial in any way. "It's not possible to be human and not discuss the trial," Mrs. Fritz said. "Marshals were human beings, too, and in five months some things would be said." There were apparently a number of things said. But Mrs. Fritz and Mrs. Seaholm insisted that the "four" were careful about talking. "We were afraid they were watching us."

In late December, 1969, the government finally corroborated through the FBI that on December 18, when Rennie Davis spoke at Northern Illinois University, one of Mrs. Fritz's daughters, a student who was perhaps overly enamored with her mother's participation in a great historical event, got up in the audience and told Davis that "her mother did not believe the government had proved its case." If it could have been proven that Mrs. Fritz discussed the trial with her daughter, she could have been held in contempt. On December 31, the defendants overheard that the government might raise the matter that day. Kunstler, first thing that afternoon, urgently made a motion about "a government attack upon the jury," upon a juror, within the hearing of Mrs. Fritz while the jury was filing out of the room. This may have been one of the most appropriate "contempts" that Kunstler committed. The government, aware of potentially contradictory responses and reactions, did not carry through with the possibility of bumping Mrs. Fritz from the jury.

The jurors were taken out of the courtroom while Seale was bound and gagged. "Some of the jurors thought Bobby Seale had it coming to him." The marshals said to the jurors, "You're going to see something a little different when you go in," trying to prepare them. Jean Fritz cried openly, and Shirley Seaholm bit back her tears, at the sight of Seale. Mrs. Fritz said she was shaking so hard that she literally had to sit on her hands. It infuriated her that Kay Richards tried to call the attention of the marshals to her, as if Mrs. Fritz were ill. "Yes, we wanted to ask questions," the two jurors said, "lots of questions."

Perhaps judges and lawyers altogether tremble at the prospect of this invasion of common law rights into their established, self-protective rituals. It would change the nature and appearance of courtroom behavior if jurors could ask questions on matters that confuse them, of evidence, law, and even perhaps of the claims in closing arguments.

*The Closing Arguments: The Telling of the People
and the Unpeople*

When I walked in the door of the courtroom on Tuesday morning, February 10, Richard Schultz was at the lectern. "Ladies and gentlemen of the jury. . . ." The jurors were nervous, as if they hardly wished or hoped that the trial would ever come to this moment. "The first question you must ask yourself," Schultz said, "is why would they want to incite a riot."

"They wanted to wreck this fucking society," he echoed his cross-examination of Abbie Hoffman. By now, the word "fucking" sounded almost natural, almost easy, from Richard Schultz. He argued that the defendants wanted to make the government responsible for the war, for racism, for poverty, in order to get people to come to Chicago to protest. The government, Schultz said, in a modest tone, couldn't answer these questions. "People would only join the demonstrators if they thought they were peaceful and the government was violent." He worked the single line of his argument as if he were trying to split a rock with a jackhammer. Yet it was an oddly soothing fantasy that he was telling, oddly fascinating. "They told it to McCarthy supporters. They told it to Julian Bond. They told it to Jesse Jackson." Schultz listed all the people the defendants duped.

He then argued how the jury could determine "credibility" of witnesses, and sure enough every behavioral sign that was negative to the eyes of the defense was positive to the eyes of the prosecution. Ann Froines got up in sudden disgust and went out, hitting the courtroom door with the flat of her hand.

Then Schultz said that he would go into each count of the indictment. "Rubin—let's take him first—Count Six—Rubin was most active of the defendants on the street in urging crowds to fight back." This choice showed what might be considered lack of confidence on the part of the government, because Schultz apparently wanted to use the lurid testimony about Jerry Rubin to put an overshadowing tone in the minds of the jurors concerning the "evidence" about all of the defendants. He leaned hard on Mailer's testimony. "Jerry Rubin told Judy Collins, 'We want it to be peaceful,' but he told Norman Mailer about one hundred thousand young people just by their presence causing the establishment to smash the city." Schultz did not mention that Mailer said that Rubin said "the secret guilt of the establishment" would cause them to do it. Schultz liberally used the language attributed to Rubin, "fucker" and "motherfucker." The sensitive reader will remember his asking for "blank" words and "f" words long ago.

"Better than Iwo Jima," Schultz reiterated Rubin's comment about kids running up the Logan Statue hill. The jury represented a generation whose sentimentalities were formed during World War II. They might not feel kindly toward anyone who made fun of heroic memories. Schultz said it again to native Chicagoans: "They came from New York." He repeated the testimony of Pierson that Rubin said he was pleased newsmen were clubbed by police. "That'll put them on our side," Rubin said. "When somebody showed Rubin a bagful of human excrement, he said, 'We have to show the world that this is a police state.' " That's what he thinks of you, Schultz was signaling to the jury.

The Assistant U. S. Attorney developed the overshadowing visions and tones of a visitant and visitations from hell. He pointed casually to Rubin at the defense table. "Rubin, who is wearing that star on his chest right now." It was the Star of David. Marshals, spectators, newsmen, and defendants were struggling against the drowse in that conflict-stymied atmosphere. "We proved that Rubin came here to incite violence, and on Count Six he's charged with that, and he's guilty."

Judge Hoffman was leaning forward and beaming at Schultz with unconcealed pleasure. Schultz called the jury's attention to the August 9, 1968, meeting reported by Bock, Frapolly, and Oklepek, where the agents testified that Davis said things that indicated his violent intentions for inciting riots in the demonstrations in Chicago. Richard Schultz stood behind the lectern gripping both sides of it, with his shoulders hunched up, and looked at the jury, jaw level, in that way that would put a crick in the neck of anyone else. "Where are the other people present?" he said, and his voice was calm and full of implications. "Defense didn't bring a single one to the stand to rebut." It was a telling moment.

Officer Thompson testified that Davis said "disrupt the Democratic convention" at Judd Hall at the University of Chicago in November, 1967. Schultz looked at the jury. "Where are the fifty people who were there in Judd Hall? Why didn't they bring one here to testify?" The telling moment was becoming a telling point.

Schultz quoted Davis as saying before the Democratic convention, "There will be war in the streets until there is peace in Viet Nam." "Right now," he said, as if whatever Davis said in his speeches now certainly convicted him for what he had said and done two years before, "Davis goes out to campuses to call for resurrection—excuse me—*in*surrection—"The rising energy of Schultz's evangelical accusation betrayed him. He became level and earnest again, perhaps driven and wary in his instrumental consciousness by that beast of contrary perception in him.

During the noon recess some of the defendants acted as if, for the first time, they distinctly realized what was happening to them.

Ann Froines came upon the prosecutors in the hallway. She immediately needled Richard Schultz by telling him that he would be sorry for his remarks to the jury about "those girls who are always with the defendants." Schultz said, "And how will I be sorry for that, young lady?" Then Foran moved in between her and Schultz to cool them. The women of the defense had tried to make themselves apparent to the women of the jury, in the hope that they might gain some sympathy of identification. To cancel the defense's possible gain, Schultz, in his remark to the jury, spoke of "those girls" who were the defendants' companions in violence during Convention Week also.

But "those girls who are always with the defendants" and other members of the Conspiracy staff had, in fact, intimidated many of the marshals. Their insistence on their rights, their vocal protest, their laughter, their way of acting forthrightly and with a purpose when the spirit of declaration moved them, made many of the marshals think two or three times before "causing an uproar" by attempting to eject any one of them.

In the afternoon, Schultz meditated yet once more upon the parade marshals' training in Lincoln Park, and upon the image of demonstrators using a rolled-up magazine to deflect a club and deliver a kick in a cop's groin to give demonstrators a moment to get away. He thrust with his left arm at the jury. "It *shows* you what was their intent." He had not tried for a single laugh. Edward Kratzke had smiled only once.

Schultz's mother and father were among the spectators today, a sort of graduation day. Schultz gestured as if a tight spring were drawing his gestures back, and as if there were notations in the margins of his notes to tell him when to gesture, when to smile. He was effective in the morning, but unable to let himself be sustained by a story to its end. That happened in his cross-examinations too.

Schultz was really yelling, letting his voice get wildly indignant, about Abbie Hoffman's "falsifying" testimony even though "Thompson and Riggio saw him and he wrote about it in his book." That was the conspiracy to "kidnap" Deputy Superintendent Rochford. Again it was odd for me to remember the "kidnap plot" being laughingly voiced from person to person at the Logan Statue.

" 'The United States is an outlaw nation,' " Schultz quoted the testimony of a speech of Tom Hayden's. " 'The United States has broken all the rules, and so peace demonstrators should break all the rules too, and shed blood.' " He mentioned a WBAI tape that was withdrawn by the defense—because it would reflect badly on Hayden, Schultz tried to suggest. Kunstler with pleasure said the defense withdrew the tape because the government would not accept it since the defense could not produce for cross-examination the man who recorded it. Schultz was hunched at the lectern during Kunstler's statement of objection.

The next morning Kunstler argued that some persons were guided past hopeful young spectators, who had slept in sleeping bags all night on the Federal Plaza. Foran made the move of frankly admitting the special privilege and said that Kunstler and Weinglass had also been extended, and had used, the privilege. The courtroom was packed with people seeking a touch of sensation, something to tell friends and grandchildren. "One lady represented herself to my secretary as my cousin," Judge Hoffman said to the assembled court. "She happened to have the same name as myself and one of the defendants."

Schultz listed several defense witnesses—such as Professor Kalish and Linda Morse—who were present at the Wednesday morning meeting where the most fanciful egg of the prosecution's conspiracy, Dellinger's diversionary march, was hatched. But the defense asked those witnesses nothing about that meeting. Rennie Davis alone testified about it. Schultz asked the jurors, "Why did the defense skip this meeting except for Davis's testimony?"

He said that the defendants planned the events of Wednesday afternoon in Grant Park so that the "regrouped" demonstrators would encounter police specifically at Michigan-Balbo.

It was a small shock when he said crassly, for guerrilla, "A gorilla isn't even mobile. A monkey is," as he explained Froines's supposed remark about "mobile tactics" to an audience before Convention Week.

"All seven defendants worked together for the common purpose, with the mutual understanding that they were going to incite violence by bringing in people here and inciting them to riot." In this context, yet again, "I want to very briefly discuss marshal training," he said, and gave a wide, set smile to the jurors, as if he had reached that point in his notes where "smile" was penciled in the margin. Schultz quoted Hayden as saying, "Snake dance gets people aroused, keeps their spirits up, gets them excited." Schultz put space around and emphasis upon the word "aroused," and poured a positively illicit energy into the word "excited." Schultz quoted Lee Weiner as saying, "It gets people together."

He recapitulated the concept of the "liberated zone," in which people could do whatever they wanted to do, smoke dope, fuck in public, have nude-ins, do anything they wanted to do. "The city was not going to give permits for such activities," Schultz said. He again suggested that the Yippies and demonstrators came from out of town and it was "not their park." It was most irritating that the defense, along with not calling a troop of Chicago witnesses, never qualified the charge of the prosecution that the Yippies and demonstrators were mostly from out of town. In fact, more than a majority of participants in street and park actions during Convention Week came from Chicago and nearby areas.

The defendants, Schultz said, "wanted a confrontation at the Amphitheatre. Nonnegotiable."

It was 12:31, time for noon recess, and Schultz, as if humiliated, said, "I can finish in about twelve minutes, your honor." The judge did not react at first, rocked quickly in his chair, then said in an undertone, "Keep going." There was laughter in the courtroom.

Schultz ended with a quiet intensity. "We proved it beyond all doubt that these seven defendants came here for purposes of inciting people to riot. They are guilty."


*Leonard Weinglass*

"The whole structure of this case is just not acceptable as a rational explanation," began Weinglass. I wondered how it was possible that the courtroom did not disintegrate into gales, storms, and buffets of laughter.

"In the final analysis this room is only a place where two sides try to create an event that happened some time before." That was exactly what had not happened. But Weinglass was a fine counter-puncher, always at his best in attacking the weaknesses and the openings in the thrust of the government's case, or in arguing the law. In short, wherever the use of reason could expose a charade of reason, he could regularly make telling points.

He gave a statistical characterization of the government's witnesses that should have indicated their unavoidable bias. Three city government witnesses, four high in the police department, five from the youth division of the police department, six from the internal investigation division of the police department, two surveillance detectives, three paid informers, two persons connected with military intelligence, two Chicago *Tribune* reporters, not to mention the young FBI agents in the rebuttal case, and only three ordinary citizens, Barbara Lawyer, Sidney White, and Dr. MacDonald. "Why are they so isolated? Why couldn't the government get all those people who were here on the street? . . ."

"We don't have to rebut every fact of the government," Weinglass said. The statement jolted because Weinglass used "fact" in the academic sense, and the jurors and the audience did a double take on the word. The defense did not feel they needed any other witnesses from those meetings because Bock's and Frapolly's testimony "was not believable" and Davis's testimony was "entirely believable." Schultz objected to that characterization. But Weinglass did not answer why Professor Kalish and Linda Morse were not asked, when they were on the witness stand, about the Wednesday morning meeting.

"Did he say disrupt the sham or did he say disrupt the Convention? That's very important." Weinglass had often argued in the trial that records of public speeches and testimony about public speeches could not be brought as evidence, because the speeches were exercise of constitutional rights. A daring defense might decide to let the matter rest entirely on constitutional grounds. But if it was important for this jury to decide whether Davis said "disrupt the sham" or "disrupt the Convention," then there should have been a witness to help them, if one were available.

"I come before you not to bring peace but a sword." If there had been a Caspar there, Weinglass said, and the sentence were reported out of context, it would be reported as a violent statement. Jesus actually meant, said Weinglass, that there was a new generation, son against father, daughter against mother. Jesus meant the youth revolution.

In the long shadow of Jesus' enigmatic incitement, the listening in the courtroom became intense as Weinglass tried to explain Mailer's remark about what Rubin "intended."

"By virtue of the language they use," Weinglass said, "these men are to be considered as criminals. Men with strong convictions use strong words." He told the jurors that they had an obligation to their conscience to question a law if they thought it was unjust and not a good law. Judge Hoffman sharply admonished Weinglass. But there exists a tradition in England and the United States for jurors to answer to their conscience about the justice of a law.

The next day Nancy Kurshan was telling friends and reporters that John Froines and Jerry Rubin had spoken at the University of Wisconsin the previous night. "The auditorium was full, ten thousand people heard it, and it was piped throughout the Student Union by TV." Newspapers reported "marauding in the streets" after the speeches. That supposedly contrasted with the tepid response among students at the trial's beginning. The defendants were excited, and they were also worried that their bail might be revoked.

The prosecutors consistently showed the more acute, manipulative sense for the sentiments of "ordinary" white, middle-class, middle-aged people, the majority of the jury. For instance, Richard Schultz objected to Weinglass's talking about the "government's theory" of Convention Week, but he did not object to Weinglass's talking about "the government's facts." Schultz knew very well that ordinary people think of "theory" as something removed from reality, but they do not have the same academic understanding of "facts."

Weinglass attacked the government's "theory" of Dellinger's march as a "diversionary action." He made the point that the crowd crossing at Jackson Bridge could have gone straight into the Loop and busted it up. But instead the demonstrators saw the three mule-drawn wagons of the SCLC Poor People's campaign and enthusiastically massed behind them to march to the Amphitheatre. "Deputy Superintendent Rochford said, 'If I thought they were going to the Amphitheatre I would have let them go.'" Then Weinglass said, "The government has not been able to bring before you a single tape, photograph, or anything else to show these men encouraging a crowd to riot."

The government said that Dellinger's nonviolent march was part of a three-pronged plan that included the "violent" alternative in a speech by Tom Neuman. But Weinglass characterized Neuman as a man angry at Dellinger for trying to force nonviolence upon a people who were being beaten mercilessly by the police. Unfortunately two witnesses whose testimony would have supported this view were excluded from the witness stand. Henry DeZutter, reporter for the Chicago *Daily News,* was sitting behind the microphone in the bandshell and he heard the angry remarks directed at Dellinger. DeZutter was excluded from the witness stand because he had been present as a reporter in the courtroom. I too would not have been allowed to testify to the parade marshals' systematic exclusion of kids with rocks and sticks from the nonviolent march, and to the hostility between the MOBE parade marshals—who were trained in Lincoln Park—and the younger people. The reason behind this rule was that an eyewitness could sit in a courtroom and listen to other witnesses and form testimony accordingly.

Weinglass followed the line of the development of action Wednesday afternoon and night with accuracy, but, in effect, disavowed the magnitude of the energy and avoided most objects thrown by demonstrators and other forms of demonstrator assertion and declaration.

When he spoke of the marshals' training in Lincoln Park, and of the snake dance in particular, he said, "It was never used. Wouldn't the ideal time be when a police line was coming through the park?" No, there was no use at all for the snake dance at such a time. The purpose of the snake dance was to get large numbers of people rapidly out of a situation in which they were surrounded. Weinglass was playing into the fantasy of the government that the snake dance was a method of attack.

Then he attempted to discuss the state of mind—that was "the substance of the crime"—that brought the defendants to Chicago. He was—in an important argument—trying to extend the doctrine of the "total situation" and "surrounding circumstances" to the enormity of the social, cultural, and historical "circumstances."

He mentioned "the decade of the nineteen-sixties and Martin Luther King." Schultz objected that King would "do nothing like this, and have nothing to do with these men." Roars and hoots came from the defense's audience. Kunstler said that he "represented King for five years," and Dellinger said that he knew King personally. The irate Judge Hoffman struck Kunstler's remark. Then Kunstler asked that Schultz's remark about King "not doing this sort of thing" be stricken. Judge Hoffman told him heatedly to sit down and directed the marshals to make him sit down. "Oh, your honor," Kunstler said, "I wasn't going to jump the rail."

After the noon recess, Abbie Hoffman was saying conspiratorially to his excited eight-year-old son, "Go sit in this chair, and when the judge comes in, you'll be on trial. Hoooo." That was from a man who wanted to be tried for "telling kids to kill their parents."

Weinglass continued his closing argument, chatty, reasoning, easy, convincing. He said that it was "a trial of what did they intend. Not of what happened. And of the use of interstate commerce to make it happen."

Weinglass emphasized again and again that Rennie Davis, who had been the most frequent representative of National Mobilization in permit negotiations, was in the presence of U. S. Attorney Tom Foran himself in those conferences before Convention Week. "No one at that meeting on July 25 told Rennie Davis in the presence of the United States Attorney that it was illegal to have a nighttime assembly at the Amphitheatre. . . .

"Roger Wilkins said on the witness stand in this courtroom if there had been permits there would have been no violence." Raymond Simon, corporation counsel for the city of Chicago, called the Park District "and got a permit just like that," Weinglass snapped his fingers. "The fact that they wanted the permits is established by the fact that they filed a lawsuit to get it."

Then he told the story of another person from Illinois, Abraham Lincoln. As a freshman congressman, Lincoln introduced a resolution denouncing the immorality and illegality of the war in Mexico. Lincoln was so vilified and derided, Weinglass said, that he couldn't run the next time for Congress. Naturally Weinglass compared Lincoln to the spokesmen of the modern peace movement.

Jesus Christ, Clarence Darrow, and Abraham Lincoln. Emotion was rising. Jurors were blinking. Then Weinglass mentioned the Salem witch trials.

"Oh, *ob*jection, your honor," Schultz said, disrupting the rise of emotion and turning it into smiles and laughter both with and against himself. Judge Hoffman sustained the objection.

Weinglass ended by speaking directly to the "impartial" jurors for the defense. "I think while you deliberate on this case, history will hold its breath. . . ."

He was asking for a hung jury.

## *William Kunstler*

That afternoon defendants and reporters said that a great many cops and marshals in plainclothes were increasing the jam of people in the courtroom.

"This is the last voice that you will hear from the defense," Kunstler said to the jury. "The government has the last word." It was not long before he had said of the defendants, "What happens to them happens to all of us. . . ."

"Objection," Foran said.

"Oh, I would question the validity of that," Judge Hoffman said to Kunstler. "Sustain the objection."

Tall, angular, and loose, Kunstler held onto the lectern with both hands and dipped his hips forward occasionally, as he started or turned a thought. "You have one of the most difficult tasks that any twelve human beings could have . . . to weigh the evidence the way a computer would," and he was apparently speaking to Kay Richards, who was known to be a systems technician. "I remind you if you don't do that you will be living a lie the rest of your life."

Then he tried to impeach the statute under which the defendants were being tried, a statute brought about by Southern congressmen, he said. Foran objected and Kunstler said, in his most innocent tone, "The history of a statute is proper summation."

Judge Hoffman said, "It is *never* appropriate."

Kunstler was unabashed by each setback. "Outside agitators have led to all the reforms," he said. "Birmingham, Selma, Montgomery." He may have been aiming those remarks at the sentimentality of the black women and the white liberals on the jury, but he was also practically accepting the government's charge.

Kunstler analogized the demonstrations at the Customs House in Boston in 1770 to Chicago's Amphitheatre, the Boston Massacre to Michigan-Balbo. "Your honor," Foran said, "I've sat here quite awhile; the purpose of summation is to sum up the evidence. I object."

After the objection was sustained, Kunstler said, "Since the judge has prevented me . . ."

"*I* have not prevented you," Judge Hoffman said. "The *law* prevents you."

"I'm going to get down to how the government stoops to conquer," Kunstler said. He was particularly happy, and forceful, in contrasting the testimony of Sergeant Murray and Commander Clarence Braasch on the outcome of the supposed incitement Sunday night, August 25, of Rubin's flicking a cigarette at "surrounded cops."

When Kunstler discussed the testimony of Chicago *Tribune* reporter Murray about the VC flag that Murray had so much trouble describing, Edward Kratzke in the jury went red in the face and partly choked again. Kunstler appeared to be bringing to the forefront the salient laughs, the most preposterous episodes of his cross-examinations, as if to color the government's case with absurdity.

Then came an incident in which Kunstler said, in an ingratiatingly righteous tone, that if what he was saying was not true, about the police having caused a sawhorse to go up in the air and break the window of the Haymarket Lounge in the Conrad Hilton, then he would eat the paper of the transcript of testimony on the lectern. After an examination of the relevant documents by Thomas Foran and Judge Hoffman, the judge said, grinning, "You will have to eat that paper, Mr. Kunstler." In the spectators' seats Foran's teen-age daughter let a smile flicker on her face. Kunstler denied that he was wrong.

None of Kunstler's great moments, from the beginning of the defense's case to the summations, occurred in the presence of the jury. He could be so commanding in his voice and manner, and so engaging, that there was a feeling of obscenity when he didn't trust himself or didn't trust the intelligence or receptivity of his listeners. He trusted the responses of the press, but, in the latter part of the trial, apparently not the jury. Defense counsel and defendants ought to have permitted themselves to respect the possible intelligence of the jury as much as the government respected the jurors' prejudices.

But the movement of Kunstler's story and Kunstler's plea and Kunstler's argument was under way, and there was a warm, if not wholly trustful, feeling in the audience as he developed his notions of what happened during Convention Week and in the testimony of the trial. He reached Count Seven of the indictment. "This is the most frightening concept—to *bomb* the underground garage." He shaped it and coaxed it into existence. "They don't call anyone else chemist except John Froines. That's because chemist sounds strange and mysterious." Then he received a note from the defendants telling him that Grant Park garage was all concrete and could not burn.

Kunstler spent a deal of time emphasizing the social, professional, and academic credentials of the defendants, and of the celebrities who appeared as witnesses for the defense. He sounded patronizing. He said that only direct knowledge of tone and inflection could reveal the intent of many remarks made by the defendants during Convention Week.

Kay Richards was rocking in her chair. A psychiatrist who was taking notes on Judge Hoffman said that her rocking indicated severe anxiety. The other jurors were more dead than alive with their anxiety.

Kunstler said that Abbie Hoffman was arrested on Wednesday of Convention Week for having the word FUCK on his forehead. But for supposedly instigating the move "to kidnap"

Deputy Superintendent Rochford at the Logan Statue hill on Thursday, he was not arrested, even though plainclothes policemen testified that they saw and heard him. "In some states," Kunstler said, "kidnapping is a capital crime."

Kunstler recited the history of the defendants' involvement in the activities and developments of the social protest movements of the decade of the sixties.

Then he addressed his personal charge to the "impartial" jurors. "We have young people who are depressed and dismayed at what they see about them. . . . You have an obligation to stand on what you believe, if you believe these men are not guilty."

Foran objected.

Judge Hoffman said to Kunstler, "You are getting involved in my part of the case."

But Kunstler repeated his "charge," and Foran objected again, and Judge Hoffman ordered Kunstler to stop. Kunstler was asking for a hung jury. Jean Fritz was biting the nail of her thumb, listening intensely, as she heard Kunstler's charge both times. Kay Richards nodded firmly, earnestly, for all the world to see.

"The right of men to speak boldly, to live and die free, the right to deal with problems is in your hands."

The courtroom was sweating with sentiment and nightmare suspicion as Kunstler moved away from the lectern.

## Thomas Foran

He came dressed for the occasion, in dark blue suit, light blue shirt, and what could only be described as a subdued but colorful tie, his view of the tone of Camelot. He paced before the beginning of his summation as if he wanted to punch his fist into his palm but that would not be cool. He was keeping his psyche up, not speaking to anyone. His wife was here, with piled-up blond hair, and some of his six children, including the pretty, dark-haired daughter. Richard Schultz's wife was here, too, and apparently Schultz's mother and father. Abbie Hoffman's son and daughter were here. David Dellinger's daughters and wife were here. Wives and companions of the defendants were here, those who had worked hard through the bitter winter for the Conspiracy.

"Intellectualism, intellectual intelligence, leaves out something," Foran said to the jury. "You will weigh the evidence not as a computer, as Mr. Kunstler suggested, but by using every sense you got. You're not an automaton as Mr. Kunstler suggested, but you are a human being, you are a human spirit." Then he dropped his dart into the pride of the jury. "You cannot ignore the way people look or act."

Everyone in the courtroom watched the divided future emerge, locked, pure and shining. "You are bound by your oath to decide without fear, without favor, without sympathy, within the framework of the law as given you by the judge." Foran sounded his theme again. "How did the witness act, how did he sound, did he dodge questions, was he candid, did he exhibit bias or friendliness? . . .

"Our system of justice was conceived on a basis that counsel and litigants would respect each other, and the judge's rulings under the law." He was going straight for the nerves in the middle-aged, middle-class jury, the self-righteous nerves, the nightmare nerves. "Outbursts in the courtroom are not something you need ignore. You may look, sense, listen." You may be, you *are,* free to find the defendants guilty and to celebrate it.

He spoke of the crimes with which the defendants were charged. "It would be hard to believe that any decent people would do such wild things. But is it hard to believe that these men," and he pointed at the defendants, "would do such wild things?" They stared at him as if presented with an obscene Second Coming.

Foran made short, abrupt gestures with his always stiff hands, or by twisting with his fist, or jabbing with a finger, or tracing with a finger. "You do begin to have some concern about certain departments in certain colleges," he said. Edward Kratzke beamed. Kay Richards smiled.

Foran audaciously put "incendiary device and butyric acid" together as if they were of equal importance. Kunstler objected, catching Foran in a shameless attempt to play upon ignorance, and Foran hunched under Kunstler's statement of objection.

Foran declared that the defendants planned exactly what actually happened, they planned the escalation of the violence from Sunday night to Wednesday night of Convention Week. "These are highly sophisticated, educated men. They are not kids. Davis is the youngest, twenty-nine." He was in front of the jury box, hacking at the defense table with his hand. "They are *evil* men." He knew the defensive bitterness, how much a man or woman with a lower middle-class job wants to laugh at or get back at those people with education who get kicks messing over their beliefs. He knew they wanted to *sense* and *act* and *live* and be *right* and *free* to do with the defendants what they *wanted* to do with them.

More than any lawyer in the summations, he used such terms as "good guys" and "bad guys," "liars" and "obscene haters," and "good" and "evil." Foran said that the cross-examination of Davis was the "hardest of my career" because Davis was "so smart" and "so alert."

"If they demand," he hit his fist on the lectern, "and don't get it, then they threaten violence—" Conspiracy staff persons, spectators, and newsmen laughed. Foran hunched under the laughter but kept his eyes on the twelve jurors and two alternates. Judge Hoffman threatened to clear the courtroom.

During the noon recess, many journalists thought they recognized Foran as a winner, and their tone was that of finding a winner in the boxing ring.

Foran stroked and stoked the locomotive of his summation. "Rubin gets going good now," he said of Sunday night, August 25, 1968, in Lincoln Park. "It's almost dark. Predators always work best in the dark." There came a collective hiss from parts of the courtroom. Two weeks ago, that hiss would have been an uncontrollable laugh, but now it was very serious to be called a "predator." Foran could be so cool in what he was saying and then suddenly he would be shooting out such words as "evil" and "predator." He kept the initiative.

He excused the startling testimony of Commander Clarence Braasch, still imprinted in the jurors' minds, by saying that "Braasch had the police retreat" in Lincoln Park.

He named and described a cast of movement spokesmen in Lincoln Park that night and listed their "techniques." He was implying that "evil" men always use "techniques." He spoke of "Ginsberg as religious leader" and Ginsberg's "pretty filthy poetry," which was "not exactly religiously inspired." I remembered Allen Ginsberg sitting in the midst of a group om-ming on Sunday night in Lincoln Park. "Call a man a pig," Ginsberg said to the young people, "and you bring out the pig in him." Foran said the defendants were "luring young people with sex and music" to Lincoln Park. Kunstler objected, on the grounds that there was no evidence of this. He was overruled by the judge.

"It's a simple technique," Foran said, to explain the success of the defendants' actions during Convention Week. "Done in complicated situations, and simple situations. You see it in this courtroom. Somebody violates the law. A marshal takes hold of them to take them out—*hunh!*" He threw his arms up to show the uproar that would then occur. The marshals in the courtroom grinned at their man Tom Foran, the same marshals who had "great respect," so they said, "for that man Dave Dellinger." The governor of the trial gave no obvious expression at this point.

Foran told the step-by-step story of escalating violence and feeling between police and demonstrators during Convention Week. I sat in a sort of shock of certainty that Foran had read my book, *No One Was Killed,* and wedded to it his dark, deliberate Gothic fantasies, the artistry of the indictment, the presence of the defendants inciting mob violence at every step. Suddenly, in the scenes of Convention Week, there were these ghosts, these chimeras, that we had not seen before.

"Wanting to fight, wanting to hate," Foran said of the film of Abbie Hoffman at the press conference tapping his thigh with a stick. Foran hit his fist hard three times against his thigh. I wondered why no one of the defense ever thought to compare Abbie Hoffman's nervous stick with a cop switching his thighs with his club or a National Guard officer tapping his thighs with a riding crop.

"They were successful in driving a wedge between newsmen and police," Foran said. "A good newsman will take almost any risk to get a story." He was telling the newsmen that it was not too late, they were still welcome.

Late Tuesday night, August 27, in front of the Hilton Hotel, Foran said, "Hayden is there saying how we fought in Lincoln Park and we will march to the Amphitheatre by *any means necessary.*" Foran implied that all of the defendants except Abbie Hoffman were present at the Wednesday morning meeting. "Rubin not there, either," the defendants objected in chorus. Foran was bitter and furious at Kunstler. He yelled, "I can remember because I remember every *day.*"

"Anybody knows a scalp wound is a lot bloodier than it is serious," Foran said, showing the jury a picture of Rennie Davis, head bloodied. "Propaganda picture. He's smiling and he looks very *alert.*"

"Tell it like it is," Dellinger said from the other side of the defense table.

Foran continued to develop the speeches at the Grant Park bandshell Wednesday afternoon. "That's wild talk," he was saying about "Bo Taylor's speech," as if he knew the man intimately. "I don't care how you read it. That's wild talk. Mr. Weinglass read it low." Foran made a prissy, what he would call faggoty, twitch of his face and of the pinky on his hand that rested on the edge of the lectern. He whispered to the jury occasionally and made facial expressions that conveyed his opinion of the long-haired defense counsel Leonard Weinglass, together with his opinion of Allen Ginsberg and of long-haired defendants in general.

Foran was letting his own emotion and the emotion of his audience rise in response to the emphases he gave to the emotions in the words of Neuman, Sandow, and other persons who spoke at Grant Park Wednesday afternoon. Mrs. Fritz stared intensely and glumly at Foran. Edward Kratzke, with one finger extended across his upper lip, leaned on his right elbow and listened, beaming at Foran. About Dellinger in Grant Park, Foran said, "Like a ventriloquist, he used Tom Neuman," to incite people onto the path to eventual violence at Michigan-Balbo.

Foran attempted through the trial to divest the jury of any notions that "kids" carried out, or were the catalysts of, the actions of Convention Week. "It's probably true that the guerrilla fighters"—get that terminology—"were not the very young. They were about in their middle twenties. Like that group at the Pentagon. It takes only two or three to become that cutting edge of resistance." He gave a brief gesture with the edge of his palm. He continually revealed his close knowledge of Convention Week and his concern that the defense might try to put into evidence the way it actually happened. In fact, throughout Convention Week kids in their teens carried off some of the most dramatic actions. In the early part of the week, they were the central catalysts. "There are millions of kids," he said, "who resent authority, who are impatient for change. And there is another thing about the kid, his attraction to evil. Evil is exciting."

You could wonder if Foran in some way knew about the bitter debates among the jurors concerning the raising of children. "These sophisticated, educated psychology majors know about them, the young kids. These guys take advantage of that, draw them together, and maneuver them. Use them for their purposes, their intent." He spoke of the assassinations of John Kennedy, Bobby Kennedy, and Martin Luther King. "Kids feel that the lights have gone out in Camelot," seizing upon the phrase of John Kennedy, "the banners are furled and the parade is over. These guys take advantage of them—personally, intentionally, and *evilly*—to corrupt these kids. . . .

"Are we going to get conned like that? The bad guys work for the government, and you're only a good guy if you like the homosexual poetry of Allen Ginsberg or think Paul Krassner's funny." Foran was standing right in front of the jury box, up close, nailing it into the jurors. "We can't let them use our kids like that . . . We can't let them do it because what they want to do," and his voice was strong and rising, "they want to stand on the rubble of a destroyed system of government, the new leaders of arrogance and uncertainty."

Now he caught the eye of Mrs. Fritz, the one whom everyone was certain was a juror sympathetic to the defense. "Gave them a permit for April 27, and there was violence. Gave them a permit for Central Park, and the young kids were *fucking*—" Jean Fritz blinked as if saliva had hit her in the face "—in the grass and smoking dope. Public authority couldn't give them permits . . . They wanted to discredit the United States," Foran said. "They are sophisticated and well educated and as evil as they can be."

Foran reviewed the supposed desires of the defendants for social change that would benefit most people. "They don't have the stomach to struggle for ultimate good." For them, "Law is viewed as merely a collection of casual suggestions that they can obey or not as they see fit."

Foran spoke now for his client, the United States of America. He turned and faced the defendants, confronting them and displaying them to the jury. "We will have a guy actually walking on the moon and instead, they burrow downward toward the primitive, in obscenity, vulgarity, and hate. They would have us believe that their revolution is in a lofty cause, and so they can break the laws to achieve it."

Then came a perfect event to end his closing argument. He was repeating names used by the defense to support the sentiment of its position. Jesus, Saint Matthew, Dr. King, Abraham Lincoln. "Can you imagine any of these men having anything to do with these defendants?"

"Yes, they would!" Tasha Dellinger got up suddenly from her front seat to leave the courtroom.

More voices were raised.

Judge Hoffman said furiously, "Remove those people, Mr. Marshal!"

Dellinger was standing up at the defense table. "That's my daughter!"

Dellinger's younger daughter supported her sister and went out of the courtroom too.

"Don't hit her," Dellinger cried. "He hit her. I saw him." It seemed to me, as I looked through the closing courtroom door with a clearer view than Dellinger, that the marshal was merely reaching up to direct the girl to go down the hall.

Then Susan Schultz of the Conspiracy staff rose, unclipped the aisle rope, and was already going out, her voice shaking as she said, "Mr. Foran, why did Ramsey Clark come here to testify for us?" Many jurors were watching these events with intense perplexity.

Judge Hoffman directed the marshals to make Dellinger sit down. "You see?" Foran said excitedly to the jury. "You see how it works? 'Don't hit her.' "

Dellinger said, "He did hit her."

Somebody else said, "He did hit her."

Foran said, "Oh, bunk!"

That event could only have been perceived with perfect righteousness by both sides.

"The lights that Camelot kids believe in need not go out," Foran said. "The banners can snap in the breeze again. The parade will never be over if people will remember what Jefferson said: 'Obedience to the law is the major part of patriotism.' These seven men have been proven guilty beyond any doubt. Do your duty."

There was an ambitious politician in Illinois bearing a sacred name for a liberal. He lost the chance to be named by the Democratic party—by Daley, in effect—as its candidate for the U. S. Senate in 1968 because he spoke against the Viet Nam war. He next published a scathing criticism of Mayor Daley and the Chicago police and the Democratic party for their brutal actions during Convention Week. In the fall of 1969, he was even skeptical of the government's role in the Conspiracy trial. But by the fall of 1970, with a Senate seat opened up by the death of Everett Dirksen, he had been transformed by the exuberance of perceived necessities. Adlai Stevenson III, running hard for the Senate and with a chance of winning, took as the chairman of his Citizen's Committee, Thomas Foran, the famous prosecutor of the Conspiracy Seven, the man who named an Unpeople.

Foran campaigned for Stevenson in those areas of Illinois where a liberal needed help and where the "law and order" issue guaranteed audience attention. The Chicago *Sun-Times* reported that, to a standing ovation from steelworkers in Granite City, Illinois, Foran said, "I want to tell you something that gives me a thrill every time I say it. Think of yourself on a vacation sometime in New York and someone asks who your senator is—and you reply, 'Stevenson of Illinois.

*Judge Julius Jennings Hoffman:*
*"sufficient to convict guilt of the evidence"*

The Jennings is believed to come from William Jennings Bryan, and indeed Judge Hoffman's infancy falls within the spell of Bryan's "Cross of Gold" speech.

Judge Hoffman's charge to the Conspiracy jury is here included among the closing arguments, because that is, by virtue of its apparent function, its appropriate position in any account or understanding of this trial.

The marshals were excluding the defendants' wives because of their outbursts the day before. "It's not a public trial," Abbie Hoffman said. Five defendants walked out, while Froines and Dellinger stayed at the defense table. Judge Hoffman then asked for "representation" that the wives and family would keep quiet.

"The jury cannot question the wisdom of any rule of law; it can only decide the facts." He would reiterate this instruction at the end of his charge after he had described the law whose "wisdom" the jury could not question.

Judge Hoffman would not give John Froines and Lee Weiner a directed verdict of acquittal, even though there was no evidence that they "did teach and demonstrate" the use of an incendiary device. Froines and Weiner turned out to be useful in the jury's bargaining.

"To convict any defendant under Count One the government must prove beyond a reasonable doubt that the defendant was a knowing member of the conspiracy, and at least one or more overt acts were committed to further it." The only problem here, the judge indicated, would be the definition of the "conspiracy" and of the crime intended. Now Judge Hoffman began to raise a structure of silver threads, as he savored separately but in comparison the meaning of conspiracy, of intent, of act, of advocacy, of incitement, and of thought.

"In Count One" the government need prove "only one or more of the means" of the Conspiracy were actually put into operation. "It is not necessary to prove that they all met formally," for "tacit agreement is sufficient . . .

"However, in determining if a particular defendant was a part of the conspiracy the jury must consider his acts." Now the innovative spirit of Judge Hoffman began to emerge. "You can reason from a person's act to determine if he conspired at some other point in the past with others." But, "Evidence after the period of conspiracy can be considered only against that defendant." That affirmed that what Abbie Hoffman and Rennie Davis said a year after Convention Week revealed their intent before Convention Week.

Now Judge Hoffman drew upon general conspiracy law and marshaled the historical imagination that could make him the peer of whatever inquisitors he might meet in whatever afterlife might await him. "If the acts of another are the will of the defendant, then he is guilty as if he committed it himself."

Then he dwelled upon Counts Two to Seven, the substantive counts against each defendant. The government had to prove that each defendant did travel in interstate commerce with the intent to cause riots in Chicago, and then did speak to assemblages of people in Chicago with the intent of causing riots. The jurors must determine whether the words spoken after the defendants arrived in Chicago were "(1) such as to organize, incite, promote, or encourage a riot, (2) were spoken or caused to be spoken to an assemblage of three or more persons having individually or collectively the ability of immediate execution of an act of violence which would result in danger or injury to any other person or his property and (3) were spoken or caused to be spoken with this specific intent that one or more persons who were part of that assemblage would cause injury or damage to any person or his property as an immediate result of such words."

Judge Hoffman's wording was such that intent and potential—past, present and future—were sufficient bases to declare a crime. The characterization of such intent and potential almost always is likely to be the personal projection of the witness to the words and the event, even when he is aware of his perceptual inclinations.

The Supreme Court must eventually rule whether the recently dominant First Amendment interpretation, that incitement to riot must produce an "immediate, perceivable effect" in "a clear and present danger," can be extended to such phraseology as an assemblage "having individually or collectively the ability of immediate execution" or to words characterized as being spoken with "specific intent that one or more persons who were part of that assemblage would cause injury or damage."

If the jurors did not question the law, or Judge Hoffman's instructions concerning it, then the "fair-minded" parts of his charge only emphasized the other parts and made the obvious more palatable.

Judge Julius Jennings Hoffman emerged, in tone and manner, from his dark and violent sea of supposings, and came up seemingly singing in the sunlight of rationality. "The law distinguishes between advocacy of violence," which expresses abstract doctrine, "and actual incitement." He proceeded to confuse thoroughly advocacy, incitement, intent, and act. The jury "must decide if words of defendants in speeches caused immediate acts of violence"; but he had already made potential of act sufficient. He said that rallies and assemblages were not unlawful if permits were applied for in good faith and in a reasonable length of time prior to the events. He referred to the evidence of the government and the defense about permits. "That is a factual question that you must determine." He said at another point that the jurors should weigh with caution the evidence given by an informer.

"Reasonable doubt," Judge Hoffman said, "is just what the term implies. . . . It is a doubt founded upon reason. It appeals to reason and it is founded upon reason."

He even recommended that this jury of ten women and two men elect a "forewoman or foreman," in that order, as their first order of business.

But he loosed a quiet thunderbolt when he said, and his voice made his import clear, "Such evil intent may be proven by defendants' conduct," slight pause, "and by all the facts of the case." With wonderful subtlety and clarity, he was echoing Foran in using the word "evil" and in referring to "defendants' conduct" in the courtroom.

In speaking of direct evidence and circumstantial evidence, he committed the most singular slip of the tongue of five months of trial, a sort of grand culmination of the pattern of his other slips of the tongue, mind, and ruling. He spoke, with the rising energy that betrayed him, of evidence "sufficient to convict *guilt of the evidence—*"he corrected himself—"guilt of the defendants." It was done. The transcript, taken from the judge's written instructions, reads blithely at this point, "If the facts and circumstances as shown by the evidence in this case are sufficient to convince you of the guilt of the defendants . . ."

"You have no right to ignore any one instruction or to question the wisdom of any law." Jimmy Jonesen and Ron Dobroski were sworn as marshals of the jury. Here one could not help but be reminded of the defense's request that its people be permitted to participate in taking care of the jurors too.

The "good citizens under oath" were marched to the deliberating room to find what combination of conscience, perception, bias, loyalty, and fear would win.

## The Court That Tries Men for Their Dreams

Judge Hoffman overruled the defense's objections to his instructions to the jury. "Now we have another matter here."

With the exception of their actions during the binding and gagging of Bobby Seale, there was seldom a full agreement among the defendants on how they should respond in the court. The "new tactics" came from their disposition of mind not to accept the manipulations of the legal proceedings against them and to give the trial political resonance. The reverberations in the media conceivably made the government and the judge feel accountable.

Many jurists over the country thought that Judge Hoffman's principal mistake—and illegality—was to wait until the end of the trial to deal with the contempts cumulatively. Summary contempt, a traditional weapon of a judge, should be done at the moment, on the spot, of the direct contempt. In Indianapolis, Indiana, a couple of months after the Conspiracy trial, the defendants of the Beaver 55—on trial for the burning of draft records—rose on the first day of their trial and sing-songed as the judge entered, "Good morning, your honor." He sentenced them, then and there, to thirty days in jail, summary contempt. The weakness of the "new tactics" was their dependence on public response generated through the media.

Judge Hoffman, in ruling against Weinglass at one point, admitted that there was no precedent here for legal argument because there was no precedent for his contempt action. Heretofore a contempt sentence dealt out summarily by a judge could not exceed six months. A longer sentence required a jury trial. Judge Hoffman, as in the Bobby Seale contempts, tried to circumvent this rule by giving no more than six months for each instance.

February 14 and 15, Saturday and Sunday, were two heavy days in Judge Hoffman's courtroom, as the nightmare became as enclosed as the inside of a sphere. The people in the space of the courtroom reacted repetitively to the same stimuli with the same intensity, as if hopelessly traumatized.

Judge Hoffman said that the contempts "openly challenged this court and the system of law it represents." In short, the defendants and Judge Hoffman agreed and flattered each other's importance. In another trial in Chicago, where Brian

Flanagan was acquitted for delivering a paralyzing blow during a Weatherman action to the neck of Richard Elrod, Assistant Corporation counsel of the city of Chicago, Flanagan said that he and the prosecutor, Beranek, "understood each other" clearly. Flanagan meant that the prosecutor understood that Flanagan was a revolutionary. It sounded somewhat self-congratulatory in the assumed flames and shadows of a twilight of the gods. Judge Hoffman was handing out what the defendants accepted as worth.

The defendants, their women, and Conspiracy staff members were talking excitedly in undertones and laughing with a release of tense expectation about what was about to happen, as Dellinger's citations were read first. Dellinger's daughter Tasha applauded Dellinger's speech. "Take him out," the judge ordered, presumably referring to Dellinger.

The marshals tried to drag Tasha out. Conspiracy staff members and spectators tried to prevent them from dragging her so violently. There were those who testified that she kicked a marshal in the balls. The marshal was in the hospital for a few days. A woman marshal came to apply the required force. A young woman, in the melee, ended up astride the woman marshal on the floor and was pulling at her hair. Bob Lamb and Susan Schultz, of the Conspiracy staff, would be charged with obstructing the marshals. Susan Schultz would be locked up on fifteen-thousand-dollar bail.

"Leave my daughter alone," Dellinger cried out.

"Leave that girl alone," someone else yelled.

"Leave her alone."

Jerry Rubin, with his arm upthrust in the Nazi salute, marched rigidly toward the bench, yelling, "Heil Hitler. Heil Hitler. Heil Hitler." Judge Hoffman was remarkably unmoved. Richard Schultz smiled and laughed, though he could not be heard. Tom Hayden was, as usual, asking everybody to "cool it." William Kunstler was leaning on the lectern, weeping, and

asking the judge to send him away too. Judge Hoffman stayed
unmoved.

Then the marshals made the press sit down, and the spectators sit down. "Well," Defendant Dellinger said, "you preserved law and order here, Judge."

Then the judge sentenced Dellinger to nearly thirty months,
and Dellinger went out the custody door. That was the most
violent melee of the trial, and yet Judge Hoffman regarded it
as a chore to be endured briskly, an attitude new for him in
this trial.

Three instances of Rennie Davis's contempts were for statements he made on his own behalf on the witness stand. He
said that the judge was not listening at one point, and did not
read a document at another. Dellinger could not get under
the judge's skin this day, but Davis, who had flattered the judge
from the witness stand, tried to explain how the court's handling of Bobby Seale involved him. The judge said that Bobby
Seale had insulted him. "Yes," Davis said, with his fingertips
stuck in his belt, and letting his voice rise with each word, "he
called you a racist, a fascist, and a pig many times. And not
enough." Judge Hoffman's face shook, and then went suddenly
red. In a fury, he ordered Davis to sit down.

Weinglass rose. "He has a right to answer."

"He has no right to stand there and insult me."

"You stand for everything that is old, ugly, bigoted, and
repressive in this country," Davis said. "The spirit at this defense table is going to devour everything you stand for in the
next generation." Davis was sentenced to twenty-five months
and fourteen days, on twenty-three instances of contempt. He
went with the marshals through the custody door.

The lawyers ritually made motions declaring the judge's lack
of authority for such contempt action and asked for bail which
was ritually denied by the judge.

Tom Hayden was cited for eleven contempts, and received
a sentence of fourteen months and fourteen days. When Hay-

den said that the marshals had told him that they regretted what they had done to Seale, Judge Hoffman interrupted, "I would agree with the marshals about deeply regretting it." Hayden's voice quavered now and then because of his belief that the defendants were going to disappear into jail, without bail, for years to come. There was the feeling of a victory celebration about to break out at the prosecution table. Tom Foran was grinning, while Richard Schultz stayed relaxed and inscrutable. Agent Stanley, with his arms folded, was smiling. Roger Cubbage was grinning.

Judge Hoffman interrupted Hayden at many points, and here the judge answered at length about Ramsey Clark. Hayden, simply and wonderfully, folded his arms and paced up and down by the defense table, listening and letting the judge protest and justify his actions for as long as he wished. It was a different and effective attitude on the part of a defendant toward the judge, and the judge became profoundly involved in explaining himself. Foran grinned widely without showing his teeth when Hayden talked about the Conspiracy trial as a "political trial."

"Right before your eyes the vital ingredients of the system are crumbling away," Tom Hayden said. Judge Hoffman said, "Smart man like you could do very well in this system." He said it as if he were ready to hire Tom Hayden on the spot. Abbie Hoffman said, "We don't want a place in the regiment, Julie."

Hayden said, with morbid intensity, that he had tried to think of the one thing that he would regret about punishment. "That is that I would like to have a child," he said. Sobs were heard in the courtroom.

Judge Hoffman said, "That's where the federal system can do you no good."

Hayden said, "That's where the federal system can do you no good in preventing the birth of a new world." The wife of the managing editor of a large newspaper was guided, sobbing,

out of the courtroom. Reporters were checking Hayden's last
words against each other's notebooks. Hayden went through
the custody door.

The black, empty chairs at the defense table were becoming
presences now.

When Judge Hoffman told Abbie Hoffman sharply to sit
down, Abbie said that he would fight for his right to speak.
"The way we fought in Lincoln Park," he said sarcastically to
the marshal. They saw that he meant that he would fight, and
the judge saw it and they let him continue talking. He grinned.
It was a small, but definite victory. Then he said, "I sat there
on the witness stand and Mr. Schultz said, 'What were you
wondering?' as he quoted from my book and speeches. 'What
were you wondering that night when you stood before a building?' And I said, 'Wonder? Wonder? I have never been on
trial for wondering. Is that like a dream?' He said, 'Yes, that's
like a dream.' And I have never been on trial for my dreams
before."

Some of the contempts attributed to Abbie Hoffman were
in fact said by Jerry Rubin. The same would be true of Rubin's
citations.

Abbie Hoffman came up to the first row behind the defense
table where Anita got up to meet him. "Water the plant," he
said puckering, and they kissed. The emotion in the courtroom
ached with the exit of each defendant.

Jerry Rubin said, "Can we do it now, Judge? I want to be
with my brothers."

"Mr. Rubin, do you want to ask any favors of Mr. Hitler?"


John Froines sat in his chair the next morning hugging a
fifth of whisky that he intended to take to jail with him. Outside
the courtroom the corridors of the huge Federal Building were
empty with Sunday, and outside the building the Loop streets
were desolate with Sunday and February.

The judge read Rubin's record quickly and unexpressively. He even said "sonofabitch" in quoting Rubin, rather than spelling it as he did the word F-U-C-K.

"I made many comparisons to Nazi Germany," Rubin said. "Everything done in Nazi Germany was legal." He said that millions of kids identified with the defendants.

Jerry Rubin was sentenced to twenty-five months and twenty-three days. Jerry Rubin and Nancy Kurshan hugged and kissed, and then Jerry Rubin went through the custody door shouting at the judge, "Sadist!"

The contumacious conduct of the defendant Lee Weiner, who was in some ways a courtroom dropout, took only six minutes for Judge Hoffman to read. Weiner's position on the faculty of the sociology department at Northwestern University intrigued Judge Hoffman. Here was another son of the system gone wrong. "This court as an institutional form supports your feeling of omnipotence," Weiner said, in a reasonable tone. "I don't personally forgive you, but neither do I personally condemn you."

He also let the judge interrupt and speak as long in self-justification as the judge wished. "Years ago," Judge Hoffman said, "I was a member of the faculty of your school." He said there was even a plaque with his name on it on an auditorium of the Law School at Northwestern. Weiner grinned, looked down, looked up, and said, "I'm pleased to report to you that it's been ripped off the wall." Weiner caught the judge in an expansive, generous moment.

"Did they tear the sign off the door?"

Weiner said that the sign had been ripped off.

Then he thanked the judge for making "the struggle real." He was sentenced to two months and eighteen days. Sharon Avery called out, "I love you," as Weiner went through the custody door.

John Froines gestured with his fist affirmatively to his wife Ann when the judge read one instance of contempt that occurred in the presence of the jury. Those were the ones that got the large sentences. Not so oddly, defendants, their women, and staff persons, took a feeling of pride in the number of contempts and the amount of sentences. It was a counting of coup. Reporters were keeping track and weighing one defendant in comparison with another as if they were talking about batting averages.

Then the judge almost continued into the lawyers' contempts without sentencing Froines. The first time I talked with John Froines, just before the trial, he called himself a "media unknown." Now he said, "It's part of being a media unknown," beginning his speech and getting a laugh, "that even the judge finally forgets you're here."

"I didn't hear that," Judge Hoffman said.

"It's perhaps an in-joke, your honor," Froines said.

He too did not personally accuse the judge with his attitude and tone, and therefore the judge again tried to explain himself. Judge Hoffman felt guilty before men whose academic credentials made him suspect that they were rational according to definitions that he accepted, and capable of forming judgments that he might fear. Froines had just published an article, in collaboration with an associate, in *The Journal of Physical Chemistry,* on "the effect of high intensity light on certain molecules, the chemical transformation that occurs, and the short life, millionths of a second, of the transformed molecules." He spoke of his "childlike curiosity" in pursuing research.

At the end of one of Judge Hoffman's particularly long interruptions, Froines said, "You have that a little backward because we didn't ask actually to come here."

"If the law enforcement agencies of the government were to wait," Judge Hoffman said, "for all alleged lawbreakers to invite themselves here, I am afraid that most of the courthouses in the land could be burned down."

"Right on, right on," came the laughter and agreement from spectators.

Froines read an article from the constitution of his home state, Oregon, about the people having the right to reform the government in any way they deem fit and proper. He said he wanted the judge to "understand our emphasis just as we have understood *your* emphasis." Froines got five months and fifteen days.

Bobby Seale's voice arose again, speaking eerily out of the mouth of Judge Hoffman as he read Kunstler's contempts. When the judge imitated the "om-m-m" in the specification concerned with Ginsberg's testimony, there was laughter. The judge was more within his rights in leaving the lawyers' contempts to the end of the trial, because of Sixth Amendment considerations of intimidating lawyers in the course of the trial.

Kunstler's hair was much longer now at the end of the trial, with curly, white tufts of sideburns.

"Do you desire to be heard, Mr. Kunstler?"

Kunstler then read the statement that launched him into the orbit of his fame. He said that until this day he had never been disciplined by any court, and he gave a list of the circuits and states where he had practiced. "I can only hope that my fate does not deter other lawyers throughout the country who, in the difficult days that lie ahead, will be asked to defend clients against a steadily increasing government encroachment upon their most fundamental liberties. If they are so deterred, then my punishment will have the effect of such terrifying consequences that I dread to contemplate the future domestic and foreign course of this country. However, I have the utmost faith that my beloved brethren at the bar, young and old alike, will not allow themselves to be frightened out of defending the poor, the persecuted, the radicals and militant, the black people, the pacifists, and the political pariahs of this, our common land." Then he spoke to those lawyers who might "waver because of what was happening to him.

"I would like to remain standing while I am sentenced."

There was great applause. In the back row, his wife seemed moved and proud of him.

"Marshals," Judge Hoffman ordered, "remove those from the courtroom who applauded. This circus has to end some-time . . .

"If crime is on the increase," the judge said, "it is due in large part to lawyers waiting in the wings to defend . . . to go beyond professional responsibility, in their defense . . . I think it has a stimulating effect." Judge Hoffman, who thought him-self to be so strict about the Rules of Evidence, drew huge conclusions from scattered impressions.

"I'm glad your honor spoke," Kunstler said, not missing a single chance to seize a moving moment. "Because I now feel nothing but compassion for you. Everything else has dropped away." Kunstler did not expect the sentence that came—over four years. It was postponed so that he would be able to act as attorney for the defendants in preparing their appeal.

Then Judge Hoffman read the counts of contempt against Leonard Weinglass. He had now come to the lawyer for whom the Conspiracy staff and many of the defendants felt especial affection and admiration. "The U. S. Attorney referred to the Seven as evil, and I believe that he meant it personally and seriously," Weinglass said. "The defendants have referred to him as fascistic. It was a political trial, though the court refused to see it as such." Most of Weinglass's instances of contempt came because he tried to continue legal argument after the judge's ruling had cut him off.

Now, at the end of the trial, Judge Hoffman wronged We-inglass's name again, called him Weinruss. "With respect to our different understandings of respect," Weinglass said to the judge, "I was hopeful when I came here that after twenty weeks the court would know my name and I didn't receive that which I thought was the minimum—" The judge tried haplessly to explain about a friend of his named Weinruss and nobody named Weinrob and the issue of Weinglass's name was as moot at the end of the trial as at the beginning.

"I'm not as strong a man as Bill Kunstler," Weinglass said, adding that he perhaps tended to feel what he perceived to be intimidation more strongly than Kunstler.

"Does your honor really believe," Weinglass asked, "that what was in conflict here in this courtroom could have been dissipated by an admonishment from Bill Kunstler or myself?"

Ten marshals stood in the aisle before the courtroom doors with their arms folded and their legs spread, listening to their long-awaited vindication. Weinglass spoke of the "rich association" with the young people who worked for the Conspiracy and slept on the floor of his apartment, working until three and four in the morning. "I would have paid out of my own pocket," Judge Hoffman said, piously, imploringly, "for a bed for them to sleep in a respectable place," if only Weinglass had admonished his clients and young workers to respect the court. "I think they would respect you even more if you had admonished these men—"

The voice of Ann Froines rang out. "There is no man in this courtroom whom I respect more than Leonard Weinglass!" She grabbed her long yellow scarf from under the front pew and went straight out of the courtroom. Mickey Leanor jumped up and brandished the power salute at Judge Hoffman. "You *are* a racist, and a fascist, and a pig!"

"Take that young woman out!" Judge Hoffman said. "She has been shown the *ut*most deference, the *ut*most respect, by members of my staff!"

Nancy Rubin said loudly, near weeping, "There *is* a conspiracy in this country, a conspiracy to overthrow the death culture! "

Weinglass was applauded. The judge ordered the marshals to take out those who applauded.

"I welcome the chance to continue my association with Bill Kunstler," Weinglass said, "which I consider to have been the richest of my life."

Weinglass was sentenced to twenty months and nine days for fourteen citations of contempt. His sentence was also postponed.

The judge said that he had no authority to do anything about the bail, and if he did have the authority, in view of the findings in the contempt action, he would not fix bail for such persons as the defendants.

## *Like the Last People on the Face of the Earth: The Jury's Deliberations*

"If we had known that the government would not try this case again, or if we'd known about the contempt proceedings, we would still be in that deliberating room to this day if that was the way Judge Hoffman wanted it," said Mrs. Fritz.

I asked Jean Fritz and Shirley Seaholm what did they think Judge Hoffman meant was going to happen when he noted instances of protest for the record throughout the trial, saying each time, "And we will deal with this at the appropriate time." They said they thought he meant "a bawling out." I asked if they didn't know during the trial what happened to Bobby Seale—four years' total sentence for sixteen citations of contempt. They said they knew only that Bobby Seale was going to get a separate trial, and they knew about his sentence only because the defendants, in some of their "outbursts," told them the impermissible information that Bobby Seale had been "railroaded" for four years. But the defense was not able to impress on the mind of the jury that the sentence was for contempt.

The jury was deliberating in a room on the twenty-third floor. If the jurors stood close to a window they could hear the small, persistent demonstration for the Conspiracy Seven on the plaza below.

"We don't ever have saints on the jury," Judge Hoffman had retorted to William Kunstler during jury selection many months before, "just good citizens under oath." The hundreds of prospective jurors belly-laughed, along with many other people in the courtroom. They had all lived long enough, with enough moral ambiguity, to appreciate the remark.

The jury may have been divided into two sides on the first day of the trial, since the trial itself may have been rooted in a profound division in the American middle class, if not in a two-sided character of all human society.

The four "acquittal" jurors sat at one end of the deliberating table, and the convict-on-all-counts jurors at the other end. The jurors first elected Edward Kratzke as their foreman, "because he was a man," and apparently to avoid the feelings and conflicts that would result if they didn't. Their first vote was 8-4 for conviction, and that basic grouping would never change. The surprise was Kay Richards, whom everyone thought was for acquittal. "See," the convict-on-all-counts jurors said, "Kay is young, and she thinks they're guilty."

The convict-on-all-counts jurors were saying: "Is this the sort of world [the defendants' life-styles] that you want your children to grow up in?" . . . "They *are* evil!" . . . "This is like Nazi Germany—hippies want to take over the country! [that was a novel image]" . . . "They had no right to come into our living room! [again echoing Foran, though Foran's assistant attorneys supposedly argued that right in their wonderfully unsuccessful civil rights cases against the eight scapegoat cops who were indicted for Convention Week rioting]" . . . "Walk through a Polish neighborhood, and they'd shoot them!" . . . "They need a good bath!" . . . "Put their feet on the government's furniture!" . . . "You're afraid to find the defendants guilty because you have young people in your families!"

The "acquittal" jurors had young people in their late teens and early twenties in their immediate families, but so did one convict-on-all-counts juror who was afraid that the defendants' life-styles would overtake her son. The "acquittal" jurors argued that none of these things were matters on which the defendants were being tried. The "acquittal" jurors talked a great deal in the deliberating room about their belief in the unconstitutionality of the antiriot statutes. That was Leonard Weinglass's plea to them.

The prosecution made the point that the defendants as "leaders" or "spokesmen" were never present when the going got rough with the police. That would mitigate any reasonable doubt about whether the defendants incited those actions directly. If the defendants were present, they incited the actions. If they weren't present, they were cowards who deserted people to slaughter. "The things we didn't like about their actions were not in the indictment," Mrs. Seaholm said.

The prosecution had also made another impression on the convict-on-all-counts jurors that, though the judge said the jurors were to disregard conduct, deportment, language, manner of dress and life-style, the jurors had every right to use "all their senses" and not leave out what had happened in the courtroom. That was Prosecutor Foran touching the nerves of the jury again. He was the one attorney who was able to touch the jury in ways that directed them toward a conclusion.

"There was more silence than anything in the deliberating room," Mrs. Fritz said. "There was a feeling of hate in the room, between the two factions."

The days of deliberation began to flow feverishly one into another. On Sunday, February 15, a hung-jury message was written by Kay Richards and read aloud to the jurors. Then Edward Kratzke knocked on the jury door and handed the message to the marshal to take to Judge Hoffman. The judge's response came back through the marshal: "Keep deliberating!" The marshal said, in addition, "The judge can keep you here as long as he wants!" This sort of assertion from the U. S. marshal gave backing and credibility to the jurors' recently acquired fear of the United States government.

Mrs. Seaholm remembered the marshal jabbing his finger emphatically at one time when he said, "Remember the judge's instructions!" The judge's instructions had seemed to be a clear spelling out of the possibilities of negotiation.

"When we voted hung jury," said Mrs. Fritz and Mrs. Seaholm, "somebody said the judge would poll us individually in his chambers, and we all said, 'I'm not afraid.' Yes, we said, 'I'm not afraid.' I think Kay was the one who said the judge would poll us individually in his chambers if we were a hung jury." The jury was aware that it was so seriously divided that it could not hope for any agreement that would satisfy any of its members. "We would not listen to them, and they would not listen to us. The conviction jurors kept saying, 'Well, they want a hung jury. All that money [the government's expenses] gone to waste.' They said that over and over again, about the money being wasted."

On Monday, February 16, the jury sent another hung-jury message to Judge Hoffman. The two jurors say Kay Richards wrote the message slips each time. The judge's response came back again through the marshal: "Keep deliberating!" The marshal also said at one time, "The Krebiozen trial jury was out two weeks!" and, "The judge can keep you here as long as he wants!" and, "This is your duty!" implying that it was their duty to deliberate and reach some sort of verdict. It was, of course, possible for the judge to keep the jury deliberating a "reasonable" length of time. But he should have notified the defense and the prosecution of the hung-jury messages and impaneled the jury so the defendants could be present at all points in the process of their trial.

The jury also sent a request to Judge Hoffman to see transcript for accounts of the defendants' speeches, and this request was denied. Again, the defense (and presumably the prosecution) were not notified. The jurors had only a speech by Tom Hayden and another by Dave Dellinger in evidence. Yet it was specifically speeches of each defendant that were cited in the substantive counts in the indictment. For lawyers, jurists, and legal scholars the most difficult point for the government to prove in the substantive counts was that the defendants were possessed of intent to incite riots at the moment of crossing state lines. Such intent could only be inferred from other evidence. For the jurors, however, the most important point apparently was the intent of the defendants at the moment of making their speeches.

"We finally voted them guilty on speeches that we don't even remember," Mrs. Fritz said, with a tone of the most solemn candor. "What we did—and this I'll never get over—we gave in to ourselves, we compromised with ourselves. Kay didn't have anything to do with our decision. You might say that we used her as much as she used us. We didn't know if it was a hung jury that they wouldn't be tried again." That was the refrain.

That was another important factor in the process by which the "acquittal" jurors came to decide that they must compromise. It could not have been predicted and apparently the defense did not know about it. Mrs. Fritz and Mrs. Seaholm feared that the case would be re-tried if the jury stayed hung. This was because Mrs. Fritz—since jurors were called for a thirty-day period of jury duty—had served as an alternate juror on a Mafia case just before the Conspiracy trial. That jury was a hung jury, and she remembered seeing in a newspaper just before she was sequestered that the trial was rescheduled for October 6, 1969. She had every reason to believe that the government would, if the jury were hung, re-try the Conspiracy case too.

This was an important factor among the feelings, fears, hopes, and interpretations discussed and worried over by the four "acquittal" jurors.

"We knew," Mrs. Fritz said, "we could never get the defendants out of that courtroom innocent."

"We didn't know the law," Mrs. Seaholm said, "we didn't know that Judge Hoffman would have to accept a hung jury eventually."

In its ceaseless ambivalence the defendants did believe that a hung jury would be a political victory. But they who were so explicit about other "impermissible" matters when they spoke to the jury were not so blunt or clear with this suggestion. Nevertheless, it was their convenient assertion that the government would not try such a difficult, expensive case again.

In retrospect, the jurors' reasoning appears to have been based, both legally and politically, better than they thought in their chagrin directly after the trial. Certainly the government, to justify its prestige and credibility in the public furor of a hung jury right at the end of this fantastic trial, would have been forced to try it again. Because of the conspiracy charge, the government could have continued trying the defendants as a group.

Mrs. Fritz and Mrs. Seaholm believed that because of the media representation given the defendants' behavior in the courtroom, it would have been nearly impossible to find a jury that would not convict them on all counts.

But the government's prestige and credibility could be vindicated by initial verdicts of guilty on the substantive counts. Then, with the conspiracy count thrown out, the convictions could be overturned at a convenient time in the future by an appeals court on the ground that the First Amendment protected the defendants' speeches. The jurors could put the law itself on trial.

Now we have to try to understand the person who used the two jurors, or was used by them, or both, to reach a verdict, and then almost immediately, despite a group oath to keep forever silent about what happened in the jury room, began publishing her story of how she did it—a story whose facts were often questioned by Shirley Seaholm and Jean Fritz, and whose omissions were at least as important as the expressed "facts."

By the end of the trial, it was hard not to review the steps by which such an earnest and apparently forceful young woman as Kay Richards came onto the jury. When the defense at the time of jury selection, with seven peremptories remaining, took the government by surprise by accepting the jury as it stood, they were glad to have young Kay Richards as the first alternate. Kristi King was also a young woman on the jury at that time. "She kept to herself until Kristi left," Mrs. Fritz said. "She sat by herself. She didn't say much."

Kay Richards said in her account in the Chicago *Sun-Times* that the defendants were "right" about Kristi King. "She was sympathetic to the defense. If she had stayed, it might have been a hung jury." In answer to this writer in the post-trial interviews, Mrs. Fritz said, "Kay had no right to assume that. How could she know? Kay Richards never talked with Kristi. I had no idea how Kristi felt. I was her roommate for two days."

In the middle of the second week of the trial, Kristi King was excused from the jury because of the so-called Black Panther letter, which she had not even read before the judge showed it to her. Alternate Kay Richards was welcomed onto the jury proper.

The two jurors said: "From the beginning, we had a peculiar feeling about her."—"She wanted a lot of information, but she never gave any."—"She used people."—"It just seems funny that the four of us sensed it immediately." The two jurors said that Mary Butler—one of two black women on the jury, and one of the "four"—called attention to the fact that Kay Richards would, if she saw any two of the four conversing, try to find out what they were talking about. Three of the four became worried when one of their number, Frieda Robbins, started showing Kay Richards how to sew in her room after the day at the trial. "We approached Frieda to warn her, and Frieda said, 'Don't worry, we never talk about anything important. I don't trust her.'"

Kay Richards always associated with the four. She was not liked by the convict-on-all-counts group. When she sat slumped in her chair in the jury box, she irritated the proper women of the majority. "Sit up like a lady," Milly Burns said to her sharply. "Be quiet," Kay Richards said right back.

In her story in the Chicago *Sun-Times* she claimed that the jurors "played games" with the defendants, "smiling occasionally" and things like that. That was an example of understatement that amounted to omission, because everyone in the courtroom saw Kay Richards laugh outright on the side of the defense, earnestly and consistently, for five months of trial. For whatever purpose, she was right that she was playing a game, and it was quite a game to play every day for five months.

The two jurors said that Kay Richards thought that Abbie Hoffman had "a crush" on her. In the last month of the trial, she exclaimed once, outside the courtroom, "I can't stand it anymore, everybody is watching me." She was right, people *were* watching her, as they watched all of the jurors for clues to their feelings. She apparently had a sense of drama about herself. Why would she make it seem to all parties, fellow jurors, and observers in the courtroom, that she was for acquittal, and then reveal herself suddenly in the deliberating room to be for conviction on all counts?

"Her boyfriend, Tom, now husband, works for City Hall," the two jurors said. In fact, he worked for Cook County, as head of a department concerned with personnel classification. "She wouldn't give her home address when she was selected alternate; she gave another address. She also wouldn't sign her name to a list of addresses that we made for ourselves to keep track of each other."

When Judge Hoffman questioned the prospective jurors, one of the few questions he would ask was about the job association of members of immediate family. The defense, if it heard that a family member worked for any level of government, would exercise a peremptory challenge to dismiss that prospective juror. If the defense had known about the job of Kay Richards' boyfriend, who would soon become her husband, they would certainly have used a peremptory against her. "We didn't trust her, and we didn't know why," the jurors said. When her boyfriend came to see her, the marshals did not monitor them as closely as the other jurors and visitors. Sometimes they even left Kay Richards and Tom Stevens alone.

"Her most important thing" in the deliberating room, Mrs. Fritz said, "was to get out of there. She was urgent about it. I think it had something to do with those articles she was going to publish in the *Sun-Times.* She changed very willingly when she heard we wouldn't agree with the other jurors." Kay Richards had, on her own insistence, a single room at the Palmer House. Other jurors also had single rooms. "She must have been typing her story for the papers, already working on it; you could hear it when she went to her room," Mrs. Fritz said. In the post-trial jury hearing, Kay Richards Stevens admitted to having kept voluminous notes on the trial.

The two jurors remembered that Kay Richards was at first angry that the jury could not agree. She sat in a corner of the deliberating room embroidering a tablecloth. "No sense in me saying any more. I'm just going to sit in a corner," she said. But by Sunday she began acting, in effect, as foreman of the jury. She was the one, throughout the trial, who took charge of things here and there, such as ordering lunch or getting a glass of water for a juror having a coughing fit.

The majority jurors avoided the four "acquittal" jurors and were angry with them. Shirley Seaholm said she was looking through photographs that were in evidence at the table when Kay Richards came out of her corner and said demandingly, "We have to come to an agreement!" After the trial, Ruth Peterson, the most bitter holdout for conviction on all counts, said that if it had not been for Kay Richards the jurors "would still be in that deliberating room."

Kay Richards said in her account that the jury came to an agreement because she "insisted" on a verdict. "We didn't know anything about her insisting on a verdict," Mrs. Fritz said. In her compelling voice she called Kay Richards "that little Joan of Arc." Kay Richards said in her account that it "came to" her that the jury had to reach a verdict. She was implying that she felt a responsibility to the nation. "It *came* to her," Mrs. Fritz said, "after we said we'll sit here forever before we'll find them guilty on the First Count. We told her we thought the indictment of Weiner and Froines was utterly ridiculous. That's how it *came* to her."

It was Tuesday, February 17, after nearly four days of hopeless deadlock, when Kay Richards started to read the indictment out loud. "We can't do it that way," Mrs. Fritz said. "We have to read it individually." It turned out that several of the convict-on-all-counts jurors had not yet read the long indictment. "There was only one copy of the indictment for twelve jurors." The jurors began to see the many alternatives and could not help but hear the voice with which Judge Hoffman read it to them months ago.

"Kay said that she would like to talk to us. We knew that we could never get the defendants out of there not guilty. We had a fear in us that you shouldn't have in a jury room, a fear that Judge Hoffman would not accept a hung jury, a fear that a hung jury would do no good." They had a perpetual fear of the government and the undercover action that it might take against them. Two hung-jury messages had already been refused by Judge Hoffman. Like most people in a situation where the validity of their choices will be determined by factors unknown to them, the two jurors were possessed by different rationales and contradictory feelings about the possibility of a hung jury.

The "acquittal" jurors in general were overtaken by a feeling of defenseless terror, and a consequent inability to eat, sleep, or do any normal activity while they tried to reach a decision. Mrs. Fritz said that she was almost hysterical, weeping more than once during the deliberations, wanting desperately to get out of there. Mrs. Seaholm shared the desperation. "Kay said, 'If I talk to them, would you mind?' We thought maybe we'd misjudged her. We were grateful."

But on Tuesday night, February 17, still without a verdict, the jurors left the Federal Building and went in their bus to the Palmer House. "We were never excused because of hate and tension from the jury room as Kay Richards says. We were excused because our foreman was so sick he could not work. He had a very bad coughing fit." I could not help but remember that each of Mr. Kratzke's coughing fits in the course of the trial were directly related to impugned patriotism. At the Palmer House that night "Kay Richards wasn't shuttling between rooms as she says in her articles, not between our rooms and their rooms. The four of us never met with Kay Tuesday night. She was talking to the three of the conviction jurors who would still talk to her, and someone else was talking with the two conviction jurors who wouldn't have anything to do with Kay. Then we knew three had come over because Kay was no longer working on them. She convinced them—no, nobody was convinced of anything—she talked them into this, this . . ." The word Mrs. Fritz could not say was either "compromise," or "agreement," or "deal," or a word to that effect. "We used her as much as she used us," the jurors said again.

Late, very late, Tuesday night, February 17, two jurors still wanted the defendants guilty on both counts and would not relinquish their position, and one juror wanted them innocent on all counts and would not give in. "It was hard for the conviction jurors to give up the conspiracy count and find Froines and Weiner innocent." It would take much effort before finally even convict-on-all-counts Ruth Peterson—remember she received a "Black Panther" letter and told the judge she could still be "impartial" and she also occasionally laughed on both sides during the proceedings—would say that "half a chicken is better than no chicken at all." The four "acquittal" jurors were not able to sleep Tuesday night.

Right after they gave their verdicts in the courtroom, somebody said to the jurors during their last minutes in the jury room "Don't you see Weiner and Froines were written into the indictment so you would be able to find someone not guilty'?" Then the jurors were confronted with the possibility that the "preposterous and horrible" conspiracy count had been put into the indictment for a two-level, and maybe three- or four-level, purpose. It would be a stupendous bonus for the government if the defendants were actually found guilty of such a charge, but it also provided a variety of items for bargaining in the jury room to ensure some kind of guilty verdicts. "The First Count [the conspiracy count] was fantastic," Mrs. Fritz said. "Burning hotels—that sort of thing. And we thought we were really doing something when we kept fighting to get them off of it. Seven men who hardly knew each other."

When the jurors threw out the conspiracy count, they were left with the relatively simple substantive counts, each of which charged an individual defendant with crossing state lines and making specific speeches with intent to incite riots. If there had been only the substantive counts, and Froines and Weiner had not been included in the indictments, there might never have been a verdict. There would have been no way for differing egos and consciences to work out a resolution. It would truly have taken "saints" rather than mere "good citizens under oath" to reject the bountiful array of charges.

The defense had pointed out that the government had not "proven" the conspiracy count, and not "proven" the use of interstate commerce, and not "proven" the count against Froines and Weiner. The prosecution pointed out that the defense had not brought any contradictory witnesses for the words spoken by the defendants in meetings, which presumably implied the presence of "intent." Therefore, the substantive "speech" counts, though contradicted by some defense testimony, became the setup for juror agreement.

Judge Hoffman said in his charge to the jury that the jurors could reason from results to intent. The jurors might have asked themselves if they could apply the same principle to the relationship of the verdicts to the indictment.

Six of the defendants were incarcerated on the upper tier of Cook County jail, while David Dellinger was on the lower tier with the older men. Cell doors were left open so the defendants could move in and out.

It was Wednesday morning, February 18, 1970. Kunstler was going to make a motion for a mistrial, because if the jury cannot reach agreement after five days, that "constitutes reasonable doubt." Several reporters—one TV reporter in particular who was close to Foran—knew what the votes had been in the jury room.

In the courtroom the defendants, come from the jail, were cheerful and looked rested, even though Rennie Davis would say in his sentencing speech that he could not sleep because of a man screaming in the cell next to him. Defendants and wives and staff members greeted each other excitedly.

Kunstler was just getting his papers together when Judge Hoffman's marshal Ron Dobroski came swiftly into the courtroom. "The jury has reached a verdict, your honor," he said. There was no time to warn anyone on the outside. The defendants stirred with confused anticipation.

Richard Schultz made a motion that no spectators be allowed. He also advised that, under federal rule, criminal action be taken against anyone who caused disturbance. Judge Hoffman then committed another one of his inspired slips of the tongue when he made a motion himself for exclusion of "wives of jurors." Schultz told him he meant "wives of the defendants." Judge Hoffman again put the defendants into a position of judging his case.

Seventeen marshals manned the courtroom, standing arms folded in the aisle, by the doors, or sitting in empty spectator seats. Foran was flushed and solemn, anxious in appearance. The two marshals in charge of the jury, Jonesen and Dobroski, also did not look happy, afraid perhaps that some of the jurors might become emotional.

Kunstler said that this was the most lonely moment that a man can face, verdict from a jury, and to be deprived of family and friends in such a moment was cruel. Schultz argued that Kunstler had done nothing to cool defendants and supporters. Schultz characterized their acts as "miniature riots."

The marshals indicated to the defendants' women that they were to leave. The government was obviously fearful that the women or the defendants would inform the jury of the contempt sentences, and fearful of the effect that might have upon some jurors. Anita Hoffman, not normally given to enthusiasm for demonstrations of any kind, shouted, "The ten of you will be avenged. They will dance on your grave, Julie, and on the grave of the pig empire." Sharon Avery said to Lee Weiner, "I love you."

Kunstler asked for a voir dire of the audience, and a scattered examination of unfamiliar faces in the press section revealed a Sergeant O'Malley of the Chicago Police Department, and Frank Sullivan, who was head of public relations for the Chicago Police Department. Judge Hoffman told the two policemen to leave. "How did the police know to be here today, your honor?"

Judge Hoffman said abruptly, "Mr. Marshal, please bring in the jury."

The courtroom watched the jurors enter.

At the sight of Mrs. Fritz, you understood the Victorian use of the descriptive term "ashen." She was ashen—pale, drawn, haggard, looking down and swinging her legs as if she were extremely preoccupied, biting back tears. Shirley Seaholm was also pale. Frieda Robbins, too. Kay Richards, too. Mary Butler's expression was set as in black stone.

The clerk of the court read aloud that all of the defendants were not guilty on the conspiracy count. Dellinger, Davis, Hayden, Hoffman and Rubin were guilty on the substantive counts Two through Six while Lee Weiner and John Froines were not guilty on Count Seven.

Then John Froines was sobbing, because he did not wish to be cut off from the comradeship at the table. "Goddammit," he was saying. Many observers once more revealed their distinguished perceptual faculties by reporting that Froines was so glad to be found innocent that he sobbed with relief. Kunstler came around the table to hug John Froines.

Then Kunstler asked that the jury be polled to answer if these were, in fact, their verdicts. Now was the last chance for the defendants or their attorneys to inform the jurors with "improper" remarks that they were all sentenced and in jail for contempt.

One by one the jurors rose to say, "Yes, they are," our verdicts. Both Shirley Seaholm and Jean Fritz were waiting for the other to say, "No, they are not my verdicts." But the moment passed and "it just would not come out." They each heard the other say, "Yes, they are."

Months after the trial when Leonard Weinglass was reading the story of the two jurors, he said that something told him to get up and make a motion when it came Mrs. Fritz's turn, in order to give her time to realize what was happening. But he didn't obey that voice.

In the jury room directly after the reading of the verdicts, the four "acquittal" jurors were sobbing and weeping. Mrs. Fritz said, "I went to pieces. I started to cry, and I couldn't stop. I kept saying over and over again, 'I just voted five men guilty on speeches I don't even remember.'" Kay Richards and the marshal Ron Dobroski were trying to comfort her, and trying to comfort Mrs. Seaholm, Mrs. Robbins, and Mrs. Butler, too. "I don't see how you could have done anything else," the marshal said.

The jurors were driven to their homes by U. S. marshals in special cars. "Tom says no marshal can take me home," Kay Richards said. "Only Tom can take me home." She meant her boyfriend who worked for Cook County.

Thomas Foran and Richard Schultz sat at a table in front of TV cameras and lights, giving their first press conference about the trial in the room on the second floor for that had seemed to be defendants' territory for five months. Foran praised the jury for "its hard work" which "proved just what the judiciary system has been under attack for," that "the system works." Foran emphasized, "I'm for the jury system. . . . The prosecution, of course, wins no matter what the verdict."

Foran gave the feeling of having been rescued. He was asked about the constitutionality of the antiriot statutes. He said, "The Seventh Circuit has already said that the antiriot law is constitutional. Three other circuits have said the same thing." He repeated his aria about the "rules of evidence and five hundred years of the adversary system." About the morality of jury bargaining, he said, "Lots of people forget that's the way we got the Constitution."

I was standing on top of a table watching Foran and the reactions in the audience. He analogized the trial to playing "a football game." Tom Weinberg, a young long-haired reporter, said, "Is this a football game?" Foran's wife, nearby, looked sharply at him.

"How could the defendants complain about the jurors' verdict? The system works." Foran injected the word "system" whenever possible.

Schultz said, "This is the first time I've tried a case where I not only had to try the case but hold the whole system together, too." He said about the defendants, "They raised serious questions as to whether the delicate balance of our judicial system can be maintained under such assaults."

"You gentlemen of the press," Foran said, apparently not referring to the women of the press, "gave major assistance to the cause and actions of the defendants and the threat that that brought against the system." Foran again called the jurors "patriots." He said, "It shows once again that the system works."

Foran privately asked the jailers at Cook County not to shave or give haircuts to the defendants, so long as the trial was prominent in the news.

In Cook County jail, the defendants saw Foran on TV in the dayroom saying, "The system works." It gave them a laugh. not without anguish. They were in daily association with poor black men and poor white men who had been in jail for months awaiting trial because they could not raise three hundred dollars' bond money, or even less. "You guys want to burn your draft cards," one man told Tom Hayden. "We'd like to burn our birth certificates."

Months later the defendants, free on appeal bond, raised money to provide bail for a number of their former companions in Cook County jail who were being punished with long, indefinite terms before they were even tried.


Judge Hoffman was well known in the Northern District of Illinois for small delay between a finding of guilty and imposition of sentence. On Friday, February 20, he acted routinely in setting a landmark precedent by making his long postponed ruling on the wiretaps, which "should not require a warrant if the President or the Attorney General find the security of the United States is at stake." It was an elaborate ruling. "I find that the electronic surveillance was lawful, and not subject to disclosure." Having annihilated certain Fourth Amendment protections, he smiled smugly—that is the appropriate word— at Richard Schultz.

He slipped again on Dellinger's name, saying, "Count Two against David T. Dillinger." Kunstler said that he had never heard of defendants not being warned of sentence. Judge

Hoffman said, "Well, you've heard of it now." Actually, the defense had found out the night before.

"If you tell me that I'm *morally* wrong in this case," the judge said. "I might add to your difficulties."

Kunstler said, "Are you *serious?*"

Judge Hoffman said, *"Yes,* I *am!"*

The judge, acting oddly upset, perhaps in anticipation of the defendants' language, said to them, "I give you the right to speak."

David Dellinger stood up as if he were in the middle of a town meeting, his voice quavering now and then with a feeling of irreparable loss. "You are a man who has had too much power over too many people for too many years." But Dellinger said that he could not help but admire the judge in a way, "because there is something spunky about you, however misguided."

Rennie Davis stabbed his hands into the tight front pockets of his pants, and spoke to the judge across the length of the defense table. "Since I did not get a jury of my peers, I will rely on the jury in the streets." When he got out of jail, he said, "I intend to move next door to Tom Foran, and bring his sons and daughter into the revolution." Foran, at the prosecution table, acted as if he'd been stuck in the face. Perhaps the word-of-mouth gossip was accurate that there was more than a little dissension in the Foran household about the trial. "We're going to turn the sons and daughters of the ruling class into Viet Cong."

Tom Hayden puzzled aloud about the indictments. "Our jury is now being heard from. . . . They're doing things in the streets that this prosecution was designed to avoid. . . . Which leads me to ask"—and he was speaking directly, personally, to Foran now—"do you want to prevent it?"

Abbie Hoffman did not, in fact, laugh much in jail. It was in the context of talking about his rebellious lethargy that a marshal told me that there were "many ways to break a man" without laying a hand upon him, such as putting him into a room without blankets and opening an unreachable window to subzero air. Whether or not that happened to him, Abbie Hoffman huddled now as if he were irredeemably chilled, far from the energy and defiance of his contempt speech. He began by agreeing with Napoleon that "history is the sum of men's lies," which was the pomposity of a military figure satirizing the pomposity of an academic figure. "I'm still waiting for the permit," Abbie said, shivering. Then, in a bereft voice, he made a remarkable statement: "I don't know whether I'm innocent or guilty."

He too spoke of jail. "It's not a nice place for a Jewish boy with a college education. I'm sure my mother would have said that." Richard Schultz laughed. Foran laughed. There was obscenity in the laughter in the courtroom.

"They're waiting to shave our heads," Abbie said. It would only be a few days after the sentencing when Sheriff Joseph Woods would speak to a cheering suburban group and show them pictures of his Republican achievement, the shorn defendants.

Unbound copies of Jerry Rubin's book *Do It!,* wrapped in jackets that brought the flash of red into the courtroom, were stacked on the defense table. It was a curious sort of publication party. "Fantastic," Rubin said. "Think back to August, 1968, and the Democratic convention and try to imagine how it really happened and then think of David Dellinger, Rennie Davis, Tom Hayden, Abbie Hoffman, and Jerry Rubin going to jail for it. Fantastic."

He tried to hand a copy of his book up to Judge Hoffman, but he had to give it to the clerk. "To Judge Hoffman, top Yippie, who radicalized more young Americans than we ever could" was the inscription that Rubin read.

Judge Hoffman, feeling hints of the warmth of Florida vacation coming, asked the government if they had any comment.

"The government has no comment," Foran said. "The evidence speaks for itself."

With a fine sense of routine, Judge Hoffman sentenced each defendant to five years' imprisonment to run concurrently with the contempt sentences, plus a five-thousand-dollar fine, and the cost of prosecution. Dellinger laughed, and reached into his back pocket. "I got it right here." Defendants and newsmen laughed among themselves. The judge meant about fifty thousand dollars of costs concerning witnesses that could be charged to the defendants.

Reporters jumped up and pounded out of the courtroom. "Wait a minute," former young reporter Jerry Rubin cried out, pointing at the reporters, "a riot."

Judge Hoffman held that the defendants were "clearly dangerous persons" and were to be confined without bail or appeal bond.

"Let's clear the court, please," the marshals were saying. There was the feeling that the defendants might well be going into jail for the full five years right now—a dead, dull, end-of-the-world feeling. I squeezed Tom Hayden's arm, and Hayden looked back and nodded as he went to the custody door.

The captain of the janitors of the Federal Building leaned on the rail of the jury box, with the empty black seats behind him. He grinned the vengeful grin of a man who has worked hard all his life for modest blandishments.

In the press conference room on the second floor, the TV cameramen were readying themselves. "Jack, how much you got?"

"I'm out."

Another cameraman yelled, "Reload."

William Kunstler sat at the table in the lights facing the tall, tripod cameras. "Tell me when you're ready," he said. "I've got to go."

An old newsman said, a little sadly, "This country ain't ready for their new society yet."

Inside Christ-the-King storefront church just south of the Federal Building, a cameraman said, "Resume your seats," to a host of Conspiracy staff members and women of the defense. Bob Lamb announced to the TV men that a statement would be made by Anita Hoffman and Nancy Kurshan outside the church, because it was of such a nature that it could not be made inside. "Are you going to desecrate the church? Burn down Chicago?" Such are the anticipations that cause our newspapers and networks to be filled with what is called news.

On the cold corner outside the church, Anita Hoffman and Nancy Kurshan stood back to back in black robes, as if comparing heights, the same sort of robes that Jerry Rubin and Abbie Hoffman used in the court. Then they heaped the robes on the sidewalk. Nancy sprayed a charcoal lighter fluid from a squeeze can onto them as fast as she could. Anita awkwardly struck one match after another and threw them onto the robes, as if afraid the cops would soon stop her. For the cameras, Anita and Nancy stood behind the flaming little pile of robes, with their fists held high in the air. "We will avenge the ten," they cried. "We will dance on your grave, Julie. Right on." Anita Hoffman, whose lack of enthusiasm for demonstrations had been immortalized in the prose of her husband, was laughing with discomfort at the formula of their actions. Nancy, too.

Then three cops came, big broad guys in the black leather jackets that made them seem bigger, with all their death-dealing equipment hanging on their belts. They made the young people of Conspiracy seem slight and frail as they shouldered their way calmly through the crowd. The image was done when the cops entered the frame of the picture approaching the women and the dying blaze of the pile of robes.

Students were rioting in one university town after another from the day of the verdicts. Kunstler spoke in Santa Barbara, California, and a branch of the Bank of America was burned by angry students, whose actions in the streets there had actually been under way for several days. Wherever Kunstler spoke, so it was charged by university presidents and trustees over the nation, students rioted. The defendants were granted appeal bond on February 28 by the appellate court.

Judge Hoffman went to Palm Beach, Florida, as soon as the trial ended, and from all accounts he enjoyed every basking minute of it. He breakfasted in Washington, D. C., with President Nixon.

Many campuses simmered with the indignity of the Conspiracy trial, and then reacted violently in May 1970 over the murder of four students at Kent State in Ohio by National Guardsmen, and of two black students in Jackson, Mississippi, by police. Colleges were closed, sometimes by protesting students, sometimes by administrators out to teach the students a lesson.

Two and a half months after the trial and the sequestration ended, Shirley Seaholm was still saying, in her new apartment on the far north side of Chicago, "I just can't get organized." For a couple of weeks Mrs. Fritz found herself so dazed it was hard for her to do even small chores around her home. At the Fritz's auto supply store, "When a customer came in, I couldn't wait on him," she said.

The Fritzes were the recipients of some standard American "hate" treatment in the form of letters, phone calls, and personal allegations. Mrs. Seaholm experienced similar pressure.

"I have never done so much talking in all my life," Jean Fritz said, "since I got out of the trial, about the issues in our country."

In the spring, Mrs. Fritz went to buy a bush for her lawn from a man who spoke to her about his certainty of the guilt and evil of the defendants. Evidently he was trying to bait her. "They should have been innocent," she told him, "if you don't mind my saying so."

The reasons the jurors came to fear the United States government emerged in the very circumstances of their lives.

I interviewed the two jurors in May and June of 1970. But before their story was even published in *Evergreen Review* in the last week of August, Jean Fritz, in the *first* week of August, received a phone call from the woman marshal who helped take care of the jurors during the sequestration. "Thomas Foran wants to know which juror said which marshal said, 'The judge can keep you here forever.' " The revealing word here was "forever." Jean Fritz responded that she didn't say "forever," she said that the marshal said, "The judge can keep you here as long as he wants." I was the author of the story based upon the interviews with the two jurors. I used the word "forever" on the phone to New York and in conversation with a few persons. The two jurors reacted again with their fear of government agents and government reprisals.

The handsome results of the dynamic of Convention Week and the Conspiracy trial were to be seen in the image, election night, Tuesday, November 3, 1970, when Adlai Stevenson III, winner of the senatorial election in Illinois, came to the victory celebration in his headquarters with cocampaign managers Thomas Foran and Daniel Walker. Daniel Walker was the head of the federal task force that investigated Convention Week violence, called it "a police riot," and published the book *Rights In Conflict,* commonly known as the Walker Report. The book effectively, by virtue of paperback distribution of over a million copies through popular outlets, deflected heavy criticism of the mayor and the administration of the city of Chicago and of the Democratic party to the policeman on the street. But at the same time it suggested that the provocations of demonstrators were so intense that cops had no choice but to beat heads wildly. It wholly avoided the fact that the cops had "their orders," as they often shouted during Convention Week.

Foran praised Stevenson for his work in passing anticrime legislation in the Illinois legislature, and Stevenson praised himself for being early in getting passage of his bill to control the sale of dynamite. Stevenson said that in 1968 he would have voted against the antiriot provisions to the 1968 Civil Rights Act, under which the defendants were tried and convicted, but now he would vote for it.

The danger of a dynamic social-democratic movement growing in the United States, born of the impeachment of the electoral process during Convention Week, had been successful forestalled by the parties of the government. The mass of American liberals were deflected from it. Foran said, "The system works." Americans believe that this system of struggle between two sides that goes back far and deep in our history and culture works—and attempts seemingly against it are part of its ways of stimulating itself to work.

There they were, the liberal team, winners on election night. Stevenson credited Mayor Daley with the essential help that elected him.

In the fall of 1970, college teachers all over the country noticed and were not able to hide their surprise that college students were more cautious and introspective in their interests, and more concerned about studies that contributed to their careers.

# PART SEVEN
*The Jury Hearing*

BECAUSE OF THIS WRITER'S STORY "Like the Last Two People on the Face of the Earth" (*Evergreen Review*, September, 1970, included in this book in different form), based upon exclusive interviews with jurors Jean Fritz and Shirley Seaholm, Judge Julius Jennings Hoffman was ordered by the Seventh Circuit Court of Appeals to conduct a virtually unprecedented hearing. He was ordered to take testimony from the twelve Conspiracy jurors, from the six marshals assigned to them, and to give his personal recollections, if he wished, so that the Court of Appeals could determine what communications, written and oral, occurred between judge, jury and marshals, in what surrounding circumstances, during the time of the jury's deliberations.

I signed the affidavit in late September, 1970, that accompanied the extensive motion on the jury written by appeals attorneys—mainly by Helene Schwartz—to which a complete copy of the story in *Evergreen* was attached. The motion was submitted to the judges of the Seventh Circuit Court of Appeals. The affidavit affirmed, among other facts, that the two jurors had read through the story three times to make sure that it accurately reflected what they had said in the interviews. The story was not published until they approved every line of it.

What particularly interested the Court of Appeals were the two "hung-jury" messages that the jurors said were sent to Judge Hoffman and refused by him, and also such remarks by marshals to jurors as "The judge can keep you here as long as he wants!" Generally, according to the rulings of the higher courts, when a judge receives a message from a jury in deliberation, he must reveal the message and its contents to both the prosecution and the defense. Then the two sides may offer argument concerning what advice or ruling the judge should give the jury. In order that defendants can be guaranteed their constitutional right to a fair trial by being present at all of its proceedings, the judge is required to impanel the jury publicly and make their messages known. Also, the judge absolutely cannot keep a jury deliberating "as long as he wants"; he can only keep a jury a "reasonable" length of time. Everything in the law, finally, proceeds from one or another interpretation of what is "reasonable." Nothing was publicly known of these messages between Judge Hoffman and the Conspiracy jury until the revelations of Jean Fritz and Shirley Seaholm in "Like the Last Two People on the Face of the Earth."

Back I went, in the middle of November, 1970, with a most particular interest, to Judge Hoffman's courtroom on the twenty-third floor of the Federal Building in Chicago. Now at last we would hear the twelve jurors speak in their personal voices, and a voice can tell more about a person and about a group or class of persons than almost any other medium of expression. Whether the jurors, considering their often expressed fear of the government and its undercover operations, would hold up in their testimony was a question that concerned some observers.

Appellants' Attorney Helene Schwartz asked that the judge read a simple statement informing the jurors that they were not on trial and that the purpose of the hearing was to send the transcript of the testimony to the Court of Appeals. Some of the jurors believed, as did many observers, that the judge could make a ruling on their conduct. Most ordinary people believe that the law and its proceedings are dangerous to all living things. Judge Hoffman denied the appellants' request that he read that simple message to each of the jurors.

In fact, Mrs. Seaholm, because of "pressures" in several areas of her life resulting from the story in *Evergreen,* including a particularly raunchy piece of threatening mail, had spent five weeks in the hospital with a hemorrhaging ulcer. Mrs. Fritz, in the suburb of Des Plaines, received a number of threatening phone calls and the letter that was also addressed to Mrs. Seaholm. The jurors had come to believe that it was likely that anyone they met could be a government agent, and that reprisals were probable. That was the measure of the courage that they showed in giving their testimony from Judge Hoffman's witness stand.

The government made its play when it called, with a sense that alarmed this writer, the four "acquittal" jurors first. Mrs. Seaholm. Mrs. Fritz. Mrs. Robbins. Mrs. Butler. But by the time Mrs. Robbins left the witness stand, the appellants could breathe easier because the charges were being steadily backed up and filled in, creating the main coherent core of testimony in the hearing. Most of the twelve jurors, whether they were "acquittal" jurors or convict-on-all-counts jurors, remembered three or two messages. But no matter what the deviation of the testimony, or the contradiction, it gave a sense of reality to that main core. Most of the jurors also remembered the marshal's saying, "The judge can keep you here as long as he wants!" or words to that effect. At least one convict-on-all-counts juror remembered a stronger version to the effect that the judge could keep them there forever.

Mrs. Seaholm had said in her interviews with me, and in the story that caused the jury hearing, that Marshal Ron Dobroski had "jabbed" his finger "emphatically" when he told the jurors, "Remember the judge's instructions!" She said to me that she remembered it with special clarity, and even demonstrated it in the living room of Mrs. Fritz's home in Des Plaines. The Assistant U. S. Attorney did not ask her if the marshal "jabbed" his finger "emphatically"; he asked her and every other juror if they remembered the marshal ever waving his finger in a *"threatening"* or *"menacing"* manner and saying, "Remember the judge's instructions!" It was the government's way of mitigating the impression that this jury had felt terror and felt intimidated. Everyone familiar with this courtroom and its personae was aware of Ron Dobroski's habit of waggling his finger strongly in one of the stereotyped ways of chastising a child, when he emphasized something. The possibility that the Court of Appeals judges might not compare the wording of the transcript with Mrs. Seaholm's original wording in the jury story made me shake with a sort of rage, a need to stand up then and there and correct the record for everyone to hear. The government's misrepresentation was obvious in its intention. It gave me to understand the motivations of the defendants in many of their "contempts." Many people are simply unable to accept that it is merely part of a prosecutor's job to misrepresent events in order to win at any cost.

The most damning and intimidating words spoken by the marshal to the jury were, "The judge can keep you here as long as he wants!" Sure enough, a few reporters, as if by reflex, shifted around the events of testimony in the jury hearing, of the government's "waggling finger," and declared that the jurors did not feel "threatened" or "menaced" or "intimidated" by the marshal's saying that the judge could keep them there as long as he wanted. No juror was ever asked such a question. In fact, the wording of the Court of Appeals in ordering the jury hearing specifically precluded the attorneys from asking any questions at all about such subjective reactions of the jurors. The jurors could have said that they felt absolutely at peace with themselves after hearing that Judge Hoffman could keep them there as long as he wanted, and the communication would still be utterly improper and in error.

What need does a "system" have for editorial conspiracies when many of its reporters, by reflex and hardly conscious of it, do the approved distortion and alteration of event on the spot of perceiving it?

The other core of testimony was created by Judge Hoffman's marshal Ron Dobroski and Judge Hoffman himself. In addition, the two black jurors showed an attitude in testimony that was revealing of the hearing, of the trial, and perhaps of the law in general. They were guarded.

Another tense expectation centered on the testimony of Kay Richards Stevens, because she had acclaimed herself as the negotiator of the verdicts in her personal story published in a newspaper serial, originating with the Chicago *Sun-Times,* almost immediately after the end of the trial. Some of the jurors. and Kay Richards herself, have said that without her driving effort this divided jury might never have reached a verdict. When appellants' attorney Thomas Sullivan questioned her about whether there came a time when she "took over" as foreman of the jury, she said that she didn't like that phrase and its connotations; she preferred the term "negotiator." Jury negotiation is also frowned upon by the rulings of the high court because it means the jury has not delivered its verdict from individual conscience and perception of fact.

Kay Richards wrote the notes that were sent to the judge. That was said by every juror. Yet she had made no mention of the "hung-jury" messages in her newspaper articles, though she *did* mention that the jury asked to see transcript of speeches by the defendants. Nevertheless, she testified in this hearing clearly and readily about the two "hung-jury" messages in addition to the request for transcript of speeches. She also testified that the marshal had said words to the effect, "The judge can keep you here as long as he wants!" These remarks had also not been included in her newspaper articles. Because she wrote the messages, and remembered their contents and that they were read aloud to all of the jurors, and because her dates for each of the messages coincided with the dates given by Mrs. Fritz and Mrs. Seaholm in "Like the Last Two People on the Face of the Earth," what she had to say made the main core of testimony quite formidable.

The attorneys for the appellants were interested in many things about Kay Richards, particularly in whether there were any communications during the deliberations between her and the Chicago *Sun-Times,* which published the first article drawn from her recollections only a day after the end of the trial. They were also interested in the fact that her then fiancé, now husband, Tom Stevens, worked for "City Hall" or "Cook County." If Kay Richards had been married to Tom Stevens at the time of the jury selection, she would never have been a juror, because that was the one question of the defense that Judge Hoffman consented to ask prospective jurors—if any of their immediate family worked for any level of government.

The hearing was so unprecedented—such a phrase is possible in legal proceedings—that there was no law specifically developed for its conduct. Attorneys for the government and for the appellants were trying to dig up law from coast to coast that might apply.

Because of the lack of law on the conduct of the hearing, appellants' attorney Thomas Sullivan was able to move into an Offer of Proof in his cross-examination of Kay Richards. The Offer almost certainly would not be sustained in the end, but until that time Sullivan could ask almost any question for which he could lay a foundation. He pursued Kay Richards with all the persistence and cunning of the fox of the fables, while she showed that she might be everything the appellants thought she was, but she was bright and determined, too. When she turned suddenly to a hapless Judge Hoffman and said in a clear strong voice, about a question of Sullivan's, "Is that within the scope of the hearing, your honor?" she sounded as if she might be the one who was directing the trial.

Sullivan went nimbly from question to question, amidst much heated feeling on part of the judge, government, and witness. Finally, he asked Kay Richards Stevens about the employment of her husband. She folded her arms and said—with more than a hint of desperation and indignation—that she was not going to answer that question. That absolutely electrified the courtroom. What *did* her husband do? Sullivan asked more questions, and then, in slightly different form, asked that question again. Again she folded her arms and refused to answer. She was not required by the judge to answer in the courtroom, but reporters quickly found out that day that Tom Stevens was employed as the Director of Position Classification with the Cook County Board. He was Assistant Director of Position Classification at the time of the trial. She said that he had arranged for her newspaper serial without her knowledge. She did not admit to any direct communication between herself as a juror and the Chicago *Sun-Times,* and she could not remember how much she was eventually paid. She did admit that she typed voluminous notes throughout the trial.

Five of the six marshals testified that they did not remember any messages or remarks at all. Appellants' attorney Helene Schwartz made a startling attempt to impeach the testimony of one marshal because recently, while guarding a prisoner in a hospital in Madison, Wisconsin, he had reportedly blabbed to another patient in that room about the "two hung-jury messages" and about the marshal's telling the jurors that the judge could keep them there as long as he wanted. The marshal grinned on the stand as he denied it.

But Judge Hoffman's personal marshal Ron Dobroski, considered to be a good guy by jurors and most persons present in the courtroom during the trial, told the story that this writer predicted the judge himself would tell. Marshal Dobroski said there had been two messages. He located the one hung-jury message only four to six hours after deliberations began, and the "transcript" request the next day. He testified that when jurors asked him how long they would have to deliberate, he had said, "It's up to the court. It's up to the court."

Judge Hoffman mystified everyone by postponing his "recollections" three times, each time several days apart. When he finally gave his "recollections," he located the hung-jury messages to which he would admit at about the same time on the first day of deliberations as his marshal testified. It was obviously too early for the jury, after such a long trial, he said, to decide that it was deadlocked. He said that he did not inform the lawyers of either side and did not impanel the jury publicly because of the many "improper" remarks made by defendants and their lawyers to the jurors in the course of the trial. He also said that at the time the messages were received "certain contempt proceedings" were being conducted and the hostility in the courtroom "markedly increased." That was surely one of the most sanctimoniously matter-of-fact phrases ever uttered.

He said that the second message, the "transcript" request, also contained a statement to the effect that the jury could not agree. This suggested that the several women were suffering a lapse of memory in recalling a second, separate hung-jury message.

Judge Hoffman left it up to the Court of Appeals to decide whether he acted appropriately—and constitutionally—in not impaneling the jury in front of defendants who more than likely *would* have informed the jurors with "improper" remarks that they were being sentenced for contempt. The judge may have suspected the effect that this information would produce upon this jury. Mrs. Fritz and Mrs. Seaholm had said flatly in their interviews that if they had known about the contempt proceedings, they would still be in that deliberating room to this day if that was the way Judge Hoffman wanted it.

The two black women, one an "acquittal" juror and one a convict-on-all-counts juror, did not recall anything at all about messages or marshals' remarks. So symmetrical was their testimony that it stood in vivid contrast to the testimony of the eight white women and the two white men. I found out that one of the black women said before the hearing that she would never testify about the messages because she feared reprisal. "I'm black," she reportedly said, "and I know how things happen."

During the time of the jury's deliberations Mrs. Fritz and Mrs. Seaholm and the other "acquittal" jurors feared, among their many contradictory fears and rationales, that if they were a hung jury the defendants would be re-tried by the government and found guilty on all counts by another jury. The jurors may have shown foresight, and conceivably the appellants were in a better position now than if the jury had been hung, though certainly their pride was offended. They could no longer be tried as a group because they were found innocent of the conspiracy charge.

If, because of the jury point, the convictions of Dave Dellinger, Rennie Davis, Tom Hayden, Abbie Hoffman, and Jerry Rubin were overturned, they and their case would be remanded to the U. S. Attorney's Office of the Northern District of Illinois. They could be re-tried. But the government could not lump them together in one trial because the conspiracy charge had been put aside. The conspiracy charge against Bobby Seale was also dropped. Seale was still scheduled to be tried on the charge of individually crossing state lines with intent to incite riot.

There were three appeal briefs, the trial brief and the contempt brief for the seven white defendants and their attorneys, and the contempt brief for Seale. If the Court of Appeals ruled—as then recent rulings of the higher courts would indicate—that defendants must receive jury trials for summary contempt sentences in excess of six months, then the U. S. Attorney's Office faced the possibility of *sixteen* separate *jury* trials resulting from the substantive counts and the contempts.

It was not surprising that one heard in certain conversations in Chicago that the new U. S. Attorney, James Thompson, and his staff felt that the Conspiracy case had turned into a "nightmare" for them.

Liberal lawyers and observers, always surprised by the actions of the judge and the government throughout the trial, felt that the government would not put out the energy or the expense to mount all of these cases. Nevertheless, the government in March, 1971, confessed error in the contempt charges against the seven white defendants, the error being that Judge Hoffman should not have handled the contempt cases personally but should have sent them to a different judge. The government asked that the seven white defendants be remanded to a different judge for hearing on the contempt charges. The Court of Appeals, however, did not grant the government's request for immediate remand. The Court said that it wanted to hear argument on the appeal of both the trial convictions and the contempts first.

The government's attitude seemed to indicate that it would prosecute every possible outcome of the Conspiracy trial to the limit.

# AFTERWORD
*Constitutional Morality Play*

## The Conspiracy on Appeal

IN HEINRICH VON KLEIST'S powerful novella "Michael Kohlhaas," the hero starts the story as a respected and prosperous horsetrader. Because of a capricious wrong done to him by a corrupt nobleman, Kohlhaas' sense of justice drives him through escalating stages to become a revolutionary and a popularly supported threat to the rulers of the German states in the 1530s. In the end, the Elector in Berlin, in order to preserve the shaken state, arranges to exact for Kohlhaas the justice originally requested, but, in turn, Kohlhaas must pay with his life for the "crimes" of his revolutionary enterprise. In accepting this tragic resolution, Kohlhaas becomes unbearably personal to us. We have identified with the rightness of his rage and have felt the commonalty of such rage in the injustices that we suffer.

Something like the same tragic principle is at work in the American constitutional system. We see it in the compromises that went into the original Constitution in 1789, such as the negotiated differences between the authoritarians and the democrats and, strikingly, in the compromises concerning black slavery, justified by the convenient assumption that slav-

ery would soon wither and die. We see the Constitutional system, *Novus Ordo Seclorum* [New Secular Order], under critical
stress as it seeks to maintain its mission of being enduring in
nature through a process of deep compromise, of forward
movement and retreat, in every major national convulsion
since 1789. As in Kleist's story, those who challenge the system
at its root *may* have justice, but *will* pay dues for it, even ultimate dues. This principle, with various levels of dues, is what
we see at work in the protracted legal and political struggle
which, in an atmosphere of government repression, resolved
contentious issues of the Conspiracy trial and hundreds of
other "political" and "quasi-political" cases in the early 1970s.

Not a rock or firecracker would have been thrown during
the Convention Week, August 1968 police-demonstrator confrontations in Chicago, not a single police officer insulted with
the word "pig," and not an untoward remark spoken during
the Conspiracy trial in the fall and winter of 1969-1970, but
for the outrage, dismay, and uncertainty felt by millions of
Americans about the Vietnam War. The Democratic Convention would have been very different, and the Conspiracy trial
itself would never have occurred. This outrage and uncertainty
about the Vietnam War was as much a matter of practical
self-interest, in terms of lives and resources, as morally driven
anger. The expenditure of national resources in a morally and
strategically ambiguous war cost this country virtually the entire Great Society program of 1965, much of it never tried,
and wreaked a distortion upon our economy well into the
1990s.

Rather than lift either the Democratic Convention of 1968
or the Conspiracy trial out of the history to which they are
attached by so many nerve ends, we must see them within the
context of this war that nearly fractured the nation. To try to
justify the war or any of the events that occurred in protest
against the war by charting public opinion polls, only shows
how a democracy boggles in attempting to deal with issues

about which the electorate has deeply contradictory perceptions. An off-and-on majority of Americans wanted out of the war in Vietnam, depending on how the question was put. A majority of Americans also fairly consistently disapproved of the anti-war movement, though often agreeing with its goals, depending on how the question was put.

In reaction to the Vietnam war, a strongly articulate proportion of an entire generation of youth was disaffected from the social, cultural, and political policies of the governing powers. Not only the contradiction-riddled mainstream of America, but the Nixon administration itself, was shocked in February, March, April, May and June of 1970 by the rapid sequence of massive campus demonstrations and "riot" reactions nation-wide to the Conspiracy trial verdicts, to President Nixon's bombing of Cambodia, to the always provocative issue of the Vietnam war which set the context for all of the demonstrations and the shooting deaths of four students at Kent State in Ohio on May 4, 1970 and two at Jackson State in Mississippi a few days later.

The mainstream majority's contradictory, war-inflamed uncertainties cut both ways, for and against the anti-war movement, throughout the 1960s and 1970s. Chicago Deputy Mayor David Stahl said in a *Chicago Tribune* interview in 1988 that long before the Democratic Convention in 1968 Mayor Richard J. Daley, on a visit to Washington, confidentially advised President Lyndon Johnson to get out of the war. Because of party loyalty and to maintain the leverage he had on the war-diminished flow of Federal funds to cities, Daley publicly continued to support the administration's position. Never did the nation so badly need highly placed persons to take exception to the prevailing policy of acquiescence. The polls had no way to measure these contradictions.

Supporters of civil liberties throughout American history have become well acquainted with tyrannies of the majority. James Madison and other writers wrote the Bill of Rights to

answer calls from the states for protections for minority opinion, since the leaders of the former Colonies had just gone
through a historical upheaval, the American Revolution, in
which they had been in the minority that prevailed.

Like it or not, the United States has one of the most enduring governmental systems in the world. Vigorous minority
opinion has been crucial to the viability of majority rule
throughout our history (you need only think of the social
movements concerning anti-slavery, child labor, the 8-hour
day, women's suffrage, labor/management conflicts, social security, civil rights, anti-war protest during the Vietnam war,
the environment, and so on). Without minority opinion, which
has often been developed by activism into majority opinion,
the United States would have foundered in authoritarianism
and blown apart at several points. Bill Clinton, who as a young
Rhodes scholar helped organize anti-Vietnam War demonstrations in England in 1969, was in November 1992 elected
President of the United States.

This historical context sets the dramatic staging of how the
Conspiracy worked out on appeal, an exceedingly complex morality play. In a morality play, the system, however pressed,
must work and must win, in whatever complicated way.

Federal District court judges may occasionally face threats,
even a bomb or a shot or a defendant throwing himself across
the courtroom upon the judge, but for the appellate judge
there is usually no consequence except possible review by the
loftier Supreme Court or the disapproval of one's peers at the
local club or bar association dinner. The appellate courts are
thought to be the heights, removed from the strife of ordinary
relationships, where models and theories of life-as-it-ought-
to-be are meticulously argued, and the majesty of American
constitutional law is maintained. Interpretation of our Constitution developed early into a kind of secular theology.

The jury in *U.S. vs. Dellinger et. al.* had found the defendants not guilty on the conspiracy count. They could never

again be tried for it. Yet they were still identified by way of introduction, even in some appellate opinions and rulings, as the Conspiracy this-or-that. In appealing the substantive count verdicts against David Dellinger, Rennie Davis, Tom Hayden, Jerry Rubin, and Abbie Hoffman, the Conspiracy defense, almost entirely staffed by the Center for Constitutional Rights led by Arthur Kinoy, Professor of Law, Rutgers University, argued its points vigorously and received many shades of opinion and ruling. Prosecutors Thomas Foran and Richard Schultz were sidelined in the appeals process by the inexorable logic of the new Republican administration's political appointments. The new U.S. Attorney James Thompson, soon-to-be Governor of Illinois, and his new Assistant Attorneys, represented the government.

### The Constitutionality of the Anti-Riot Statute— The Rulings of the 7th Circuit Court of Appeals

Two years after the trial ended, in February 1972, a three-judge panel named by the 7th Circuit Court of Appeals accepted briefs and heard oral argument from the Conspiracy defense and the government. First, the constitutionality of the law itself was at issue. The defense argued several constitutional points concerning the Anti-Riot Statute, among them that the statute was overly broad and unconstitutionally restricted travel and infringed upon freedom of speech. They discussed the motives of Congress for writing, in a climactic year of social upheaval, the Anti-Riot statute of 1968.

Ironically, the Anti-Riot statute was piggy-backed by Southern senators onto the comprehensive civil rights bill of 1968. The bill's passage on April 18, 1968 had been given large impetus by the riots that flared in black ghetto areas of cities in response to the assassination of the non-violent civil rights leader, the Rev. Martin Luther King, Jr. Many congressmen could not believe that pre-existing conditions provoked spontaneous riots in poverty areas of cities, like heat rising in a flammable material to the combustion point. 18 U.S.C. Section 2101 made it a crime to travel in interstate or foreign commerce with "intent" to incite a riot and, "in the course of any such travel," commit "any other overt act" in furtherance of that purpose. Necessarily, intent could mainly be inferred from speech given before and after crossing state lines, which immediately stumbled into the contested territory of the first amendment.

After the presentation of written briefs and oral arguments in February 1972, the three-judge panel of the 7th Circuit Court of Appeals (Judges Fairchild, Cummings, and Pell) retired to consider the case. The panel did not render its opinion and rulings until two weeks after the national elections in November 1972. In that time, momentous political and legal events washed over the appellate process. There were the "secret" peace talks between North Vietnam and the United States in Paris, and the election campaign of 1972 pitting Nixon's cryptic assurances of peace to come against the avowedly anti-war Democrat, George McGovern. The June 17 "plumbers' gang" break-in burglarizing Democratic Headquarters in the Watergate apartments was possibly motivated by secret knowledge of the decision being handed down the next day by the Supreme Court on "warrantless" domestic wire-tapping.

On June 18, 1972, the Supreme Court ruled against a rather panicked Department of Justice by upholding the 6th Circuit Court of Appeals in "the warrantless wiretapping case," *US vs. US District Court* (Detroit), in which District Judge Damon Keith had ruled against the government's argument that the President had the power to suspend any constitutional guarantee when he deemed the national interest was at stake. The Court extended the protection of the fourth amendment to warrantless non-invasion of premises, i.e., wiretapping involving domestic matters. Subsequently, fourth amendment issues concerning domestic wiretapping remained in contention in the courts, with some government agencies resisting restraint.

Despite the initial publicity of the Watergate break-in, Richard Nixon won by a hefty landslide in November 1972 against George McGovern. But the contradiction-riddled thrust of American politics later overwhelmed even the most manipulative of presidents when Nixon resigned in 1974 to escape impeachment.

The decision against "warrantless wiretapping" opened the gates for the three-judge panel of the 7th Circuit Court of Appeals not only to rule that the Conspiracy defendants should have been shown those portions of the electronic surveillance logs that dealt with domestic matters, but to consider many controversial areas of the Conspiracy trial.

The 7th Circuit judges were also affected from February 1972 to November 1972 by vigorous discussion with their own law clerks, bright articulate young people, who argued strongly against the constitutionality of the law and against the sufficiency of the evidence. Stephen Seliger, law clerk to Judge Fairchild at the time, told me in an interview in 1992, "There was a lot of give and take between the judges and the clerks. I wrote a couple of hundred pages on issues of guilt and innocence. Another one of Judge Fairchild's clerks spent a good deal of time trying to convince him of the unconstitutionality of the law. I wrote memos suggesting that the judges should enter a verdict of acquittal. It was, in part, a generational issue. We were young. I had long hair. I did legal support work for movement groups." The appellate judges welcomed discussion of central issues with their law clerks.

In November 1972, the three-judge appellate panel ruled on the 76 points of the Conspiracy appeal. Judge Fairchild, the panel's chief judge, wrote the majority opinion finding the Anti-Riot Statute constitutional by a 2-1 vote, Judge Pell dissenting. After a constitutional discussion as intricate as any piece of theological argument, the two judges of the Appellate court concluded that the threshhold meanings of "urging and instigating" could be "carved away from the comprehensive protection of the first amendment's guarantee of freedom of speech." The opinion wound its way finally to "conclude that when . . . the statute is fairly read as a whole and all basic relations between elements are noted, the statute is not unconstitutional." However, the two judges also said, with more than a glance at their law clerks' intense scrutiny of the constitutional issues, "We do not intend to minimize the first amendment problems presented on the face of this statute . . . Arguably the statute does not require that the speech [actually result in a riot] . . . we acknowledge the case is close [as to whether the statute conflicts with the first amendment]."

In his strong dissent from the opinion of the appellate majority, Judge Pell, a new, Richard Nixon appointee and a legal and political conservative, surprised those who thought they knew the 7th Circuit when he wrote that the majority opinion of his brothers on the panel bordered "on being an apologia for inept legislative draftsmanship." Pell found that the statute did not require a "causal relationship between the travel with intent and the riot intended . . . [with] no necessary connection" and no time limitation. He agreed with Attorney General Ramsey Clark's original concerns about the Anti-Riot statute expressed to Congress in March and April of 1968.

Here is the Anti-Riot statute's (c) sub-section with its puzzling "double negative" construction:

> "(b) As used in this chapter the term 'to incite a riot,' or 'to organize, promote, encourage, participate in, or carry on a riot', includes, but is *not* limited to, urging or instigating other persons to riot, but shall *not* be deemed to mean the mere oral or written (1) advocacy of ideas or (2) expression of belief, *not involving* advocacy of any act or acts of violence or assertion of the rightness of, or the right to commit, any such act or acts." (Emphasis added.)

I defy anyone to keep track in that sentence of what is being negated and what is being affirmed. Yet, it must be said that legal boggles created by legislative syntax are infamous. The government acknowledged the "awkward phraseology." Jeffrey Cole, former Assistant U.S. Attorney and Chief of the Appellate Division in U.S. Attorney James Thompson's office, supervised the writing of the government's brief. In a 1992 interview, Cole said, "I was not troubled over the language of the statute, though I do recall having to read it more than once or twice to comprehend its meaning. The wording did not partake of any special ambiguity any more so than scores of other statutes. It's infinitely clearer than the tax code."

In his dissenting opinion, Judge Pell did not wish to believe that Congress' phrasing was deliberate, but acknowledged there were congressmen who "were of the belief that punishment should be visited upon any who merely advocated the idea of violence or expressed belief in the rightness thereof." Under the language of the Anti-Riot statute, Thomas Jefferson, third president of the United States, could conceivably have been convicted for his statement that the tree of liberty needs to be watered by the blood of revolution every twenty years or so. Pell came to the inevitable,

> "I am able to reach no conclusion other than that the added phrase was intended to preclude, under pain of prosecution, advocacy of violence even though only an idea or expression of belief . . . the distaste [for the advocacy of violence] must be over-ridden in the preservation of the essential freedom here at stake."

Pell held that "the statute was not drawn sufficiently narrowly to avoid" conflict with the first amendment. He cited the Supreme Court's decision in *Brandenburg vs. Ohio* which took precedence over the *Foran vs. National Mobilization to End the War In Viet Nam* decision of the 7th Circuit which had upheld the constitutionality of the Anti-Riot law in the fall of 1968.

The *Foran* ruling had come as a result of a challenge to the law growing out of the Chicago Federal Grand Jury investigation of the Convention of 1968. The *Brandenburg* decision found that the Constitution did not permit laws on the state level to "proscribe advocacy," except when advocacy was "directed" to "producing imminent lawless action" and was "likely" to do so. Pell cited Judge Will in the 1968 case of *Landry v. Daley* (Mayor Richard J.), "New ideas more often than not create disturbances, yet the very purpose of the first amendment is to stimulate the creation and dissemination of new concepts," and quoted the philosopher/mathematician Alfred North Whitehead, "Great ideas often enter reality in strange guises and with disgusting alliances."

To try to attain a society made free of violence through "the suppression of the free interchange of ideas and beliefs would be a pyrrhic sacrifice of a precious freedom for an illusory safety . . . "

## Errors and Grounds for Reversal

After the constitutional issue, the court decided for, or leaned toward, the defense on all but a few of the remaining points. The judgments of error and grounds for reversal mount as the rulings address one after another the 76 points.

In discussing Communications by the Trial Judge and Marshal with the Deliberating Jury, the court said: "Several months after the verdict defendants discovered through a magazine article about the jury in this case [this writer's jury story] that there had been communications between the district judge and jury during its deliberations without knowledge of counsel . . ." The judge should have discussed the messages with both the defense and the prosecution and might have instructed the jurors "that no juror should surrender his honest conviction for the mere purpose of returning a verdict . . ." The panel concluded that the suppression of the hung jury messages was "grounds for reversal."

The appellate panel was none too happy with Judge Hoffman, the prosecutors, the defendants, or their defense counsel. "We conclude that the demeanor of the judge and the prosecutors would require reversal if other errors did not." The appellate opinion noted, among other things, " . . . the judge was more likely to exercise his discretion against the defense . . ." Yet, "It must be said that defense counsels' trial technique often seemed inadequate, but even so, gratuitous implications of ineptness before the jury [by the judge and prosecutors] . . . were not justified . . . In final argument, the United States Attorney went at least up to, and probably beyond, the outermost boundary of permissible inferences from the evidence in his characterizations of defendants. He referred to them as 'evil men' etc. . . . He told the jurors they need not ignore 'how these people look and act'. . . . Dress, personal appearance, and conduct at trial were not probative of guilt. . . . The United States Attorney should not have urged the jury to consider these things."

The appellate court reversed and remanded the substantive count convictions for new trial, in fact, for new *trials*, because the government could no longer try the defendants as the Conspiracy, but had to try them individually.

> "In deciding that the record contains evidence sufficient to support a verdict of guilty, we do not suggest any opinion that the defendants are in fact guilty of the offenses charged under the Anti-riot Act. There is evidence in the record which, if believed, and inferences favorable to defendants drawn, would lead a jury to acquit. The decision whether to bring the matter to trial again is one for the government to make."

"All they were saying," Stephen Seliger, Judge Fairchild's law clerk, said twenty years later, "was that they were not going to direct the judge to a finding of acquittal. They were really very solicitous of Judge Hoffman. They didn't want to embarrass him. They would often have lunch together at the Standard Club [near the Federal Building in Chicago]."

In event of a new trial, the panel ruled that former Attorney General Ramsey Clark would be permitted to testify, but did not support the defense's claim that undercover agents' testimony was unconstitutional, citing Justice Brennan that the risk of being deceived "is probably inherent in the conditions of human society." They ruled that in a new trial it would be at the judge's discretion to allow defendants to address the jury, making it possible that a jury might hear those passionate, vivid, and well-argued statements concerning the defendants' "state of mind," "the substance of their crime," their committment to getting the United States out of the war in Vietnam.

Yet government attorneys were quick to claim that the appellate judges believed the defendants were guilty. In 1992 former Assistant U.S. Attorney Jeffrey Cole discussed his argument for the constitutionality of the law: "I remember in the oral arguments, Arthur Kinoy saying, 'The government's brief is an incredible intellectual tour-de-force in that it completely removes the first amendment from this case.' I honestly thought that one could remove the first amendment from this case. Certainly there are risks to free speech in this kind of statute. But if you accept the constitutionality of the act and these two premises that it is a crime to (1) cross state lines with intent to incite a riot and (2) commit some overt act in furtherance of that intent, and that the defendants did this, then you have to look at the defendants in a different way. I don't know if they're guilty or not. Based on the evidence, as reviewed by the appellate court, they could be found guilty, guilty as sin.

"After twenty years, my perspective on the case in its social and political context has changed. In hindsight, there is a credible argument to be made that it would have been better to have left it to the political arena rather than bring it into the court. I haven't made that judgment myself, but that argument could be made. On the basis of the evidence, they [the defendants] used people, their behavior was cynical, perfidious, to further their own political ends.

"If you look at the thing realistically, they altered the course of history through a crime. It may have been for the good. But there is also a substantial argument to be made that it was a crime. It isn't o.k. to commit a crime, to advance political purposes by inciting a riot. But there is a huge substantial argument that other considerations should be weighed."

In the course of the Conspiracy trial, the defense reminded the court and the prosecutors that The Boston Tea Party, so revered in grade-school history texts, had been a sort of political theater, very similar to what occurred during the Democratic Convention of 1968. The British certainly argued that The Boston Tea Party involved criminal destruction of property, just as the prosecution argued that the demonstrators destroyed police cars during the Convention of 1968. Our courts have occasionally held, following the example and thinking of Henry David Thoreau, that the magnitude of the condition protested must be weighed against the crime committed in protesting it. In 1987, in Northampton, Massachusetts, Leonard Weinglass successfully argued a "necessity" defense in the trial of Amy Carter [President Jimmy Carter's daughter] and Abbie Hoffman et. al. for seizure of a University of Massachusetts building in protest against Central Intelligence Agency recruitment activities on campus. In another similar case in Northampton, only months apart, another judge did not allow the scope of a necessity defense.

On January 4, 1973, the government announced that it did not elect to re-try the Conspiracy defendants on the substantive counts of individually crossing state lines to incite riots at the Convention of 1968.

*The Issue of the Contempts*

Despite the grave constitutional issues concerning the law itself, despite the documented facts of wholly improper government intervention in the judicial process, the dominating issue in the public mind about the Conspiracy trial has been the much ballyhooed "disruptive" protest on the part of the defendants and their attorneys. Twenty two years later attorneys otherwise committed to the defense of civil liberties said that the defendants and their counsel were "completely out of line, no excuse for contumacious behavior," as if this were the one issue still alive. Others said, "What else could they do?" Whenever courts take on political or quasi-political trials, serious concerns about outspoken behavior come to the fore.

At issue were the very fundamentals of United States and English contempt law. Before, during, and after the writing of the Constitution, there had been a cultural division in the new secular order of the United States between those who wanted a more authoritarian state and those who wanted a more democratic state. The authoritarians wanted a country more like England, a nation among equals. The authoritarian and the democratic were really two sides of a deep cultural division. English contempt law, based upon "immemorial usage," was weighted heavily toward upholding the judge's actions and the court's dignity, no matter how despotic. In the late 1820s an important change was made in the practice of Anglo-Saxon contempt law in the United States. District Judge James Peck in St. Louis ruled against a lawyer named Lawless, who was doing a brisk business in land litigation coming out of Jefferson's Louisiana Purchase. The Judge's opinion was published in a newspaper. Lawless responded by publishing an unsigned criticism of Judge Peck in the same newspaper. Peck called in the publisher, got Lawless' name, cited Lawless for contempt, imprisoned and disbarred him. Instead of appealing in St. Louis, Lawless went straight to Washington, D.C., to the Senate Judiciary Committee chaired by James Buchanan of Pennsylvania, an effective and important senator who would later be the not-so-effective President on the eve of the Civil War. Judge Peck was tried in an impeachment hearing before the Senate. Peck cited English precedent and argued that lawyers should uphold the dignity of the judge, no matter what. There was strong feeling at the time about freedom of the press. Buchanan argued against an oppressive English contempt law interpretation, in effect saying, We've had a revolution here, a Bill of Rights, and a First Amendment. These should make our contempt law different from English contempt law. On the record, Buchanan said, "I will venture to predict that [whatever happens] . . . Judge Peck has been the last man in the United States to exercise this power, and Mr. Lawless has been its last victim." Judge Peck was not impeached, in a close vote of 22-21. Buchanan immediately introduced a bill that passed in 1831, rewriting the Federal Statute concerning contempt power so that a judge could only exercise his powers against behavior "so near thereto as to obstruct the administration of justice."

The phrasing "so near thereto," and interpretation of what constitutes "obstruction," have allowed a lasting struggle in our courts over what behavior is allowed and what isn't, rooted deeply in the cultural division between the authoritarian and the democratic. Responding to the pressures of different historical moments as perceived by its changing membership, the Supreme Court has swung back and forth interpreting Buchanan's wording, in one historical period regarding any speech that affronts the dignity of a court, as contumacious, and in another period requiring the contempt to be such as to actually obstruct a court in the performance of its duties. Usually mere remarks and sarcasm have been protected by the first amendment, as they were not originally protected under English law.

In 1962, the Supreme Court in *McConnell* continued the everlasting struggle over the definition of contempt with a ruling in which it said "by our resolving doubts in favor of advocacy [rather than in favor of the judge], an independent and unintimidated bar can be maintained while actual obstruction is dealt with appropriately." Other rulings, such as *Mayberry*, held that if a judge waited as did Judge Hoffman to the end of a trial to cite and sentence for contempt, the contempt hearing had to be held before another judge and jury. In the 1960s, with outspoken defendants in one "political" trial after another seizing the attention of a country convulsed over issues of war, racism, civil rights, and poverty, the courts were tending toward the earlier English principle of finding contumacious any behavior that offended the court's dignity.

In the trial of the Conspiracy contempts, the government attorneys argued a position similar to that of English precedent and Judge Peck's. Lawyers and defendants should, as Assistant U.S. Attorney Richard Schultz suggested that the government had to do, sit there tight-lipped and take it. Assistant U. S. Attorney Jeffrey Cole, who participated in writing the government's brief in the contempt trial, was less prescriptive: "The first amendment does not have the same contours in a criminal trial as outside the court." Both sides had to cope with Buchanan's wording, the defense arguing that its behavior did not constitute "obstruction," the prosecution that the defense behavior came "so near thereto . . ."

There were 159 "contempts" against the 7 white defendants, and 16 against Bobby Seale—175 all told. The 7th Circuit Court of Appeals did not want its reversal of the substantive count convictions to give an imprimatur of approval to the defense's aggressive approach. Nor did the court wish to wipe out the first amendment in the area of courtroom behavior.

Early in their pre-trial preparations, the defendants were aware of the risky tug-and-pull in the interpretation of contempt law. Tom Hayden recounted in *Reunion, A Memoir* that in the summer of 1969, the defendants' chief counsel-to-be Charles Garry, in agreeing to take the case, "lectured" the defendants "against any outbursts or disrespectful behavior" and if there were any they could all " 'go to hell.' In the light of later history," Hayden wrote, "it might seem amazing, but we all agreed." Defendant Lee Weiner, who was not present for the meeting with Garry in San Francisco, said in 1992 that there was no agreement at this point. Judge Hoffman did not grant the continuance of six weeks that would have allowed Charles Garry to recover from his gallbladder operation and enabled us to see if the vortex of forces in the Conspiracy trial would have drawn in Garry as it did everyone else.

The Conspiracy trial defendants and lawyers had virtually no contemporary models of political trials to draw wisdom from. Their turn came right at the beginning of the spate of political trials that started in the late 1960s as the government upped the ante in its repression of anti-war and urban black protest movements. Historical models were not clear in supporting a carefully obedient attitude toward the court. In another Chicago case, the Haymarket defendants in 1886 faced a blatantly prejudiced judge and jury and behaved carefully according to strict English precedent up to their sentencing speeches. Three of them were executed, one blew his head off with a blasting cap in jail, one got a fifteen years' sentence, and three were finally pardoned by Governor Peter Altgeld.

The Conspiracy defendants' statements in the media after their indictments in March 1969 would not have assuaged the fears of any judge, much less one so easily aroused as Judge Hoffman. It would seem that the seven white defendants not rising when the judge entered on the first day of trial, while Bobby Seale rose in stony respect, indicated a degree of agreement among the white defendants on strategy. Yet, this particular incident hardly figured in the final trial of the contempts. Even at this, the beginning of the trial, the actions of all eight defendants were, so to speak, proactively defensive, for Judge Hoffman had already denied their right to counsel Charles Garry, denied access to the electronic surveillance logs, ruled the "substance" of their "crime" was "a state of mind," issued bench warrants for the four pre-trial attorneys, and refused questions to prospective jurors. Lee Weiner said in 1992, "I have a vague memory that Bobby was pissed [at the white defendants for prejudicing Seale's case], and our judgment was that we should support Bobby." So the next day the seven white defendants stood with Bobby Seale in traditional respect to the judge.

Shortly before the trial began in September 1969, Northwestern University Professor of Law Jon Waltz, a man to whom Judge Hoffman had turned, but who was also helpful to the defense, told the defendants and their attorneys, "If you step out of line in any way, the judge is going to send you to prison." The judge had fired a law clerk, one of Waltz's students, in the summer of 1969.

Two weeks into the trial, after Judge Hoffman had arrested the four pre-trial attorneys in a move that still shocked lawyers twenty years later, Leonard Weinglass, on a worried weekend in his home state of New Jersey, asked State Judge Raymond Del Tufo for advice. Del Tufo thought, looked up and said, "About the only thing you can do is fight like hell. You have to make sure you make a record." He meant, said Weinglass, "that that was the only way we could legally survive."

The defendants acted rarely in concert, most of the time according to their personalities and their different political approaches. Most days of trial were relatively free of outspoken behavior. This strategy of act-as-you-are-moved-to-act was illustrated, in part, by Hayden's account in *Reunion* (1988) of how he secured one "contempt," after the judge excluded former U. S. Attorney General Ramsey Clark from testimony.

> We definitely weren't going to accept this suppression quietly, no matter what the judge instructed. The only question was which defendant was going to take the contempt to let the jury know. For a change, I was more than

glad to do it. I sat quietly, secretly enjoying the search for the proper moment. A few days later, Foran made one of his many remarks about the irrelevance of the defense testimony, and I blurted out as the jury was leaving the room, "*You* should talk. You wouldn't even let Ramsey Clark testify for us." For that the judge sentenced me to six months, the maximum for a single count of contempt.

## Seale Goes First

Seale's case was tried first, in February 1972, a year and a half before the white defendants were tried for contempt, and the *Seale* decision was handed down in May 1972, several months before the three-judge appellate panel reversed the substantive count convictions against the seven white defendants. This time Charles Garry was Seale's chief attorney. During the trial itself Garry, from his hospital bed in San Francisco, had advised Seale through Conspiracy staff members to keep pushing his sixth amendment rights.

Judge Hoffman had needed, so the government argued, to personally cite and sentence Seale as a deterrent to the remaining defendants, to prevent a complete breakdown of the trial. The appellate court said, "We cannot agree," and added that Judge Hoffman could have, and should have, cited Seale the instant of each contempt rather than wait to the time he declared a mistrial for Bobby Seale. The court split the difference between Seale's right to counsel and Judge Hoffman's right to dignity and orderly procedure. While Judge Hoffman's misbehavior reduced the degree of Seale's culpability, it did not exonerate Seale. The court suggested that if Seale had not called the judge "fascist," "racist," and other such names, he might have been within the bounds of first and sixth amendment protections, but that it would have been impossible for any judge to remain unbiased after the names Seale called

Judge Hoffman. The court reversed the conviction and remanded Seale for trial by a new judge and jury.

A politically astute U.S. Attorney, such as James
Thompson, needed only to glance at the likely spectacle and
political consequence of giving Bobby Seale a forum before a
jury. The government did not elect to re-try Seale on the substantive count or the contempts.

## *The Contempt Trial of the Seven White Defendants*

If the white defendants initially thought Seale's case meant
their contempt convictions would be dismissed, the court
rather promptly dangled them over the fires of anxiety again.
The 7th Circuit Court of Appeals had thrown out a few of the
contempts against the seven white defendants and remanded
the remaining ones for trial by a judge other than Hoffman.
No federal judge in the states covered by the 7th Circuit
wanted to be responsible for, in effect, trying Judge Hoffman.
Warren Burger, Chief Justice of the U.S. Supreme Court, a
Richard Nixon appointee, was asked to appoint a judge.

The conservative Burger was known for seeing that a part
of his mission was to shrink the broad liberalization of the Earl
Warren court whose civil rights and civil liberties decisions
had given such impetus to the social and cultural energy of the
nineteen sixties. Burger had already spoken out publicly
against the outspoken actions of the Conspiracy defendants
and their attorneys. The defense held its breath on Burger's
choice of a judge. Burger looked the country over and settled
on New England as the veritable repository of judicial virtue.
He chose the tall, athletic Edward T. Gignoux, U.S. District
Judge from Maine.

Gignoux looked and acted in every way the opposite of
Judge Hoffman. Jon Waltz wrote in *The Nation* that Gignoux,
in charge of the courtroom, smiled, spoke firmly, and engaged
in no "exacerbating games of one-upmanship." This time

rather than the judge mispronouncing lawyers' and defendants' names, it was Gignoux who heard "his name mispronounced twenty different ways" and kept his disposition intact.

In an interview with this writer in 1992, Morton Stavis, who led the Conspiracy team in the contempt trial, said that he perceived Judge Gignoux as "a real New Englander, ramrod up his spine, but very gracious," and that the defense felt concern and trepidation at the prospect of being tried by him. Stavis recalled, "Gignoux approached the case as if the defense attorneys and the defendants had misbehaved. He felt that he had to protect the court from Judge Hoffman's misbehavior and also from the defense attorneys' and the defendants' behavior."

In April 1973, the defense's motion for a jury trial was denied. To avoid the jury trial required for any contempt sentence of six months or more, the possible cumulative sentence for each defendant was reduced to 177 days. In October 1973, the case was tried before Gignoux.

Anyone who expected Gignoux to do the repressive will of the Nixon administration—it was widely thought that that was why he had been named—was in for a surprise. If the Conspiracy trial itself had been an education for William Kunstler and just about anyone else associated with it, the contempt trial became an education for Judge Edward T. Gignoux, as he himself taught how exquisitely the Constitutional system could work. In 1992 William Kunstler said, "Gignoux was a very patrician type of man. Very concerned about the appearance of the law," and added ironically, "A dangerous man. He makes the system look good."

The trial was in many ways as full of sudden turns as the first trial, but aesthetically more muted, chamber rather than epic drama. The U.S. Attorney's office had reduced the number of charges to 52 "solid" contempts. U.S. Attorney James Thompson, accepting the responsibility of the government's case and the government's honor, made his appearance at the beginning of the trial, and answered some of Judge Gignoux's initial questions. Leonard Weinglass recalled that Gignoux at the opening of the hearing read scenes from the transcript and the defense's brief aloud and asked the U. S. Attorney, " 'Did this happen?' and to each item Thompson had to answer, 'Yes, your honor, it did . . .' or, as in the case of Judge Hoffman's arresting the four lawyers, 'Yes, your honor, I'm afraid it did.' " Weinglass added, "You could see the judge physically changing up there on the bench as Thompson answered, 'Yes, your honor, it did happen . . .' "

Thompson clearly recognized that the record of the trial, in transcript and in eyewitnesses' recollection, cut both ways. With the masterful political touch that he showed throughout his career, he let the government's case consist of presenting the transcript of the trial. Rather than try to defend Judge Hoffman, he concentrated the government's approach on what could be perceived as the obstructive contumacious behavior of the defense. Two junior Assistant U.S. Attorneys in Thompson's office, Gary Starkman and Royal B. Martin, were then left in charge of cross-examining defense witnesses and presenting rebuttal witnesses.

If Gignoux was initially disposed to take a firm-lipped attitude toward the defense, the dramatic recitation of what had happened in the Conspiracy courtroom appeared to work some change of his attitude. He was impressed, as noted by Professors of Law Harry Kalven and Jon Waltz, that the largest portion of the contempts clustered around key incidents such as the binding and gagging of Bobby Seale and the revocation of Dellinger's bail.

In late October 1973, at conclusion of the government's starkly abbreviated case, Judge Gignoux acquitted the defendants of 24 "solid" contempts and dismissed two. Froines and Weiner were entirely removed from the case. 26 contempts remained against the two attorneys Kunstler and Weinglass and against Dellinger, Davis, Hayden, Rubin, and Hoffman. These 26 contempts were now tried before Gignoux.

In order to make its argument stand against the government's argument that the lawyers and the defendants' outspoken verbal responses constituted "obstruction" of the court, the defense needed to bring the trial alive before Judge Gignoux, just as we need to see the Democratic Convention of 1968 and the Conspiracy trial alive in their historical contexts. Stavis, chief attorney for the defense, knew that Dorothy Brackenbury, the court recorder, had tape-recorded much of the trial, partly as a backup for her transcript record and partly as a matter of business, since court recorders operate as independent contractors. In a sense, Stavis agreed with Judge Hoffman's preface to the original contempt proceedings, that no written record could "adequately portray" the laughter, murmurs, snickering, venom, sarcasm, and tone of voice, "and other subtle tactics employed" in the courtroom. The defense needed to counter the written transcript, which made Judge Hoffman look better than the live experience of him had been. Stavis subpoenaed the tapes.

"John Froines' students [Froines was teaching at Bard College] came down to help. They listened carefully to day after day of four and a half months of tape, isolating significant passages. There was one passage," Stavis said, "when Bobby Seale was bound and gagged. On transcript, the judge sounded reasonable. On the tape, the same passage sounded very different. As we played it in the courtroom, I was looking out of the corner of my eye and I saw Gignoux change in response to hearing Judge Hoffman's voice."

When Northwestern University Professor of Law Jon Waltz entered the courtroom as a witness, he saw Rennie Davis trying to sit in a lotus position in his courtroom chair. Davis had become a devotee of the fifteen-year-old guru, the Maharaj-Ji, partly in reaction to his depression at the success of police in breaking up the Mayday 1971 anti-war demonstrations in Washington, D.C., arresting some 13,000 people. With Gignoux's permission, the talented Waltz gave a theatrical but uncomfortably accurate imitation of Judge Hoffman, along with testimony of Judge Hoffman's behavior in this and other trials, reinforcing what Gignoux heard on the tape. Testing this new representation of things, Gignoux asked Waltz, who was a registered Republican, "Are you a movement lawyer?"

U.S. Attorney James Thompson returned only once, as a defense witness, called because the defense had heard so many rumors of Thompson's supposed displeasure with his predecessors' conduct of the Conspiracy trial. He surprised the defense by letting them know that Acting Attorney General Robert Bork had wanted to drop the contempt case but Thompson had persuaded him to continue because "it was not too much to expect the defendants to obey the law, too," another example of Thompson's sensitivity to the pull-and-tug among positions in the legal and political system. Former U. S. Attorney Tom Foran was also called to the stand during the government's rebuttal, and admitted, under cross-examination, that he'd indulged in some name-calling, too.

Judge Gignoux's newly heightened sense for the misbehavior of the government stopped short of accepting former 113th Military Intelligence agent John O'Brien's testimony about efforts of the U. S. Army's domestic agents to "infiltrate" the defense's staff of volunteers. Gignoux later declared O'Brien's testimony to be unbelievable. In the United States Senate's 1970s select committee hearings that exposed domestic spying and illegal counter-intelligence work of the Army, FBI, and other Federal agencies, O'Brien's testimony joined that of others in pulling up the curtain on the government's massive attempts to infiltrate and disrupt hundreds of political, religious, and community groups.

Now Gignoux showed that the Constitutional system could be exacting to a fault. The twenty six contempts that were finally tried, and the thirteen contempt convictions that Gignoux finally let stand, revealed the different patterns for each defendant's personality and political approach, and highlighted the kind of behavior the court regarded as requiring a price. Hayden, Davis, Froines, and Weiner had, Gignoux decided, kept their "contempts" within the bounds of first amendment protections and none of these reached the final thirteen. Rubin and Hoffman carried out much more striking, theatrical behavior and were found guilty of two contempts each, including the wearing of choir robes as "judicial" robes and throwing the robes on the floor and stomping on them, all committed in the tumult around the revocation of Dellinger's bail. Dellinger's outspoken, continued arguments with Judge Hoffman were ruled as being beyond mere remarks and constituted obstruction, giving the one pacifist in the trial seven contempts in the final thirteen, among them the "barnyard epithet," which Judge Gignoux regarded evenly but not lightly. None of the white defendants' contempts that concentrated around Bobby Seale's binding and gagging, and none in the first two and a half months of the original trial, made it to the final thirteen. Leonard Weinglass' attempts to continue argument over Judge Hoffman's rulings, though they came to the "brink," did not pass over into obstructive behavior and would not be included. William Kunstler was judged guilty of two contempts, centering around the incident involving Judge Hoffman's denial of Ralph Abernathy as a witness. Ironically, these were instances in which Kunstler gave himself over to passionate advocacy. One of them undoubtedly would have been set aside if he had not said that Judge Hoffman could hold him in contempt if he wished to do so. To Judge Gignoux, it indicated that Kunstler voiced his thought that what he was doing might be contempt.

Jeffrey Cole, former Assistant U. S. Attorney, said in 1992 about the contradictory problems postulated by the Constitutional system in dealing with the contempts, "The court cannot deal effectively with crimes of a quasi-political nature. The people who play that way do not play by the rules. If you have people dedicated to the goals of using the court to further their own political ends, the court cannot work effectively. Judge

Hoffman played into the defendants' hands. They were wonderfully adept at manipulating him. They had a view of the case
that he was prejudiced against them and they weren't going to
go down without fighting. The defendants were not under a
constitutional imperative to be fair. But the judge is under an
imperative to be fair. They manipulated him exquisitely.

"But twenty years have persuaded me it isn't so easy to say
that only the defendants were at fault. There's blame enough
for everybody in that case. The system itself can profit in examining from a balanced perspective what happened on both
sides." However, "You cannot simply excoriate the judge. There
was a symbiotic involvement between him and the defendants."

Gignoux revealed in his final ruling that he was a veritable
theologian of *Novus Ordo Seclorum:*

> "The Court of Appeals made clear in *Seale* and *Dellinger*
> [the two previous Appellate cases concerning the Con-
> spiracy contempts] that impropriety on the part of the
> trial judge cannot justify or excuse contemptuous con-
> duct. However, the Court of Appeals made equally clear
> in those cases that judicial error, judicial or prosecutorial
> misconduct, and judicial or prosecutorial provocation are
> to be considered in extenuation of the offense and in
> mitigation of any penalty to be imposed."

The thirteen contempt convictions were allowed to stand as
the system's witness against one attorney and three defendants, the price exacted for their outspoken protest in the
courtroom. It was a price of great importance to the Constitutional system, a symbol for the more tragic price at the center
of the system's process. No sentence would be imposed.

*The Jury Strategy in Subsequent Trials—*
*The Jury in its Classic Role*

The "Whole World Is Watching" sort of publicity generated
by the startling events of the Conspiracy trial, and the embroil-

ment of the media and the judiciary system in the issue of outspoken political or "quasi-political" behavior in the court-room, cut more than one way in the conduct of the political trials that multiplied after the Conspiracy trial. The possible effects that Kunstler so eloquently warned about were as brac-ing as they were chilling. The government preferred to gang-try defendants with conspiracy charges—the Harrisburg 7, the Beaver 55, the Minnesota 8, and so on. Movement lawyers turned to rigorous development of the art of jury selection and of factual and legal case. At the same time they chose not to take lying down any court's hostility or arbitrariness.

"We had a considerable debate [when the first movement trials began in the late sixties]," Morton Stavis of the Center for Constitutional Rights said, "on whether it would be better to go before a jury or before a judge [bench trial]. In the Smith Act cases in the early 1950s [the Smith Act, among other specifications, made it a crime to be a member of an organi-zation that merely advocated forcible overthrow of the gov-ernment and was effectively neutralized by the Supreme Court in 1956], attorneys found it impossible to win Smith Act cases before American juries; anti-communism had taken such deep root in the American people. In the late sixties we decided to go for juries, because we felt the country was deeply divided about the Viet Nam war."

The movement lawyers got help from psychologists and so-ciologists and honed the process of jury selection to make sure the defendants' side of the cultural division showed up in the juries of political trials. Lawyers began to ask untraditional questions of prospective jurors, some allowed by judges, some not. In New York City, Gerald Lefcourt, defense attorney in the Panther 21 trial, went so far as to ask questions about prospective jurors' feelings about childrearing. The judge looked at Lefcourt, puzzled, and denied that line of question-ing because it didn't seem to him to be "relevant."

Originally conceived as a form for insulating the citizenry from governmental oppression, the jury began to function in its classic role. In a host of quasi-political trials in the early 1970s, juries perceived evidentiary weakness and political bias in state and federal prosecutions. The Panther 21 were acquitted. A Chicago jury freed Brian Flanagan from all charges of assault upon Richard Elrod who was crippled by a blow to the neck during the Weatherman "Days of Rage" action in October 1969. Another Chicago jury freed members of the Black P Stone Nation on charges of murdering a police officer. In New Haven, Connecticut, Charles Garry's defense secured a hung jury in the trial of Bobby Seale and Ericka Huggins for conspiracy to commit murder. In each of these cases, the jury was much more rigorously selected than in the Conspiracy trial. The lawyers in these trials worked hard to build a persuasive legal and factual case. Counting draft resistance and conscientious objector cases, there were hundreds, even thousands of movement trials.

Morton Stavis tried the only other case brought to trial under the Federal anti-riot statute, the Gainesville 8 in Florida, involving Vietnam Veterans Against the War, indicted for actions planned against both the Republican and Democratic conventions of 1972. "The judge was no picnic," Stavis said. "He wanted a conviction so bad he could taste it. But the jury voted acquittal."

## Were They Guilty? Guilty of what?

Another question that has titillated the public mind concerning the Chicago Conspiracy trial is whether the defendants were guilty or not. The question is buoyed to the fore by the amazing imagery of police-demonstrator confrontations outside, and inside, the Democratic Convention of 1968. Guilty of *what*? Guilty in terms of the Federal Anti-Riot law? Guilty before God and one's conscience? In 1976, three years after

Judge Gignoux's finding on the contempts, Jerry Rubin electrified the nagging debate by writing in the *Chicago Sun-Times*: "WE WANTED disruption. We PLANNED it. We WERE NOT innocent victims . . . Guilty as hell. Guilty as charged." Judge Hoffman and the prosecution crowed, and so did that 71% of the American electorate who had known it all along. Movement people were angry at Rubin. Years later, Rubin told Abe Peck, "It was a mistake to say 'we' and 'guilty.' What I was saying was that we"—ironic word, as Peck observes in *Uncovering the Sixties*—"wanted a confrontation. We were not innocent." Rubin had described the Conspiracy indictment as the "greatest honor" of his life. After the Conspiracy trial, in 1970, Jerry Rubin had pleaded guilty to state charges of mob action during the Convention and served sixty days in Cook County jail. Lee Weiner, defendant and sociologist, said in 1992, "Jerry's article was a piece of reconstructing himself in 1976, as he wanted himself to have been in 1968."

Stew Albert, an unindicted co-conspirator in the Conspiracy case, one of the twenty J. Edgar Hoover originally wanted Judge Campbell's Grand Jury to indict, was in Rubin's 'affinity group' during August 1968 and was a friend and associate for many years. Albert said, in an interview with this writer in 1989, "Anybody who knows Jerry knows he's anything but consistent . . . Jerry has fallen in love with the prosecution's case. The prosecution portrays you as brilliant, courageous, consistent, audacious, imaginative. You like the image. The defense portrays you as a victim, weak, not attractive. Jerry believes that history will vindicate him as having been an architect of what happened in Chicago. Actually, Jerry had little or no control over the crowds. None of the leaders had much control over the crowds.

" . . . I agree that we weren't innocent victims. We knew how the police could respond. But there's an after the fact quality to what Jerry is quoted as saying . . . What we wanted to do kept changing. Festival of Life was falling apart. Jerry and Abbie had their falling out [patched up by the time of the Conspiracy trial] . . . We had rapidly changing tactics because the situation was changing . . . There were so many different groups. Fundamentally, what we did in Chicago was spontaneous, with some degree of influence from the organizers on people immediately near them.

"Specific plans? . . . The chief strategist was whoever gave the orders to the police to attack us, attack reporters, photographers, anyone who happened to be on the streets . . ."

Thomas Foran and Richard Schultz said in a retrospective article "The World Is Still Watching" in the *Chicago Tribune* (July 1988) that in 1987 Tom Hayden, working very successfully as an elected assemblyman in California, visited them as a part of gathering material for his book *Reunion* and said in private to them that he was guilty. Hayden was shocked to hear they had said that, and denied it. In the same *Tribune* article, Hayden speaks of a distributed responsibility for the Convention of 1968.

Leave it now to a man who passed to other realms long before his fellow defendants, to speak with Dostoyevskian insight on the issues of guilt and innocence. At the time of sentencing at the end of the Conspiracy trial, with no knowledge that the convictions would be overturned, Abbie Hoffman addressed the court with the remarkable statement, "I don't know whether I'm innocent or guilty." At other times, he seemed to want to celebrate, if not specifically take responsibility for, "the perfect mess" of the Democratic Convention of 1968. In the "perfect mess," Abbie wrote in *Revolution for the Hell of It*, everyone gets what he wants. In the summer of 1968, during planning for Convention Week demonstrations, he unnerved Chicago area Yippies by pencilling in his cryptic "Riot" for Wednesday night, August 28, nomination night, as told by Abe Peck in *Uncovering the Sixties*. To Abbie, the word "riot" could mean riot of fun as well as any other put-on of double-meanings. I interviewed Abbie Hoffman three times in March and

April 1989. For himself he said, "I'm proud of what I did. Oh, very. I have no regrets. I wasn't guilty. Even given the law, I was not guilty. And the law [the Anti-Riot statute] is unconstitutional. Every speech I gave, there were microphones in front of me." And there were no immediate acts of violence committed as a result of his speeches. On the night of April 6, three days before he died, in a depression-slurred but clear voice, he discussed Jerry Rubin's statements,

"Yes, we talked about it. Most clients don't know if they're guilty or not. It was a state of mind trial. I told him he didn't know enough about the law."

Abbie Hoffman wanted the last defense witness in the Conspiracy trial to be Groucho Marx. He wanted Groucho as expert witness to say that many of the things the defendants were accused of doing during Convention Week 1968, such as the so-called plot to kidnap Deputy Superintendent of Police James Rochford at the Logan Hill statue, were within the bounds of American humor. "I called Groucho," Weinglass said, "and he seemed willing to testify, but he said, 'Hey, this judge is sending people to prison. I'm too old to become a homosexual. You'll have to talk to my lawyer and agent.' " Lawyer and agent said no. The prosecution was spared having to cross-examine Groucho Marx on the boundaries of American humor, within which Americans have always sought the resolution of their daily trespasses. We lost what could have been an amazing transcript. Would Groucho have dwelled on small-town Halloween pranks that included theater in the streets and such acts as leaving telephone poles on the mayor's porch? The sort of prank stories that people in their "mature" years laugh about around a convivial table? Would he have dwelt on the use of violence in humor? Pies in the face? Sudden trapdoors? Big guys looming over little guys, and little guys making fools of big guys? Community leaders costumed as Indians and dumping unwanted commercial goods into nearby waters, like The Boston Tea Party? How would the jury have regarded his expert statements?

## The Government's Drive to Trial and Invasion of the Judicial Process

During the trial itself Judge Hoffman's slips of the tongue appeared to point to guilt of the government.

It is not enough that in political cases the prosecution can muster the enormous resources of the Federal Government against ordinary citizens, using the taxpayer's money to employ agents and informers and sophisticated electronic surveillance and talented lawyers and research staff in building and trying a case. It is not enough that the judge favors the prosecution, suppresses hung jury messages from the jury, and sends through his marshals messages that intimidate the jury toward decision. In this case, and in other political trials of the late 1960s and early '70s, the government interfered in the judicial process in a variety of ways concentrated toward securing a verdict of guilty. Ramsey Clark, in his public confrontation with J. Edgar Hoover, Director of the FBI, in September 1968 said in response to police violence during the Convention, "What are the people to do when the police break the law?" The further question looms, What are the people to do when the government interferes in the citizen's last bulwark, the judicial process and the jurors' deliberations?

At the earliest points in the process of driving to trial, the government sent often highly biased agents and observers to see and hear "evidence" before "crimes" had been committed and to use their "eyewitness" presence as a way to develop further, rather questionable testimony. The extent of this invasion is illustrated by documents I have obtained through the Freedom of Information Act and seen in the Chicago Police Intelligence files revealing, for example, that of six people present in one anti-war meeting in the summer of 1968 at least five were agents, unbeknownst to each other, reporting on each other, the meeting even chaired by an agent. In the middle of August 1968, about ten days prior to the Convention, the Assistant Attorneys in the Northern District of Illinois were briefed in the U.S. Attorney's Office on the new Anti-Riot statute and what to look for as evidence, including presumably speeches (overt acts) to take notes on. (Such briefings were not necessarily "out of the ordinary," said Tom Sullivan, a counsel for the Conspiracy defense, later U.S. Attorney.) Anti-war organizers were already angry about the troubling insinuations in the air concerning the new Anti-Riot statute. Some of them began to warp their phrasing, becoming elliptical and somewhat obscure when they spoke to crowds. Were they hiding a criminal impulse? Were they suppressing their thoughts? Is this an example of the "chilling effect" abhorred by the Supreme Court?

On Tuesday afternoon, August 27, 1968, the second day of the Convention proper, Abbie Hoffman played with contradictory statements in a worried, humorous talk that he gave to young people and anybody who stopped to listen under a tree in Lincoln Park, saying for instance, "I'm worried about the conspiracy thing . . ." On the same afternoon J. Edgar Hoover in Washington, D.C., sent an Airtel to Chicago asking that his agents be alert for evidence for possible charges to be brought under the Anti-Riot statute. The next day, August 28, Hoover re-affirmed his request, even before "The Whole World Is Watching" televised police attack upon demonstrators and the general melee at Michigan-Balbo in front of the Hilton Hotel in downtown Chicago.

In the first week of September 1968, directly after the Convention, Attorney General Ramsey Clark called U.S. Attorney Thomas Foran and said that the Department of Justice should not convene a Grand Jury to bring charges under the Anti-Riot statute. Clark said this while Hoover's FBI, only nominally within the purview of Clark's Department of Justice, was already mounting the investigation aimed toward producing indictments of demonstration leaders, and the Grand Jury was already being initiated by Foran. On September 9, the Federal Grand Jury was convened by Judge Campbell, Mayor Daley's ally.

The government's purpose in seeking the trial was explicitly to destroy the burgeoning political rebellion that was multiplying exponentially in the late 1960s throughout the country. The Chicago Federal Grand Jury proceeded apace for several weeks. October 23, 1968, Hoover sent a memo to FBI offices across the country saying that indictments were imminent against "approximately twenty principal leaders and activists of various new Left organizations," charging them with conspiracy to cause violence and violate the new Federal anti-riot statute at the Democratic Convention in August 1968. Hoover concluded, "A successful prosecution of this type would be a unique achievement for the Bureau and should seriously disrupt and curtail the activities of the New Left."

In fact, Ramsey Clark did succeed in slowing down and frustrating the efforts to bring indictments. Later in the fall of 1968, LBJ said that everyone in his cabinet wanted the indictments except "Ramsey, who is hemming and hawing." The Chicago Grand Jury investigating the Convention "disorders" was stalled by Johnson's divided administration. In February 1969, with John Mitchell appointed Attorney General, the Nixon administration resumed the push for indictments. The Grand Jury came up with eight rather than twenty.

From March 27, 1969, directly after the indictments, the FBI and police intelligence departments in Newark, New York, and Chicago used surveillance of several kinds to spy on strategy meetings of the defense. There are also FBI memos that point to wholly improper communications between U.S. Attorney Foran, Judge Hoffman, Chief Judge William Campbell, and Chicago FBI Special Agent in Charge, Marlin Johnson. On April 14, 1969, SAC Marlin Johnson reported to

Hoover that U.S. Attorney Foran had "confidentially advised that he had talked with trial judge Julius Hoffman and strongly feels that, subsequent to the trial . . . the defendants and their lawyers may well be held in contempt because of their behavior and public statements prior to and during the trial." Two weeks into the trial itself, an FBI memo dated 10/7/69 declared, "Judge Hoffman has indicated to USA [U.S. Attorney] Foran, and USA Foran is in full agreement, that many of the statements made by the defendants, their lawyers, and possibly others, such as the unindicted co-conspirators, may well be in contempt of court. Judge Hoffman has indicated in strictest confidence that following the trial he definitely plans to consider various individuals for possible contempt of court." On December 7, 1969, in response to a defense attempt to subpoena FBI Director Hoover himself to testify, an internal FBI memo noted that the subpoena also requested "data relating to surveillance," which the FBI rather fearfully saw as requiring "the most extensive file search throughout the field . . ." and expressed relief that "Chief US District Judge [Campbell] in Chicago has given his assurance the subpoena will be quashed . . ."

"Flatout untrue," Tom Foran said, when told about the Freedom of Information-obtained documents in the late 1970s. "I never talked to Judge Hoffman except in open court." Judge Hoffman also denied any improper conversations with the U.S. Attorney.

If a defense person had broken into the government's offices to get information on the prosecution's case, the defense would have been guilty of breaking and entering. If a government Cointel-Pro [Counterintelligence-Project] agent, or right wing group inspired by the FBI or local "Red Squad," broke into a citizen's office illegally, without a warrant, as they actually did, to get information or just to mess things up, there was nothing the citizen could do. Justice Brandeis wrote, "Decency, security and liberty alike demand that government officials shall be subjected to the same rules of conduct that are commands to the citizen."

Former Assistant U.S. Attorney Jeffrey Cole said in 1992, "After twenty years, I've come to recognize that the government does not always play a noble role. When I was a young prosecutor, I used to think the government was always on the right side. Now I see that the government is not always noble, and not always right when it tries to play a noble role. Young prosecutors often do not truly appreciate that there are human pain and human values that get lost in striving to win. As a young prosecutor one sees agents and government representatives as the embodiment of good and nothing but evil on the defense's side. Defendants are just entities, beyond the pale of redemption. Most young prosecutors come into the role straight out of law school. Nobody should be a prosecutor unless you've had at least six months as a defense lawyer."

Because of the evidence in the FBI memos of improper government intervention, Dellinger, Hoffman, Rubin, and Kunstler filed a motion in 1979 to have the trial declared a "non-trial" and their thirteen contempt convictions vacated and expunged. Judge Gignoux denied the motion in 1980, in effect protecting the government's intervention ex post facto and declaring that the trial had been real, unexpungeable. The 7th Circuit Court of Appeals upheld the denial in 1981:

> The scales of justice must be tipped more steeply than here to justify our regarding courts of law as mere street scenes or theaters in the round . . . The documents submitted at this time suggest additional improprieties [on the part of the government], but we do not believe that anything shown here requires us to abrogate without condition *all* sanctions undergirding orderly judicial process.

The Constitutional system insisted not only on the maintenance of its own enduring nature, but on the appearance of being to some degree right.

*What Happened to Them Afterward?*

Directly after the trial Leonard Weinglass was distinctly concerned about his lawyerly future. Back in his home state of New Jersey, Weinglass recalled, "U.S. Attorney Frederick Lacey moved to have me disciplined—censured, suspended, or disbarred. At a dinner, Lacey was guest speaker, calling for me to be disciplined. I stood up and requested the opportunity to respond. There were voices pro and con on all sides of me, but finally they let me speak for five minutes. One of the things I asked Lacey in that five minutes was 'Have you read one page of the 20,000 page transcript?' Lacey's attempt to discipline me was somewhat discredited, and that was the end of it.

"My name recognition went up. I did feel endangered. When I was admitted to the California bar, the committee started questioning me on my contempts in the Conspiracy trial. They said, 'If we can't question you on this, who can we question?' When I was admitted to the New York bar, I had to answer questions.

"For six or seven years after the Conspiracy trial, every time I appeared in out-of-state court, the judge would appear on the bench with that volume of the Federal Reporter that contained my contempts, look down at me, and ask, 'Are you the Leonard Weinglass who . . . etc . . .'" Subsequently, Weinglass was barred once—from the trial of the Minnesota 8. He became a successful criminal lawyer with an interest in political and "quasi-political" cases.

In 1992 William Kunstler remembered, "I felt kind of exhilarated at the end of the trial. I felt instinctively that it would come out all right, a reasonable chance for success on the appellate level. I did have this marvelous sense of exhilaration that we had come through and done the right thing—by attacking, by not kowtowing, by protesting every wrong decision. On one level, I didn't care. Personal fears should not play a part in it. The mark of a civilization is that you can stand up and speak your mind.

"The Whole World Watching [the media focus on the Conspiracy trial] made me feel distinctly safer. If that trial had been done in anonymity we wouldn't have had much of a chance. We were galvanizing the young people. I'm in favor of TV in the courtroom [not allowed in the Conspiracy trial]. It keeps the prosecutors and the judge within bounds. It removes the mystique.

"Up to the Chicago trial, I'd been practicing law for 30 years. I was convinced that you follow the rules and you will do all right, and the lawyer's job was not to be a partisan, the lawyer's job was to be a good lawyer. Chicago taught me that the system is evil and oppressive. Lawyers should stand up and speak out. The government commits perjury, fabricates evidence, influences the judge, intimidates the jurors, and can't be sued for it. If you listen to a tape that Judge Hoffman's secretary forgot to turn off, when the Judge was watching the defendants on TV before the trial, you hear an FBI agent saying, 'Judge, you've gotta put a lid on those people.' They programmed him. They will do anything to win. After Chicago, I was a different lawyer.

"Controversial cases should be tried by lawyers from out of state. This was very true in the Deep South in the sixties. Justice Douglas [Supreme Court] spoke of the need for itinerant lawyers. The extremely controversial case requires the travelling, out-of-state lawyer.

"After Chicago, at the Wounded Knee trial in Minnesota [in 1974], I got disbarment papers from New York [because of reaction to the Conspiracy trial and the two contempts held against Kunstler in Judge Gignoux's final ruling]. We found out that the New York Bar grievance committee had not got the o.k. of the executive committee and it was forced to withdraw. That was the end of it." Kunstler wrote articles, a book, *Trials and Tribulations*, and became Vice-President of the Center for Constitutional Rights. "When Tom Hayden [like other moderate Democrats in the early 1990s] politically positioned himself in favor of the death penalty in certain cases, I wrote and published sonnets attacking Hayden's stand." Kunstler played a judge in the 1992 Spike Lee film *Malcolm X.*

No defendant or attorney served a day of jail time for either the substantive counts or the contempts. Dellinger spent the last days of the trial in Cook County jail when his bail was revoked. All of the defendants waited in jail for several days before adequate funds were raised to post bail for them in February 1970.

David Dellinger continued vigorously as a peace activist, living and writing at his home in Vermont. His son died in 1988 and Dellinger commented how painful it was that the parent should outlive the child. His daughter won the Vermont Lottery, something like a $50,000 yearly stipend for the rest of her life. Tom Hayden married actress Jane Fonda in 1973 and divorced in 1990, became first an assemblyman and then state senator in California, an important figure in California's Democratic Party, fulfilling Judge Hoffman's admonition that "a young man like you could do very well in our system." Rennie Davis, one of the most skilled organizers of the 1960s, eventually dissassociated himself from the boy guru Maharaj-Ji, became director of what he characterized as a think tank for inventors in Colorado, concentrating on environment-protecting inventions, and worked for an insurance company. In New York, Jerry Rubin started an employment business, famous for its parties for young professionals and business people, then married, became a doting father (in 1969-70 he had said that children should kill their parents), and in the early eighties toured campuses with Abbie Hoffman debating their different positions. Abbie Hoffman, pursued on a charge of possessing a small amount of cocaine (his "one lapse of judgment," said columnist Mike Royko), went underground, had his nose broken and underwent other facial surgery to change his appearance, and did not surface until 1980, when he went on ABC-TV with interviewer Barbara Walters. Literally hundreds of people knew where he was at various times and places but no one turned him in to the FBI. Underground, as Barry Freed, he was organizer of the Save-the-River (the St. Lawrence River) campaign in upstate New York, had his picture taken with Senator Daniel Patrick Moynihan, and went to Washington to testify before Congress. He was diagnosed as a manic-depressive in the early 1980s. On April 9, 1989, he was found dead of a massive dose of phenobarbital and nearly a fifth of liquor in his cabin-like house in a sort of artists' colony in New Hope, Pennsylvania. He left no note.

Bobby Seale wrote a book, *Seize the Time*, and after years of struggling for the Black Panther Party and surviving its infighting, court cases, and the vicious FBI Cointel-Pro campaign against the Panthers, left Oakland, California, for Philadelphia, Pennsylvania, where he pursued graduate studies and taught in the African-American Studies Department at Temple University. In the introduction to his cookbook *Barb-que'n with Bobby*, he refers to recipes he used to entertain Jerry Rubin with when they were in jail together. He played a street speaker role in the film *Malcolm X*. John Froines, already possessing his Ph.d. in Chemistry at the time of the trial, worked in OSHA during the Carter administration in the late 1970s, and wrote federal workplace standards for lead and cotton dust. "I thought we veterans of the sixties had a responsibility to work within government." He became a Professor of Toxicology at UCLA, a leading scientist concerned with environmental policy implications of scientific research. "My life has been a constant fight to maintain my position as a respected scientist." He has two children. Lee Weiner taught sociology at Rutgers University, became father of five children, and Director of Special Projects for the Anti-Defamation League in New York.

Juror Jean Fritz and her husband Marvin continued living in Des Plaines, retired, taking fishing trips to Wisconsin and other vacations together with their grown children. Her interest in political causes heightened through the years. Kristi King, the young juror bumped so precipitously by Judge Hoffman because of the "Black Panther Letter," called Jean Fritz months after the trial and said she wished she had stayed and thought she would have supported Mrs. Fritz.

Denied his chance at elected office, prosecutor Tom Foran, with a strong record as U.S. Attorney in securing convictions in mobster and other cases, started a law firm with Richard Schultz. They prospered.

Judge Hoffman retired by degrees from the bench, because of age and some reluctance on the part of the Northern District of Illinois to give him any cases. The zealous Julius Hoffman became as much of a confused martyr in his own eyes, as much used by the establishment that he sought to uphold, as the defendants themselves. In the beginning, after the trial, feted by the forces that celebrated the guilty verdict, he breakfasted with President Nixon. Yet, as the years went by, and one appeal after another went against him, he found the very people who had used him shunning and distancing themselves. He endlessly sought justification for the way he conducted this one trial. Jeffrey Cole, who had been married by Judge Hoffman, said, "There is no doubt this case became the sum total of his existence." Judge Hoffman cut Northwestern University Law School out of his will, then made another will re-including it, but this version was found unexecuted. After he died July 1, 1983, his effects were auctioned, down to his gavel, by his step-son. Abbie Hoffman, we are told, was invited to bid on the gavel.

## The System Works—At What Cost?

For the government's representatives who participated in the trial, victory evaporated before them like watery mirages on a highway. In fact, though the government's effort in the

Conspiracy trial was seemingly discredited, the Nixon administration's bottom-line was met (to put it in terms of the ac-
counting mythology of later decades). In fact, the bottom-line
of both sides was met, at a tremendous cost.

The Conspiracy trial (and other trials) did assist in serving
the purpose outlined in J. Edgar Hoover's October 23, 1968
memo by lending impetus to the fragmenting and curtailing
of what Hoover identified as the New Left, i.e., the general-
ized, grass-roots rebellion that was called the "movement" in
this country. Motion was denied. Yet successful repression cut
more than one way. The Conspiracy verdicts triggered sudden,
massive protest, followed in rapid succession by anti-war demonstrations and riots erupting on campuses across the country,
coming close to social conflagration in May and June 1970
after the National Guard shootings of four students at Kent
State in Ohio and police shootings of two students at Jackson
State in Mississippi. Henry Kissinger, former Secretary of
State, later wrote of this period, "The very fabric of government was falling apart. The Executive Branch was shell-
shocked. After all, their children and their friends' children
took part in the demonstrations." A couple of hundred university presidents advised President Nixon to get out of the
boggle of the war where it seemed the U.S. military could
"win" only by literally bombing Vietnam foot by foot back into
the Stone Age, as General Curtis LeMay had recommended.

After the summer of 1970, the grass-roots spirit of common
opposition to "the government of death and its deathly policies," which gave the variety of movement groups some cohe-
sion of purpose, was eroded by exhaustion of willpower and
vision within, as the organized groups and the broad-based
counter-culture movements choked on their accusatory intol-
erance of ambiguity among themselves. Movement people
were numbed and depleted by the endless trials and the divisive
fragmentation exploited by the massive Cointel-Pro invasion
and disruption of political, religious, and counter-culture

groups all over the country carried out by the FBI, Army, other government and local police intelligence agencies. Yet, the government had to find a way out of the Vietnam War or create fascism at home to support it, and most Americans would not go along with such a solution. The protest movement would have been stronger, and its willpower less vulnerable to erosion and governmental repression, if all of its groups had recognized in those bitterly divisive days of late 1969 and early 1970s that it was a petitioning, not a revolutionary, movement.

Ultimately, the American constitutional "system" requires in the center of its process a kind of tragic compromise, or sufficient threat and echo of it. In the end of Kleist's novella, the revolutionary Michael Kohlhaas finally receives the justice he asked for, but must, in return, pay with his life. With us, this has taken on the status of a civil religion. The political and quasi-political trials of the late 1960s and early 70s punished the movement with years of anxiety and resource-consuming effort, and cost taxpayers a good deal of money.

The government's effort in the Conspiracy trial and other political trials prolonged the war in Vietnam, at a horrible cost in lives and resources. Had the government followed Justice Black's (building upon Justice Holmes' free-market-of-ideas) dissenting prescription of letting the remedy to the difficulties caused by speech be *more speech*, the United States would have done what it finally had to do—get out of the war without winning it—sooner.

It seems that many of the ritual trials that have occurred during political crises throughout our history, from the trial of William Penn in England in 1680 to the Haymarket trial in 1886 to the Chicago Conspiracy trial in 1969-70, have brought two sides of a deep cultural division into a courtroom governed by a seemingly arbitrary, tyrannical, highly involved and emotional judge. Cryptic or not, the pattern may suit the ritual. Given its personae and their dispositions and its long moment in history, the watershed event of the Conspiracy trial happened the only way it could have happened, offering much to learn, but there is no taking back one word of it.

## Acknowledgments

For the revision and updating of the main body of the story and the writing of the Afterword, I want to acknowledge my extensive conversations with Arthur Kinoy, Professor of Law, Rutgers University; Morton Stavis and William Kunstler, the Center for Constitutional Rights; Leonard Weinglass, Thomas Sullivan, Stephen Seliger, and Jeffrey Cole, attorneys; Jon Waltz, Professor of Law, Northwestern University; Lee Weiner, John Froines, Rennie Davis, and Abbie Hoffman, former "fulltime" defendants; Nancy Kurshan, former Conspiracy staff member; Jean Fritz, former juror; and Stewart Albert, former unindicted co-conspirator, all of whom were generous with their time and thought. I would like also to acknowledge my conversation in the fall of 1969 with Kenneth Gaines, former law clerk to Judge Hoffman. Many aspects of the trial were reawakened and informed by my re-reading of *The Great Conspiracy Trial*, by Jason Epstein; *The Barnyard Epithet and other Obscenities*, by J. Anthony Lukas; *The Conspiracy Trial*, edited by Judy Clavir and John Spitzer; *Contempt*, edited by David Dellinger, with Foreword by Ramsey Clark and Introduction by Harry Kalven, Jr.; *The Tales of Hoffman*, edited by Mark L. Levine, George C. McNamee and Daniel Greenberg; *Conspiracy on Appeal*, by Arthur Kinoy, Helene E. Schwartz, Doris Peterson; *Reunion, A Memoir*, by Tom Hayden; *Uncovering the Sixties*, by Abe Peck; and *The Contempt Power*, a historical examination of the use of contempt power, by Ronald Goldfarb; and my viewings of the play, "The Chicago Conspiracy Trial," directed by Frank Condon, which played at the Remains Theater in Chicago and Odyssey Theater in Los Angeles. I want also to note my references to the Convention Week 1968 retrospective

"The World Is Still Watching" by Jeff Lyon in the *Chicago Tribune* (July 24, 1988) and "The Great Conspiracy Trial of '69" by William M. Kunstler and Stewart E. Albert and "Wind-Up of the Chicago 7" by Jon R. Waltz, both in *The Nation* (respectively, September 29, 1979 and January 19, 1974); also, to thank the Northwestern University School of Law Library; my editor at Da Capo Press, Bea Friedland, for insight and faith, and Ruth Jensen, for resourcefulness. Finally, a special thanks to Betty Shiflett.

# Other DA CAPO titles of interest